A CURIOUS HISTORY OF SEX

For SWOP NSW

A CURIOUS HISTORY OF SEX

KATE LISTER

unbound

First published in 2020

Unbound
6th Floor Mutual House, 70 Conduit Street, London W1S 2GF
www.unbound.com

Text Design by carrdesignstudio.com

A CIP record for this book is available from the British Library

ISBN 978-1-78352-805-9 (hardback)
ISBN 978-1-78352-806-6 (ebook)

Printed in Barcelona by Novoprint

1 3 5 7 9 8 6 4 2

For my family (sorry!)

Contents

Introduction

*Unexpressed emotions will never die. They are buried alive
and will come forth later in uglier ways.*

Sigmund Freud

S ex is one of the great universal levellers; to paraphrase Geoffrey
Rush's Marquis de Sade, 'we eat, we sleep, we shit, we fuck and
we die'.[1] Desire cuts across boundaries of culture, gender and class. It
cares little for our 'rules' and, as anyone who has ever been caught with
their pants down will tell you, it cares even less for common sense. Of
course, humans do far more than eating, shitting and fucking – our
intellect is what really sets us apart from the beasts. And herein lies
the problem. To say that humans have overthought sex is something of
an understatement.

All life on this planet shares the desire to reproduce, but what makes
humans unique are the infinitely complex and varied ways we seek
to gratify our sexual desires. In *Forensic and Medico-legal Aspects of
Sexual Crimes and Unusual Sexual Practices* (2008), Professor Anil
Aggrawal listed 547 different paraphilic sexual interests, and noted
that 'like allergies, sexual arousal may occur from anything under the
sun, including the sun'.[2] And, in case you're wondering, sexual arousal
caused by the sun is called 'actirasty'.

Humans are also the only creatures that stigmatise, punish and create
shame around their sexual desires. While all animals have courtship
rituals, no wildebeest has ever gone into therapy because it's struggling to express a latex fetish. The queen honeybee will shag up to
forty partners in one session, return to her hive dripping in semen

and clutching the severed cocks of her conquests, and not one drone will call her a slut. Male baboons will happily bugger each other all day long and never fear being sent to a gay conversion camp. Yet the guilt we humans feel around our desires can be paralysing, and severe punishments have been doled out to those who break 'the rules'.

Colombian novelist Gabriel García Márquez once wrote that 'everyone has three lives: a public life, a private life and a secret life'.[3] Paradoxically, our secret life is us at our most honest. We force this honest piece of ourselves into secrecy because the systems we have created have rendered it incompatible with our public and private lives. In an effort to control this secret part of ourselves, humans turned sex into a moral issue and developed complex social structures to regulate our urges. We invented categories to try to control it: gay, straight, monogamous, virginal, promiscuous, etc. But sexuality does not fit neatly into man-made boxes; it spills over, and that's when things get messy. When we try to suppress our desire, it becomes a fault line running underneath our structures of morality, ethics and decency. But when the pink mist descends, people will still risk the earthquake to have an orgasm.

The act of sex itself has not changed since we first worked out what went where. Penises, tongues and fingers have been probing mouths, vulvas and anuses in search of an orgasm since humans first crawled out of the primordial sludge. What does change is the social script that dictates how sex is culturally understood and performed. For example, according to Pornhub, the largest pornography site on the internet, 'lesbian' has remained the number one search term used on their site worldwide since they first launched in 2007. In the Netherlands, 'lesbian' searches on Pornhub were up by 45 per cent in 2018 from 2016.[4] So, it's fair to say that the Dutch are giving lesbian sex a big thumbs up. However, they have not always been so appreciative of V-on-V love. Between 1400 and 1550, fifteen women were burned alive in the Netherlands as 'female sodomites'.[5] Those who were not put to death still faced severe punishments. In 1514, Maertyne van Keyschote and Jeanne van den Steene of Bruges were both publicly flogged, had their hair burned off, and were banished from the city for the having committed 'a certain great kind of the unnatural sin of sodomy with several young girls'.[6] Six hundred years later, 'the unnatural sin of sodomy with several young girls' is the most watched porn category among the descendants of the same people who thought it reasonable to chuck lesbians on a bonfire.

Pornhub searches for 'porn for women' were up by 359 per cent in 2018, with women viewing lesbian pornography 197 per cent more often than men did in the same year. This would have come as quite a shock to Dr William Acton (1813–1875), who claimed that 'the majority of women (happily for them) are not very much troubled with sexual feeling of any kind'.[7] And what the *Sunday Express* editor James Douglas (1867–1940) would have made of all this is anyone's guess. In 1928, Douglas attacked Radclyffe Hall's landmark lesbian novel, *The Well of Loneliness*, writing, this 'pestilence is devastating the younger generation. It is wrecking young lives. It is defiling young souls.' Douglas urged society to 'cleans[e] itself from the leprosy of these lepers'.[8] And yet here we are, ninety years later, with millions of women around the world jilling off to such 'pestilence' with our leprous souls intact. What a time to be alive.

This is a book about how attitudes to sex have changed throughout history. It is the curious history of sex and some of the things we have done to ourselves and to each other in the pursuit (and denial) of the almighty orgasm. This is not a comprehensive study of every sexual quirk, kink and ritual across all cultures throughout time, as that would entail writing an encyclopaedia. Rather, this is a drop in the ocean, a paddle in the shallow end of sex history, but I hope you will get pleasantly wet nonetheless. I have tried to choose subjects that provide valuable context for issues today, particularly issues of gender, sexual shame, beauty, language, and how desire has been regulated. I have chosen subjects that are close to my heart, such as the history of sex work, deeply emotive subjects, such as abortion, and also subjects that made me laugh, like 'cocklebread' and orgasming on a bicycle. Although it is easy to laugh at the silly things people have believed throughout history, and I hope you do, it is far more valuable to see how similar we are to people who have gone before us and question our own beliefs as a result. Sex remains a deeply divisive issue around the world, and in many places is a matter of life and death. These attitudes will turn and turn again – hopefully for the better. But we will never arrive at a place where sex is free of stigma and shame unless we first know where we have come from.

A note on the use of language. As far as offensive language goes, you are now entering a hard hat area. This is a book that uncovers historical attitudes to sex and gender. Our ancestors had little understanding of gender fluidity and understood gender as binary and biologically determined. As a result, much of the historical material in this book defines women as having vulvas and men as having penises. For example, in the chapter on the history of the word 'cunt', 'cunt' is understood to be the genitals of a woman. Today, we know that some women have cunts and some do not, just as some men do and some do not. But our ancestors did not view gender or biology in such terms – they understood 'cunt' as being a woman's genitals. While this may be offensive to modern ears, understanding historical attitudes to gender identity and sexual morphology is essential if we are to fully appreciate how heteronormativity and constructs of the binary of masculine and feminine came to dominate cultural narratives today.

The slang used throughout this book is all genuine historical slang and is followed by the date it was first recorded. My primary source for the historical slang is Jonathon Green's *Dictionary of Slang*, which I cannot recommend enough if you want to learn more.

SEX
AND
WORDS

'Tis Pity She's a Whore

The 'Whore' in Whores of Yore

Language is an important battleground in the fight for social equality. As the linguist Daniel Chandler succinctly put it, 'language constitutes our world, it doesn't just record it or label it'.[1] Language is fluid and malleable; it drives social attitudes, rather than simply expressing them. To see the evolution of language we only have to look at what was once everyday terminology to describe people of colour: 'half caste' was once perfectly acceptable for a person of mixed race, just as 'coloured' was an accepted term for a black person. Such words were not thought of as offensive, merely descriptive, and can occasionally still be heard in usage, though thankfully less often. But when we break down the power structures implicit in such phrases, we can begin to understand how words do reinforce and create our reality. A person who is 'half caste' is, by definition, half of something; they are half formed, half made, half a person rather than a whole person in their own right. A person who is 'coloured' has been metaphorically coloured in, which suggests an original state of not being coloured in (or, white); it reinforces difference and tacitly suggests racial hierarchy. We might not immediately recognise the implications of such phrases, but describing someone as half formed simply reinforces racial attitudes; as Chandler argued, it makes our reality, it does not record it.

Language that reflects the humanity of the person or people being described is a constantly evolving process, and while political correctness frequently comes in for scorn, we cannot and will not achieve social equality if the language we use to describe marginalised groups only reinforces stigma. Language informs much of the debate around LGBTQ rights, body issues, ageism and, of course, gender.

The reclamation of terms of abuse is a linguistic minefield where no one has written down the rules, but we all know there are rules. 'Fag', 'ho', 'bitch', etc., can function as terms of inclusion and even affection when used within specific groups. As a straight, white woman, I cannot call a gay man a 'queer', but I can call my female friend a 'bitch', whereas a straight man cannot – though a gay man might be able to (minefield, indeed). When a term of abuse is reclaimed and owned by the people it once stigmatised, it is a defiant action, one that takes the power away from the oppressor, galvanises an identity within the formerly oppressed, and sticks two politically incorrect fingers up at the establishment. Of course, many argue that such

The Whore of Babylon from the Luther Bible, 1534 edition.

words, used in any context, only serve to reinforce a prejudice as such words are never shaken free of historical baggage; they create reality, rather than recording it. The word 'whore' is also in a state of reclamation among certain groups of the sex work community (others reject it entirely).

The truth is that I should not have used 'whore' in the Whores of Yore website; it's not my word, and if you're not a sex worker, it's not yours either. It's a term of abuse that sex workers hear every day by those seeking to devalue and shame them, and I had not fully appreciated that. I used 'whore' to refer to transgressive sexuality, like 'slut' or 'slag', rather than a woman who sells sex. I've always considered the word to be far bigger than that. I have had feedback from many sex workers questioning my use of the term, and for a while I gave serious consideration to changing it. But the history of that word is an important one, and one that I want to emphasise. Debate around what 'whore' actually means is a conversation worth having.

The German dramatist Georg Büchner (1813–1837) once wrote that 'freedom and whores are the most cosmopolitan items under the sun'.[2] But what does the word 'whore' actually mean? Where has it come from, and what does someone have to do to earn that particular title? Why was Joan of Arc, who died a virgin, called the 'French Whore'? And why was Elizabeth I, the 'Virgin Queen', attacked as the 'English Whore' by her Catholic enemies? French revolutionaries called Marie Antoinette the 'Austrian Whore'; Anne Boleyn was the 'Great Whore', and in the 2016 presidential campaign, Hillary Clinton was repeatedly attacked by Trump supporters as a 'whore'.[3] Perhaps we think we know perfectly well what we mean should we ever choose to drop the W-bomb, but the word is historically and culturally complex. This simple monosyllable is loaded with over a thousand years of attempting to control and shame women by stigmatising their sexuality.

The word is so old that its precise origins are lost in the mists of time, but it can be traced to the Old Norse *hora* (adulteress). *Hora* has multiple derivatives, such as the Danish *hore*, the Swedish *hora*, the Dutch *hoer*, and the Old High German *huora*. Going back even further to the Proto-Indo-European language (the common ancestor of the Indo-European languages), whore has roots in *qār*, meaning 'to like, desire.' *Qār* is a base that has produced words in other languages for 'lover', such as the Latin *carus*, the Old Irish *cara* and the Old Persian *kama* (meaning 'to desire').[4] 'Whore' is not a universal word; the indigenous Aborigines, First Nation people and native Hawaiians have no word for 'whore', or indeed for prostitution.

From the twelfth century, whore was a term of abuse for a sexually unchaste woman, but it did not specifically mean a sex worker. Thomas of Chobham's thirteenth-century definition of a whore was any woman who had sex outside marriage (hands up all those who have just learned they are a thirteenth-century whore).[5] Shakespeare used 'whore' nearly a hundred times in his plays, including *Othello*, *Hamlet* and *King Lear*; but in these plays it doesn't mean someone who sells sex, it means a promiscuous woman. John Webster's *The White Devil* (1612) explores narratives around badly behaved women. In one memorable scene Monticelso defines what a whore is:

> Shall I expound whore to you? sure I shall;
> I'll give their perfect character. They are first,
> Sweetmeats which rot the eater; in man's nostrils
> Poison'd perfumes. They are cozening alchemy;
> Shipwrecks in calmest weather. What are whores!
> Cold Russian winters, that appear so barren,
> As if that nature had forgot the spring.
> They are the true material fire of hell:
> Worse than those tributes i' th' Low Countries paid,

Exactions upon meat, drink, garments, sleep,
Ay, even on man's perdition, his sin.
They are those brittle evidences of law,
Which forfeit all a wretched man's estate
For leaving out one syllable. What are whores!
They are those flattering bells have all one tune,
At weddings, and at funerals. Your rich whores
Are only treasures by extortion fill'd,
And emptied by curs'd riot. They are worse,
Worse than dead bodies which are begg'd at gallows,
And wrought upon by surgeons, to teach man
Wherein he is imperfect. What's a whore!
She's like the guilty counterfeited coin,
Which, whosoe'er first stamps it, brings in trouble
All that receive it.[6]

Monticelso doesn't admit it, but what is driving this rant is a fear of women, fear that they can wield power over men; they can 'teach man wherein he is imperfect'. Here, a whore is not a sex worker, she is a woman who has authority over a man and must be shamed into silence at all costs.

Historically, 'whore' has been used to attack those who have upset the status quo and asserted themselves, usually in an attempt to reassert sexual control and dominance over her. But unlike the word 'prostitute', whore is not tied to a profession but to a perceived moral state. Which is why many powerful women, with no connection to the sex trade, have been attacked as 'whores'; Mary Wollstonecraft, Phulan Devi, even Margaret Thatcher were all labelled whores. The word is an attempt to shame, humiliate and ultimately subdue its target, and your average woman on the street is just as likely to be called a whore as a world leader, perhaps even more so.

'Whore' is a nasty insult today, but calling someone a whore in the early modern period was regarded as such a serious defamation of character that you could be taken to court for slander.* By far the most frequent insult cited in these cases where a woman has been slandered is 'whore' and myriad creative variants thereon: 'stinking whore', 'ticket-buying whore', 'drunken piss-pot whore', 'lace petticoat whore' and 'dog and bitch whore' have all been recorded.[7]

In 1664, Anne Blagge claimed that Anne Knutsford had called her a 'poxy-arsed whore'.[8] Poor Isabel Yaxley complained of a neighbour alleging that she was a 'whore' who could be 'fucked for a pennyworth of fish' in 1667.[9] In 1695, Susan Town of London accused Jane Adams of shouting to 'come out you whore, and scratch your mangy arse as I do'.[10] In 1699, Isabel Stone of York brought a suit against John Newbald for calling her 'a whore, a common whore and a piss-arsed whore … a Bitch and a piss-arsed Bitch'.[11] And in 1663, Robert Heyward was hauled before the Cheshire courts for calling Elizabeth Young a 'salt

bitch' and a 'sordid whore'. In court he claimed he could prove Elizabeth was a whore and she should just go home and 'wash the stains out of thy coat'.[12]

Examples of 'unfeminine language' from *New Art of Mystery of Gossipping*, 1770.

---

* Three excellent sources to read more about Tudor slander courts are Dinah Winch, 'Sexual Slander and its Social Context in England *c*.1660–1700, with Special Reference to Cheshire and Sussex' (unpublished PhD thesis, The Queen's College, Oxford University, 1999); Bernard Capp, *When Gossips Meet: Women, Family, and Neighbourhood in Early Modern England (Oxford Studies in Social History)* (Oxford: Oxford University Press, 2003); and Rachael Jayne Thomas, '"With Intent to Injure and Diffame": Sexual Slander, Gender and the Church Courts of London and York, 1680–1700' (unpublished MA, University of York, 2015).

In order to prove a case of slander, you would need a witness to the insult, to prove the accusation was untrue with a character witness, and to show how your reputation had been damaged by being called such names. The punishment for slander ranged from fines and being ordered to publicly apologise, through to excommunication (though this was rare). One example of punishment occurred in 1691, when William Halliwell was ordered to publicly apologise in church to Peter Leigh for defaming his character:

> I William Halliwell forgetting my duty to walk in Love and Charity towards my neighbour have uttered spoken and published several scandalous defamatory and reproachful words of and against Peter Leigh ... I do hereby recant revoke and recall the said words as altogether false scandalous and untrue ... I am unfeignedly sorry and I hereby confess and acknowledge that I have much wronged and injured him.[13]

The accusation of 'whore' was particularly damaging as it directly affected a woman's value on the marriage market. So when Thomas Ellerton called Judith Glendering a 'whore' who went from 'barn to barn' and from 'tinkers to fiddlers' in 1685, he was doing more than being abusive, he was preventing her finding a husband.[14] In 1652, Cicely Pedley alleged she had been called a 'whore' with the intention 'to prevent her marriage with a person of good quality'.[15] It could even affect business. In 1687, a Justice of the Peace decided that calling an innkeeper's wife a 'whore' was actionable because it had affected trade.[16]

There are numerous slander cases brought by a husband whose wife had been called a whore. Calling someone's wife a whore was a particularly devastating insult as it not only insulted the wife, but also impugned the husband as a cuckold and questioned his ability to sexually satisfy the missus. In 1685, for example, Abraham Beaver was accused of ordering Richard Winnell to 'get thee home thou cuckold thou will find Thomas Fox in Bed with thy Wife'.[17]

Although cases of men alleging slander were less frequent, they too were often sexual in nature. In 1680, Elizabeth Aborne of London was taken to court by Thomas Richardson for saying that his penis was 'rotten with the pox'.[18] Men were also attacked as 'whoremongers', 'cuckolds', 'bastard-getters', 'rogues', and in one case a 'jealous pated fool and ass'.[19] Men brought cases against people who had called them thieves, beggars or drunkards. In 1699, for example, Thomas Hewetson was brought before the courts in York for calling Thomas Daniel a 'mumper' (beggar): 'he was a mumper and went about the Country from door to door mumping'.[20]

By the end of the seventeenth century, there was a notable decline in the number of slander cases brought before the Church courts. Historians have long debated why this may have been the case. It may be that as cities swelled and the population grew, the courts became more concerned with crimes other than women calling each other 'hedge whores' and 'poxy-arsed whores'. It may just be that there was a shift in culture and taking your slagging matches before a judge became less

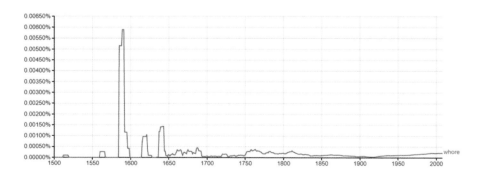

Google Ngram Viewer: frequency of the word 'whore' recorded in English literature from 1500 to 2008.

the done thing. By 1817, UK law ruled that 'calling a married woman or a single one a whore is not actionable, because fornication and adultery are subjects of spiritual not temporal censures'.[21]

As the above chart shows, since the seventeenth century there has been a notable decline in the use of the word 'whore'. Until the end of the seventeenth century, 'whore' was still a legal term and turns up in no less than 163 trials at the Old Bailey from 1679 until 1800. Historians such as Rictor Norton have examined how 'prostitute' or 'common prostitute' came to replace 'whore' as the legal terminology for a person who sells sexual services.[22] I suspect the sharp decline in the usage of 'whore' at the end of the seventeenth century is linked to the linguistic shift from legal terminology to a pure insult.

Today, 'whore' is largely confined to abusive and coarse speech. However, like the word 'slut', 'whore' is also in a state of reclamation and can be used to directly challenge the shame the word has carried for hundreds of years. 'Whore' may be a term of abuse, but it is one rooted in fear of female independence and sexual autonomy. Its progression from meaning a woman who desires, to an insult seeking to shame that desire, traces cultural attitudes around female sexuality. I do not use 'whore' to shame, I use it to recognise all those who rattled cultural sensibilities enough to be called a whore. I use it to deflate the shame within it. I use it to remember that our language shapes how we view each other, and it is constantly evolving. Historically, if you desire, you are a whore; if you have sex outside of marriage, you are a whore; if you transgress and threaten 'the man', you are a whore. We are all historical whores.

'A Nasty Name
for a Nasty Thing'

A History of Cunt

Ilove the word cunt. I love everything about it. Not just the signified vulva, vagina and pudendum (which are all kinds of cunty goodness and will be returned to shortly), but the actual oral and visual signalled sign of cunt. I love its simple monosyllabic form. I adore that the first

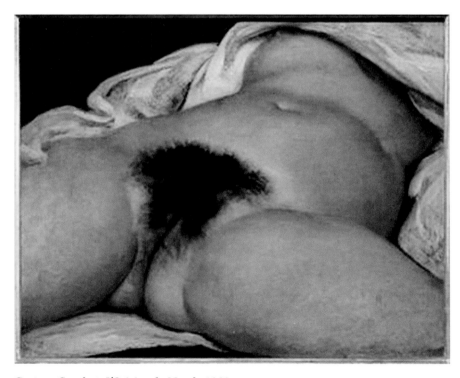

Gustave Courbet, *L'Origine du Monde*, 1866.

three letters (c u n) are basically all the same chalice shape rolling though the word until they are stopped in their ramble by the plosive T at the end. I love the forceful grunt of the C and the T sandwiching the softer UN sounds, enabling one to spit the word out like a bullet, or extend the *un* and roll it around your mouth for dramatic effect: cuuuuuuuuuuuunt!

I love it because it's deliciously dirty, endlessly funny and, like an auditory exclamation mark, is capable of stopping a conversation in its tracks. Walter Kirn called cunt 'the A-bomb of the English language', and he's absolutely right.[1] I love its versatility. In America, it is spectacularly offensive, while in Glasgow it can be a term of endearment; 'I love ya, ya wee cunt' is an expression heard throughout Glaswegian nurseries. That's not true, but Scottish folk do possess a dazzling linguistic dexterity with cunt. Irvine Welsh's 1993 novel *Trainspotting* contains 731 cunts (though only nineteen made it into the film).

But more than anything else, I love the sheer power of the word. I am fascinated by cunt's hallowed status as, to quote Christina Caldwell, 'the nastiest of the nasty words'.[2] There are other contenders for the 'most offensive' word in the English language; racial slurs are obvious heavyweights. The N-word is a deeply offensive word because of its historical context. It is not just a descriptive word, it is a word that was used to dehumanise black people and justify some of the worst atrocities in human history. It enabled the enslavement and brutalisation of millions of people by linguistically denying black people equality with white people. We can understand why racial slurs are hideously offensive, but cunt? Does it not strike anyone else as odd that one of the most offensive words in English is a word for vulva? Or that this word could even be considered in the same league of offence as racist terms spawned from the darkest and most rank of human atrocities? As far as I am aware, cunt has not enabled racial genocide, so we have to ask: how did cunt get to be so offensive? What did cunt do wrong?

Let's turn to the etymology first. Cunt is old. It's so old that its exact origins are lost in the folds of time and etymologists continue to debate where in the cunt cunt comes from. It's several thousand years old at least, and can be traced to the old Norse *kunta* and Proto-Germanic *kunt*, but before that cunt proves quite elusive. There are medieval cunty cognates in most Germanic languages; *kutte*, *kotze* and *kott* all appear in German. The Swedish have *kunta*; the Dutch have *conte*, *kut* and *kont*, and the English once had *cot* (which I quite like and think is due a revival).* Here's where the debate comes in: no one is quite sure what cunt actually means. Some etymologists have argued cunt has a root in the Proto-Indo-European sound *'gen/gon'*, which means to 'create, become'. You can see 'gen' in the modern words gonads, genital, genetics and gene. Others have theorised cunt descends from the root *gune*, which means 'woman' and crops up in 'gynaecology'.[3] The root sound that most fascinates etymologists is 'cu'. 'Cu' is associate with the female, and forms the basis of 'cow' and 'queen'.[4] 'Cu' is linked to the Latin *cunnus* ('vulva'), which sounds tantalisingly like cunt (though some etymologists claim it is unrelated), and has spawned the French *con*, the Spanish *coño*, the Portuguese *cona*, and the Persian *kun* (کون).[5] My favourite cunt theory is that the 'cu' also means to have knowledge. Cunt and 'cunning' are likely to have descended from the same root – 'cunning' originally meant wisdom or knowledge, rather than sneak-iness, while 'can' and 'ken' became prefixes to 'cognition' and other derivatives.[6] In Scotland today, if you 'ken' something, it means you

---

* 'Oxford English Dictionary', *Oed.Com*, 2018 <http://www.oed.com/view/Entry/45874?redirectedFrom=cunt#eid> [Accessed 7 September 2018]. Other excellent sources that cover the etymology of cunt include Mark Daniel, *See You Next Tuesday* (London: Timewell, 2008); Pete Silverton, *Filthy English* (London: Portobello Books, 2009); Jonathon Green, *Green's Dictionary of Slang* (London: Chambers, 2010); Melissa Mohr, *Holy Sh*T: A Brief History of Swearing* (Oxford: Oxford University Press, 2013); and Matthew Hunt, 'Cunt', *Matthewhunt.Com*, 2017 <http://www.matthewhunt.com/cunt/> [Accessed 3 September 2018].

understand it. In the Middle Ages 'quaint' meant both knowledge and cunt (but more of that later). The debate will rage on, but the bottom line is that cunt is something of a mystery.

Here is what we do know: cunt is the oldest word for either the vulva or the vagina in the English language (possibly the oldest in Europe). Its only rival for oldest term for 'the boy in the boat' (1930) would be yoni (meaning vulva, source or womb). The English language borrowed yoni from ancient Sanskrit around 1800 and today it has been appropriated by various neo-spiritual groups who hope that by calling their 'duff' (1880) a yoni they can avoid the horror of cunt and tap into some ancient veneration of the 'flapdoodle' (1653). Of course, the irony is cunt and yoni may even have sprung from the same Proto-Indo-European root. Furthermore, cunt is far more feminist than vagina or vulva could ever dream to be.

Vagina turns up in seventeenth-century medical texts and comes from the Latin *vagina*, which means a sheath or a scabbard. A vagina is something a sword goes into; that's its entire etymological function – to be the holder of a sword (penis). It relies on the penis for its meaning and function. We may as well still be calling the poor thing 'cock alley' (1785) or the 'pudding bag' (1653). There are many cunning linguists who rightly get their proverbials in a twist when you confuse vagina with vulva: to be clear, the vagina is the muscular canal that connects the uterus to the vulva, and the vulva is the external equipment (comprising the mons pubis, labia majora, labia minora, clitoris, vestibule of the vagina, bulb of the vestibule, and the Bartholin's glands). Vulva dates to the late fourteenth century and comes from the Latin *vulva*, meaning 'womb' – some have suggested it comes from *volvere*, or to wrap. In his 1538 Latin dictionary, Thomas Elyot defined a vulva as 'the womb or mother of any female animal, also a meat used of the Romans made of the belly of a sow, either that hath farrowed or is with farrow'.[7] So, yet again, the meaning of vulva is dependent on being the container for a penis – or a questionable cut of a pregnant Roman pig.

Cunt, however, predates both these terms and derives from a Proto-Indo-European root word meaning woman, knowledge, creator or queen, which is far more empowering than a word that means 'I hold cock'. Plus, cunt is the whole damn shebang, inside and out. There's no need to split pubic hairs when it comes to cunt. Words like vulva and vagina are linguistic efforts to offer sanitised, medicalised alternatives to cunt. And if that wasn't enough to sway you over to team cunt, in 1500 Wynkyn de Worde defined vulva as 'in English, a cunt'.[8] Cunt is not slang; cunt is the original. So, cunt is the godmother of all words for 'the monosyllable' (1780) – but then the question arises: has cunt always been such an offensive word as it is today?

The simple answer is no. To the medieval mind, cunt was simply a descriptive word, a little bawdy perhaps as cunts tend to be, but certainly not offensive. The fact that cunt would make it into de Worde's dictionary and medical texts shows how everyday the word was. John Hall's sixteenth-century translation of Lanfranc of Milan's medical text *Chirurgia Parua Lanfranci* is not cunt shy and describes 'in wymmen neck of the bladder is schort, is made fast to the cunte'.[9] The earliest cunt citation in the *Oxford English Dictionary* dates to 1230, and is a London street in the red-light district of Southwark – the beautifully named 'Gropecuntelane'.[10] It did exactly what it said on the tin: it was a lane for groping cunts. There were Gropecuntelanes (or variations of Grapcunt, Groppecuntelane, Gropcunt Lane) found throughout the cities of medieval Britain. Keith Briggs locates Gropecuntlanes in Oxford, York, Bristol, Northampton, Wells, Great Yarmouth, Norwich, Windsor, Stebbing, Reading, Shareshill, Grimsby, Newcastle and Banbury. Sadly, all of these streets have now been renamed, usually as 'Grape Lane' or 'Grove Lane'.[11]

While Scottish folk may be calling their friends cunts, medieval people seem to have been calling their children cunts. Cunt actually turns up in a number of medieval surnames (though they are quite possibly aliases): Godwin Clawecunte (1066), Gunoka Cuntles (1219), John Fillecunt (1246) and Robert Clevecunt (1302) have all been recorded. And if the possibility of meeting Miss Gunoka Cuntles on Gropecuntelane was not an exciting enough prospect (and it should be), a Miss Bele Wydecunthe appears in a Norfolk Subsidy Roll of 1328.[12] While we are on the subject of cunt monikers, in his study of humorous names, Russell Ash found a whole family of Cunts living in England in the nineteenth century: Fanny Cunt (born 1839), also her son, Richard 'Dick' Cunt, and her daughters, Ella Cunt and Violet Cunt.[13]

Medieval literature is similarly awash with cunts. *The Proverbs of Hendyng* (c.1325) contains this advice to young women: 'Give your cunt cunningly and make (your) demands after the wedding' (ʒeve þi cunte

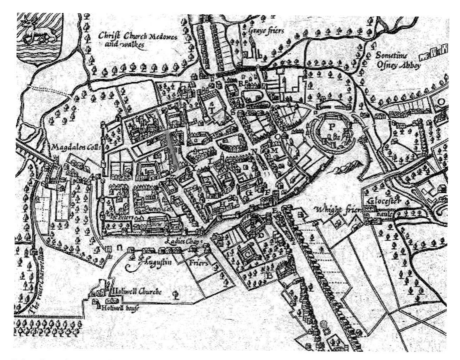

John Speed, *Map of Oxfordshire and the University of Oxford*, 1605. Gropecuntelane is shown in blue.

A twelfth-century sheela na gig on the church at Kilpeck, Herefordshire, England.

to cunni[n]g, and craue affetir wedding).[14] The fifteenth-century Welsh poet Gwerful Mechain advised fellow poets to celebrate the 'curtain on a fine bright cunt' that 'flaps in a place of greeting'.[15] Medieval society was far more sexually liberated than we give them credit for, and one reason cunt wasn't considered offensive is because sex wasn't that offensive to them. It was certainly not a sexually liberated utopia, but neither were medieval people waddling about in chastity belts, as popular mythology would have us believe. Sex was a source of great humour, eroticism and absolutely central to married life; finding sex deeply offensive is something that came into its own during the early modern era.

Historically, the most heavily tabooed language has shifted from the blasphemous to bodily functions, and is now in a process of moving to race. Swear words that would get you into serious trouble in the

Middle Ages were blasphemous ones. If you caught your soft areas in a zipper in the thirteenth century, you might cry out something like 'God's teeth', 'God's wounds' (Z'wounds) or 'God's eyes'. Cunt, by comparison, was a descriptive word and suitable for all occasions. It was not euphemistically twee, overly medicalised or humorously grotesque – cunt was cunt.

One medieval author who dropped the C-bomb with the precision of a military drone is Geoffrey Chaucer (1343–1400). The word that Chaucer uses in *The Canterbury Tales* and *House of Fame* is not 'cunt' but 'queynte'. However, the reader is left in little doubt as to what a queynte is – the Wife of Bath is quite clear:

> What eyleth yow to grucche thus and grone?
> Is it for ye wolde have my queynte allone?

> (What ails you that you grumble thus and groan?
> Is it because you'd have my cunt alone?)[16]

Chaucer's most famous cunt joke is in 'The Miller's Tale', where 'queynte' means both knowledge and cunt (remember the root to both cunning and cunt?):

> As clerkes ben ful subtile and ful queynte,
> And prively he caughte hire by the queynte,
> And seyde, 'Ywis, but if ich have my wille,
> For deerne love of thee, lemman, I spille.'

> (The clerk had been subtle and cunning,
> and quickly he caught her by the cunt,
> and said, 'If I cannot have my will,
> for love of thee, darling, I will spill.')[17]

The use of 'quaint' as a synonym for cunt is seen in a variety of other works. In his 1598 Italian/English dictionary, John Florio uses 'quaint' as a synonym for cunt and defines *potta* as 'a cunt, a quaint', and a *pottuta* as 'that hath a cunt, cunted, quainted'.[18] The playful double meaning of 'quaint' turns up again in Andrew Marvell's 'To His Coy Mistress':

> Thy beauty shall no more be found;
> Nor, in thy marble vault, shall sound
> My echoing song: the worms shall try
> That long preserved virginity:
> And your quaint honour turn to dust;
> And into ashes all my lust.[19]

It has also been suggested that William Shakespeare's 'acquaint' in his Sonnet XX (1609) is a play on 'quaint' and 'cunt'. And if any man knew the comedic power of a well-placed cunt it was Shakespeare. In Act III, Scene 2 of *Hamlet*, the eponymous hero asks Ophelia, 'Lady, shall I lie in your lap?' Ophelia replies, 'No, my lord.' Hamlet then asks her, 'Do you think I meant country matters?'[20] When David Tennant played Hamlet, he paused on the first syllable to emphasis this: 'Cunt-ry matters'. In *Twelfth Night* (Act II, Scene 5) Malvolio describes his employer's handwriting: 'There be her very Cs, her Us, and her Ts: and thus makes she her great Ps' – making for a simultaneous pun on 'cunt' and 'piss'.[21] The immortal bard's status as a smut peddler has been discreetly swept under the cultural rug, but his work is full of innuendo and nob gags. In 1807, a shocked Thomas Bowdler edited out all the rude jokes so women and children could safely read it, and published *The Family Shakespeare* (which was completely cunt free). Among the many changes made in *The Family Shakespeare*, Ophelia doesn't commit suicide in *Hamlet*, the character of Doll Tearsheet (a sex worker) is entirely edited out of *Henry IV*, and in *Romeo and Juliet*, Mercutio's saucy 'the bawdy hand of the dial is now upon the prick of noon' was altered to read 'the hand of the dial is now upon the point of noon'.[22] This led to the addition of the word 'bowdlerise' to the English language, which means to remove passages of a text that are considered objectionable.

Cunt was also used freely in the bawdy ballads of Shakespeare's contemporaries, who felt no such compulsion to veil their cunts in double entendres. *Ragionamenti della Nanna e della Antonia* (1534–36) by Pietro Aretino tells readers to shun flowery euphemisms and just say cunt: 'Speak plainly, and say fuck, cunt and cock; otherwise thou wilt be understood by nobody'.[23] The Scottish play *Philotus* (1603) contained the lines 'doun thy hand and graip hir cunt'.[24] And the *Mercurius Fumigosus* (1654) celebrates 'cunt and good company'.[25] But the fact that big-name writers, such as Shakespeare and Marvell, used cunt as a saucy punchline and camouflaged it in puns and cheeky hints suggests that, by Shakespeare's time, cunt was starting to be censored.

It is no coincidence that it was around this time that the first laws banning sexually obscene material came into force. In Britain, the first parliamentary bill to restrain 'books, pamphlets, ditties, songs, and other works that promote lascivious ungodly love' was drafted by William Lambarde in 1580.[26] The Licensing Act of 1662 banned the publication of any 'heretical, seditious, schismatic or offensive books, or pamphlets wherein any doctrine of opinion shall be asserted or maintained which is contrary to Christian faith'.[27] Language is a powerful tool of social control: as sex became repressed, words linking to the body became taboo. After all, how can we enjoy the sexuality of our bodies, shame free, when the very words we use to talk about them, think about them or write about them are considered obscene? Ellis Cashmore argued that cunt's banishment to the naughty step is a result of mass sexual censure and the rise of 'modesty': 'with rules came manners, and with manners came courtesy, and with courtesy came modesty, and the word "cunt" [was] referring to parts of the body that were enclosed, they were secreted away'.[28] Women's sexuality came in for particular censure and punishment, and cunt was an obvious symbol of all puritan rule sought to repress.

By the seventeenth century cunt had acquired a shock factor, and one author who revelled in the deliciously deviant embrace of cunt was John Wilmot, Earl of Rochester (1647–1680). Rochester was an English poet and courtier of King Charles II. He was the poster boy of debauchery and sexual excess and simply dripped with 'fuck you'. If Cromwell's parliament had attempted to dam up sexuality, Rochester surfed to notoriety on the tidal wave of sexual repression that was unleashed when the plug was pulled on Puritan rule. Geoffrey Hughes once perfectly described Rochester as delighting in 'a world seen from crotch level'.[29]

Wilmot's poem 'Advice to a Cuntmonger' begins as follows:

> Fucksters you that would bee happy
> Have a care of Cunts that Clapp yee,
> Scape disease of evill Tarsehole,
> Gout and Fistula in Arsehole.[30]

He described his attraction to a lover as 'A touch from any part of her had done 't, / Her hand, her foot, her very look's a Cunt' (1680). His 1684 play *Sodom* features characters such as 'Queen Cuntigratia' and her maid 'Cunticula'. His 'A Ramble in St James's Park' (1672) contains eight cunts as he grows increasingly jealous of his mistress's other lovers.

> When your lewd cunt came spewing home
> Drenched with the seed of half the town,
> My dram of sperm was supped up after
> For the digestive surfeit water.

Full gorged at another time
With a vast meal of slime
Which your devouring cunt had drawn
From porters' backs and footmen's brawn ...[31]

It's tempting to read Rochester's work as a celebration of sexuality, but he directs considerable anger and hatred towards cunts and their owners. In *Sodom* he defines cunt as 'Love's common nasty sink' and claims 'she that hath a cunt will be a whore'. His verse is full of degrading, grotesque descriptions of diseased, balding, biting, feral cunts. In 'A Ramble in St James's Park', his hatred towards the women (and genitals) he desires is projected onto the other men, whom he spurns as 'obsequious' 'curs' in their hunt for cunt.

So a proud bitch does lead about
Of humble curs the amorous rout,
Who most obsequiously do hunt
The savory scent of salt-swoln cunt.[32]

Image from *The School of Venus, or the Ladies Delight*, 1680.

By the seventeenth century, cunt was also being used as a derogatory synecdoche for women, especially a sexual woman – in much the same way as women can be charmingly referred to as 'pussy' (1699) or 'clunge' (2008) today. In 1665, Samuel Pepys writes about a powder that should 'make all the cunts in town run after him', and one 1675 ballad warns that 'Citty Cunts are dangerous sport'.[33]

By the eighteenth century, cunt was regarded as an obscene and ugly word. In his *Classical Dictionary of the Vulgar Tongue* (1785), Francis Grose defines cunt as 'a nasty name for a nasty thing', and instead employs the euphemism 'the monosyllable'.[34] Such modesty from a man who lists 'Mrs Fubb's Parlour', 'Buckinger's Boot', 'Scut' and a 'Lobster Pot' as common synonyms for 'a woman's commodity'. 'Cunny', a derivative of cunt, and 'quim' come into common usage in the eighteenth century. John Cleland's 1748 bonkbuster *Fanny Hill* was a completely cunt-free affair, and Cleland boasted he had written it without one rude word. The annual almanac on London sex workers, *Harris's List* (1757–95) also shies away from cunt, preferring instead to use 'mossy grot' and 'Venus mound'.[35]

But one eighteenth-century author who uses cunt precisely for its shock factor was the Marquis de Sade (1740–1814). There are 'little cunts', 'frigged' cunts, 'open cunts', 'pretty cunts', 'infamous' cunts, 'bloodied' cunts, 'fucked', 'licked' and 'rascal' cunts. If you shake any book by Sade, a cunt will fall out; Sade is a cunt piñata. His *La Philosophie dans le Boudoir* (1795) includes such cunt gems as:

> Next, I will lodge my prick in her anus; you will avail me of your ass, 'twill take the place of the cunt she had under my nose, and now you will have at it in the style she will have employed, her head now between your legs; I'll suck your asshole as I have just sucked her cunt, you will discharge, so will I, and all the while my hand, embracing the dear sweet

'Les charmes de Fanny exposés' (plate VIII) from *Fanny Hill*, 1766.

pretty little body of this charming novice, will go ahead to tickle her clitoris that she too may swoon from delight.[36]

Sade delighted in writing the most extreme, deviant pornography and his repeated use of cunt, rather than the twee euphemisms seen in *Fanny Hill*, is testament to the cunt's ascension to being regarded as the most offensive word in the Western world.

Despite their reputation for being sexually repressed, pornography flowed beneath the upper crust of Victorian prudery like the river of slime in *Ghostbusters II*. There is no doubt that cunt was a thoroughly obscene word. But precisely because of this, Victorian erotica is simply groaning under the weight of cunts. Erotic novels such as *The Lustful Turk* (1828), *The Romance of Lust* (1873), *Early Experiences of a Young Flagellant* (1876) by Rosa Coote, *Miss Bellasis Birched for Thieving* (1882) by Etonensis, *The Autobiography of a Flea* (1887) and *Venus in India* (1889) by 'Captain Charles Devereaux' are a veritable blitzkrieg of C-bombs. *The Pearl* was a pornographic magazine that was published in London from 1879 to 1880, when it was closed down for publishing obscene material. Most editions contained a collection of limericks, or 'Nursery Rhymes', that have a lot of fun with cunt.

There was a young man of Bombay,
Who fashioned a cunt out of clay,
But the heat of his prick
Turned it into a brick,
And chafed his foreskin away.

There was a young lady of Hitchin,
Who was scratching her cunt in the kitchen,
Her father said 'Rose, It's the crabs, I suppose'.
'You're right pa, the buggers are itching'.[37]

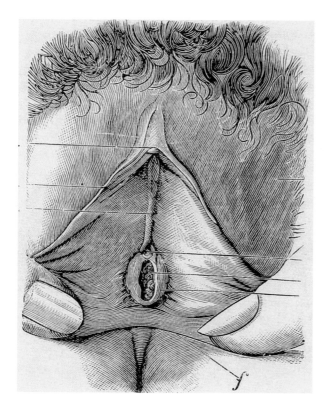

Lawson Tait, *Diseases of Women and Abdominal Surgery*, 1877.

And it is in the nineteenth century that cunt starts to be used as a general term of abuse. The *Oxford English Dictionary* places the first known use of cunt as an insult at 1860: 'And when they got to Charleston, they had to, as is wont/ Look around to find a chairman, and so they took a Cunt'.[38]

Perhaps one of the most significant cunt moments in the twentieth century was the banning and subsequent obscenity trial of D. H. Lawrence's *Lady Chatterley's Lover* (1928), which contains fourteen cunts (and forty fucks). When Gerald Gould reviewed an edited version in 1932, he noted that 'passages are necessarily omitted to which the author undoubtedly attached supreme psychological importance – importance so great, that he was willing to face obloquy and misunderstanding and censorship because of them'.[39] The book caused

Invocation A L'amour, 1825.

a sensation not only because of its graphic descriptions of sex and women's sexual pleasure, but because it uses sex to smash down class boundaries. Sex is one of the supreme levellers, and for all her titles, money and privilege, Lady Constance Chatterley has a cunt: she is a sexual being. Sexual desire and pleasure have no understanding of the class system. Lawrence uses the word cunt throughout because it is the only word that can express the yearning, primal sexuality of Constance and subvert the pretensions of a society that viewed women as sexless wives and mothers. Lawrence's use of cunt is shocking, but also incredibly tender and passionate; for Lawrence, cunt is a truly wonderful thing. One of the pivotal scenes in the novel is where Mellors teaches Constance the difference between cunt and fuck:

'Th'art good cunt, though, aren't ter? Best bit o' cunt left on earth. When ter likes! When tha'rt willin'!'

'What is cunt?' she said.

'An' doesn't ter know? Cunt! It's thee down theer; an' what I get when I'm i'side thee, and what tha gets when I'm i'side thee; it's a' as it is, all on't.'

'All on't,' she teased. 'Cunt! It's like fuck then.'

'Nay nay! Fuck's only what you do. Animals fuck. But cunt's a lot more than that. It's thee, dost see: an' tha'rt a lot besides an animal, aren't ter? – even ter fuck? Cunt! Eh, that's the beauty o' thee, lass!'[40]

Cunt: 'that's the beauty of thee, lass' — I don't think I have heard a more marvellous definition of cunt. Sadly, despite Lawrence's best efforts and a jury that agreed a work stuffed with cunts does have artistic merit, cunt has yet to be welcomed back to polite society. James Joyce uses one cunt in *Ulysses* (1922) and calls the Holy Land 'the grey sunken cunt of the world'.[41] (Though he freely uses cunt in his private erotic letters to his wife, Nora, whom he delightfully calls 'fuck bird'.) The American Beat poets like the shock of the cunt. In 'Howl' (1956) Ginsberg writes about a 'vision of the ultimate cunt'.[42] But cunt is there to shock. Cunt didn't make it into mainstream cinema until 1971, in *Carnal Knowledge*, starring Jack Nicholson and Ann-Margret. Jonathan Fuerst, Nicholson's character, screams at Bobbie (Ann-Margret): 'Is this an ultimatum? Answer me, you ball-busting, castrating, son of a cunt bitch!'[43] *The Exorcist* (1973) uses 'cunting' as an adjective twice (i.e. 'cunting daughter'). There is a third cunt that was cut from the final edit where the troubled Regan tells her doctor he must keep his fingers away from her cunt.[44] Notice that the only cunt that was cut was the one that actually means vulva? This has been true of most cinematic uses of cunt — it is far more often used as an insult than it is to mean the genitals.

As the twentieth century wore on, cunt settled into its role as a powerful insult. The *Oxford English Dictionary* did not admit cunt until the seventies. But in 2014 the OED added 'cunty, cuntish, cunted, and cunting' to the entry under cunt; 'cunty' is defined as 'highly objectionable or unpleasant'; 'cuntish' means an 'objectionable person or behaviour'; 'cunted' means to be drunk and 'cunting' is an intensifier that means 'very much'.[45] There is no doubt that cunt is a very versatile word (noun, adjective, verb), but it still shocks. In 2016, Ofcom (the regulator for UK communications) ranked swear words in order of offensiveness, and cunt came out on top.[46] The British Board of Film Classification's guidelines state that the word cunt can only be used frequently in films that are rated 18+.

Cunt maintains an uneasy relationship with feminists, who are undecided if the word is empowering or demeaning. Various feminist movements have tried to reclaim cunt. Judy Chicago led the 'Cunt art' movement of the 1970s and created works of art that aggressively used 'cunt' to cut through prudish attitudes around female sexuality. Inga Muscio's 1998 *Cunt: A Declaration of Independence* inspired a movement called 'Cuntfest' – 'a celebration of women'. In 1996, Eva Ensler premiered a new play called *The Vagina Monologues* at the HERE Arts Centre. The play features different characters talking about their sense of self, their sexuality and how they feel about their vaginas. One monologue is entitled 'Reclaiming Cunt' and is a tour de force of cunt:

> I love that word
> I can't say it enough
> I can't stop saying it
> Feeling a little irritated at the airport?
> Just say CUNT and everything changes
> 'What did you say?'

'I said CUNT, that's right, SAID CUNT, CUNT, CUNT, CUNT.'

It feels so good.

Try it. Go ahead. Go ahead.

CUNT.

CUNT.

CUNT.

CUNT.[47]

The audience are encouraged to shout CUNT in unison and to feel the explosive power of the word as one. *The Vagina Monologues* was a landmark production in feminist theatre. But although I am very much in agreement with Ensler and also consider shouting cunt at Ryanair baggage reclaim services to be highly therapeutic, Ensler's work hasn't forced the mass renegotiation with cunt we may have hoped for. Perhaps cunt is beyond reclaiming now. But it remains a deeply powerful and special word.

Words for women's genitals tend to be clinical (vagina, vulva, pudendum, etc.), childlike (tuppence, foof, fairy, minky, Mary, twinkle, etc.), detached (down there, bits, special area, etc.), highly sexual (pussy, fuck hole, etc.), violent (axe wound, penis flytrap, gash, growler, etc.), or refer to unpleasant smells, tastes and appearance (fish taco, bacon sandwich, badly stuffed kebab, bearded clam). Cunt doesn't convey any of these. Cunt is cunt. Words for the vulva seem to be in a constant state of trying to deny the very thing being described – your genitals aren't a 'twinkle' or 'fur pie'. Sadly, just as cunt the word has been censored, cunts themselves have been culturally censored to the point where the only cunts that we feel are acceptable are plucked, waxed, surgically trimmed, buffed, douched with perfumed cleaning products and served up covered in glitter. The vaginaplasty business is booming and you can now have your labia cut off, your hymen rebuilt and a car air freshener installed (I joke). Is it any wonder we can't cope with the directness of cunt and resort to 'down there'? Cunt may never be allowed off the naughty step, but it is surely far less offensive than many synonyms on offer. And while people insist on calling cunt a vagina or a vulva so as not to cause offence, it's worth remembering that we are actually calling cunt a scabbard – a cock holder, a sausage pocket.

Cunt may be classed as an offensive word, but it's an ancient and honest one. It's also the original word; everything else came after.

Welcome to #TeamCunt.

SEX
AND
VULVAS

Looking for the Boy in the Boat

A History of the Clitoris

Unless you're a late social bloomer who still believes women are domesticated wombs with tits, who should restrict their activities to baking cakes and darning socks, I think we can all agree that feminism has done some pretty marvellous things. Women can now vote, open bank accounts and make cheese from our own breastmilk without being molested by the patriarchal dairy overlords. There's no doubt, women have come a long way. But there's still one area that feminism is failing in. One area where the almighty penis continues to reign over the vulva unchallenged – and that area is sexual slang. However many slang words you can think of for the clitoris, there will be a thousand more for the penis, testes or semen. Of course, there are many colloquialisms for the vulva, but they rarely delineate the various important pleasure points contained within that glorious goodie bag: the clitoris, the cervix, or the much mythologised Gräfenberg spot, for example. It's just 'gash', 'pussy', 'clunge', etc. And I'm not even sure if there are any slang words for the womb or the ovaries (would 'baby-cave' or 'lady baubles' work?). The whole 'locker-room banter' register of bawdy sexual slang celebrates the vulva for the pleasure it brings to the mighty 'rod' (1591). The omission of the clit – whose only function is to pleasure its owner – is telling. In Western culture, the clitoris has been overlooked because female sexual pleasure has historically played second fiddle to male pleasure. Literally and metaphorically, the clitoris has never received enough attention.

Take, for example, that much beloved encyclopaedia of vulgarity, *Roger's Profanisaurus*, first published in 1998. The work contains over 2,500 slang entries, cataloguing all manner of obscenities from 'purple headed yoghurt warrior' (penis) to 'growling at the badger' (cunnilingus). But there are only five clitoral colloquialisms to be found within the whole damn thing: 'boy in the boat', 'bell', 'button', 'fanny flange' and 'sugared almond'.[1] Even the latest reworking of the *Profanisaurus* series, *Hail Sweary* (2013), which advertises itself as containing '4,000 new rude words and blasphemies', only manages a dismal five entries on the clitoris; 'beanis' (a large 'bean' that resembles a penis), 'clock' (again, a large clitoris and cock hybrid), and 'panic button' – under which is sub-referenced 'wail switch' and 'clematis'. Which means that the clitoris accounts for less than 0.15 per cent of all the entries. But it's not like the book is pussy light. In fact, while *Hail Sweary* only contains thirty-seven colloquialisms for the penis and/or testes, there are a whopping 104 entries for the vulva. While this might sound like a win for #TeamCunt, most of these terms are pejorative comments on what's referred to throughout as 'untidy', 'unkempt' or 'messy' vulvas. References to the labia are multiple: 'doner meat', 'pig's ears', 'Biggles' scarf'. Pubic hair also features heavily: 'ZZ Mott', 'gruffalo', 'Terry Waite's allotment'. Allusions to fish are tediously predictable: 'fishmonger's dustbin', 'trout pocket', 'haddock pasty'.[2] And so on, and so on. Despite the book's obvious obsession with the holiest of holies, the emphasis is clearly phallocentric and prioritises the pleasure the vulva gives, rather than that which it can receive. It might seem like I am picking on the *Profanisaurus*, but the colloquial drought around the clitoris is universal. Ignoring clitoral pleasure is woven into the very language of sex.

This chapter focuses on the Western fascination with the clitoris and the endless efforts by doctors to understand and 'fix' it. As female

medical encyclopaedia gives the most detailed and vivid account of this awful procedure (wince warning):

> Have the girl sit on a chair while a muscled young man standing behind her places his arms below the girl's thighs. Have him separate and steady her legs and whole body. Standing in front and taking hold of the clitoris with broad-mouthed forceps in his left hand, the surgeon stretches it outward, while with the right hand, he cuts it off at the point next to the pincers of the forceps. It is proper to let a length remain from that cut off, about the size of the membrane that's between the nostrils, so as to take away the excess material only; as I have said, the part to be removed is at that point just of the forceps. Because the clitoris is a skinlike structure and stretches out excessively, do not cut off too much, as a urinary fistula may result from cutting such large growths too deeply. After the surgery, it is recommended to treat the wound with wine or cold water, and wiping it clean with a sponge to sprinkle frankincense powder on it. Absorbent linen bandages dipped in vinegar should be secured in place, and a sponge in turn dipped in vinegar placed above. After the seventh day, spread the finest calamine on it. With it, either rose petals or a genital powder made from baked clay can be applied. This is especially good: Roast and grind date pits and spread the powder on [the wound]; [this compound] also works against sores on the genitals.[7]

'Excessively large' clitorises were thought to be analogous to a mini penis, and therefore responsible for lesbianism and abnormal sexual appetites in women. This belief dominated cultural attitudes to the sweet spot right up until the twentieth century. In modern medical terms, this is known as 'clitoral hypertrophy', a 'macroclitoris' or

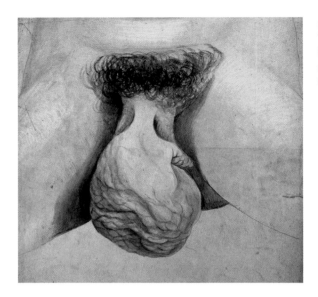

Christopher D'Alton,
'Female Genitalia Showing
Severely Diseased Tissue
and Hypertrophy of the
Clitoris', 1857.

'clitoromegaly', and it is an extremely rare condition. But given the frequency with which hypertrophied clitorises turn up in historical medical texts, you'd be forgiven for thinking our matriarchal ancestors were packing endowments that would make a donkey blush. Obviously, this was not the case, so we have to conclude that this obsession with the clitoris and uncontrolled sexuality was cultural, rather than biological. Given the fascination with cutting out offending clitorises, perhaps it's no wonder the poor thing has tried to keep its head down throughout history. There is not much mention of the 'jellyroll gumdrop' (1919) outside medical literature of Ancient Greece and Rome, but we can find it if we put the effort in.*

---

* Even the *Kama Sutra*, composed sometime around the third century AD, doesn't directly reference the clitoris, referring instead to the 'mons veneris', but it is one of the earliest texts to fully explore the female orgasm. However, ancient Sanskrit does contain a number of terms for the clitoris: *yoni-lingam* (vulva-penis), *bhagankura* (sprout of the vulva), and my personal favourite, *smara-chatra* (umbrella of the God of Love). Thank you to Professor Wendy Doniger, who was kind enough to talk me through the original Ancient Sanskrit language used for the vulva in the *Kama Sutra*.

The word 'clitoris' didn't come into use until around the sixteenth century. The Ancient Greeks and Romans would call the 'little bald man' (1997) the 'nymph', 'myrtle-berry', 'thorn', 'tongue-bag', or just plain 'bag'.[8] Charming. But the compliments don't stop there. Orally pleasuring the clitoris was considered obscene. When cunnilingus is spoken about in Classical literature it is generally regarded as something repugnant, indulged in only by lesbians and weak men whose erection had failed them. So much so that many Greek insults involved accusing someone of 'dining at the Y' (1963). The Greek playwright Aristophanes (446–386 BC) mentions cunnilingus several times to point to a character's moral failings. His character Ariphrades appears in several plays

Roman fresco from the Terme Suburbane in Pompeii AD 79.

as the 'inventor' of oral sex: 'he gloats in vice, is not merely a dissolute man and utterly debauched, but he actually invented a new form of vice; for he pollutes his tongue with abominable pleasures'.[9]

The Romans went one better and actually considered the word clitoris (*landīca*) an obscenity, in much the same way as 'cunt' is obscene today. Cicero referred to it as 'the forbidden word'.[10] It was regarded as so naughty, it really only appears in street graffiti: '*Fulviae landicam peto*' ('Seek the clitoris of Fulvia'), and '*Eupla laxa landicosa*' ('Eupla, a loose, large clitoris').[11] Poet and satirist Martial (AD 41–104) mocks the clitoris as a 'monstrous blemish' and a 'protuberance'.[12] All this big-clit bashing may be disheartening, but, as Melissa Mohr argues, 'people swear about what they care about', and it seems that the Greeks and Romans really did care about the clitoris and its stimulating effects.[13] And at least they were talking about the clitoris, because the conversation stalls somewhat when we hit the Middle Ages.

It's not really fair to say the medieval world forgot about the clitoris – they knew it was there and what it was (sort of), but they didn't really move the discussion on from the big boys of Greek and Roman gynaecology.[†] Today, we understand scientific research to have a 'half-life', meaning that information is being updated at such a rate that by the time medical students leave university, half of what they have learned will be obsolete.[14] However, European medieval doctors believed in vintage medicine and continued to trot out gynaecology's greatest hits for hundreds of years. One of the pilgrims in Chaucer's *Canterbury Tales* (1400) is a physician, who we are told is well educated because he has studied the work of...

---

* For further reading about the clitoris being used as an obscenity in the Ancient World, read Melissa Mohr, *Holy Sh*T: A Brief History of Swearing* (Corby: Oxford Academic Publishing Ltd, 2013).

† For a really excellent overview of the medieval medical understanding of the clitoris, read Karma Lochrie, *Heterosyncrasies: Female Sexuality When Normal Wasn't* (Minneapolis: University of Minnesota Press, 2005), pp. 71–102.

... old Esculapius,
And Deiscorides, and also Rufus,
Old Hippocrates, Hali, and Galen,
Serapion, Rhazes, and Avicen,
Averroes, Gilbertus, and Constantine,
Bernard and Gatisden, and John Damascene.[15]

Meaning that even by the late Middle Ages, the most up-to-date research Chaucer's physician is reading is over two hundred years old. Imagine your surgeon looming over you with a meat cleaver and a medical manual from the eighteenth century and you start to get a sense of just how bizarre that is. So, it's little wonder that medieval understanding of the clitoris circled the same conclusions drawn in the Ancient World: namely, big ones are bad, and lesbians like them. However, new Arabic medical texts were also published and translated throughout the Middle Ages and proved highly influential. The work of Islamic physicians such as Avicenna (AD 980–1037) and Albucasis (AD 936–1013) were translated into Latin by Gerard of Cremona

A woman caresses another woman who uses a root vegetable as a dildo, 1900.

(AD 1114–1187) and were still in use across the West until the seventeenth century.

Medieval Arabic texts continued to fret about large clitorises, recommending they be trimmed back to curb all manner of naughty behaviour, including promiscuity and lesbianism. Albucasis, often called 'the father of surgery', wrote:

> The clitoris may grow in size above the order of nature so that
> it gets a horrible deformed appearance; in some women it
> becomes erect like the male organ and attains to coitus ... this
> too you should cut away.[16]

Avicenna threw his hat in the ring and claimed that a large clitoris 'occurs to [a woman] to perform with women a coitus similar to what is done to them with men'.[17] But at least Avicenna recognised the clitoris's function in pleasure and advises men to the rub 'area between the anus and the vulva. For this is the seat of pleasure.'[18] Thankfully, Avicenna's work was highly influential throughout medieval Europe and advice on stimulating 'the seat of pleasure' is found in a number of later texts, such as William of Saliceto's *Summa Conservationis et Curationis* (1285) and Arnold of Villanova's *De Regimen Santitatis* (c.1311).[19]

The Middle Ages may not have significantly advanced the field of gynaecology, but the translation of Arabic texts into Latin led to several new terms for the love button. 'Nymph', 'myrtle' and '*landīca*' were still popular, but 'tentigo' and 'virga' (both alluding to an erection) came into medical parlance. 'Bobrelle' pops up in fifteenth-century Britain, which sounds delightfully like 'bobble' and probably means something that's raised (to 'bob' up and down).[20] 'Kekir' is another fifteenth-century term that is cited alongside bobrelle in Wright's *Anglo-Saxon and Old English Vocabularies* as meaning 'tentigo' (or erection).[21] But despite all this medieval bobbling, the clitoris was not widely discussed in surviving medieval sources. Even when it was, most medieval physicians were simply repeating much earlier medical opinion and threatening to cut the poor thing out. But things really start to get going when we hit the Renaissance.

In possibly the most champion act of mansplaining in the whole of human history, two Renaissance anatomists proudly claimed to have 'discovered' the clitoris in 1559. (Cue slow-clapping.) Italian anatomist Realdo Colombo (1515–1559) was Chair of Anatomy at the University of Pisa and claimed the 'quimberry' (2008) was his discovery in *De re Anatomica* (1559).* (Note this discovery belongs to Colombo, and not Columbo, the man in the mac.) The runner-up in this gynaecological game of 'Where's Wally' is Gabriele Falloppio (1523–1562), of Fallopian tube fame. Falloppio published *Observations Anatomicae* in 1561, but maintained he wrote it in 1550. He claimed that he was the first to plant his flag in Mount Clit and that 'if others have spoken of it, know that they have taken it from me or my students'.[22] Of course, both men are talking utter nonsense as not only had doctors been aware of the clit for some time, but women had long had an inkling of its whereabouts as well.

Colombo and Falloppio 'discovered' the clitoris in much the same way Columbus 'discovered' America to the bemusement of the natives some sixty-nine years previously. But they were both so proud of their discovery! Colombo wrote excitedly:

> Since no one else has discerned these processes and
> their working; if it is permissible to give a name to things
> discovered by me, it should be called the love or sweetness

---

* For further reading, see Mark D. Stringer and Ines Becker, 'Colombo and the Clitoris', *European Journal of Obstetrics & Gynaecology and Reproductive Biology*, 151.2 (2010), pp. 130–3 <https://doi.org/10.1016/j.ejogrb.2010.04.007>.

of Venus. It cannot be said how much I am astonished by
so many remarkable anatomists, that they not even have
detected [it] on account of so great advantage this so
beautiful thing formed by so great art.[23]

Falloppio was adamant that 'it is so hidden that I was the first to
discover it'.[24] To be fair, their claim that this was new terrain speaks
more to the lack of medical information available than to arrogance on
their part. And as Colombo and Falloppio based their work on extensive cadaver dissections, they did finally provide new anatomical information about this 'sweetness of Venus'. True, Colombo thought that the
mighty 'bean' (1997) produced a kind of lady sperm he called 'Amor
Veneris', but at least he wasn't trying to cut it off. They also understood
the clitoris was an organ and not just a sweet spot to be rubbed, and
this was brand new information. And more than this, the Renaissance
anatomists emphasised the clitoris's role in sex and pleasure. Colombo
wrote that his discovery 'is the principal seat of women's enjoyment in
intercourse; so that if you not only rub it with your penis, but even
touch it with your little finger, the pleasure causes their seed to flow
forth in all directions, swifter than the wind'.[25] Swipe right, ladies.

To confuse things even more, in 1672 Dutch anatomist Regnier
De Graaf re-rediscovered the clitoris in his landmark *Treatise on the
Generative Organs of Women*, where he chastised his fellow physicians for ignoring it: 'We are extremely surprised that some anatomists
make no more mention of this part than if it did not exist at all in the
universe of nature ... In every cadaver we have so far dissected we
have found it quite perceptible to sight and touch.'[26] But crucially De
Graaf did away with all this 'tentigo', 'sweetness of Venus', 'bobrelle'
and 'nymph' nonsense and insisted on using 'clitoris' throughout
his work. The word itself is something of an etymological mystery,
but most likely derives from the Greek 'kleiein', meaning 'to shut',

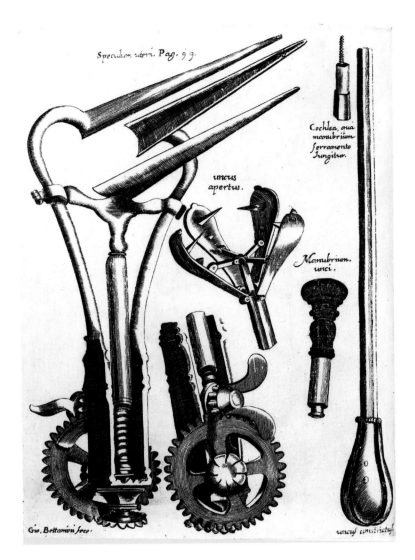

Vaginal Speculum, 1678.

which may be a reference to its being covered by the labia minora, or
possibly to much earlier theories that the clitoris was a kind of door for
keeping the womb warm. The first recorded use of the word 'clitoris'
is in Helkiah Crooke's *Mikrokosmographia* (1615), an encyclopaedia of
human anatomy where he correctly identifies the location, structure

and muscle make-up of the clitoris.* From here on out, 'clitoris' was on the rise.

Despite the giant medical leaps forward in sixteenth-century lady-lump appreciation, the obsession with the hypertrophied clitoris continued. In 1653, Dutch anatomist Thomas Bartholin called the clitoris *'contemptus viorum'*, or 'the contempt of mankind' because he believed women who overused theirs would become *'confricatrices'* ('rubsters') or lesbians. He even claimed that he knew of one woman who had so abused her 'contempt of mankind' that it had grown the length 'of a goose's neck'. (Repeat: a GOOSE'S NECK.) Bartholin wrote:

> Its size is commonly small; it lies hid for the most part under
> the Nymphs (labia) in its beginning, and afterwards sticks out
> a little. For in Lasses that begin to be amorous, the Clitoris
> does first discover itself. It is in several persons greater or
> lesser: in some it hangs out like a man's yard, namely when
> young wenches do frequently and continually handle and
> rub the same, as examples testify. But that it should grow as
> big as a goose's neck, as Platerus relates of one, is altogether
> preternatural and monstrous. Tulpius hath a like story of
> one that had it as long as half a man's finger, and as thick
> as a boy's prick, which made her willing to have to do with
> women in a carnal way. But the more this part increases, the
> more does it hinder a man in his business. For in the time

---

* Antecedents to 'clitoris' had been in circulation in Latin and Greek since Rufus of Ephesus (first century AD) used both κλειτορίς (clitoris) and κλειτοριάζειν (clitorising) in his anatomical works. Rufus uses 'clitorising' as a verb to mean stimulating the clitoris. See Carolyn J. Gersh, 'Naming the Body: A Translation with Commentary and Interpretive Essays of Three Anatomical Works Attributed to Rufus of Ephesus' (unpublished PhD thesis, University of Michigan, 2012); Helkiah Crooke, *Microcosmographia* (London: Printed by William Iaggard, 1615), p. 129.

of copulation it swells like a man's yard, and being erected, provokes to lust.[27]

It would be nice to think that Bartholin was a lone, crank voice, but this was far from the case. In his enduring popular sex manual, *Conjugal Love; or, the Pleasures of the Marriage Bed* (1686), Nicolas Venette warns of some clitorises that swell 'to such a bigness, as to prevent entrance to the yard' and of labia that are 'so long and flouting that there is a necessity in cutting them in maids before they marry'.[28] In 'A Faithful Catalogue of Our Most Eminent Ninnies' (1688), the Earl of Dorset attacks Lady Harvey as a predatory lesbian, writing that her 'clitoris will mount in open day' – meaning it was so big she could use it as a penis.[29]

Even women got in on the act. Jane Sharp was a seventeenth-century midwife who published a landmark text on pregnancy and childbirth in 1671: *The Midwives Book*. Here, Sharp gives detailed anatomical descriptions of the vulva and the function of the clitoris. She writes that the clitoris 'makes women lustfull [sic] and take delight in copulation, and were it not for this they would have no desire nor delight, nor would they ever conceive'.[30] While this might seem like something of a win for the 'love-nub' (2008), Sharp also warns about large clitorises that 'shew like a man's yard'. She goes on to compound this with a hefty dollop of racism, writing that 'lewd women' in India and Egypt frequently use their large clitorises 'as men do theirs', though she has never heard of a single English woman behaving like this.[31] She continues:

> In some countries they [clitorises] grow so long that the chirurgion [surgeon] cuts them off to avoid trouble and shame, chiefly in Egypt; they bleed much when they are cut ... Some sea-men say that they have seen negro women go stark naked, and these wings hanging out.[32]

This marks the beginning of a Western obsession with the genitals and sexuality of women of colour that persists to this very day.

We don't know if any of this medical 'advice' around clitorectomy was actually followed, or what your everyday women on the street made of all of this because (sadly) their voices are lost to us. We know that some doctors fretted about big clitorises, but how much of this filtered down to the consciousness of the general populace is anyone's guess.

But there may be one controversial body of evidence available for us to examine just how medical theories of hypertrophied clitorises impacted outside the medical community in the early modern period: the witch trial records. It has long been hinted at by various historians that the fabled 'witch's teat' may have in fact been the clitoris.[33] Various online articles have got a bit carried away with this idea and claimed that the clitoris was referred to as 'the witch's teat' in the early modern period, but this isn't true. The witch's mark was left by Satan to symbolise his ownership of the witch (think the 'dark mark' in *Harry Potter*), whereas the witch's teat was a kind of nipple where the witch suckled Satan in the guise of a familiar. The difference between the two is academic, as both were used to condemn a witch to death. Absolutely anything could be identified as a teat or mark:

T. Norris, *The History of Witches and Wizards*, 1720.

boils, burns, warts, moles, scars, haemorrhoids, or any kind of lump or bump. Although this mark could be found anywhere on the body, it was regularly found on the genitals.

When James VI of Scotland (later James I of England) published his witch-hunting guide *Daemonologie* in 1597, he advised people where to look for this secret mark and why.

> The Devil doth generally mark them with a private mark, by reason the Witches have confessed themselves, that the Devil doth lick them with his tongue in some privy part of their body, before he doth receive them to be his servants, which mark commonly is given them under the hair in some part of their body, whereby it may not easily be found out or scene, although they be searched.[34]

There are recorded incidents of the teat turning up in the throat, on the belly, the breast, and on men, so it is clear in these cases the teat is not the clitoris. But there is no denying the similarity between the hypertrophied clitorises fretted over in medical texts and sexualised descriptions of the witch's teat, raising the possibility that the clitoris itself was interpreted as the witch's teat by overzealous witch hunters.

After seventy-six-year-old Alice Samuel was executed as a witch in 1593, the gaoler examined her body and found irrefutable proof she was guilty.

> [H]e found upon the body of the old woman Alice Samuel a little lump of flesh, in manner sticking out as if it had been a teat, to the length of half an inch; which both he and his wife perceiving, at the first sight thereof meant not to disclose because it was adjoining so secret a place which was not decent to be seen.[35]

In a final act of indignity, poor Alice's body was put on display for the public to inspect her genitals for themselves. In 1619, Margaret Flowers confessed to having a black rat that sucked upon the teat on her 'inward parts of her secrets'.[36] In 1645, Margaret Moone was interrogated by the self-styled 'Witch-Finder General', Matthew Hopkins. Poor Margaret was one of several victims that Hopkins found to have 'long teats or bigges in her secret parts, which seemed to have been lately sucked'.[37] In Bury St Edmunds, 1665, elderly widow Rose Cullender was found to have three teats in her vulva. One 'it appeared unto them as if it had lately been sucked, and upon the straining of it there issued out white milkie matter'.[38] All the women were executed for witchcraft. We will never know precisely what these teats were, but the descriptions of them as long, fleshy protrusions from the vulva

Richard Boulton, *The Witches of Warboyse*, 1720.

that were sucked by demons to pleasure the witch certainly has echoes of the irrational fears over long clitorises we have seen.

By the end of the sixteenth century, the clitoris was well and truly out of the bag (so to speak), and not just in medical texts, or the ravings of witch hunters. It was recognised as an organ and one that provided pleasure. It was even a source of humour. Our favourite potty-mouthed aristocrat, John Wilmot, 2nd Earl of Rochester, names one of the characters in his *The Farce of Sodom, or The Quintessence of Debauchery* (1689) 'Clitoris'. Clitoris is a maid of honour and she regularly brings her queen, Cuntigratia, to orgasm. And the notoriously naughty libertine Sir Francis Fane made jokes about 'cunt bay' and 'pier clitoris' in the city of Bath.

The eighteenth century was a boom time for the print industry. Production and distribution methods improved, costs dropped and literacy rates rose, bringing newspapers, magazines, almanacs and cheap broadsides to the masses. Where technology leads, sex soon follows, and the trade in erotic literature similarly flourished. Eighteenth-century pornographic literature offers a very welcome second opinion on the clit to that of the scalpel-wielding physicians.* Nicolas Chorier's *A Dialogue Between A Married Lady and A Maid* (1740) is fictionalised erotic exchange between a MILF and her maid where the older woman teaches the younger all about sex. Part of this lesson covers clitoral pleasure. Hurrah!

> ... towards the upper part of the cunt, is a thing they call *clitoris*, which is a little like man's prick, for it will swell, and stand like his; and being rubbed gently, by his member will, with excessive pleasure, send forth a liquor, which when it comes away, leaves us in a trance, as if we were dying, all our senses being lost, and it were summed up in that one place,

---

* A really great source to read about eighteenth-century pornography is Julie Peakman, *Mighty Lewd Books* (London: Palgrave Macmillan, 2014).

and our eyes shut, our hearts languishing on one side, our
limbs extended, and in a word, there follows a dissolving
of our whole person and melting in such inexpressible
joys, as none but those who can feel them can express or
comprehend.[39]

The work of the Marquis de Sade is a predictable clitfest. Even
though Sade does devote a considerable amount of time to clitoral
torture, there is also cunnilingus, fingering and clit tips aplenty – such
as always 'insist your clitoris be frigged while you are being buggered'
and 'Madame; don't be content to suck her clitoris; make your voluptuous tongue penetrate into her womb'.[40] Which is sound advice for
all, really.

One genre of erotic texts known as the 'Merryland Books' were
published throughout the eighteenth century. These texts write about
the female body as if it were a landscape to be explored. There are
many puns on rising hillocks, mossy valleys and fertile soil, and just
occasionally the clitoris gets a look-in too. As you can see, despite a
notable swell in clit appreciation, the medical obsession with large

Hubert François
Bourguignon
D'Anville and John
Cleland, *Memoirs of
a Woman of Pleasure*,
1766.

58

clitorises finds space in the dogeared pages of eighteenth-century pornography as well, where it was further fetishised as an indicator of sexual deviancy.

> Near the Fort is the metropolis, called CLTRS [clitoris]; it is a pleasant place, much delighted in by the Queens of MERRYLAND, and is their chief Palace, or rather *Pleasure Seat*; it was at first but small, but the pleasure some of the Queens have found in it, has occasioned their extending its bounds considerably.[41]

Whereas large clitorises had been thought to be analogous to a high libido and lesbianism, eighteenth-century anxieties around masturbation gave rise to new reasons for the Goose's Neck – overuse through excessive 'diddling' (1938). In 1771, M. D. T. de Bienville, a little-known French doctor, published his treatise on the dangers of nymphomania. Bienville believed that masturbation was the cause of this unhappy state, and warned that women who masturbated would soon 'throw off the restraining, honourable yoke of delicacy, and without blush, openly solicit in the most criminal, and abandoned language, the first comers to gratify their insatiable desires'. Well, who hasn't? What's more, Bienville was confident that in women afflicted with 'uterine fury', the clitoris would be considerably larger than in 'discreet women'.[42] Although many ridiculed Bienville's work, he was one of several doctors around this time who medicalised masturbation and viewed the size of the clitoris as an indicator of whether or not a woman had been rubbing one out – a kind of clitmus test, if you will.

Despite the clitoris being thoroughly enjoyed in Victorian pornography, a small but vocal section of the medical community continued to have serious concerns about the clitorati and the clitmus test persisted into the nineteenth century.* French doctor Alexandre Parent du Châtelet (1790–1836), for example, studied the genitals of over five thousand Parisian sex workers and was surprised to find that, contrary to popular belief, 'the genital parts of the prostitute … present no special alteration which is peculiar to them, and in this respect they do not differ from those of married women of unblemished character'.[43] What's more, 'there is nothing remarkable either in the dimensions or the dispositions of the clitoris in the prostitutes of Paris, and that in them, as in all married women, there are variations, but nothing peculiar'.[44] However, this study did little to dissuade other doctors from poking and prodding about women's hoo-hahs searching for signs of sexual degeneracy. The 1854 editions of *Medical Lexicon: A Dictionary of Medical Science* included the word 'clitorism', which was defined as 'a word invented to express the abuse made of the clitoris. Also, an unusually large clitoris.'[45] Whereas the *American Homeopathic Journal of Gynaecology and Obstetrics* (1885) claimed that in 'evidences of masturbation' the 'clitoris is much elongated, and the prepuce is hypertrophied and thrown into wrinkles'.[46] Some doctors believed a hypertrophied clitoris was caused by masturbation, others that it was the other way around.

The most notorious English proponent of the anti-clit brigade was gynaecologist Dr Isaac Baker Brown (1811–1873). Brown was a widely respected physician. He was a founding member of St Mary's Hospital, London, elected a Fellow of the Royal College of Surgeons, and in 1865 he was elected president of the Medical Society of London. Everything was on the up for Brown until he published *On the Curability of Certain*

---

* Despite vocal medical opinion, the anti-clit agenda had limited influence as Victorian erotica shows no such concerns. *The Pearl Magazine* (1879–80) regularly includes clitoral pleasure. The anonymous *Romance of Lust* (1873) contains no fewer than 166 instances of the word 'clitoris', all of which are positive and pleasurable depictions. Even that homage to gay love, *Sin of the City of the Plain* (1881), details bringing women to orgasm through clitoral pleasure.

Forms of Insanity, Epilepsy, Catalepsy, and Hysteria in Females in 1866. Here, Brown told of his success in performing clitorectomies as a cure for everything from hysteria to back pain, epilepsy, infertility, paralysis, blindness, insanity and much more. In one 1863 case, Brown cut the clitoris out of a thirty-year-old woman who had developed 'a great distaste for her husband'. Brown declared the operation an 'uninterrupted success' and the patient returned to give her marriage another try.[47] (Deep breath.)

> The patient having been placed completely under the
> influence of chloroform, the clitoris is freely excised either by
> scissors or knife – I always prefer the scissors. The wound is
> then firmly plugged with graduated compress of lint, and a
> pad, well secured by a T bandage.[48]

Brown's theories were not well received, and in 1867 he was expelled from the Obstetrical Society of London. His hearing was widely reported, and Brown was clearly at a loss as to why he had been singled out when so many of his peers had themselves performed clitorectomies. 'I maintain my late colleagues in this room have all performed this operation … not my operation, recollect gentlemen, but an operation, as Dr Haden has showed, that has been practised from the time of Hippocrates.'[49] And he may have had a point. Brown is very much the pantomime villain of Victorian gynaecology, but his butchery did not exist in a vacuum. I have no doubt that many of the good doctors who presided over Brown's expulsion were equally guilty, if just a bit quieter about it. But none of this saved Brown, whose career never recovered, and he died in poverty in 1873 – possibly the only man in history to regret his success in finding the clit.

Sigmund Freud once described female sexuality as the 'dark continent' of psychology.[50] Given the amount of time he seemed to spend

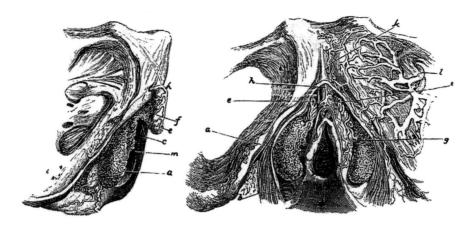

Lateral view of erectile structures of external organs in female (left). Blood vessels were injected, and skin and mucous membrane were removed. *a*, bulbus vestibule. *c*, plexus of veins named pars intermedia. *e*, glans clitoridis. *f*, clitoral body. *h*, dorsal vein of clitoris. *l*, right crus clitoridis. *m*, vestibule. *n*, right gland of Bartholin. Front view of erectile structures of external organs in female (right). *b*, sphincter vaginae muscles. *e*, venous plexus of pars intermedia. *f*, glans clitoridis. *g*, connecting veins. *k*, veins passing beneath pubes. *l*, obturator vein.

'Dissected Clitoris' from Georg Ludwig Kobelt's, *The Male and Female Organs of Sexual Arousal in Man and Some Other Mammals*, 1844.

wandering around it, clearly lost and terrified of the natives, I am inclined to agree with him. One of Freud's less than gold-star brilliant theories was that clitoral orgasms are sexually immature. In his *Three Essays on the Theory of Sexuality* (1905), Freud argued that the female child's sexuality is entirely clitoral and masculine until she reaches puberty, when she must transfer her 'erotogenic susceptibility to stimulation ... from the clitoris to the vaginal orifice' for her to become mature and feminine.[51] Freud might not have been circumcising the clitoris, but his ideas had the effect of metaphorically cutting the clitoris out of 'healthy' sexuality nonetheless. And although Freud wasn't the only doctor distinguishing between 'vaginal' and 'clitoral' orgasms, he was certainly the most influential.[*]

---

[*] An excellent source of nineteenth- and twentieth-century medical practices of clitorectomy is Sarah B. Rodriguez, *Female Circumcision and Clitoridectomy In the United States* (New York: University of Rochester Press, 2014).

One of Freud's most famous patients was Princess Marie Bonaparte (1882–1962), great-grandniece to Emperor Napoleon I. Princess Marie married Prince George of Greece and Denmark in 1907 and she had several lovers on the go as well, but she was never able to achieve an orgasm through vaginal penetration. Heavily influenced by Freud's

Princess Marie Bonaparte (1882–1962).

theories and being a scientifically minded kind of woman, Marie began to research her own sexual 'frigidity' and arrived at the conclusion she couldn't achieve the almighty vaginal orgasm because her clitoris was too far away from her vaginal opening. She confirmed this by conducting a survey of 243 women and published her results in the 1924 edition of the *Bruxelles-Médical*, under the name A. E. Narjani. Marie identified women with a short distance between the clitoris and the vaginal opening, who orgasm easily, as *'paraclitoridiennes'*, and those with a difference of more than two and a half centimetres, who struggle to orgasm, like Marie, as *'téleclitoridiennes'* (with the *'mesoclitoriennes'* being somewhere between the two).[52] Marie became Freud's patient in 1925, which further reinforced her belief that she would only be satisfied if she came through penile penetration (listen carefully and you can hear the lesbians laughing). The upshot of Princess Marie's obsession with mature and immature orgasms was that in 1927 she employed surgeon Josef Halban to operate and reposition her clitoris closer to the vaginal opening. When this operation did not achieve the desired result, Halban operated again in 1930 and yet again in 1931. Poor Princess Marie never got her vaginal orgasm and wound up with a clit that must have been left dangling like a loose button. Poor, poor Marie.

And not just poor Marie. As Freud's theories about the difference between vaginal and clitoral orgasms took hold across the medical world, women were routinely told that they were sexual failures if they could only orgasm through clitoral stimulation. In 1936, Eduard Hitschmann and Edmund Bergler published their highly influential *Frigidity in Women*, where they claimed that the 'sole criterion of frigidity is the absence of the vaginal orgasm'.[53] In 1950, Dr William S. Kroger claimed that women for 'whom sexual response occurs only after clitoral stimulation' were 'frigid'. He went on to explain that the vaginal orgasm was the 'optimum type of sexual response'.[54] In America, this led to numerous gynaecologists operating to 'free' the clitoris from its hood, which would supposedly allow a frigid wife to climax with her husband. Even Alfred Kinsey recommended this 'very simple' procedure; 'with a tool the physician can strip the clitoris, allowing the foreskin to roll back and may make a distinct difference in the response of the female'.[55] Bizarrely, there are still plastic surgeons today who offer clitoral hood reduction surgery to improve orgasm, despite partial or total hoodectomy being classed as female genital mutilation by the World Health Organisation.[56]

But what is particularly galling about all this vaginal versus clitoral orgasm nonsense is that as we have learned more about the structure of the clitoris, it has become glaringly obvious that ALL orgasms are clitoral. The structure of the clitoris is as complex as it is extensive, comprising clitoral glans, prepuce, body (or corpora), crura, bulbs, suspensory ligaments and the root – the only visible parts being the glans and the hood.[57] The structure descends downwards from

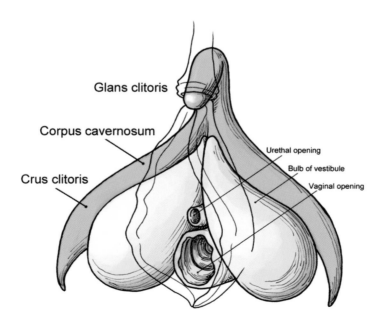

Anatomy of the clitoris.

the pubic bone into the adiposity of the mons pubis. It was only in 2009 that Pierre Foldes and Odile Buisson used 3-D sonography to get a complete picture of a stimulated clitoris, and we finally started to understand what the hell is going on down there. They found that when the clitoris was engorged, it swelled to touch the anterior walls of the vagina.[58] Then, in 2010, Buisson and Foldes joined forces with Emmanuele Jannini and Sylvain Mimoun and scanned the vagina and clitoris of a volunteer woman during sex in the missionary position. The results showed that the penis stretched the clitoral root and during the (ahem) thrusting, the now stretched root crashed repeatedly into the anterior vagina wall – offering clear evidence that the much lauded G-spot has actually been the C-spot all along.[59] A kind of clitoral Scooby-Doo ending to a debate that has raged throughout medicine for centuries.*

The question remaining is surely 'why?' Why has the 'pussy pearl' (2007) been so horribly victimised throughout history, and indeed continues to be abused throughout much of the world, when all it wants to do is bring pleasure? The World Health Organisation cites numerous reasons why FGM is carried out today, including to 'reduce a woman's libido and therefore... to help her resist extramarital sexual acts'.[60] Looking back throughout history, this certainly rings true here.

---

* Not everyone was happy with this theory, most notably Vincenzo Puppo, who was adamant that there was no such thing as an internal clitoris (Vincenzo Puppo, 'Anatomy of the Clitoris: Revision and Clarifications About the Anatomical Terms for the Clitoris Proposed (Without Scientific Bases) by Helen O'Connell, Emmanuele Jannini, and Odile Buisson', *ISRN Obstetrics and Gynecology*, 2011, pp. 1–5.) However, although others debate how the vagina, clitoris and urethra all work together in orgasm, the concept of the G-spot as a distinct anatomic sensory entity has now been widely debunked (e.g. Kilchevsky et al., 2012). Various Neotantra groups (such as 'The New Tantra') continue to teach that clitoral orgasms are inferior to vaginal ones, claiming that a clitoral orgasm is a 'peak orgasm' that causes a crash of various neurochemicals in the brain. There is no evidence to support this. It is nonsense.

Although the clit was recognised as the 'seat of pleasure' very early on, it was not regarded as a very stable seat. Rather, it was thought the clitoris could provoke an excessive libido in women, which had all manner of health problems attached – both somatic and psycho-somatic. But attacking the clit is about more than just curbing female desire, it's about protecting the primacy of the penis. The clitoris brings pleasure without penetration, and it doesn't need a man operating the controls to do so. The fears that an overused clitoris would morph into a penis, which could be used to penetrate other women, speaks to an anxiety that the penis is redundant or that the man is being replaced. Freud's insistence that the only orgasm it was worth a woman having required a penis also speaks to a need to pay deference to the mighty rod. Likewise, the ridiculing of men who performed cunnilingus in the Ancient World, the clitoral association with lesbianism and 'clitorism' caused by masturbation all tacitly accuse the clitoris of ignoring the penis.

We will never know how many clitorises have been cut, cauterised and circumcised throughout history, but we do know that virtually none of these procedures were necessary. The clitoris is a truly magnif-icent organ, and one that is still mysterious – why can some women orgasm through penetration and others can't? Exactly how does all the equipment work together to produce an orgasm? But here is what we do know: the clitoris is the only organ on the human body that has no other purpose than to bring pleasure. It has 8,000 nerve endings, double the amount in the glands of the penis, and almost 75 per cent of women need to have their glans clitoris (the external part) stimulated to orgasm. It has taken us a long time to get here, and there is still work to be done, but we are finally beginning to see just how important the clitoris is in sexual fulfilment.

Colonising the Cunt

A History of Racial Fetishization

Sir Mix-a-Lot's 1992 smash-hit 'Baby Got Back' hit the airwaves as a tongue-in-cheek celebration of black women's bodies – an auditory fuck you to the super-thin, white women that dominated Western beauty narratives. The video opens with two white girls criticising a black woman's appearance and likening her to a 'prostitute'.[1] Although 'Baby Got Back' has often been dismissed as novelty rap, it succeeded in raising numerous issues around race, sexuality and women that remain unresolved twenty-six years later: the whitewashing of the beauty industry, the marginalisation of the black voice and the hyper-sexualisation of women of colour, particularly black women.

The main focus of this chapter is on the historic sexualisation of black women by white colonisers. I am a white woman and I am in no position to speak for the black woman's experience. I do not know what it is like to be a black woman in a world that fetishises black bodies. But I am a historian, and I see parallels in the language white colonisers historically used to talk about – and disempower – women of colour, and modern 'bootylicious' narratives. This is not a chapter that further fetishises women of colour, or offers any kind of comment on black culture. This is a history of how white people have viewed, talked about and claimed ownership over black women's bodies, specifically their genitals.

When Europeans first arrived in Africa, they encountered a culture vastly different from their own in almost every single way. But something that immediately struck the sexually repressed Roman Catholic explorers was that Africans did not share their doctrine of 'thou shalt not'.

When Prince Henry the Navigator (1394–1460) arrived at the coast of West Africa from Portugal in 1441, he came from a deeply repressive culture where women could be put to death if their husbands accused them of adultery.[2] By comparison, African women danced, wore clothes that exposed their bodies and were not shamed sexually. To the buttoned-down Europeans, this could only mean that they were highly sexed. Black women were not only heavily eroticised, but also held up as sexually savage and therefore in need of controlling – presumably by white men. In *A New Voyage to Guinea* (1744), William Smith described African women as being 'hot constitution'd Ladies': 'They miss no Opportunity and are continually contriving Stratagems how to gain a Lover. If they meet with a Man they immediately strip his lower Parts, and throw themselves upon him, protesting if he will not gratify their desires they will accuse him to their husbands'.[3] A British report on the African slave trade dated 1789 blamed the poor fertility rates of black women on the 'prostitution of all the women in the young part of their lives, going from one estate to another during the night, and thereby contracting disorders...'[4] Such texts understood black women as being promiscuous by nature, and their very bodies seemed to offer all the evidence that was required for white colonisers to accept this as a scientific fact.

The sad case of Sarah (Sara, or Saartje) Baartman (1789–1815) has come to represent the epitome of the white West's obsession with, and ultimate commodification of, the black female erotic body.[5] Baartman was a South African Khoikhoi woman who was taken to London in 1810 by William Dunlop, a Scottish military surgeon, and her employer Hendrik Cesars, and exhibited in sideshows as a 'Hottentot Venus'.*

---

* The word 'Hottentot' dates to the late seventeenth century and was the name white Europeans gave to the Khoikhoi people of South Africa.

Sartjee the Hottentot Venus, 1810.

Baartman was one of several Khoikhoi women put on display around Europe for white audiences to gawk at, though she would become the most well known. As late as 1840 a black Englishwoman by the name of Elizabeth Magnas was exhibited at Leeds as a 'Hottentot Venus' for six years before she died of chronic alcoholism.

What was it that white Europeans found so fascinating about these women? It was their bodies, specifically their buttocks and genitals. Steatopygia is a genetic characteristic frequently found among the Khoisan of southern Africa, whereby substantial levels of fat build around the buttocks and thighs. To white European eyes, women like

Sarah Baartman and Elizabeth Magnas had excessively large buttocks, and this was enough to warrant placing them in a freakshow.

As if to justify claims that black women were promiscuous, travel writers such as François Le Vaillant (1753–1824) and Sir John Barrow (1764–1848) described African women as having large buttocks and hypertrophied, protruding labia, which they called 'the Hottentot apron'. François Le Vaillant wrote at length about his efforts to persuade South African women to show him their genitals: 'confused, abashed and trembling, she covered her face with both her hands, suffered her apron [*tablier*] to be untied, and permitted me to contemplate at leisure what my readers will see themselves in the exact representation which I drew of it'.[6] In his *Travels into the Interior of Southern Africa* (1806), Barrow described a Khoisan woman's buttocks and thighs as being a 'protuberance consist[ing] of fat, and, when the woman walked, had the most ridiculous appearance imaginable, every step being accompanied with a quivering and tremulous motion as if two masses of jelly were attached behind'.[7]

It was to audiences like this that Sarah Baartman was exhibited. Onstage, Sarah wore tight, flesh-coloured clothing, necklaces of beads and feathers, and smoked a pipe. In 1810, *The Times* recorded that 'she is dressed in a colour as nearly resembling her skin as possible. The dress is contrived to exhibit the entire frame of her body, and the spectators are even invited to examine the peculiarities of her form.'[8] Even at the time, the prospect of a woman being exhibited for her buttocks caused an outrage, and many petitioned for Sarah's freedom. Anti-slavery activist Zachary Macaulay (1768–1838) and the African Association succeeded in taking Sarah's case to court in 1810, where she was cross-examined for several hours by an attorney to ascertain if she consented to her treatment. William Dunlop was allowed to remain in the court as Sarah testified, and even produced a contract signed by himself and Sarah agreeing to her working conditions.[9] We will never know if his presence prohibited Sarah from saying otherwise, but she told the court she was 'under no restraint' and was 'happy in England'.[10] The case was dismissed.

Sarah was never exhibited naked, nor did she allow French surgeons to examine her genitals when she was sold to be shown at the Palais Royal, in 1814. But after she died of alcoholism in 1816, aged just twenty-six, Georges-Frédéric Cuvier (1773–1838) dissected Sarah's body and published a detailed account of her anatomy. His report is well known, as is his lengthy, voyeuristic description of Sarah's vulva, buttocks and brain – which he likened to that of a monkey.[11]

Cuvier preserved her brain and skeleton, and put her genitalia in a specimen jar. Several body casts of Sarah were made, as was a wax mould of her vulva, which were put on display at the Muséum d'Histoire Naturelle until 1974. In 2002, the president of South Africa, Nelson Mandela, secured the repatriation of Baartman's body and the various plaster casts from France to South Africa, and she was finally laid to rest in Hankey, in the Eastern Cape province.

The nineteenth century was the golden age of physiognomy, a thankfully debunked practice of 'reading' a person's character through their physical appearance. Early criminologists such as Cesare Lombroso

---

THE HOTTENTOT VENUS.

They are now employed in one of the rooms of the Museum of National History in forming a cast of the Hottentot Venus, who died the day before yesterday of an illness that lasted only three days. Her body exhibited no visible trace of this malady, except some spots of reddish brown round the mouth, legs, and sides. Her size and enormous protuberances are not diminished, and her hair, extremely curled, has not become lengthened, as is usual with negroes in illness and after death.— The dissection of this woman will furnish an extremely curious chapter in the history of the variety of human species.—(*Moniteur.*)

Belfast Commercial Chronicle, Monday 15 January 1816.

(1835–1909) theorised criminal tendencies could be predicted by studying physical features. One 'criminal' trait that physiognomists believed they could read in a person's body was prostitution. Considerable research was undertaken by scientists such as Adrian Charpy (1848–1902) to examine the genitals of sex workers, which were directly compared to those of black women to deduce a highly sexed woman.[12] Charpy claimed that both the prostitute and the 'Hottentot' had hypertrophied labia, which signified a base sexuality. In his 1893 book *La donna Delinquente*, Lombroso directly compared images of the body of the black woman with that of the prostitute in order to 'prove' the deviant, animalistic nature of both.[13]

Although this chapter is primarily concerned with the colonising of black women's genitals, it's important to acknowledge that Europeans were equally fascinated with, and threatened by, black men's genitals. The mythology of the 'big black cock', or 'BBC' as it is categorised on porn sites today, also finds its roots in earliest colonial propaganda that black men are sexually savage, animalistic and dangerous.* Just as the black woman's genitals and buttocks were read as 'evidence' of her promiscuity, the black man's penis was also considered proof of a hypersexual, bestial nature. In 1904, Dr William Lee Howard published 'The Negro as a Distinct Ethnic Factor in Civilization' in the journal *Medicine*. Here, Howard claimed that the 'large size of the African's penis' would prevent him from ever being 'civilised' or 'moral' like the white man. Howard suggested that the black man's cerebral development stopped at puberty, and that 'genetic instincts [become] the controlling factor of his life ... He will walk the alleys late at night with a penis swollen from disease, and infects his bride-to-be with the same nonchalance that he will an hour later exhibit when cohabiting with the lowest of his race.'[14]

---

* For a detailed history of race and the penis, see David M. Friedman, *A Mind of its Own* (London: Hale, 2001).

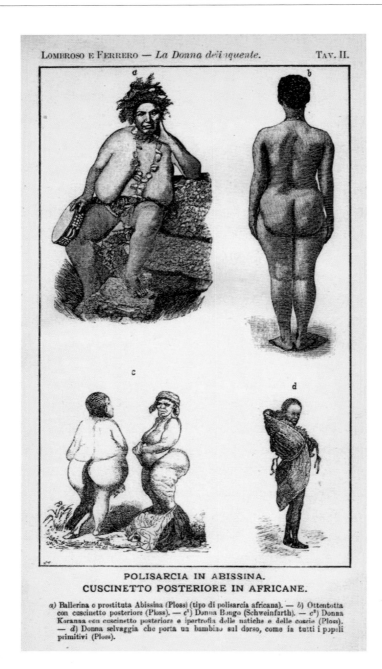

Large buttocks and pronounced labia were linked to promiscuity and racial inferiority in this nineteenth-century Italian study of the female criminal.

The effect of this pseudoscientific racism was far reaching and served to justify the brutalisation and sexual exploitation of black men and women well into the twentieth century. Military propaganda campaigns of the 1920s and 1930s actively drew on entrenched sexual stereotypes of women in the colonies in an attempt to lure European men into the colonial armies.

The colonial postcards of the time emphasised the breasts, exaggerated buttocks and nakedness of women of colour in order to signify their sexual availability to European men. The women in these postcards are simply window dressing – props to affirm colonial power. They are reduced to their physicality, just as Sarah Baartman

A German postcard reads 'Another city, another girl!' From Inge Oosterhoff, 'Greetings from the Colonies: Postcards of a Shameful Past'.

These postcards reveal more about the colonial fantasies of the photographer than the woman being photographed. Photograph from Malek Alloula, *The Colonial Harem*.

Jean Jules Antoine Lecomte du Noüy, *Rhamsès Dans Son Harem,* in Louis Enault, *Paris-Salon,* 1887.

Eugène Delacroix, *Jewish Wedding in Morocco,* 1841.

was: consumables for a white audience. And it was not just black bodies the Europeans sexualised. As Africa, Asia and the Americas were colonised by Europeans the same process of sexually othering non-white women as 'exotic' took place.

We have no record of Sarah Baartman's own voice. Many people spoke for her, or about her, but her own voice has been lost to us completely. We will never know her thoughts on her life, her body and her treatment. Sadly, all the evidence we have is mediated through white writers. Her experience may be shocking, but it is part of a wider history of sexualising women of colour – and of using women's bodies to justify their oppression. We will never know what Sarah's choices were, but women today can at least choose to be part of a narrative that fetishises them. Many women find reclaiming sexuality on their own terms empowering and work to redefine their stories on their own terms. But it is important to fully understand the history that frames such choices today.

'As Easily Made as a Pudding'

A History of Virginity Tests

In 2017, researchers at the University of Minnesota published a systematic review of all available, peer-reviewed research into the reliability of so called 'virginity tests' where the hymen is examined, as well as the impact on the person being examined. The team identified 1,269 studies. The evidence was summarised and assessed, and this was the conclusion:

> This review found that virginity examination, also known as two-finger, hymen, or per-vaginal examination, is not a useful clinical tool, and can be physically, psychologically, and socially devastating to the examinee. From a human rights perspective, virginity testing is a form of gender discrimination, as well as a violation of fundamental rights, and when carried out without consent, a form of sexual assault.[1]

The following year in 2018, the World Health Organisation, the United Nations Human Rights and the United Nations Women issued a statement calling for the elimination of virginity testing; stating that '"Virginity testing" is a violation of the human rights of girls and women, and can be detrimental to women's and girls' physical, psychological and social well-being. "Virginity testing" reinforces stereotyped notions of female sexuality and gender inequality.'[2] There is no reliable virginity test. You can no more tell if someone has had sex by looking between their legs than you can tell if someone is a vegetarian by looking at their belly button. However, the fact that virginity cannot be proven, tested or located on the body has not deterred people from claiming otherwise.

Sadly, a woman's virginity is still highly prized around the world today, a fact which has, in turn, led to the creation of numerous damaging rituals around keeping and proving a woman's sexual purity that are still in force today. These tests usually involve searching for an intact hymen, or what's known as the 'two-finger test', which checks for vaginal tightness. Countries where this practice has been reported include Afghanistan, Bangladesh, Egypt, India, Indonesia, Iran, Jordan, Palestine, South Africa, Sri Lanka, Swaziland, Turkey and Uganda. The FGM National Clinic Group states that female genital

Henry O'Neil, *Jephthah's daughter contemplating her virginity and her imminent death, surrounded by woeful attendants with musical instruments*, 1846.

mutilation is valued 'as a means of preserving a girl's virginity until marriage (for example, in Sudan, Egypt, and Somalia). In many of these countries FGM has been seen as a prerequisite to marriage and marriage is vital to a woman's social and economic survival.'[3] The World Health Organisation estimates that 200 million girls globally have been subjected to female genital mutilation, in no small part to preserve their virginities until marriage.[4]

The idea of female sexual purity being a prerequisite for marriage underpins many cultures and religions around the world. In Indonesia, virginity testing remains a requirement for women wanting to join the army or police force. So-called 'Purity Balls' are held all over America, where fathers take their teenage daughters on a 'date'; she pledges to stay a virgin until marriage and he, in turn, pledges to protect his daughter's virginity until she is married (presumably with a shotgun and some kind of alarm system). Women can now pay to have their hymens rebuilt for the marriage market, and the hymenoplasty business is booming. In 2016, a South African KwaZulu-Natal municipality introduced an academic bursary for young women who can prove that they are virgins.[5] And in 2017, the Russian Investigative Committee and the health minister, Vladimir Shuldyakov, caused outrage by ordering doctors to carry out 'virginity tests' on schoolgirls and to report any found without a hymen to the authorities.[6]

Not only is virginity impossible to prove, it's also quite difficult to define. We might think that virginity is a very simple thing to understand, but it doesn't hold together all that well when we start to poke it a little. Precisely what we count as sex for the first time can be more complicated than we might initially think. If two girls have sex, does that count as losing their virginity? What if they used a strap-on? If a heterosexual couple hit first, second and third base, but strike out at fourth in a sweaty, satisfied mess, are they still virgins? Can you lose your virginity to yourself? Does it have to involve penile–vaginal

"OF COURSE, UNMARRIED GIRLS CAN USE PURSETTES!"

A subject unmarried girls often ask about is *internal* sanitary protection. Here's a solution welcomed by thousands: a tiny new tampon called Pursettes®. The exclusive prelubricated tip of this tampon eliminates the need for a cardboard applicator...makes insertion easy, medically correct. No larger than a lipstick, Pursettes proved as much as 25% more absorbent than regular applicator-type tampons in a university laboratory test. That's why women—both married and unmarried—are switching to Pursettes. At drug and department stores—Pursettes.

FREE OFFER: For a trial supply of Pursettes tampons, send 10¢ for postage-handling to: Campana, Box WD-15, Batavia, Illinois.

Name_____
Address_____
City_____ State_____

1960s advert for Pursette tampons that reassured 'unmarried girls' (virgins) that they too can use tampons.

penetration? If so, does that preclude same-sex sex? Is gay pride really a mass virgin rally? How about if a heterosexual couple just have anal sex? Does he lose his, but she keeps hers on a technicality?

Despite considerable research into hymens, many myths still surround them. People still believe exercise and horse-riding can rupture the hymen (they don't), and Tampax were still reassuring young women that they couldn't 'pop their cherries' (1988) on a tampon as late as the 1990s.

Even the language surrounding virginity is loaded. The concept of 'losing' or 'keeping' your virginity suggests that once lost, we are all lacking something and no longer whole. It also suggests that virginity is something tangible that we had in the first place. You can metaphorically 'give' someone your V-card, but it's not like they can hang it above their fireplace, or resell it on eBay (although several women have tried).

The concept of virginity is undeniably gendered, and the reason we think we know what we mean when we discuss 'losing' said 'cherry' (1933) is because we subconsciously understand virginity as belonging to penis-in-vagina sex. This is what is meant by 'compulsory heterosexuality'. This doesn't mean that heterosexuality is literally compulsory, but that our cultural scripts around sexuality focus more on heterosexual sex than any other kind: it has become our 'normal'. Now, this is undeniably cis-gendered privilege, but it is the product of thousands of years of cultural conditioning. It is only with the tremendous work done by LGBTQ activists over the last fifty years that we have begun to create space to discuss alternatives to boy–girl sex at all. But there is still a long way to go.

When anyone is concerned about virginity it is almost always a woman's virginity. Even the word 'virgin' comes from the Latin *virgo*, meaning a girl or a woman who is not married. Men and boys have never been valued by their virgin status in the same way women have. At various points in history, women have been disowned, imprisoned, fined, mutilated, whipped and even killed as punishment for losing their virginity outside of marriage, whereas funny films are made about forty-year-old male virgins.[*]

Quite why it is female rather than male virginity that has been so rigorously sanctioned is a matter of some dispute, but it is likely all down to paternal legacies. It's unfair, but in the pre-Pill world, pregnancy out of wedlock was a far more immediate physical and

---

[*] Despite the social emphasis on keeping your flower unplucked, research published by the *Journal of Sex Research* found that adult virgins of both sexes (aged over twenty-five) face considerable social stigma in the US, and believe that they are not desirable as romantic partners. Male adult virgins felt their masculinity was called into question and women believed they were written off as 'old maids' (Amanda N. Gesselman, Gregory D. Webster, and Justin R. Garcia, 'Has Virginity Lost its Virtue? Relationship Stigma Associated with Being a Sexually Inexperienced Adult', *The Journal of Sex Research*, 54 (2016), 202–13).

financial concern for the mother than the father; consequently, it was her shenanigans that were scrutinised rather than his. But more than this, in a paternalistic society where wealth and power are passed down the male line, female chastity is heavily policed to ensure legitimate offspring, and that your worldly goods pass to your children (and not the milkman's). This theory holds some weight when we consider that in the few matriarchal societies around the world, wealth is passed down the female line. In these cultures, female sexuality is regarded very differently.*

Today, the most well-known 'proof' of virginity test is blood produced from a ruptured hymen. But our ancestors didn't even use the word 'hymen', and certainly didn't go rooting around inside vaginas like they were digging for buried treasure to find one. In fact, medical texts don't start talking about a hymen until the fifteenth century.[7] None of the Classical physicians make mention of it (Galen and Aristotle, for example). Greek physician Soranus suggests that any post-coital vaginal bleeding was the result of burst blood vessels, and categorically denied any kind of membrane inside the vagina.[8] Many early texts acknowledge that virgins may bleed when they have sex for the first time, but this wasn't linked to the hymen. Rather, it was thought that the bleeding was caused by the trauma of penile penetration and was not proof enough of virginity. It was the Italian physician Michael Savonarola who first used the word 'hymen' in 1498, describing it as a

---

* The Minangkabau of West Sumatra, Indonesia, the Mosuo of Tibet, the Ghanese Akan, the Bribri of Costa Rica, the Garo of Meghalaya, India and the Nagovisi of New Guinea are all regarded as matriarchal societies and all share matrilineal inheritance lines. When property passes from mother to daughter (regardless of paternity), who's the daddy is of little consequence. The sexual customs of these cultures are far more permissive; unions between men and women are easily dissolved without shame, women are free to have multiple sexual partners, and concepts of adultery, promiscuity and illegitimacy are not known as they are in the West (H. Gottner-Abendroth, 'The Structure Of Matriarchal Societies', *Revision*, 21.3 (1999)).

membrane that 'is broken at the time of deflowering, so that the blood flows'.[9] After this, references to the hymen and its links to virginity become increasingly common. But just because our ancestors didn't search for intact hymens does not mean that virginity was not subject to rigorous tests before the hymen became the benchmark for proof of tampering.

The most famous virgins in the Ancient World were Rome's Vestal Virgins. The Vestal Virgins were priestesses, dedicated to the goddess of hearth and family, Vesta. They were chosen at a young age and had to dedicate thirty years of worship and chastity to the city of Rome and tend the temple flame of Vesta; the punishment for a Vestal having sex was to be entombed alive and left to starve to death.

So, how do you test a Vestal's virginity? Well, some praying is involved. The priestesses were believed to have a special connection

Pietro Saja, *Vestal Virgin Condemned to Death*, 1800.

with the gods, so when the Vestal Tuccia was accused, she was given the opportunity to conjure a miracle and prove she was still a virgin. According to Valerius Maximus, Tuccia proved her virginity by carrying water in a sieve. Tuccia called out, 'O Vesta, if I have always brought pure hands to your secret services, make it so now that with this sieve I shall be able to draw water from the Tiber and bring it to Your temple.'[10] The sieve has since become a symbol of virginity and Queen Elizabeth I was often painted holding one to symbolise that no one had taken a bite of her cherry bun. But if you did not happen to have a sieve to hand there were other virginity tests available to you – as long as you had a snake, some ants and a cake. The Roman writer Aelian (AD 175–235) describes a ritual for testing virginity that took place on holy days:

> In a grove is a vast deep cavern, the lair of a snake. On fixed
> holy days maidens bring barley cakes in their hands, their
> eyes bandaged. Divine inspiration guides them straight to
> the serpent at a gentle pace without stumbling. If they are
> virgin, the snake divines the answer and accepts the food,
> if not, it remains untasted. Ants break up the cakes of the
> deflowered and carry the pieces outside the grove and thus
> cleanse the spot. The people get to know of the results and
> the girls are examined and the one who shamed her virginity
> is punished.[11]

Quite what this 'punishment' was is not elaborated upon, and given that snakes are not widely known for their love of Battenberg, this test seems rather unfair.

But to really confirm the seal had not been broken, you needed a bottle of wee. The thirteenth-century text *De Secretis Mulierum* explains that the urine of virgins is 'clear and lucid, sometimes white,

A Physician Examining A Urine Flask, after Gerrit Dou (1613–1675).

sometimes sparkling'. The reason that 'corrupted women' have 'muddy urine' is because of the 'rupture' of skin and 'male sperm appear on the bottom'.[12] Pissing Perrier is a neat party trick, but there are other signs to look for. William of Saliceto (1210–1277) wrote that 'a virgin urinates with a more subtle hiss', and if you had a stopwatch handy, it 'indeed takes longer than a small boy'.[13]

Medieval virginity tests are quite urine-focused, and fifteenth-century Italian physician Niccolo Falcucci was also a piss prophet, but he had a few other tricks up his sleeve.

> If a woman is covered with a piece of cloth and fumigated
> with the best coal, if she is a virgin she does not perceive
> its odor through her mouth and nose; if she smells it, she
> is not a virgin. If she takes it in a drink, she immediately
> voids urine if she is not a virgin. A corrupt woman will also
> urinate immediately if a fumigation is prepared with cockle.
> Upon fumigation with dock flowers, if she is a virgin she
> immediately becomes pale, and, if not, her humor falls on the
> fire and other things are said about her.[14]

The anonymous, thirteenth-century Hebrew text *Book of Women's Love* says, 'The girl must urinate over marshmallows in the evening, and bring them in the morning; if they are still fresh she is modest and good, if not she is not.'[15] Before you start pissing into a bag of flumps, the marshmallow referred to here is a medicinal plant.

But perhaps you are struggling to inspect, listen to or time your intended's waterworks. In which case, you will need to study her general appearance for the tell-tale clues that her flower has been plucked. Before explaining that a virgin's piss sparkles, Pseudo-Albertus Magnus's *De Secretis Mulierum* explains what to look out for. 'The signs of chastity are as follows: shame, modesty, fear, a faultless gait and speech, casting eyes down before men and the acts of men.' (FYI, these are also signs she ordered and ate the Pizza Hut family feast on her own and is praying you don't find the evidence in the bin.) Magnus continues:

> If a girl's breasts point downwards, this is a sign that she has
> been corrupted, because at the moment of impregnation the

menses move upwards to the breasts and the added weight causes them to sag. If a man has sexual intercourse with a woman and experiences no sore on his penis and no difficulty of entry, this is a sign that she was first corrupted. However, a true sign of the woman's virginity is if it is difficult to perform the act and it causes a sore on his member.[16]

Of course, once the hymen became the go-to virginity test, checking for sparkling wee that whistled, perky boobs and the ability to smell coal without wetting oneself largely fell out of favour. Virginity testing became all about tightness and blood.

Producing bloodied bedsheets as proof of a wife's virginity does still occur around the world today, although it's rare. In certain regions of Georgia, brides have a 'Yenge', usually an older family member, who will instruct her in what to expect on her wedding night. Traditionally, it was the Yenge's responsibility to take the bloodied sheets from the marital bed and show them to both families to 'prove' the bride was a nookie newbie. Although the Yenge's role is largely ceremonial today, in some areas the practice of showing bloodied sheets still goes on.[17]

The bloody sheet test also has a long pedigree. It is found in the Bible, old medieval romances, and it's even said that Catharine of Aragon was able to produce blood-stained sheets to prove she married Henry VIII as a virgin.[18] Of course, as long as people have subscribed to this deeply flawed test, there have been ways of faking it. Given what was at stake should the gift of a bride's virginity be unwrapped by someone else before the 'I dos', you can understand why a girl might tell a fanny fib on her wedding night, and for as long as medical texts have been telling us how to prove virginity, they've also been giving advice on how to restore it. The *Trotula* is the name given to three twelfth-century Italian texts on women's health. At least one of the three was authored by a woman, Trota of Salerno, who practised medicine in the southern

Italian coastal town of Salerno. The *Trotula* has this exceptionally devious advice for a girl whose cherry is on the blink:

> This remedy will be needed by any girl who has been induced to open her legs and lose her virginity by the follies of passion, secret love, and promises ... When it is time for her to marry, to keep the man from knowing, the false virgin will carefully deceive the husband as follows. Let her take ground sugar,

Silver-bound hinged cowrie shell containing a painting of a man unlocking the chastity belt of a reclining woman.

the white of an egg, and alum and mix them in rainwater in which pennyroyal and calamint have been boiled down with other similar herbs. Soaking a soft and porous cloth in this solution, let her keep bathing her private parts with it.

But the best of all is this deception: the day before her marriage, let her put a leech cautiously on her labia, taking care lest it slip in by mistake; then blood will flow out here, and a little crust will form in that place. Because of the flux of blood and the constricted channel of the vagina, thus in having intercourse the false virgin will deceive the man.[19]

The *Book of Women's Love* recommends the following to restore virginity: 'take myrtle leaves and boil them well with water until only a third part remains; then, take nettles without prickles and boil them in this water until a third remains. She must wash her secret parts with this water in the morning and at bedtime, up to nine days.' However, if you're in a real hurry you can 'take nutmeg and grind to a powder; put it in that place and her virginity will be restored immediately'.[20] Nicolas Venette (1633–1698), the French author of the seventeenth-century *L'amour Conjugal*, gave this advice to fake a maidenhead:

Make a bath of decorations of Leaves of mallows, Groundsel, with some handfuls of Line Seed and Fleabane Seed, Orach, Brank Ursin or bearfoot. Let them sit in this Bath an hour, after which, let them be wiped, and examin'd 2 or 3 hours after Bathing, observing them narrowly in the mean while. If a Woman is a Maid, all her amorous parts are compress'd and joyn'd close to one another; but if not, they are flaggy, loose, and flouting, instead of being wrinkled and close as they were before when she had a mind to choose us.[21]

NOCTURNAL REVELS:

OR, THE

HISTORY

OF

KING's-PLACE,

AND OTHER

MODERN NUNNERIES.

CONTAINING THEIR

MYSTERIES, DEVOTIONS, and SACRIFICES.

Comprifing alfo, The

ANCIENT and PRESENT STATE of PROMISCUOUS GALLANTRY:

WITH THE

PORTRAITS of the moft CELEBRATED DEMIREPS and COURTEZANS of this PERIOD:

AS WELL AS

Sketches of their Profeffional and Occafional Admirers,

By a MONK of the ORDER of St. FRANCIS.

IN TWO VOLUMES.
VOL. I.

THE SECOND EDITION, CORRECTED AND IMPROVED, WITH A VARIETY OF ADDITIONS.

Il vero eft, quod ego mihi puto palmarium,
Me reperiffe, quo modo adolefcentulus
Meretricum ingenia & mores poffit nofcere:
Mature ut cum cognorit, perpetuo oderit.
TER. EUN. Act 5. Sc. 4.

LONDON:

Printed for M. GOADBY, Pater-nofter-Row.
1779.

Cover page from Monk of the Order of St Francis, *Nocturnal Revels: or, The History of King's-Place, and Other Modern Nunneries*, 1779.

As Hanne Blank argued in her marvellous *Virgin: The Untouched History*, many of the ingredients listed here are astringents or anti-inflammatories that were thought to tighten the vagina. Although Venette doesn't list it here, one of the most well-known twinkle tighteners was alum water. In Francis Grose's *Dictionary of the Vulgar Tongue* (1785) he cites 'pucker water' as 'Water impregnated with alum, or other astringents, used by old experienced traders to counterfeit virginity'.[22] Alum is a class of chemical compound that is used widely today in food preservatives and industry. Insanely, there are numerous websites out there that still recommend alum for tightening the vagina. I will just take this moment to say, dear God, please do not do that to your poor chuff; do your Kegels and keep the faith.

Other than wishing to fake it on their wedding night, another reason a girl would want to pass as a novice is that maidenheads came at a premium. By the eighteenth century, virgins were a lucrative business, and any working girl or madam would know how to fake a hymen for maximum profit. *Nocturnal Revels* (1779) provides explicit details about women selling their virginity several times over, and quotes the famous madam Charlotte Hayes as saying a virginity is 'as easily made as a pudding'. Charlotte goes on to say that she sold her own 'thousands of times'.[23] The eponymous heroine of the original bonkbuster *Fanny Hill* (1749) tells the reader precisely how virginity is faked in the sex industry.

> In each of the head bed-posts, just above where the
> bedsteads are inserted into them, there was a small drawer,
> so artfully adapted to the mouldings of the timber-work, that
> it might have escaped even the most curious search: which
> drawers were easily opened or shut by the touch of a spring,
> and were fitted each with a shallow glass tumbler, full of a
> prepared fluid blood, in which lay soaked, for ready use, a

sponge, that required no more than gently reaching the hand to it, taking it out and properly squeezing between the thighs, when it yielded a great deal more of the red liquid than would save a girl's honour.[24]

Other sneaky tips include having sex during menstruation to ensure blood, and placing a bird's heart, or a pig's bladder stitched up and containing blood, into the vaginal cavity so it will 'bleed' on cue.[25]

Despite a deeply engrained historical belief in the bleeding virgin, this has never been unanimously accepted by the scientific community. There have always been lone voices of reason who recognised this as a load of cobblers. Physicians such as Ambroise Paré not only denied that

Francisco Goya, *A Young Woman Casting Aside Her Virginity to Become a Prostitute*, 1798.

virginity could be proven with a hymen, he claimed there was no such a thing as a hymen back in 1573. Since then there have been occasional whispers that the hymen is not quite the certificate of authenticity it is touted to be. By the nineteenth century, these whispers had become an audible grumble. Dr Blundell questioned the value of this 'mystic membrane', and Erasmus Wilson stated that the hymen 'must not be considered a necessary accompaniment to virginity' in 1831.[26] Edward Foote wrote that 'the hymen is a cruel and unreliable test of virginity' and that 'physicians know it is a very fallible test of virginity'.[27] By the twentieth century, the grumble had become a deafening shout and by the twenty-first century the shouting had been replaced by dramatic eye rolls and exasperated cries of 'for fuck's sake! Not this bollocks again!' The research I referred to at the beginning of this chapter identified some 1,269 studies in electronic databases that research the validity of virginity testing and hymen reliability, and they overwhelmingly reach the conclusion that you cannot 'prove' someone is a virgin and hymens tell you naff all about the owner's sexual past.[28] And yet the myth persists, and women are routinely subjected to pointless and invasive examinations to try and establish their sexual experience.

Today virginity examinations are largely carried out on unmarried females, often without consent or in situations where individuals are unable to give consent.[29] Virginity testing on schoolgirls has been reported in South Africa and Swaziland to deter pre-marital sexual activity. In India, the test has been part of the sexual assault assessment of female rape victims. In Indonesia, the exam has been part of the application process for women to join the police force.[30] But even if you could prove someone's virginity, the issue isn't really the examination itself (although it's bad enough) – it's cultural attitudes that value women based primarily on whether they are sexually active that are the issue. There is no way of 'proving' if someone has had sex by examining their genitals, because 'virginity' is not something tangible.

The hymen is simply a stretchy tissue inside the vagina, but it doesn't seal it up like a Tupperware lid. Hymens come in many different shapes and thickness – some bleed when torn and others do not. The hymen absolutely does not 'pop' when broken and cannot prove anyone's sexual history any more than your elbow can. You cannot 'lose' your virginity because virginity is an invention, not a physical fact – no matter how sparkly your piss may be.

SEX
AND
PENISES

Spilling the Beans
Orgasm and Onanism

T he female orgasm is often spoken of as if it were a hidden treasure to be found only with the aid of maps, detailed instructions and a packed lunch. The intrepid sexual adventurer boldly sets out, like Indiana Jones, to navigate the mystery of the female body, read the clues, solve the puzzle and choose wisely before drinking from the Holy Grail. The male orgasm, on the other hand, is spoken of in terms of a bottle of Coke: shake it up until it explodes out the end and makes everything sticky. Job done.

Almost all slang terms for orgasm throughout history refer to male orgasms, rather than female. When it comes to orgasm slang, women share with men rather than owning their own: cumming, spending, climaxing, orgasming, etc. are all unisex, with the possible exception of squirting. While there are thousands of nouns for semen, how many can you think of for the natural lubricant women secrete during sex? It doesn't even have a word of its own in English. In medical parlance, it's called vaginal mucus, or vaginal secretion. The French call this fluid *cyprine*, from 'Cyprus', the birthplace of Aphrodite, goddess of love. Not to be outdone by the French, *Roger's Profanisaurus* arrived in the 1990s to nourish the English lexical wasteland with such gems as 'fanny batter' and 'gusset icing'. However welcome such additions may be, the fact remains that slang for semen and the male orgasm could fill a dictionary, and the female equivalent could fill a footnote.

Perhaps it's not too surprising that male and female orgasms are discussed in very different terms. Elisabeth Lloyd's comprehensive analysis of thirty-three studies of sexual behaviour, conducted over the past eighty years, reveals that up to 80 per cent of women have difficulty orgasming from vaginal intercourse alone and between 5 per cent and 10 per cent of women never experience an orgasm.[1] Ever. To date, there have only been a handful of studies into the orgasms of trans women after penile-inversion vaginoplasty, but this research has shown that 18 per cent of trans women could not orgasm by masturbation alone, 14 per cent of trans women complained of anorgasmia, and up to 20 per cent experienced difficulty orgasming post-surgery.[2] Studies have shown that most women require at least twenty minutes of sexual activity to climax and there are myriad factors that can kibosh a lady's snap, crackle and pop: age, stress, atmosphere, smells, self-esteem.[3] Frankly, it's a known flight risk.

Comparably straightforward a male orgasm may be, but the history of male orgasm is anything but simple. The historical understanding of what happened to a man's body and soul once he had 'blown his beans' (1972) is a dark and deeply troubling one. From the medieval theologians who actually recommended beans to cure impotence as they believed an erection was caused by air inflating the penis, to Roman priests of Cybele who castrated themselves in frenzied ceremonies, it's been a bumpy ride for the 'hot rod' (1972). But it's the link between orgasm and energy that I want to focus on here, the ancient theory that orgasm weakens a man's strength and drains his masculine virility. You know the one. In *Rocky* (1976), the Italian Stallion's legendary trainer, Mickey, tells him 'women weaken legs'.[4] British sprinter Linford Christie used to say making love the night before a race made his legs feel 'like lead'.[5] Boxer Carl Froch abstained from sex for three months before knocking out George Groves in their world title fight.[6] Each world cup, rumours abound about which coach has imposed a nookie embargo on his players before a match.

It's important before going any further to state that there is absolutely no scientific data to support this theory. A 2016 systematic review of all the current scientific evidence on the effects of sexual activity on sport performance found that 'evidence suggests that sexual activity the day before competition does not exert any negative impact on performance'.[7] The New York Yankees manager Casey Stengel once said, 'it's not the sex that wrecks these guys, it's staying up all night looking for it'.[8] However, the myth persists.

The theory that orgasm creates an energy leak stretches back to ancient China and Taoism. A key belief within Taoism is seminal vitality (*yuan ching*), and that semen must not leave the body, but be reabsorbed to nourish the brain (*huan jing*). While a man is encouraged to have sex, he must not orgasm if the life force is to be preserved. *The Classic of Su Nu* (*c.* AD 200–500) is a text in the form of a debate between the Yellow Emperor and the goddess Su Nu. The emperor asks the goddess how he can preserve his vital energies, and she tells him to cease ejaculating during sex.

> One act without emission makes the ch'i strong. Two acts
> without emission makes the hearing acute and the vision
> clear. Three acts without emission makes all ailments
> disappear. Four acts without emission and the 'five spirits'
> are all at peace. Five acts without emission makes the pulse
> full and relaxed. Six acts without emission strengthens the
> waist and back. Seven acts without emission gives power to
> the buttocks and thigh. Eight acts without emission causes
> the whole body to be radiant. Nine acts without emission and
> one will enjoy unlimited longevity. Ten acts without emission
> and one attains the realm of the immortals.[9]

Taoism taught that ingesting vaginal secretions would strengthen the Yang (male) essence. Therefore, pussy was not only celebrated,

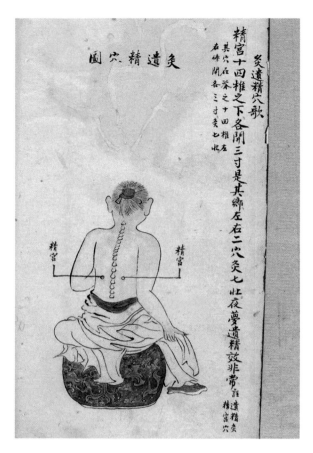

圖穴精遺灸

精宮

精宮

精宮十四椎之下各開三寸是其鄉左右二穴灸七壯夜夢遺精效非常註遺精灸精宮穴

灸遺精穴歌

其穴在茶之十四椎左右傍開各三寸灸七壯

Acu-moxa point chart, showing the *jinggong* (Palace of Essence/Semen) point, from *Chuanwu lingji lu* (Record of Sovereign Teachings), by Zhang Youheng. This work survives only in a manuscript draft, completed in 1869 (eighth year of the Tongzhi reign period of the Qing dynasty).

it was a superfood. Suck on that, kale crisps. Semen retention is still widely practised in Taoism and Neotantra groups today, who believe energy and health can be increased by corking the cum. But before you all start saving up your 'axel grease' (1983) for some cosmic spunk dump, research from Harvard University has linked not ejaculating with a marked increase in prostate cancer. 'Men who ejaculated 21 or more times a month enjoyed a 33 per cent lower risk of prostate cancer compared with men who reported four to seven ejaculations a month throughout their lifetimes.'[10] An Australian study had similar findings, and found that men who ejaculated four to seven times a week were

Xiuzhen miyao, a gymnastic (*daoyin/qigong*) text of unknown origin, was rediscovered and published with a preface by Wang Zai in 1513. It records forty-nine exercises. This illustration depicts *Jiang niu zhuo yue* (dismounting from the ox to catch the moon), a technique used to treat involuntary seminal emission.

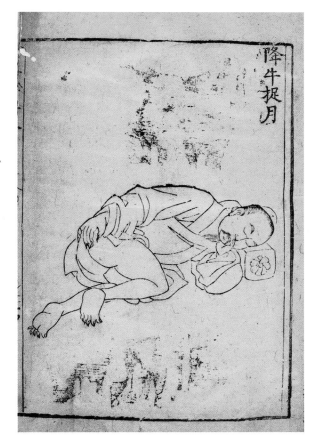

36 per cent less likely to develop prostate cancer than men who ejaculated less than two or three times a week.[11] But I digress.

The Ancient Greeks and Romans also believed that constantly 'cracking your marbles' (1967) was damaging to your health and depleted essential energy reserves. Hippocrates taught that a healthy body required a balancing of the humour fluids (blood, yellow bile, black bile, and phlegm). Logically, losing too much 'baby juice' (1901) could disturb this delicate balance and affect health. Aristotle believed that too much sex activity could stunt your growth. Plutarch advised men to 'store up his seed'. Plato wrote, 'if any man retains his semen, he is strong, and the proof is athletes who are abstinent'. To make sure there were no nocturnal emissions, Galen recommended athletes sleep on lead plates.[12]

This belief persisted throughout the Middle Ages. St Albert the Great (1200–1280) firmly believed that 'coitus drains the brain', and that dogs followed lustful people around as 'the body of a person who has had a great deal of intercourse approaches the condition of a cadaver because of all the rotten semen'.[13] Of course, if you could lose too much 'dilberry' (1811), conversely you could have too much of the stuff, which would also unbalance the humours. In 1123, the First Lateran Council imposed compulsory celibacy on all priests. As you can imagine, this decree was met with considerable opposition from the clergy, and medical reasons were often cited. Gerald of Wales was archdeacon of Brecon in the twelfth century and wrote of a number of cases where celibacy had caused the death of various priests and bishops. Gerald recorded the death of an archdeacon of Louvain, whose 'genital organs swelled up with immeasurable flatulence' because of his vows of celibacy.[14] The archdeacon refused to break his vows, and died shortly afterwards. This is by no means the only example of such medical advice in medieval Europe. It may seem strange that the Church would encourage sex, but the medieval Church understood lust to be sinful, whereas sex was essential to fulfil God's command to 'go forth and multiply'; so functional, fun-free intercourse was the order of the day. The medieval Church operated like a semen satnav, directing a chap's 'duck butter' (1938) to its lawful uterine destination with minimal wrong turns and in the most efficient way possible. Semen that had missed its mark was dangerous stuff indeed. Some medieval theologians taught that demons stole semen from masturbators and couples practising coitus interruptus, and used it to impregnate women. St Thomas Aquinas in his *Summa Theologica* wrote that demons took the form of beautiful women called succubi, inflamed lust in men,

Indian gouache painting of a giant penis copulating with a female devil, *c.*1900.

seduced them and harvested his seed.[15] Then the demon would take the form of a man (incubus) and impregnate a willing woman.

This nice little theory is repeated and expanded upon in Heinrich Kramer and James Sprenger's guide for hunting witches, *The Malleus Maleficarum* (1487). Although the text acknowledges that men can be witches too, it argues 'a greater number of witches is found in the fragile feminine sex than among men'.[16] It goes on to argue that unlike men, women 'know no moderation in goodness or vice', and that 'all witchcraft comes from carnal lust, which is in women insatiable'.[17] The fear of women dominating men, castrating them or stealing their 'oyster soup' (1890) and draining their strength runs throughout the *Malleus*. 'And blessed be the Highest Who has so far preserved the male sex from so great a crime: for since He was willing to be born and to suffer for us, therefore He has granted to men the privilege.'[18] The fear that an orgasm drained men of their strength is palpable.

But it is easy to understand why orgasm would be linked to a loss of strength and potency. The French call an orgasm *la petite mort* (the little death), and with good reason. Ask yourself how you feel after orgasm when the mist has lifted. I'm generalising but, for those of us with vulvas, the orgasm is like an end-of-level boss; a violent showdown, after which we level up and want more – only harder. Though many women experience painful sensitivity in the genitals post-orgasm, we can keep going and, as *Cosmo* keeps assuring us, can achieve multiple orgasms. But once the penis has 'shot his snot' (1709) it's all over, and before you can say 'I'm ready, darling' he is snoring in the wet patch. This special time is known in medical terms as the 'male refractory period'. It is defined as 'the transient period of time after ejaculation associated with detumescence, reduced interest in sexual activity, inability to ejaculate or experience orgasm, and increased aversion to genital sensory stimulation'.[19] The finger of blame for this period is often pointed at central serotonin and prolactin fluctuations in the brain. But as pre- and post-orgasmic elevations in prolactin and serotonin are observed in both men and women, this is not regarded as an explanation as to why men and not women experience a refractory period.[20] Whatever the reason, the MRP is very real, and the post-orgasm crash from super horny sex god to sleeping bear seemed irrefutable proof that an orgasm sapped men of their potency.

This all seemed perfectly obvious to Dr Samuel-Auguste Tissot when he published *Onanism: A Treatise on the Maladies Produced by Masturbation* in 1758. Tissot argued that semen was a vital body fluid, and that masturbation was the most damaging way to lose precious *liqueur séminale*. The picture Tissot painted of a man who ejaculated too frequently is not a pretty one. He argued excessive masturbation, nocturnal emission and coitus interruptus caused the body to simply waste away:

> I have seen a patient, whose disorder began by lassitude,
> and a weakness in all parts of the body, particularly towards
> the loins; it was attended with an involuntary motion of the
> tendons, periodical spasms and bodily decay, Insomuch as
> to destroy the whole corporeal frame; he felt a pain even in
> the membranes of the brain, a pain which patients call a dry
> burning heat, and which incessantly burns internally the
> most noble parts.[21]

Tissot's work set in motion a crusade against masturbation that would last for the next two hundred years. The solitary vice, self-pollution, onanism, or 'jerkin the gherkin' (1938) would come under increasing medical scrutiny and men's soft-and-danglies were subject to various quack cures, ranging from the mildly amusing to the outright dangerous.

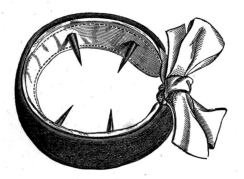

Nineteenth-century four-pointed urethral ring for the treatment of masturbation. The ring would be fitted around the penis before bedtime and if the wearer had an erection during the night, the teeth would bite into the penis and wake the poor chap up.

FOUR-POINTED URETHRAL RING.

By the nineteenth century, medical theories that a loss of semen was seriously injurious to health had been firmly established. Physicians all over the Western world were warning that masturbation was not only dangerous, but could be fatal. Dr Léopold Deslandes (1797–1852), for example, wrote that 'the patient is unconscious of his danger, and perseveres in his vicious habit – the physician treats him symptomatically, and death soon closes the scene'.[22]

Men were warned to conserve their 'essence' by avoiding fornication and masturbation, and by limiting sex within marriage. Numerous anti-masturbation devices were available to prevent 'nocturnal emissions', or to stop young boys interfering with themselves. Physicians are recorded as applying acids, needles and electric shocks to the penile shaft in an attempt to cure what was then known as 'spermatorrhea' (weakness caused by loss of semen). Sparse diets were recommended to subdue lust, and purity crusaders such as John Harvey Kellogg (1852–1943) manufactured plain cereals to suppress urges. Kellogg argued that masturbation could cause all manner of illnesses, from cancer of the womb to epilepsy, insanity and impotency. But Kellogg went much further than just peddling a cock block in a box. He was full of useful information for parents on how to 'cure' a child from masturbating.

Nᵒ1

A young lad has become withered and aged because of his constant masturbating, 1845.

Representing the debilitated state of the body from the effects of Onanism or Self-pollution.

Bandaging the parts has been practised with success. Tying the hands is also successful in some cases; but this will not always succeed, for they will often contrive to continue the habit in other ways, as by working the limbs, or lying upon the abdomen. Covering the organs with a cage has been practised with entire success.[23]

But the method Kellogg felt most successful in stopping the 'knuckle shuffle' (2001) was circumcision – without anaesthetic.

A remedy which is almost always successful in small boys is circumcision, especially when there is any degree of phimosis. The operation should be performed without administering an anaesthetic, as the brief pain attending the operation will have a salutary effect upon the mind, especially if it be connected with the idea of punishment, as it may well be in some cases. The soreness which continues for several weeks interrupts the practice, and if it had not previously become too firmly fixed, it may be forgotten and not resumed.[24]

If women were habitual masturbators, Kellogg recommended burning out the clitoris with carbolic acid as an 'excellent means of allaying the abnormal excitement, and preventing the recurrence of the practice'.[25] It is in no small part thanks to anti-masturbation crusaders, such as Kellogg, that circumcision is still so widespread in America today. Although circumcision rates are declining, almost 80 per cent of American babies are circumcised today. It's important to remember that doctors like Kellogg truly believed they were helping people, and that orgasms were debilitating.

The 1911 *Boy Scout Handbook* by Robert Baden-Powell (1857–1941) devoted an entire chapter to instructing young boys in 'storing up natural forces' in order to conserve 'power and manliness'.

> In the body of every boy, who has reached his teens, the
> Creator of the universe has sown a very important fluid. This
> fluid is the most wonderful material in all the physical world.
> Some parts of it find their way into the blood, and through
> the blood give tone to the muscles, power to the brain, and
> strength to the nerves. This fluid is the sex fluid ... Any habit
> which a boy has that causes this fluid to be discharged from
> the body tends to weaken his strength, to make him less able
> to resist disease, and often unfortunately fastens upon him
> habits which later in life he cannot break.[26]

Although the Boy Scouts were still being cautioned not to 'box the Jesuit' (1744) right up to the 1950s, the early sexologists were already dispelling masturbation myths. In 1908, Albert Moll identified four phases of orgasm, and defined orgasm as a 'voluptuous acme' that gave way to a 'sudden cessation of the voluptuous sensation' and detumescence.[27] Wilhelm Reich described orgasms as a 'bioelectric discharge' and the work of Kinsey revealed that masturbation was an almost universal human experience.[28] It was the work of Masters and Johnson in 1966 that finally revealed exactly what happens

Victorian spermatorrhoea urethral ring.   TOOTHED URETHRAL RING.

to the male body before, during and after orgasm, and identified the 'refractory period'.[29] And while you may hesitate to bring up the subject of rubbing your nubbin over tea with the vicar, I like to believe we're now in a place where ejaculation and masturbation are no longer subjects shrouded in mystery and shame.

The instrument consists of a ring (A), which is hinged for the purpose of keeping the circuit open when the organ is quiescent. Upon the ring is a flat plate of ivory (*a*), furnished with a bolt (*b*), which, upon erection, is pushed backwards so as to complete the

circuit at this point. With the ring and bolt are connected two insulated wires (B, B), which convey the current to two binding screws (C1, C2). Of these C1 is in communication with one of

'The Electric Alarum', for treatment of masturbation. This lovely device was designed to electrocute the wearer's penis if he got an erection, 1887.

But better than that, new science is emerging all the time to show how important orgasm is within human relationships. In 2004, Bartels and Zeki demonstrated that the areas of the brain activated during orgasm are also activated when looking at pictures of the person's lover.[30] The work of Komisaruk and Whipple (2008), Kurtz (1975) and Yang et al. (2007) all show that the brain activity during orgasm in humans and animals is linked to memory consolidation, meaning orgasms bond partners together.[31] The work of Genaro (2016) builds on this and demonstrates that orgasm is key to pair-bonding partners, even in developing an attraction to certain 'types'.[32] In 2007, Stuart Brody studied the vaginal orgasms of some 1,256 women and concluded regular orgasms led to 'greater satisfaction' with sex life, mental health and general well-being.[33] In 2011, Cindolo et al. showed that not ejaculating regularly led to a notable decline in the micturition reflex (the ability to pass urine from the body). One study found that 32 per cent of 1,866 US women who reported masturbating in the previous three months did so to help them go to sleep. The same study also found that orgasm can increase levels of endorphins and corticosteroids that raise pain thresholds, easing discomforts associated with arthritis, menstrual cramps, migraine and other conditions.[34] In 2001, research showed that orgasm relieved the pain of migraines or cluster headaches for up to a third of patients.[35] And I have only just scratched the surface of research into why an orgasm is good for you.

So please, 'walk your ferret' (1785), 'flub your dub' (1966) and 'pull your pud' (1986); as long as no one else on the bus minds, orgasm to your heart's content. It's medically recommended. And every time you do, think of your orgasm as a tribute to all those before you who have paid an incredibly high cost for enjoying what Quentin Crisp called the ultimate 'expression of self-regard'.[36]

Gland Larceny

Testicular Transplants in the Twentieth Century

The link between ejaculating too often and a physical decline in health was an established medical fact until the twentieth century. So, what was a chap to do if his sexual potency had been drained and his manhood was in need of a reboot? An obvious remedy for depleting semen levels was to restock the reserves. The early twentieth century saw a medical craze for surgically rejuvenating ageing men by operating on their genitals to increase the amount of semen and/or sex hormones in the body. Depending on which physician you opted to visit, this could mean being subjected to a bilateral vasectomy, or having a monkey testicle grafted into your scrotum. These were the early days of endocrinology and hormone replacement therapy, and the doctors pushing these procedures touted them as a fountain of youth, albeit a fountain full of semen. But before you head off to look up 'monkey balls' on eBay, you should know that these procedures were discredited by the 1930s, when they were found to cause more harm than good (for both humans and monkeys alike).

In the 1880s, French physiologist Charles-Édouard Brown-Séquard (1817–1894) started injecting himself with testicular extracts from guinea pigs and dogs.[1] He called his concoction the 'elixir of life', and believed it would replenish his own 'seminal losses'. 'I put forward the idea that if it were possible without danger to inject semen into the blood of old men, we should probably obtain manifestations of increased activity as regards the mental and the various physical powers.' He continued:

> It is well known that seminal losses, arising from any cause, produce a mental and physical debility which is in proportion to their frequency. These facts, and many others, have led to the generally-admitted view that in the seminal fluid, as secreted by the testicles, a substance or several substances exist which, entering the blood by resorption, have a most essential use in giving strength to the nervous system and to other parts.[2]

Charles-Édouard Brown-Séquard (1817–1894) was a Mauritian physiologist and neurologist.

Convinced the ageing process could be reversed by boosting semen in the body, Brown-Séquard started to experiment on animals, trying to graft parts of guinea pigs into male dogs, and injecting ageing rabbits with the blood or semen taken from the testicles of younger rabbits, that kind of thing.[3] Convinced all this seminal swapping was having a positive effect on his subjects, Brown-Séquard began injecting himself with a mixture of blood, semen and 'juice extracted from testicles' of dogs and guinea pigs.

> To the three kinds of substances I have just named I added distilled water in a quantity which never exceeded three or four times their volume. The crushing was always done after

the addition of water. When filtered through a paper filter
the liquid was of a reddish hue, and rather opaque ... For
each injection I have used nearly one cubic centimeter of the
filtered liquid.[4]

Immediately after these injections, Brown-Séquard reported being
able to work for longer hours, experienced an increase in mental focus,
and, at the age of seventy-two, could run up and down stairs again.
Brown-Séquard published his findings in *The Lancet*, and legitimised
organotherapy as a credible medical discipline.[5]

Brown-Séquard may have been an early pioneer, but the man
responsible for making surgical rejuvenation mainstream was the
Russian-born French surgeon Serge Voronoff (1866–1951). Voronoff
was a laboratory director at the prestigious Collège de France when he
made his name implanting monkey testicles into men who complained
they were not as sprightly as they used to be. An expert manipulator
of the press, Voronoff's work became the subject of intense media focus
around the world.

Mr Monkey Nuts himself,
Dr Serge Abrahamovitch
Voronoff (1866–1951).

Before turning his full attention to monkey 'bollocks' (1000), Voronoff was a respected gynaecologist and had pioneered new surgical techniques in *Les Feuillets de Chirurgie et de Gynecologie* (1910). Influenced by the work of Brown-Séquard, Voronoff began experimenting on animals to see if grafting testicle glands from one animal into the body of another held rejuvenating properties. Convinced that it did, Voronoff presented his findings to the French Surgical Congress in 1919. *Le Petit Parisien* reported his findings the next day.

> Doctor Serge Voronoff, director of the physiology laboratory at the Collège de France, offered a stunning communication to the surgical congress yesterday. He claims to have rejuvenated and reinvigorated aging goats and rams by grafting an interstitial gland taken from one of their own species ... The entire human race will benefit from the success of Mr Voronoff's projects, since he is working hard to obtain similarly successful results while operating on aging men by grafting the interstitial gland of a monkey. It does not matter what glands these might be. If their introduction, through the scalpel of Doctor Voronoff, can give our tired organisms youth and vigour, then long live interstitial glands.[6]

After repeating his experiment hundreds of times on sheep, dogs and bulls, in 1920 Voronoff began transplanting monkey glands into humans. He had originally wanted to use human testicles, taken from corpses and criminals, but soon realised he would never be able to secure a regular supply, so monkey nuts it was. Eventually, Voronoff had to buy a monkey colony near Nice to keep up with demand.[7]

The procedure was as simple as it was horrific. The chimp's testicle would be removed and finely cut into longitudinal segments. An incision was then made into the patient's scrotum to expose the testicles and membranes. The cut-up chimp testes were implanted underneath the tunica vaginalis membrane, and the incision was sewn back up. The theory was that the monkey glands would be absorbed directly into the patient's own sex glands. The monkey was euthanised.

Voronoff knew the value of customer testimonials, and in his 1924 book, *Forty-Three Grafts From Monkey to Man*, he meticulously detailed his many successes, including a seventy-four-year-old Englishman, Arthur Liardet. Voronoff grafted a baboon's 'bobble' (1889) into Arthur Liardet in 1921 and declared, 'his man has truly been rejuvenated by 15 or 20 years. Physical state, genital vitality, all has radically changed from the results of the testicular transplant that transformed a senile old man, powerless and pitiful, into a vigorous man with all his capacities.'[8] Despite being transformed 'from tottering old age to the activity of a man in the prime of life', Liardet died just two years later.[9] Undeterred, in his 1925 book, *Rejuvenation by Grafting*, Voronoff declared that his ageing patients appeared fifteen years younger, and common ailments such as constipation, cramps, fatigue and colitis were all hugely improved. In cases of depression, post-surgery patients appeared to be 'more alert, displayed increased vigour, jovial eyes, and had more energy'.[10] Of course, one of the most commonly cited ailments Voronoff claimed to be able to cure was impotency and a lack of libido. One sixty-seven-year-old post-operative patient claimed that his sexual libido had returned to an 'extraordinary degree'.[11]

Despite Voronoff's confidence, the scientific community were less and less convinced that sewing monkey balls into an old man's scrotum was a good thing. Scientists began trying to replicate Voronoff's remarkable success and couldn't. French veterinary surgeon Henri Velu experimented with testicular grafting on sheep to try and improve their health, but found this only resulted in grumpy sheep. He presented his findings before the French Veterinary Academy in 1929 where he called Voronoff 'delusional'. Similar studies in Australia and Germany also found gland grafting produced no positive effects.[12] To make matters worse, Voronoff was denied a licence to operate in Britain on grounds of animal cruelty. Leading anti-vivisectionists in the UK denounced Voronoff as 'an offence against morality, hygiene, and decency'.[13]

But at least Voronoff was an established medical surgeon, which is more than could be said for the American John Richard Brinkley (1885–1942), who started grafting goat testicles into human subjects armed only with a bought medical diploma and a can-do attitude.[14] Brinkley became known as the 'goat gland doctor', and made a great deal of money from convincing men he could restore their erection with a billy goat's scruff. Inspired by the work of rejuvenists like Voronoff, Brinkley operated on hundreds of people (men and women) and given he really didn't have the qualifications to be doing so, infections were common, and a number of patients died. Between 1930 and 1941, Brinkley was sued more than a dozen times for the wrongful death of a patient in his care.[15] Eventually, Brinkley was exposed in court as a 'charlatan and a quack in the ordinary, well-understood meaning of those words', and was subsequently ruined by an avalanche of lawsuits.[16] He declared bankruptcy in 1941, and died in poverty the following year.

While Voronoff escaped such a fate, by the closing years of the 1920s, the once great surgeon was attracting more mockery than praise. In 1928, shortly before Voronoff's lecture series in London, George Bernard Shaw wrote a letter to the *London Daily News* from the perspective of a monkey:

> We apes are a patient and kindly race, but this is more than we can stand. Has any ape ever torn the glands from a living man to graft them upon another ape for the sake of a brief and unnatural extension of that ape's life? … Man remains what he has always been; the cruellest of animals. Let him presume no further on his grotesque resemblance to us;

he will remain what he is in spite of all of Dr Voronoff's efforts to make a respectable ape of him.

Yours truly,

Consul Junior, The Monkey House Regents Park, May 26, 1928.[17]

By 1929, Voronoff claimed to have carried out almost five hundred gland transplants, but he had lost credibility with the public and his peers. Not only was new research disproving his theories, but his patients continued to age, deteriorate and die. Eventually, Voronoff's name faded from the press, his work was widely condemned, and he was painted as just another quack. Voronoff and his theories may be long gone, but in one final disturbing twist, it has been suggested that the vogue for transplanting monkey tissue into humans may have been responsible for transferring simian immunodeficiency virus (HIV-1) from apes to humans, leading to the global AIDS crisis today.[18]

Voronoff may have been one of the most notorious surgeons mangling scrotums in the quest for eternal youth, but he certainly wasn't the only one.* Austrian physiologist Eugen Steinach (1861–1944) believed that a bilateral vasectomy (tying the tubes of both testicles), would act like a kind of plug to keep semen in the body, which would boost a flagging sex drive. After experimenting on rats, Steinach refined his technique and moved on to human subjects. Steinach claimed his early experiments not only cured impotence, but his patients were younger, 'more buoyant and alive'.[19] Patients before the operation were described as being 'subject to paralysing fatigue, disclination to work, failing memory, indifference and depression; all of which hinder or preclude

---

* Other physicians working in gland and rejuvenation surgery included Victor Darwin Lespinasse (1878–1946), George Frank Lydston (1858–1923) and Leo Leonidas Stanley (1886–1976).

Eugen Steinach
(1861–1944) pioneered
a partial vasectomy
to prevent ageing –
despite this, he still died
of old age.

progress and every kind of competition', and, of course, they were 'impotent'.[20] The promise of eternal youth and a raging 'hard-on' (1864) are extremely seductive, and it's little wonder the public responded to Steinach's work so enthusiastically.

Word of the 'Steinach operation' soon spread and physicians such as Harry Benjamin, Robert Lichtenstern, Victor Blum and Norman Haire set up their own clinics and started twisting the 'nuts' (1704) of men across Europe and America. But not everyone was convinced surgical rejuvenation worked. In 1924, an editorial in the *Journal of the American Medical Association* denounced surgical rejuvenation as open to 'abuse and fantastic exploitation' and scorned those who 'are willing to grasp at such new suggestions towards accomplishing an invigorating end'.[21] But this didn't stop several high-profile figures from going under the knife.

Sigmund Freud was reported to have undergone a vasectomy at the hands of Dr Victor Blum in 1923 to try and cure him of cancer.[22] The Irish poet and Nobel Prize winner William Butler Yeats (1865– 1939) went to Dr Norman Haire in London for a bilateral vasectomy to try and boost his libido and the quality of his work. Shortly after the procedure, Yeats wrote to a friend that he now felt 'marvellously strong, with a sense of the future'.[23] However, Ethel Mannin, who had a brief relationship with Yeats after the operation, later pronounced the Steinach operation a 'failure'.[24] Ouch.

Failure or not, in the first half of the twentieth century, glands were big business. Newspapers reported huge consignments of rhesus monkeys being transported to Australia to 'meet the demands of patients for rejuvenation operations'.[25] In 1924, Dr William Bailey, director of the American Endocrine Laboratories, outlined seven possible methods for surgical rejuvenation to the American Chemical Society:

1. Transplantation of a gland from one position to another.
2. Grafting portions of animal glands to human ones (Voronoff's methods).
3. Cutting and binding the gland-ducts or vasoligature (Steinach's operation).
4. Application of X-rays.
5. Use of radium emanations, or gamma rays.
6. 'Drugging' the gland with iodine or alcohol.
7. 'Diathermia', or the application of heat through high-frequency electricity.[26]

There was no shortage of surgeons who were willing to subject men's 'tallywags' (1680) to all manner of quackery, but the Holy Grail (and most expensive) of the gland treatments was the transplant. Men feeling their youth slip away desperately clambered to get their hands on a pair of springy young gonads, through legal means, or not. The extent that some were willing to go to was laid bare in 1922.

On a bright summer morning in Chicago, in 1922, a man in his early thirties was found unconscious in a doorway at the corner of

Ranch Avenue and Adam Street. Unable to rouse him, concerned residents took the man to the local country hospital where he was soon identified as Henry Johnson, an electrical employee who lived with his sister, Beryl Heiber. Johnson was examined by one of the hospital's surgical interns who discovered that both Johnson's testicles had been removed from the scrotal sack, and that the wound had been cleaned with antiseptic and 'expertly' stitched closed. Johnson recalled he had been drinking with a friend on Madison Street the night before. His last memory was getting into a streetcar to go home, and after that, everything was blank. Surgeons treating Johnson at the time believed he had been drugged prior to the attacks, and noted the level of surgical skill required to excise a man's testicles without severing the testicular artery. Johnson was too embarrassed to report this to the police, and instead went home and returned to work.

Four months later in October, thirty-four-year-old Polish labourer Joseph Wozniak awoke lying in a vacant lot, with little recollection of how he came to be there. Wozniak had been out drinking with his friend Kuchnisky in Milwaukee Avenue, and the last thing he recalled was hailing a taxicab to go home. His head ached, he felt disorientated and he had a strong chemical taste in his mouth. Wozniak managed to stagger home to Seventeenth Street in the north of Chicago. A severe pain in his groin had grown steadily worse throughout the day until Wozniak admitted himself to hospital to be treated by Dr Sampolinski, who discovered that Wozniak's testicles had also been removed. The strong chemical taste Wozniak had in his mouth was chloroform.

Shocked, Dr Sampolinski called the police, and as soon as the media picked up the story, Joseph Wozniak was reported around the world as a victim of 'gland larceny'. Wozniak's drinking buddy Kuchnisky was missing, and police believed he must have suffered a similar fate to his friend, but was too embarrassed to come forward and had gone into

Reports of the case of testicular theft even made it to the UK. *Dundee Evening Telegraph*, Monday 16 October 1922.

hiding. Upon reading about the Wozniak case in the papers, Henry Johnson came forward to report his attack. It quickly became apparent that not only were these cases linked, but they were most likely carried out by a surgeon.

It is believed that this outrage was committed by gang of thieves to supply the new demand for glands for human rejuvenation. The greatest indignation prevails in Chicago medical circles. Dr Sampolinski, who was called in to treat Wozniak, said that the removal of the glands was made presumably to supply the want of some wealthy aged patient. Wozniak, who is a Polish war veteran, informed the police that he met a stranger who appeared to take an interest in him, and when he learned that Wozniak was hunting for a job gave him £2 and treated him to several drinks. 'He ordered a taxicab to drive me home,' said Wozniak. 'Four men were in the taxicab, and before I knew what had happened a sack was thrown over my head, and I lost consciousness. When I regained consciousness I was in a vacant house. My mind was befuddled, and I did not at first know that I had been operated on. I was dazed from the drink ... Then I tasted chloroform in my mouth, and felt intense pain. I managed to get home, and called [Dr] Sampolinski, who told me what had happened to me.'[27]

The following year, there were two more attacks within twenty-four hours of each other. Taxi driver Charles Ream was drugged and had both testicles removed, and John Powell of North Chicago was mutilated, but escaped with his testes intact.

Leading physicians in the field of rejuvenation were swift to condemn and distance themselves from such barbarism. Voronoff himself stated that 'the surgeon who did it should be compelled to suffer a like fate himself'.[28] The case sent Chicago residents into a panic and the police braced themselves for 'an epidemic of gland robberies like the Burke and Hare epidemic in [the UK]'. Fortunately, the epidemic never came, but the attackers were never caught.

Testicles were big business in the first half of the twentieth century and numerous products hit the market claiming to provide all the benefits of testicle grafting without the expense or having to go under the knife. And unlike beauty products today, these ones were proud to be full of bollocks. 'Gland Extract Tablets' promised 'perfection without drugs'.

Gland face creams advertised themselves as being able to 'permanently remove all traces of lines, wrinkles, crow's-feet, sagging muscles, and all facial blemishes'.

Eventually, the craze for gland surgeries and gland-based beauty products fell out of favour. How many people and animals had their genitals mutilated in the quest for sexual potency and a less wrinkled forehead is unknown. Although the idea of grafting monkey bollocks into your own genitals may sound utterly horrific to us today, people still to turn to extreme and bizarre surgical options in an effort to stop the clock on old age. Plastic surgery, Botox injections, penis enlargement surgeries, vaginal tightening, and all manner of lotions, potions

'Rejuvenating Tablets'
made from glands to
prevent ageing, 1926.

Anti-ageing face cream
made from glands, 1938.

and woo-woo are sought out in the fight against old age and impotence. We might laugh at the gland surgeons, but I can't honestly say I wouldn't rub a cream made of testicles on my face if I thought it could knock out a few wrinkles. The twentieth-century craze for gland treatment is testament to both our insecurities and our vanity. Even at the height of Voronoff's fame, there were those who urged people to reject such nonsense and embrace ageing with a bit of dignity – a sentiment that rings as true today as it did then.

Tough Love
Medieval Impotence Tests

As we have seen, throughout history people have submitted to extreme treatments in order to try and combat impotence. But it was only when the US Food and Drug Administration approved Sildenafil (tradename Viagra) on 27 March 1998 that there was finally a treatment that worked. The advent of Viagra did more than offer hope to millions of men around the world, it medicalised erectile dysfunction. In fact, it's thanks to Viagra that we even have the term 'erectile dysfunction'. Until the blue pill revolution, no one had 'erectile dysfunction', they were simply 'impotent', and this had to be accepted as a fact of life along with a receding hairline and middle-aged spread. As Viagra's advertising executive Ken Begasse Jr explained:

> Just calling it erectile dysfunction, as opposed to impotence, was one of the first major decisions that was made by Pfizer and the [ad] agency, to remove that social stigma. The initial ads – many of the ads – while they were seen as Viagra ads, were actually men's health ads. They were really there to break down the stigma.[1]

The effects of Sildenafil were discovered by accident when UK scientists at Pfizer were testing it as a cardiovascular drug to lower blood pressure. The irony that Viagra was once thought to lower anything at all is almost too delicious to bear, but it is true nonetheless. The

Paintings of carousing in taverns and brothels were very popular with sixteenth-century collectors in the Netherlands. Joachim Beuckelaer, *Brothel*, 1562.

drug works by increasing blood flow into the penis during sexual arousal, which means that 'Captain Standish' (1890) can steer into port, rather than capsizing in the shallows. This unexpected side effect was reported when members of the clinical trial refused to give the medication back to Pfizer.[2]

It's easy to make jokes about Viagra, but it has spearheaded a sexual revolution. According to the *Pharmaceutical Journal*, the drug has been prescribed for more than 64 million men worldwide. According to *Time* magazine, when the drug was first launched demand was so great that doctors had to use rubber stamps just to keep up with the prescriptions.[3] Of course, we all know Viagra is used recreationally by silly sods who believe that popping a pill will morph their penis into a Power Ranger, but the drug wasn't made for them. Viagra can offer more than the opportunity to 'dance with your arse to the ceiling' (1904).

Successfully treating erectile dysfunction can have a dramatic effect on a patient's mental health. In 2006, research published in the *Journal of General Internal Medicine* found that men treated with Sildenafil produced 'substantial improvements in self-esteem, confidence, and sexual relationship satisfaction. Improvements in these psychosocial factors were observed cross culturally and correlated significantly and tangibly with improvements in erectile function.'[4]

Today, a trip to the pharmacy or an online form may be all that stands between you and your happy ending, but things were far from this simple in a pre-Viagra world. The medieval Church looked on marriage (and indeed sex) as necessary to procreation. So central was sex to married life that the twelfth-century text on canon law, *Decretum*, listed impotence as grounds for annulment.* Divorce was all but impossible in the medieval world, and even if it was granted, neither party was allowed to remarry while the other one lived. But impotence was regarded as a lawful impediment to marriage if it was kept a secret from the wife when they wed. Next time you're at a wedding and the officiator asks if anyone knows of any 'lawful impediment' why the couple cannot be joined, just remember that you are legally bound to inform the congregation if you know that the groom's 'winkie' (1962) is on the

---

* *Decretum* is an enormous collection of papal letters, penitentials and the writings of various Church fathers that was compiled by Bishop Ivo of Chartres (d. 1115). Here, Ivo printed a letter from Pope Gregory II (AD 669– 731) which declared if a husband and wife could not have sex and refused to live together 'as brother and sister', the marriage could be annulled. Given the sheer size of Ivo's work, it wasn't a bestseller. However, around 1139 a canon lawyer known only as Gratian compiled a collection of canon law, now known as the Gratian *Decretum*, that also argued impotence was grounds for annulment. The Gratian *Decretum* quickly became the textbook for European law schools, and impotence was recognised as a legal deal breaker. Quoted in Catherine Rider, *Magic and Impotence in the Middle Ages* (Oxford: Oxford University Press, 2008), p. 57 and 'The Medieval Canon Law Virtual Library', *Web.Colby.Edu*, 2018 <http://web.colby.edu/canonlaw/category/ canon-law/> [Accessed 26 August 2018].

fritz. Impotence suits allowed a medieval woman to take her husband to court to annul her marriage and, crucially, if the annulment was granted, both parties could remarry.[5]

To the medieval Church this made perfect sense: no sex, no children, no point. However, this was not as easy as a wife announcing her husband couldn't get it up, and packing his bags for the off. The Church did not trust women to tell the truth, and certainly did not like annulling marriage. As keen as they were that their flock 'go forth and multiply', several criteria had to be met before the Church would agree to a couple separating. The couple would usually have to be married for at least three years before a case could be brought. If the husband denied the charges, the wife would be requested to produce witnesses to testify that she was a truthful person. If the husband admitted that he was impotent, the couple's neighbours would have to testify that they were of honest character, and they had seen no evidence to contradict the claims. And, crucially, the Church required 'proof' of the husband's impotence.[6]

But how do you 'prove' your husband wields a less than magic 'Johnson' (1863)? Today, a doctor may carry out a nocturnal penile tumescence (NPT) test, an intracavernosal injection test or even order a Doppler ultrasound. But in the twelfth century, all that was required was a group of 'wise matrons', a priest and an event known as 'congress'. Congress was required in most annulments proceeding from a charge of impotence, and it meant a group of women subjecting the accused man to a public examination and sustained efforts to rouse the beast. In *Summa Confessorum*, Thomas of Chobham (1160–1230) recommended the following:

> After food and drink the man and woman are to be placed
> together in one bed and wise women are to be summoned around
> the bed for many nights. And if the man's member is always found
> useless as if dead, the couple are well able to be separated.[7]

The results of these tests can be found throughout medieval court records, and they do not make for comfortable reading. Take, for example, the 1370 case of John Sanderson of the city of York. John's wife Tedia took her case to the ecclesiastical court, who ordered three women to inspect poor John's 'jiggle stick' (1890). Congress was performed and the matrons reported the following back to the court:

> the member of the said John is like an empty intestine of mottled skin and it does not have any flesh in it, nor veins in the skin, and the middle of its front is totally black. And said witness stroked it with her hands and put it in semen and having thus been stroked and put in that place it neither expanded nor grew. Asked if he has a scrotum with testicles she says that he has the skin of a scrotum, but the testicles do not hang in the scrotum but are connected with the skin as is the case among young infants.[8]

In 1368, Katherine Paynel demanded her husband, Nicholas, be examined and unsurprisingly Nicholas refused to submit to this. However, this did not stop Katherine calling various witnesses to testify that Nicholas had never risen to the occasion. Thomas Waus told the court that Katherine had:

> often tried to find the place of the said Nicholas' genitals with her hands when she lay in bed with said Nicholas and he was asleep, and that she could not stroke nor find anything there and that the place in which Nicholas' genitals ought be is as flat as the hand of a man.[9]

In 1292 in Canterbury, twelve women of 'good reputation' testified that Walter de Fonte's 'virile member' was utterly 'useless'. In 1433, at the trial of John of York, things got carried away when one matron:

exposed her naked breasts and with her hands warmed at
the said fire, she held and rubbed the penis and testicles of
the said John. And she embraced and frequently kissed the
said John, and stirred him up in so far as she could to show
his virility and potency, admonishing him for shame that
he should then and there prove and render himself a man.
And she says, examined and diligently questioned, that
the whole time aforesaid, the said penis was scarcely three
inches long.

In each case, the wife was granted her annulment and given permission to find a man who could 'better serve and please her'.[10]

Medieval canon law recognised two types of impotence: *permanent impotence* caused by a physical inability to have sex, and *temporary impotence* that was thought to be caused by witchcraft. For it was well known that impotence was often caused by magic, rather than by any personal failing on the man's side.

Burchard, Bishop of Worms, warned of such things in his eleventh-century penitential:

Have you done what some adulterous women are
accustomed to do? When first they learn that their lovers
want to take legitimate wives, they extinguish the men's
desire by some magic art, so that they cannot be of use to
their legitimate wives, or have intercourse with them. If you
have done this or taught others, you should do penance for
forty days on bread and water.[11]

As we have already seen, Heinrich Kramer and Jacob Sprenger's infamous witch-hunting manual, *The Malleus Maleficarum* (1486), has a lot to say about impotence, and devotes an entire chapter to how witches 'impede the power of generation'. Using their dark powers, witches can dry up a man's semen reserves or cast a spell to 'magically injure the power of generation – that is, so that a man cannot have sex'.[12] What's more, according to Kramer and Sprenger, a witch can do much worse than simply cursing your 'jumble giblets' (1890), they can remove the entire penis if they feel like it. Or rather, they can bewitch the 'gigglestick' (1944) so it is 'hidden by an evil spirit who uses the art of illusion so that they cannot be seen or touched'.[13] Kramer and Sprenger address common gossip that some witches remove the 'family jewels' (1911) and keep them hidden in trees, nests or boxes:

> What are we to think about those witches who shut up
> penises in what are sometimes prolific numbers, twenty or
> thirty at a single time, in a bird's nest or some kind of box,
> where they move about in order to eat oats and fodder, as
> though they were alive – something which many people have
> seen and is reported by common gossip?[14]

They conclude that this too is achieved by causing victims to halluci-nate, and that witches do not really keep 'dicks' (1836) in trees as pets. Given how fascinated witches seem to be with cursing the 'dibble' (1796), it is little wonder that magical causes had to be considered in a charge of impotence.

When Hincmar, the archbishop of Rheims (AD 806–882) was asked to advise on King Lothar of Francia's attempt to divorce his wife, Queen Theutberga, he responded with the treatise *On the Divorce of King Lothar and Queen Theutberg*. Here, Hincmar suggests that the king's favourite mistress, Waldrada, had bewitched him into no longer having sex with his wife.[15] Hincmar was certain that 'sorceresses and magicians ... working of the Devil' could render a man impotent and prevent a marriage from being consummated. If this should happen,

Hincmar recommended the couple 'make a pure confession of all their sins to God and a priest with a contrite heart and humble spirit'.

> With many tears and very generous almsgiving, and prayers
> and fasting, they should make satisfaction to the Lord, by
> whose judgement, at their own deserving and unwillingly,
> they have deserved to be deprived of that blessing which the
> Lord gave to our first parents in paradise before sin.[16]

One of the most famous cases of magically induced impotence was that of King Philip Augustus of France (1180–1223), who claimed he had been unable to consummate his marriage to Ingeborg of Denmark because he had been bewitched. By all accounts the king had been looking forward to marrying Ingeborg, yet the day after the wedding he wanted the marriage declared void. Three months after the wedding, Philip's council had produced a spurious family tree to try and prove the king and Ingeborg were related and therefore couldn't marry. When Ingeborg protested about this, the king naturally claimed he had been rendered impotent through magic. He later directly accused Ingeborg herself of witchcraft and of cursing him. None of this convinced Pope Innocent III and Philip was ordered to stay married to Ingeborg. Philip's response was to lock Ingeborg away in the chateau of Étampes and marry Agnes of Merania in 1196. The pope was so enraged that not only did he refuse to recognise this marriage, but he ordered all churches in France to be shut up for nine months and imposed an edict that rendered any child born during this period illegitimate. After this scandal, Pope Innocent III ruled that marriage could no longer be annulled on grounds of magically induced impotence.[17]

Wives continued to seek an annulment to their marriages on grounds of impotence until the eighteenth century, though the practice of congress was largely abandoned by the seventeenth century.[18]

However, penile humiliation continued to be a feature of the divorce court throughout the eighteenth century as the proceedings were often published as lurid erotica. Unscrupulous publishers such as Edmund Curll and George Abbot distributed numerous compilations of scandalous court records, including *The Case of Impotency; and Cases of Divorce for Several Causes* in 1714, and *Cases of Impotency as Debated in England* in 1719. 'Wise matrons' may no longer have been required to examine a chap's 'virile member', but these texts made sure every detail of a husband's sexual dysfunction was made public.

Viagra turned twenty years old in 2018, and this is surely something worth celebrating. The successful treatment of erectile dysfunction has allowed millions of people to get their mojo back. It is also worth remembering all those throughout history who have not been able to access such treatment, and how important sexual function is to a person's well-being. If you ever pop a blue pill, please remember to give a full salute to all the 'useless members' who entered the history books because they were accused of not being able to enter anything else.

SEX
AND
FOOD

Staff of Life

Sex and Bread

There's no denying it: food and sex are two pleasures intimately connected in the human psyche. Admittedly, literally mixing the two (or 'sploshing', to use the vernacular) can lead to a steep dry-cleaning bill and a lifetime ban from the salad bar at Pizza Hut, but the point remains: food is sexy. Countless eating metaphors can be employed to describe sex acts: 'eating' pussy, 'sucking' dick, 'tasting' or wanting to 'devour' a lover, for example. Every Valentine's Day, sweethearts gift each other with taste sensations (chocolates, wine, oysters, etc.), and sex goddess Nigella Lawson made her name fellating buttered parsnips.

We employ many of the same senses when we eat as we do when we have sex: sight, smell, taste, touch, etc. Both can bring feelings of comfort and love, as well as guilt and shame. Both over- and under-eating have been linked to sexual frustration and sexual trauma.[1] And, of course, both eating and sex are pleasurable activities that can be shared, or indulged in alone. As it says in *Proverbs* 9:17: 'Stolen waters are sweet, and bread eaten in secret is pleasant.'[2]

Some foods are sexier than others. Champagne and caviar are decidedly more seductive than Um Bongo and a can of Spam, though you may disagree. Bread might not immediately strike you as erotic, but the staff of life has some surprisingly kinky secrets in its larder. For a start, the bread-making process is laden with innuendo. After it has been firmly kneaded, bread is put into a hot oven where it swells and rises, and then it's all finished off with a sticky glaze. The suggestive links

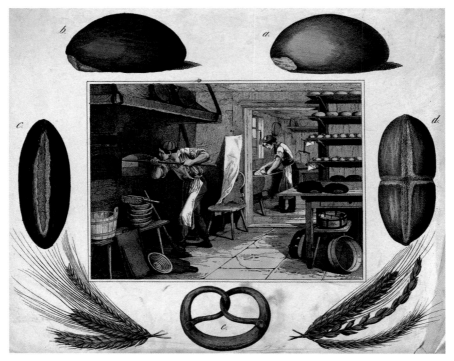

One man makes dough as another stokes the fire for the oven. There is bread on the tables and trays and baskets are piled in stacks. Sixteenth-century coloured etching.

between rising bread and rising penises, and hot ovens and hot vulvas, can be found back in AD 79, in the Roman town of Pompeii. During an excavation of the ancient city, a terracotta plaque with a projecting penis was discovered above the oven of a bakery, bearing the inscription *hic habitat felicitas* ('here dwells happiness').[3]

The potential for doughy double entendres was not lost on the Anglo-Saxons either. *The Exeter Book* was compiled by clerics sometime in the tenth century and it contains a number of gloriously smutty riddles, like 'Riddle 45':

> I have heard of something or other growing up in the corner,
> swelling and groaning, heaving up its covers.

A mind-proud woman, some prince's daughter, seized it
boneless with her hands, a tumescent thing, covered it with
her dress.[4]

The answer is, of course, bread dough (wink, wink, nudge, nudge).
As well as providing ample material for such risqué jokes, bread can
be fashioned into all kinds of rude shapes. In his epigrams, the Roman
satirist Martial (AD 40–104) joked about bread dildos, claiming that
sexual urges could be placated by nibbling on penis-shaped bread
instead of the real thing. 'If you want to satisfy your hunger you can
eat my Priapus; you may gnaw his very appendage, yet you will be
undefiled.'[5] Whether or not anyone has actually pleasured themselves
with a loaf, fertility festivals have been celebrated with phallic- and
yonic-shaped breads for thousands of years.

The Greco-Egyptian
author Athenaeus of
Naucratis (AD 170–223)
described how the harvest
goddess Demeter was
worshipped in Sicily
with a sweet bread
called *mulloi* that was
shaped like a vulva.[6]
There is also evidence
that genital-shaped breads
were baked to celebrate

A baker is loading uncooked
dough into an oven, as baked
loaves are carried away by a
woman. Woodcut by J. Amman
(1539–1591).

Easter throughout the Middle Ages and into the early modern period. Writing in 1825, French historian Jacques-Antoine Dulaure (1755–1835) quotes from a sixteenth-century book by Johannes Bruerinus Campegius that details 'the degeneracy of manners, when Christians themselves can delight in obscenities and immodest things even among their articles of food'. Dulaure goes on to describe how penis breads were still being baked to celebrate Easter in the lower Limousin and Brive areas of France, whereas the citizens of Clermont in Avignon celebrated Christ's resurrection with a vulva-shaped bread.[7] Writing in 1865, Thomas Wright claimed that phallus breads were still being baked in Saintonge 'as offerings at Easter, and are carried and presented from house to house'.[8] It is entirely possible that the Easter tradition of hot cross buns may descended from the ancient custom of celebrating fertility and the spring with knob bread.

Not only has bread been fashioned into sexually suggestive shapes throughout history, it has also been used in love spells. Throughout the Middle Ages, various church authorities were thoughtful enough to print books for priests listing the appropriate penance for various sins that parishioners would confess to; these books are known as 'penitentials'. The earliest date to the sixth century in Ireland and they are a gold mine for anyone studying medieval sexuality, as the Church was nothing if not thorough (and imaginative) when it came to indexing sexual sin. One of the best known penitentials is *Decretum* by Bishop Burchard of Worms (*c*.950–1025). Here, the good bishop lists numerous penances for sexual sin that involve ingesting bodily fluid, ranging from swallowing semen (seven years' penance on fast days), through to wives tricking their husbands into drinking their menstrual blood (five years' penance on fast days).[9] Burchard is particularly concerned with women rubbing different types of food on their bodies to cast spells over men. These spells could be designed to kill their husbands, like this one:

Have you done what some women are accustomed to doing? They take off their clothes and smear honey all over their naked body. With the honey on their body they roll themselves back and forth over wheat on a sheet spread on the ground. They carefully collect all the grains of wheat sticking to their moist body, put them in a mill, turn the mill in the opposite direction of the sun, grind the wheat into flour, and bake bread from it. They then serve it to their husbands to eat, who then grow weak and die. If you have, you should do penance for forty days on bread and water.[10]

Or, they can be love/lust spells, like this one:

Have you done what some women are wont to do? They take a live fish and put it in their vagina, keeping it there for a while until it is dead. Then they cook or roast it and give it to their husbands to eat, doing this in order to make men be more ardent in their love for them. If you have, you should do two years of penance on the appointed fast days.[11]

Before you kick off your knickers and head to the nearest koi pond, let's take a moment to think of the science at work here. To the medieval mind this made perfect sense. Touch and transference were very important to both medieval medicine and superstition. Many medieval aphrodisiacs attempt to transfer sexual potency from source to subject via ingestion. For example, sparrows were once considered to be symbols of lust. When Chaucer wants to describe one of the pilgrims in the *Canterbury Tales* (the Summoner) as being oversexed, he describes him as being as 'hot and lecherous as a sparrow'.[12] So medieval physicians believed that by eating lustful sparrows, patients with a flagging libido could absorb some of this lust themselves.[13] The vulva was obviously associated with lust, so it stood to reason that being spiked with a fish that had died in the 'glory hole' (1930) would inflame a man's senses.

Burchard of Worms was also concerned about women baking bread with their little chefs, and he has a penance for this too:

> Have you done what some women are accustomed to do? They lie face down on the ground, uncover their buttocks, and tell someone to make bread on their naked buttocks. When they have cooked it, they give it to their husbands to eat. They do this to make them more ardent in their love for them. If you have, you should do two years of penance on the appointed fast days.[14]

You might be forgiven for thinking that all this is the product of an overactive imagination and a night on the communion wine, but you'd be wrong. Kneading bread with your naughty bits is recorded again almost six hundred years later, only by this time it's called 'Cocklebread', and has a song and a dance to go with it. George Peele's 1595 play *The Old Wives' Tale* contains these lines:

> Fair maiden, white and red.
> Stroke me smooth, and comb my head.
> And thou shalt have some cockell-bread.[15]

In *A Jovial Crew* (1641), Richard Brome also refers to young women who 'mould cocklebread', dance 'clatterdepouch', and 'hannykin booby'.[16] But it is the author John Aubrey (1626–97) who gives the most detailed account of how cocklebread was prepared. Aubrey writes of young women and their 'wanton sport', the 'moulding of

Sixteenth-century woodcarving of two people making bread.

Cocklebread'. Aubrey describes how 'young wenches' would 'get upon a Tableboard, and as they gather-up their knees and their Coates with their hands as high as they can, and then they wabble to and fro with the Buttocks as if they were kneading the Dough with their Arses'. While doing their wabbling, the women would sing:

> My dame is sick, and gone to bed.
> And I'll go mould my cocklebread!
> Up with my heels and down with my head,
> And this is the way to mould cocklebread.

Once baked, the bread would be delivered to that special someone and left to inflame their lust (or at least their lower intestines). Aubrey calls this a 'relique of natural magik' and goes on to suggest that 'cockle' derives from an Anglo-Saxon word meaning 'arse', which is supported by the sixteenth-century term 'hot cockles' – meaning to have sex.[17] Think about that the next time you're 'warming the cockles of your heart'. Cocklebread turns up again in Victorian texts, only by then it's a children's game, divorced from all naughtiness (and bread), where you squat on your haunches and rock to and fro singing a song about your granny. If only they'd known.

In 2015, pussy loafs made a brief but memorable comeback when feminist blogger Zoe Stavri used the yeast of her thrush infection to bake sourdough.[18] Unlike the 'wanton wenches' Aubrey wrote about, this was not done to try and seduce someone, but to make a statement about cultural attitudes towards the vulva. It would be fair to say that Stavri's bread strongly divided opinions, and despite widespread coverage online, the recipe never really caught on.

Despite such gallant efforts, genital-based cooking techniques have witnessed a noticeable decline since the seventeenth century, though if you ask me a revival is due. Perhaps Delia Smith or Mary Berry could lead the way in reviving these old traditions. But I imagine health and safety would frown on confectionery moulded from genitalia and would mandate some kind of hair net be used. It does seem safer to stick to a box of Milk Tray. Although should a lover ever approach you carrying an oddly squashed farmhouse loaf, don't say I didn't warn you.

The Food of Love

A History of Oysters

Oyster, n. A slimy, gobby shellfish which civilization gives
men the hardihood to eat without removing its entrails!

Ambrose Bierce

Possibly the most well known and enduring of all the aphrodisiacs, the oyster has occupied a special place in our hearts and stomachs for a millennium. Quite why this fishy, lumpy mollusc, swimming in its own fluids and resembling something one might clear from the back of the throat during flu season, came to be the go-to love food is a matter of some debate. Did you know that oysters have eyes? Eyes! But first things first – do they work as an aphrodisiac?

In 2005, it was widely reported in the press that 'science' had finally proven that the oyster is an aphrodisiac.[1] However, this is not quite true. Professor George Fisher and a group of researchers from the US and Italy presented their research on the aphrodisiacal properties of marine bivalves to the American Chemical Society. Two years earlier, the same team had published research that suggested D-aspartic acid (D-Asp) and N-methyl-D-aspartate (NMDA) stimulate the release of sex hormones (e.g. progesterone and testosterone) in rats.[2] The 2005 research detected the presence of D-Asp and NMDA in some molluscs, namely mussels and clams. From this, the team theorised that this could produce an aphrodisiacal effect in humans when eaten.[3] Crucially, the research did not cover oysters, and there were no human studies conducted to back this up – it is all theoretical. But a good story is

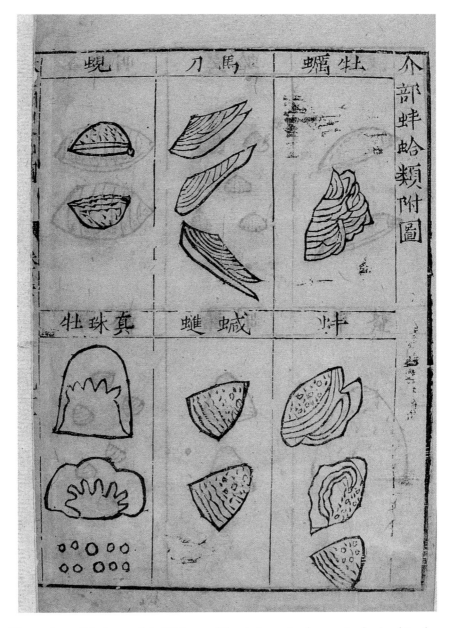

Illustrations of six types of shellfish – *muli* (oyster), *madao* (razor clam), *xian* (clam), *beng* (freshwater mussel, clam), *xianjin* (a kind of clam) and *zhenzhu mu* (pearl oyster), from Li Shizhen's pharmaceutical encyclopaedia *Compendium of Materia Medica*, 1596.

a good story and the press leapt on these findings, proclaiming 'raw oysters really are aphrodisiacs, say scientists!'[4] Except they didn't. There is no scientific evidence at all that oysters raise anything other than your toilet seat should you get a bad one. Having said that, oysters are incredibly good for you. Not only are they ridiculously low in calories, they are a powerhouse of zinc, copper, vitamin B12, vitamin C and lean protein. Interestingly, a man loses between one and three milligrams of zinc every time he cracks his oysters (so to speak), so the famed molluscs are an ideal snack to replenish sperm reserves.[5] Oysters may well be very good for you, but a marine Viagra they are not.

Oysters are a very old food, and their shells have been found at multiple Palaeolithic sites around the world. Tools for opening oysters and oyster shells that were found within a fossil reef at the Red Sea coast of Eritrea were dated to around 125,000 years old.[6] There are many different types of oyster, and they are found throughout the world's oceans. Oysters are ancient, plentiful and may be the original fast food. But why are they sexy?

Botticelli's famous painting of the birth of Venus shows the goddess riding a scallop shell, not an oyster. Sandro Botticelli, *The Birth of Venus*, 1486.

A likely reason is that oysters came to be associated with the Greek goddess of love, Aphrodite (and later, Venus). Aphrodite was supposedly born from the sea. According to the Greek poet Hesiod (c.700 BC), Aphrodite rose up out of the waves, fully formed, after Uranus's testicles were thrown into the sea by Cronus.[7] Hesiod doesn't mention molluscs in this story, but in Renaissance paintings such as Botticelli's *Birth of Venus* (c.1486), Aphrodite is shown standing atop a scallop shell, and this may be where shellfish acquired a sexy reputation – and it's not just molluscs.

Sparrows were also associated with Aphrodite, and like oysters, they came to be regarded as a potent aphrodisiac in the Classical world. Even the *Kama Sutra* gives a number of recipes to inflame the passions that use sparrow eggs.

> The chataka is the common sparrow. Take the juice of their eggs, mixed with rice and cooked in milk, then mix with honey and ghee. When eaten, one's sexual prowess is so enhanced that one can possess an unlimited number of young women.[8]

The belief in the stimulating effects of sparrow brains persisted for hundreds of years. According to Culpeper's *The Complete Herbal* (1653) 'The brain of Sparrows when eaten provokes the lust exceedingly' – but back to oysters.[9]

It's not clear if the ancient Greeks and Romans regarded oysters as an aphrodisiac, but they certainly thought of them as a luxury item. The Emperor Clodius Albinus was allegedly capable of sinking four hundred of the slippery blighters at one sitting.[10] Pliny the Elder writes about oysters being served up covered in snow at the most opulent banquets.[11] The Romans thought oysters were good for a number of ailments (ranging from indigestion to skin complaints), but there's little

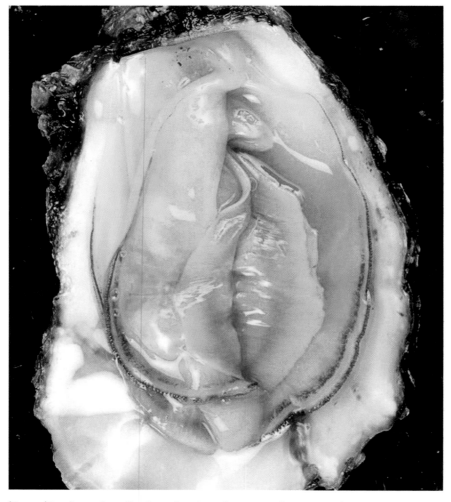

'Oyster' has been slang for the vulva since the sixteenth century. It's not hard to see why, really.

mention of their sexual benefits. For that, we have to jump forward to the early modern period, because it's here that oysters really come into their own as *the* culinary come-on food.

In 1566, Alain Chartier asked 'why were Oysters consecrated by the auncient to Venus? Bycause Oysters doe prouoke lecherie'.[12] Indeed, by the Renaissance, oysters are frequently turning up in medical texts as an aid to ardour. For example, Felix Platter's *A Golden Practice of Physick* (1664) recommends oysters to cure a 'Want of Copulation', when 'there is none or small pleasure in the act', and Humphrey Mills describes pickled oysters being served to customers in brothels in 1646.[13]

But perhaps the most obvious reason for the oyster's association with sex is its resemblance to the vulva. The soft folds of pink salty flesh and nestling pearls made for an obvious comparison, and 'oyster' has been slang for the vulva since the sixteenth century. John Marston made bawdy jokes about 'yawning Oystars' in 1598.[14] In *The Parson's Wedding* (1641), Thomas Killigrew writes 'he that opens her stinking Oyster is worthy of the Pearl',[15] and that debauched scamp, Rochester, penned the following lines in 1673:

> Arch'd on both Sides, lay gaping like an Oyster.
> I had a Tool before me, which I put in
> Up to the Quick, and strait the Oyster shut;
> It shut and clung to so fast at ev'ry Stroke.[16]

Given the dual meaning, it is little wonder the figure of the 'oyster-girl', selling her wares on the street, became a figure associated with sex workers and general naughtiness. Throughout the eighteenth century, bawdy songs about oyster girls were common. M. Randall's 'The Eating of Oysters' (1794), for example, begins like this:

> As I was walking down a London Street,
> a pretty little oyster girl, I chanced for to meet.
> I lifted up her basket and boldly I did peek,
> just to see if she's got any oysters.
> 'Oysters, Oysters, Oysters,' said she.
> 'These are the finest oysters that you will ever see.
> I'll sell them three-a-penny but I give 'em to you free.'[17]

The Irish folk heroine Molly Malone, who sells 'cockles and mussels, alive, alive, oh', was immortalised in verse in 1876 and attributed to James Yorkston. The song tells of the beautiful Molly Malone who

A young girl is selling oysters to a customer in the street. Nineteenth-century coloured lithograph produced by J. Brydone & Sons.

sells her wares throughout Dublin, and that 'she died of a fever'.[18] Since then, the song has become the unofficial anthem of Dublin, and a busty bronze statue of Molly was erected in the Georgian Quarter of the city in 1988. Dubliners affectionately call the statue 'the tart with the cart', and over the years repeated gropings have buffed her cleavage to a high shine.

In 2010, a text unknown to modern literary scholars, *Apollo's Medley* (1790), was discovered and contains an earlier version of the Molly Malone song. Here, 'Sweet Molly Malone' is not quite the wholesome young woman depicted a century later. The narrator sings,

> Och! I'll roar and I'll groan,
> My sweet Molly Malone,
> Till I'm bone of your bone,
> And asleep in your bed...
>
> Be poison, my drink,
> If I sleep, snore, or wink,
> Once forgetting to think,
> Of your lying alone.[19]

In 1805, the song was republished and put to music by John Whitaker, who attests to its popularity and calls this bawdy version a 'favourite song'.[20] 'The Widow Malone', dating to the early nineteenth century, casts Molly as a very wealthy and very horny widow.

> Of lovers she had full score, or more...
> from the minister down To the clerk of the crown,
> They were all courting the widow Malone.[21]

Although Sweet Molly Malone wasn't given her wheelbarrow full of cockles and mussels until much later, it seems she has long had a reputation for promiscuity, and her casting as an oyster girl is very much a part of this.

Perhaps the most famous devotee of the oyster aphrodisiac was the legendary lover, Giacomo Casanova (1725–1789). It's often reported that

MOLLY MILTON, the PRETTY OYSTER WOMAN.

Molly Milton, the Pretty Oyster Woman, 1788. Molly flaunts her wares to a fashionable young man who ogles her with his hand in his pocket.

Casanova ate fifty raw oysters for breakfast each day, but this isn't quite true – though he certainly ate a lot of them. On several occasions Casanova records sharing plates of fifty oysters with his guests, and there's no doubt he believed in their stimulating effects. One of his favourite seduction techniques was teaching his lovers to eat oysters properly. 'We sucked them in, one by one, after placing them on the other's tongue. Voluptuous reader, try it, and tell me whether it is not the nectar of the gods!'[22] He writes about the 'oyster game' he used to seduce two friends, Armelline and Emilie.

> I placed the shell on the edge of her lips, and after a good deal
> of laughing she sucked in the oyster, which she held between
> her lips. I instantly recovered it by placing my lips on hers ...
> [Armelline] was delighted with my delicacy in sucking away
> the oyster, scarcely touching her lips with mine. My agreeable
> surprise may be imagined when I heard her say that it was my
> turn to hold the oysters. It is needless to say that I acquitted
> myself of the duty with much delight.[23]

His diary records that they played this 'game' twice. The second time, Casanova 'accidentally' spills his oyster down Armelline's cleavage and undresses her in order to retrieve it with his teeth. You may want to try this move the next time you successfully swipe right – if you fancy fishing lumps of dead molluscs out from between a lady's tits, that is.

By the nineteenth century, the oyster industries were booming. Oysters were so plentiful they came to be dietary staples of poor and working-class neighbourhoods. In *The Pickwick Papers* (1837) Dickens noted that 'poverty and oysters always seem to go together'.[24] But just because they were widely consumed didn't mean that oysters shook off their sexy image. It's no coincidence that two of Victorian London's

A woman, with light shining on her face from a lamp, standing in front of a barrel of oysters, opening one with a knife, 1855. The caption reads 'The 4th of August. An oyster-woman of the last century. (From a painting by H. Morland).'

most famous underground erotic magazines were titled *The Pearl* and *The Oyster*.

Jonathan Swift once wrote 'he was a bold man that first ate an oyster', but I suspect the ritual around eating an oyster is another significant factor in its long association with sex.[25] As Casanova observed, there is something undeniably sensual about freeing the plump oyster from his shell, and tipping the liquored, salty flesh into your mouth to be tongued and swallowed whole. Combine this with the fact that the oyster looks like a vulva (yonic) and has strong associations with Aphrodite/Venus, and it's little wonder that this humble mollusc garnered a reputation as a decadent aphrodisiac. As Trebor Healey once wrote, 'The world is your oyster, they say, so fill it with pearls of semen'.[26]

Turning Down the Heat

A History of the Anaphrodisiac

An aphrodisiac is defined as any food, drink or drug that increases libido, and/or improves sexual pleasure and performance.[1] Aphrodisiacs are recorded in every culture throughout history, ranging from rhinoceros horn in Chinese culture to the West Indian 'love stone' and the highly toxic European 'Spanish Fly', made from crushed beetles.[2] One of the earliest references to treating impotence is found in the ancient Hindu medical text the *Sushruta Samhita*, composed around 600 BC.

> Powders of sesame, Masha pulse, and S'ali rice should
> be mixed with Saindhava salt and pasted with a copious
> quantity of the expressed juice of the sugar cane. It should
> then be mixed with hog's lard and cooked with clarified
> butter. By using this Utkarika a man would be able to visit a
> hundred women.[3]

Having spent many an evening gorging on fat, sugar and salt, I have to say that it has never endowed me with energy for anything other than experiencing an intense and greasy remorse, but maybe that's just me.

The history of the aphrodisiac has been well mapped. But what of the anaphrodisiac? An anaphrodisiac is the opposite of an aphrodisiac and is intended to suppress libido and impair sexual function – the

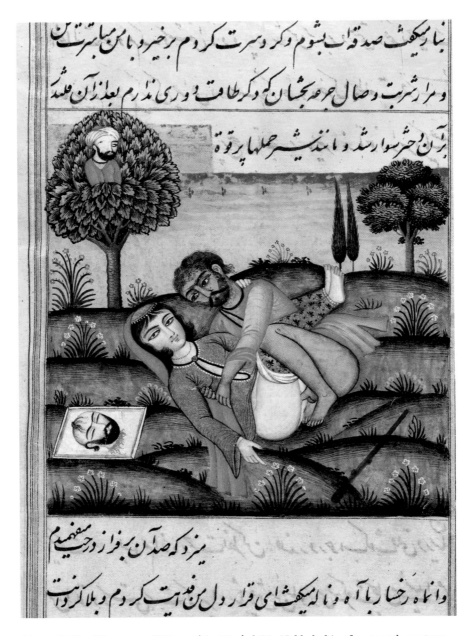

Lizzat Al-Nisa (Pleasures of Women) by Ziya' al-Din Nakhshabi, a fourteenth-century Persian physician, is derived from the Sanskrit treatise *Ratirahasya* (Secrets of Love), and covers topics such as sex, foods and aphrodisiacs. This image comes from an 1824 manuscript held by the Wellcome Library, London.

culinary equivalent of a cold shower. But why would anyone want to suppress their sexual urges, I hear you cry? Just ask yourself how much trouble your libido has landed you in and you may have the answer. Not to mention how much more productive working from home could be if we could stop 'procrasturbation'. The Greek poet Sophocles is quoted as saying he welcomed old age as it had freed him from his libido: 'I feel as if I had escaped from a frantic and savage master.'[4] This is the history of trying to escape that master.

Before the advent of chemical castration, anaphrodisiacs generally fell into three categories: cooling the body, starving the body and sedating the body. Sedating the body could be accomplished through drugs such as opium, fasting and rigorous exercise. Fasting is still practised within many religious communities today (opium less so), and is often linked with subduing lustful desires. Just google 'fasting and sexual desire' and you will be greeted with hundreds of religious websites that discuss how fasting can help to subdue lustful thoughts. This is a method that has been used throughout history. Early Christian saints, such as St Jerome (c. AD 347–419), regularly fasted to purify the body and cleanse lustful thoughts. Medieval monks would also starve themselves for long periods of time to gain mastery over food and sexual hunger.[5] And there may well be method in the madness. In 2015, a research team from Qatar found that men who fasted during the holy month of Ramadan experienced a significant decrease in follicle-stimulating hormone (FSH), the hormone responsible for stimulating the gonads.[6]

Exercise was thought to exhaust both the body and the libido. When Victorian doctors pondered how to cure women of nymphomania, the one thing that is almost universally prescribed is exercise and plenty of fresh air. Henry Newell Guernsey was one of many doctors who battled the urge with 'Out-door exercise ... taken daily during favourable weather'.[7] Unfortunately for Victorian women, we now know that exercise actually increases the sex drive. In 2012, researchers from the

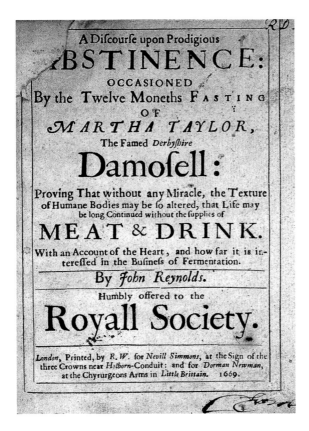

A seventeenth-century work on the benefits of fasting. John Reynolds, Nevill Simmons and Dorman Newman, *A Discourse Upon Prodigious Abstinence: Occasioned by the Twelve Moneths Fasting of Martha Taylor, the Famed Derbyshire Damosell: Proving that Without Any Miracle, the Texture of Humane Bodies May be so Altered, That Life May Be Long Continued Without the Supplies of Meat & Drink. With an Account of the Heart, and How Far it is Interested in the Business of Fermentation.*

University of Austin found that regular exercise not only increases the sex drive in pre-menopausal women, but that it can actually reverse the anaphrodisiac effect of antidepressants.[8]

Cooling the body to cool desire made perfect sense as heat was (and still is) associated with sex. Sex is 'hot', and abstinence is literally 'frigid' (from the Latin *frigere*, meaning to be cold). We still talk about taking a 'cold shower' to try and rid ourselves of the 'horn' (1695), and the effects of cooling the body were well known in the Ancient World too. As well as cold baths, Aristotle recommended going barefoot to suppress lust. He believed that the bareness of the feet 'causes dryness and cold ... it is either difficult or impossible to have sexual intercourse when the feet are not warm'.[9] Pliny the Elder went one better and recommended placing lead plates on the genitals to cool them down and 'restrain venereal passions, and put an end to libidinous dreams at night, attended with spontaneous emissions, and assuming all the form of a disease'.[10] Oversexed Victorian ladies could find themselves on the wrong end of an ice-cold vaginal douche or submerged in a bath of freezing water as doctors battled to control their lusts. 'The cold bath, the shower bath, the douche, and cold applications to the region of the uterus, have been employed with great advantage.'[11]

Spicy, hot food was thought to inflame the senses, so conversely cooling, bland foods were thought to cool things off. Cucumbers are both bland and cool, and despite their shape, they have long been considered an anaphrodisiac. One Ancient Greek proverb was 'eat the cucumber, O woman, and weave your cloak'.[12] Meaning, calm yourself down, and get on with your work.

The French writer and physician François Rabelais (1494–1553) recommended a number of foods to cool down a lustful body.

> The fervency of lust is abated by certain drugs, plants herbs
> and roots, which make the taker cold, maleficiated, unfit for,
> and unable to perform the act of generation; as hath often
> been experimented by the water-lily, Heraclea, Agnus-Castus,
> willow-twigs, hemp-stalks, woodbine, honeysuckle, tamarisk,
> chastetree, mandrake, bennet keebugloss, the skin of a
> hippopotamus, and many other such...[13]

I've never tried it, but I imagine that eating hemp-stalks and hippopotamus skin would indeed kibosh a night of passion. Although Rabelais was likely poking fun at medical quackery, most of the items on his list really were prescribed as anaphrodisiacs. As late as 1869, John Davenport was writing about medicines called 'refrigerants' that provided the iceberg to sink the SS *Libido*.

The most favourite of these are infusions from the leaves or flowers of the white water-lily (*nymphea alba*), sorrel, lettuce, perhaps also from mallows, violets, and endive (*cichorium*), oily seeds, and waters distilled from lettuce, water lily, cucumbers, purslain, and endives. In equal esteem are the syrups of orgeat, lemons, and vinegar, to which may be added cherry-laurel water, when given in proper and gradually-increasing doses. Hemlock, camphor, and agnus-castus, have likewise been much recommended as moderators of the sexual appetite.[14]

As well as eating foods to cool down the body, foods that were thought to 'dry out' the body were also recommended. This treatment is rooted in the Ancient Greek theory of the four humours. Hippocrates (460–375 BC) taught that human health is dictated by the balancing of four bodily humours: blood, yellow bile, black bile and phlegm. Galen (AD 130–210) then expanded on humoral theory by combining them with four temperaments: hot, cold, wet and dry. Greek humoral theory dominated Western medicine until the early nineteenth century. Women were thought to be guided by the wet and hot humours, which made them less controlled and more lustful than men, who were believed to be cold and dry in comparison.[15] Therefore to regain control over a lustful nature, one should try to 'dry out' the excess of the juicy humours.

Despite its stimulating effects, coffee has been accused of drying out a chap's beans since it was first introduced to Europe in the seventeenth century. In 1695, physicians at the Ecole de Médecine in Paris warned that drinking coffee every day 'deprived both man and woman of the generative power'.[16] In 1674, a remarkable petition was published in London, alleged to be from the 'buxom' wives of men who had taken to drinking coffee and were now useless in bed.

The Women's Petition Against Coffee is likely to be satirical, but it does reveal how the 'base, black, thick, nasty, bitter, stinking, nauseous Puddle-water' was believed to wither sexual potency.[17] The 'wives' accuse coffee of 'drying up' their husbands' 'radical moisture', leaving them 'as Impotent as Age, and as unfruitful as those *Desarts* [*sic*] whence that unhappy *Berry* is said to be brought'.[18] The depletion of vital juices has left their men with 'nothing *moist* but their snotty Noses, nothing *stiffe* but their Joints, nor *standing* but their Ears'.[19]

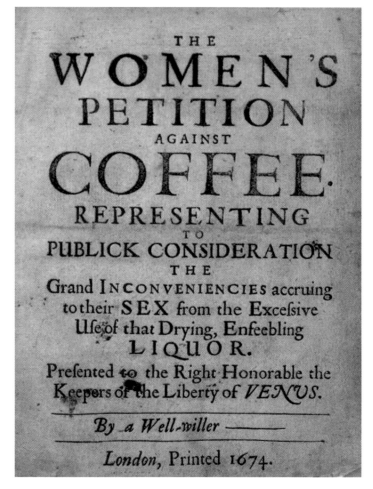

Title page for *The Women's Petition Against Coffee*, an anonymous pamphlet published in London in 1674.

In the *Physical Directory* (1649), Nicholas Culpeper recommended waterlilies to 'dry' the body out and suppress lust.[20] In *The Anatomy of Melancholy* (1621), Robert Burton recommended men rub camphor on their genitals to dry out lust, and to carry some with them in their breeches to keep the penis flaccid.[21] French scholar Joseph Justus Scaliger (1540–1609) claimed that monks regularly smelled and chewed camphor to try and keep their urges at bay.[22] In the nineteenth century, camphor was being used for its sedative effect, often in conjunction with ice-water enemas.

> Various medicines have been recommended as anti-
> aphrodisiacs... iced-water, ices taken internally, and nitre
> alone, or combined with camphor. The sedative effect of
> camphor, in large doses, on the generative organs, as in
> painful erections in gonorrhoea, proves it to be an efficient
> remedy.[23]

As well as drying food, bland food and plain diets were thought to calm the body and prevent heat building up in the first place. Davenport recommends taming the beast by eating 'less nutritious food', and avoiding 'all dishes peculiarly stimulating to the palate ... as well as the use of wine and other spirituous liquors'.[24] *The Diagnosis, Pathology and Treatment of Diseases of Women* (1868) recommends a 'plain and simple but nourishing diet', the 'avoidance of mental excitement or effort', and regular dips in a cold bath.[25]

But if you're looking for the ultimate bland, dry and boring food to derail your desire, then look no further than the humble cornflake. As we covered in 'Sex and the Penis', Dr John Harvey Kellogg (1852–1943) was an American health crusader, nutritionist and the director of the Battle Creek Sanatorium in Michigan. He was an advocate of abstinence, viewed masturbation as the root of all evil, and believed

John Harvey Kellogg (1852–1943),
co-founder of the Kellogg Company.

that diet was a vital weapon in the war on 'wanking' (1970). In *Plain Facts for Old and Young* (1887), Kellogg devotes whole chapters to discussing the importance of diet in preserving chastity. He recommends never overeating, eating only twice a day (and not after 3 p.m.), and avoiding all hot drinks. All 'stimulating foods' are to be avoided, including 'spices, pepper, ginger, mustard, cinnamon, cloves, essences, all condiments, pickles, etc., together with flesh food in any but moderate quantities'. Instead, Kellogg advises eating 'fruits, grains, milk, and vegetables. There is a rich variety of these kinds of food, and they are wholesome and unstimulating. Graham flour, oatmeal, and ripe fruit are the indispensables of a dietary for those who are suffering from sexual excesses.'[26] The Graham flour Kellogg endorses was inspired by the Reverend Sylvester Graham (1794–1851), who was a major influence on Kellogg's own work.

The Reverend Sylvester Graham was a dietary reformer and leader of the American temperance movement. He advocated plain, simple food (bread mostly), to prevent the youth of America falling into ill health and sin. He also saw a clear link between rich food and masturbation. In *A Lecture to Young Men on Chastity* (1848) he warned that steak and wine would 'increase the concupiscent excitability ... of the genital organs', and lead to all manner of 'sexual excesses', as well as affecting the 'moral facilities'.[27] His work on plain diets inspired

Graham crackers, Graham flour and Graham bread – all designed to bore the libido into submission.

Graham's work was concerned with more than 'self-pollution'; he also wanted to tackle ill health and general moral decay. But Kellogg was obsessed with 'diddling' (1938), and the cornflake was designed to suppress lust and cure serial masturbators. Kellogg and his brother William Kellogg designed bland foods to treat the patients at their sanatorium. It was here the cornflake was born. It was everything Kellogg prescribed to stifle sexual desire: bland, plain, meat-free and made of corn. The original cornflake was patented by Kellogg in 1894, and he prescribed them to all his patients, who could also look forward to daily yogurt enemas, cold-water baths and douches, lots of fresh air and daily exercise regimes.[28] Despite humoral theory having been discredited by the time Kellogg was filling his patients full of yogurt at one end and cornflakes at the other, it is remarkable just how similar his treatments were to those offered in the Middle Ages.

Today, we don't have to resort to walking barefoot or eating cucumbers to suppress the sex drive. Chemical castration is controversially used around the world to 'treat' sex offenders and provide an alternative to incarceration.[29] Anti-androgen drugs are administered to block the effects of androgens, such as testosterone. Although reversible, this is an extreme option if all you're looking to do is get more work done at home or to resist that 3 a.m. booty call.

One final option you might want to try before resorting to opiates and ice douches is mathematics. One man who knew a thing or two about uncontrolled libido was the Genevan philosopher Jean-Jacques Rousseau (1712–1778). In his *Confessions* he records desperately lusting over a young woman who sharply told him to 'give up the ladies, and study mathematics'.[30] John Davenport also recommends studying maths to rid yourself of lustful thoughts. He reasoned that:

It will, indeed, be found that, in all ages, mathematicians have been but little disposed or addicted to love, and the most celebrated among them, Sir Isaac Newton, is reputed to have lived without ever having had sexual intercourse. The intense mental application required by philosophical abstraction forcibly determines the nervous fluid towards the intellectual organs, and hinders it from being directed towards those of reproduction.[31]

Or, perhaps you would just prefer to sit in a cold bath with a bowl of cornflakes.

SEX
AND
MACHINES

Buzzkill

Vibrators and the Victorians

Iam sure you have heard this one: Victorian doctors invented the vibrator to masturbate women to orgasm because they had been 'finger-banging' (1988) so many patients in an effort to cure their hysteria that frankly their arms ached. We love this story. I love this story. Hollywood loved this story so much that both *The Road to Wellville* (1994) and *Hysteria* (2011) are based on it. But sadly it really is just a story. Like trickle-down economics and Jamie Lee Curtis's hermaphroditism, it's an urban myth. But like all the best stories, there are flashes of truth in it. We love this story because it goes straight to the hysterical heart of the Victorian sexual hypocrisy that we enjoy rolling our eyes at: 'Did you know Victorian doctors were wanking off their female patients, but considered exposed table legs to be sexually obscene? So glad we're not like that now!' (Except the table legs thing is also myth, but that's another book for another day.)

The root of the diddling doctors theory is Rachel Maines's book *The Technology of Orgasm* (1999). Here Maines hypothesises that doctors masturbated women to orgasm for health reasons, and that the vibrator was nothing short of a 'godsend' for the physicians suffering from repetitive strain injury in their index fingers. More than this, Maines makes the case that this practice can be traced back to Classical times. However, it has to be said that her evidence for medical vulva massage in the Ancient World has been severely criticised, most notably by Professor Helen King, as well as Hallie Lieberman and Eric Schatzberg, who took apart such claims in the academic equivalent of a Vulcan death grip.[1] It's also important to remember that Maines herself refers to her argument as a hypothesis; and, to be fair, it's a damn interesting one. In an online interview in 2010, Maines said:

> People just loved my hypothesis and that's all it is really, it's a hypothesis, that women were treated with massage for this disease, hysteria, which has supposedly existed since the time of Hippocrates, 450 BC, and that the vibrator was invented to treat this disease. Well, people just thought this was such a cool idea that people believe it, that it's like a fact. And I'm like, 'It's a hypothesis! It's a hypothesis!' But it doesn't matter, you know? People like it so much they don't want to hear any doubts about it.[2]

So, let's unpack this hypothesis a little further. Make no mistake, Victorian doctors were obsessed with sex and health, and there were many highly questionable medical theories flying around, from the anti-onanism crew who believed that masturbation was terminal, to Italian criminal anthropologist Cesare Lombroso's theories that sex workers had no sensation in their clitorises, as they had been rendered 'insensible' through 'overuse'.[3] But the theory that doctors invented vibrators to cure hysteria is doubtful for several reasons.

British doctor Joseph Mortimer Granville (1833–1900) patented the first electric vibrator in the 1880s, not as a sexual device but as a massager to relieve the aches and pains of men, not women – he was quite clear on that. In his book *Nerve-Vibration and Excitation as Agents in the Treatment of Functional Disorder and Organic Disease* (1883), he wrote, 'I have never yet percussed a female patient … I have avoided, and shall continue to avoid the treatment of women by percussion, simply because I do not wish to be hoodwinked, and help to mislead others, by the vagaries of the hysterical state.'[4] Furthermore,

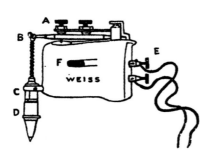

This is Granville's vibrator and, as you can see, it does not look like a machine to be used internally. Illustration from Joseph Mortimer Granville, *Nerve-Vibration and Excitation as Agents in the Treatment of Functional Disorder and Organic Disease*, 1803.

one look at this contraption and I am sure we can all agree that this is not a device you would want anywhere near your clacker without adult supervision and a safe word. This was clearly not designed for internal use. It was designed to strike the body in a hammer-like motion, which was why Granville called it 'percussing'.

Other vibrating massagers soon followed on a wave of pseudo-scientific theories about electricity, which was touted as a cure-all panacea, along with rectal dilators and radium. Vibrating massage promised to alleviate all manner of mental and physical disorders (including the mysterious 'hysteria'), but they were not designed for use on the genitals, and were not used by doctors to induce orgasm. Now, that does not mean that people did not figure out that these massage devices could be put to other, less hygienic uses. I like to define a 'kink blink' as the insanely short length of time between the introduction of new technology and its adaptation for sexual purposes. And as with the speculum, the nurse's uniform and Viagra, the vibrator went from medical to mucky in a kink blink. One early pornographic film from the 1930s, *The Masseur*, shows the vibrator

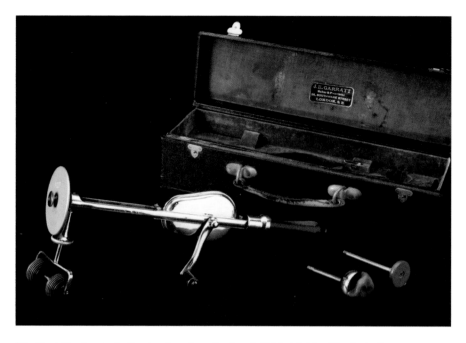

'VeeDee' Mechanical vibrator, London, England, 1900–15. The 'Veedee' vibratory massager claimed to cure colds, digestive complaints and flatulence through 'curative vibration'.

in action as two saucy masseurs vibrate it up and down the happy chap's bottom. But, crucially, the vibrator is not used internally.

And if we are to believe that vibrators were common knowledge and widely used to induce orgasm, we have to account for the fact that there is not one mention of this in any known Victorian pornography (textual or visual). Not one. However, there are many references to dildos, as well as the occasional cucumber put to good use. Sex toys are not new. And, as these pictures show, the Victorians knew how to fashion a dildo. Unsurprisingly, the design has changed very little since cavemen first started carving 'dongs' (1890) out of stone. They tend to be, well, cock-shaped.

Have a look around any modern-day sex shop and we can see that the cock shape for a sex toy is still very much in vogue. Victorian dildos

LEFT: Anonymous Victorian pornographic photograph showing 'pegging' (the woman penetrating the man with a strap-on).

BELOW: Anonymous Victorian pornography showing a woman being masturbated with a vegetable by her lover.

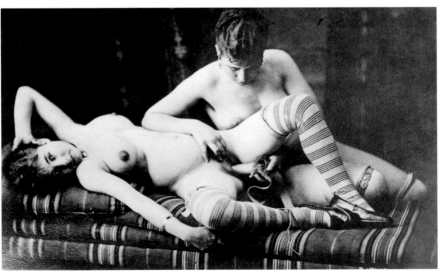

Anonymous Victorian pornography showing that the Victorians knew precisely what a dildo was.

were made from wood, leather and even ivory, and they were certainly a lot of fun, as this extract from *The Pearl* (1880) demonstrates: 'As we are five to two you will find I have a stock of fine, soft, firmly made dildos to make up the deficiency in males, which alternated with the real article will enable us to thoroughly enjoy ourselves.'[5]

Or this jolly song, titled 'The Old Dildo':

> She flew with the treasure into her room
> (Its size was the handle of a broom).
> Oh! What ecstatic moments she passed there,
> As she threw up her legs on the back of a chair.
> Through each vein in her body the fire lurked,
> Surely and quickly the engine worked;
> Face her, back her, stop her no! no!
> Faster and faster flew the old Dildoe.[6]

Not only is there no known mention of doctors and vibrators in Victorian pornography, there is also no mention of them in the work of the early and pioneering sexologists. Iwan Bloch, Havelock Ellis, Richard von Krafft-Ebing and Freud meticulously catalogued every fetish, paraphilia and known expression of sexual behaviour, but not one of them mention doctors, vibrators and orgasm. Ellis and Bloch even describe some women deriving sexual pleasure from sewing machines and sealing wax, but still there is no mention of a vibrator.* Fifty years

---

* In *The Sexual Life of our Time in its Relations to Modern Civilization* (1908), Bloch lists the motion of a sewing machine treadle as giving 'rise to masturbatory stimulation', along with horse riding, cycling and rubbing the thighs together. Iwan Bloch and Maurice Eden Paul, *The Sexual Life of Our Time in Its Relations to Modern Civilization,* trans. by M. Eden Paul (London: Rebman, 1908), p. 413. Havelock Ellis also describes women using sewing machines for sexual stimulation, as well as sealing wax, bananas, hairpins and corks. Havelock Ellis, *Psychology of Sex: A Manual for Students* (London: Heinemann, 1933), p. 104.

later, in his seminal *Behaviour in the Human Female* (1953), Alfred Kinsey does not mention vibrators in his lengthy and comprehensive chapters on female masturbation, and you'd think if doctors were wanking women to wellness, it would have cropped up somewhere in these works.

But what about the Victorian medical texts themselves? Surely there must be some mention of doctors conducting 'pelvic massage' of female patients? Well, yes! Yes, there is, and lots of it. The medical craze for pelvic massage came from the work of Swedish obstetrician and gynaecologist Thure Brandt (1819–1895), who began treating women in 1861. The 'Thure Brandt method' of pelvic massage and 'manipulating the womb' proved very popular and was widely reported at the time. The *New York Medical Journal* (1876) was one of many journals that described the technique in some detail.

> Brandt claims that his method of treatment is useful in prolapses and protrusion of the uterus; prolapse of the vagina; hypertrophy and induration of the uterus; ulcerations; abnormal haemorrhage, depending on relaxation of the uterus; tendency to miscarriage; slight hypertrophy of the ovaries. The method is simple, consisting of three motions:
>
> 1. Stroking the loins and sacral regions. In this, the patient assumes a position leaning forward, resting her hands against a wall or door.
>
> 2. Pressure with the points of the fingers of both hands on both sides, over the loins and sacral region, as well as over the upper and anterior surfaces of the ischium. The pressure is combined with vibratory shaking. The patient assumes a dorsal, semi-reclining position, and the knees are bent to relax the abdominal muscles.

3. Elevation of the uterus during the vibratory shaking. The position of the patient resembles the previous one. The operator endeavours to press the finger-points of both hands just over the horizontal ramus of the arch of the pubis of both sides down into the pelvis minor, and then to lift up the uterus. This attempt at elevation is also made during vibration.[7]

As you can see, the technique is largely performed externally and with a noticeable lack of a vibrator or an orgasm. And if you were still unsure of how to perform this massage, the 1895 book by Dr A. Jentzer, *Physiotherapy in Gynaecology and the Mechanical Treatment of Diseases of the Uterus and its Appendages by Thure Brandt*, illustrates the procedure, and contains possibly the most disturbing images of gynaecological examination ever produced.

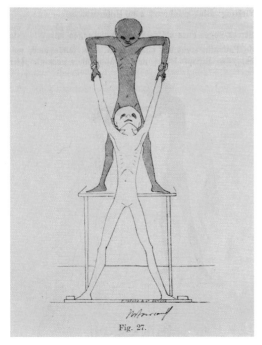

Fig. 27.

Terrifying illustrations of pelvic massage from *Die Heilgymnastik in der Gynaekologie* by Dr Jentzer.

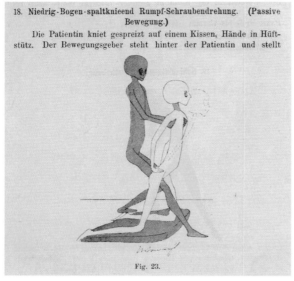

18. Niedrig-Bogen-spaltknieend Rumpf-Schraubendrehung. (Passive Bewegung.)

Die Patientin kniet gespreizt auf einem Kissen, Hände in Hüftstütz. Der Bewegungsgeber steht hinter der Patientin und stellt

Fig. 23.

Part of Brandt's massage involved stretching out the spine, as seen here.

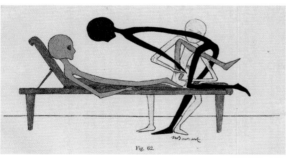

Fig. 62.

Illustration showing the internal part of Brandt's pelvic massage.

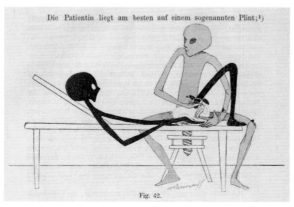

Die Patientin liegt am besten auf einem sogenannten Plint;[1]

Fig. 42.

Another illustration of the internal part of the pelvic massage.

Much of Brandt's massage involved shaking, or 'vibrating', the patient vigorously.

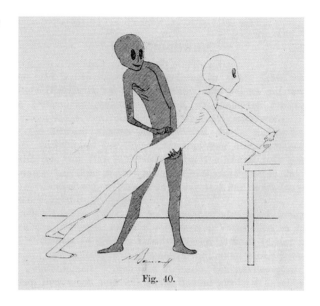

Fig. 40.

Once you have moved past the fact that the doctor and patient strongly resemble escapees from Area 51, you will notice that the technique is about applying pressure to the pelvic area in a variety of odd positions. Here we do see that some of the massage was internal (he is a gynaecologist, after all), and involved inserting a finger and applying the other hand on top of the abdomen and pushing downwards. But at no point is an orgasm mentioned or a vibrator required.

Brandt's theories were celebrated and expanded on three years after his death by Dr Robert Ziegenspeck (1856–1918) in his *Massage Treatment (Thure Brandt) in Diseases of Women: for Practitioners* (1898). Ziegenspeck gives considerable detail about the internal part of the pelvic floor massage. The good doctor strongly emphasises that this 'localised' treatment requires plenty of 'massage and stretching' with one finger in the vagina and the spare hand pushing down on the abdomen.[8] And if you were still unsure of what you were doing, Ziegenspeck supplied a handy seven-point guide:

(1) The patient's dress is not removed, not even thrown back, but merely opened around the waist. The corset likewise is loosened, so that no hook or band may interfere. The chemise is then pulled up so far that the hand can be placed upon the bare abdomen; the abdomen itself, however, is not uncovered.

(2) The finger to be introduced into the vagina, from underneath the knee of the side corresponding to the hand employed, can also be advanced beneath the dress towards the vaginal orifice without the knees being separated.

(3) Only one finger is introduced under all circumstances – preferably the forefinger, except in ventro-vaginal-rectal palpation, where the forefinger is inserted into the rectum and the thumb into the vagina.

(4) The hand laid upon the abdomen feels its way towards the finger in the vagina, not with uniform pressure, but penetrating deeper and deeper by means of gentle circular massage movements.

(5) The examiner, seated upon a chair at the end of a couch, takes the corner of the latter between his separated knees.

(6) Only a low bench, couch, or so-called plinth is used and no examining chair or table.

(7) The unemployed fingers are not flexed (examination with closed hand) but rest loosely extended in the groove between the nates (examination with open hand).[9]

It's very difficult to read through that little lot and not arrive at the conclusion that this is just fancy fingering, and it seems that this 'treatment' drew similar criticism in the nineteenth century. Ziegenspeck claims that the 'massage has been unjustly reproached' as causing 'sexual irritation' (read, 'sexual stimulation').[10]

> If we follow the rules given above sexual irritation will occur no oftener during massage than during any gynecological diagnosis. No doubt there are women of abnormal sexual excitability, who become excited by every gynecological examination, sometimes even without any such cause. Those malevolent persons, however, who time and again raise such an unwarranted objection against the method, certainly without fully understanding the same, on the one hand unjustly charge the numerous physicians using this method either with carelessness or unscrupulousness, it being an easy matter to find out whether a woman is sexually excited or not; while, on the other hand, they most grossly insult thousands of highly respectable women by maliciously insinuating that they undergo this treatment in spite of its power to cause sexual excitement, or, perhaps, even on that very account.

Clearly, for Ziegenspeck at least, sexual stimulation during pelvic massage was to be avoided. Should any patient experience 'sexual irritation', he recommended 'increasing the pressure a little, so that real pain is caused'.[11]

The theories behind 'pelvic massage' and the techniques are frankly bizarre, and although I am cautious of judging this 'treatment' by modern standards, there is something undeniably sexual going on here. I know it, you know it, and clearly people at the time knew it. But there is no vibrator, there is no orgasm, there is no hysteria, and its practitioners emphatically deny this is medical masturbating. However, it seems that it is here, in the confusing practice of pelvic massage, that the myth that

Victorian doctors collectively drained the national grid as they buzzed their patients into post-orgasmic delirium developed.

The other persistent part of the medical vibrator story is that of 'hysterical paroxysm', which Maines understands as being 'the female orgasm under clinical conditions'.[12] But when we start to investigate the medical texts of the era, a hysterical paroxysm doesn't sound like any orgasm I've ever had. *Hysterical and Nervous Affections of Women. Read Before the Harveian Society* describes a hysterical paroxysm as 'an uncontrollable attack of alternate sobbing and laughter'.[13] Andrew Whyte Barclay's *A Manual of Medical Diagnosis* (1864) describes it as a 'fit' and 'a simulation of epilepsy'.[14] John Henry Walsh describes the hysterical paroxysm as beginning with uncontrollable giggling, and lasting 'for at least an hour, and often for five or six'.[15] William Potts Dewees claims that 'It is very common for the stomach to eructate a great deal of "gas," at the termination of an hysterical paroxysm, from which the patient finds much relief.'[16] I'm sorry, but a farting, giggling fit that lasts an afternoon is not an orgasm. Whatever this is, it is described in terms very similar to a fit, or a nervous, uncontrollable episode. Medical theories of the time do link this strange phenomenon to a gynaecological cause. Walsh wrote that a 'copious secretion of pale urine accompanies the disease'.[17] George Bacon Wood wrote that hysterical paroxysm was 'apt to be worse around the menstrual period', and W. W. Bliss was certain that 'hysterical paroxysms are usually an accompaniment of painful menstruation'.[18] But this should not be surprising as the word 'hysteria' comes from Latin *hystericus*, meaning 'of the womb', and from the Greek *hysterikos*, meaning 'suffering in the womb'.

The mysterious medical phenomenon known as hysteria has attracted considerable research in modern scholarship, precisely because no one really knows what it is. The word covers a multitude of psychological and physical ailments and, until Freud's work, was predominantly a woman's malady. At the risk of oversimplification, hysteria meant the physical or behavioural manifestations of physiological distress in women. This could be aggression, fainting, nymphomania or a farting fit. The theory that the womb caused emotional instability can be traced back to Ancient Greece and the 'wandering womb' theory. Aretaeus, a physician contemporary with Galen in the second century AD, describes how the womb moves around the abdomen, causing madness:

> In the middle of the flanks of women lies the womb, a female viscus, closely resembling an animal; for it is moved of itself hither and thither in the flanks, also upwards in a direct line to below the cartilage of the thorax, and also obliquely to the right or to the left, either to the liver or the spleen, and it likewise is subject to prolapses downwards, and in a word, it is altogether erratic. It delights also in fragrant smells, and advances towards them; and it has an aversion to fetid smells, and flees from them; and, on the whole, the womb is like an animal within an animal.[19]

By the nineteenth century, the wandering womb theory had fallen out of favour, though the link between the womb and hysteria clearly enjoyed a last hurrah in theories of pelvic massage and womb manipulation. A hysterical paroxysm was simply another ill-defined category of hysteria that can be found in nineteenth-century medical manuals, along with the hysterical coma, hysterical headaches, hysterical excitement, hysterical convulsive affections and (of course) hysterical flatulence.

But more than this: the Victorians knew what an orgasm was! There was no need to dress it up in euphemistic language. Even a cursory glance at the erotic literature of the time will tell you that the Victorians were well aware of orgasms. *The Pearl* (1879–80) is crammed full of women orgasming: 'I felt her crack deluged with a warm, creamy spend whilst my own juice spurted over her hand and dress in loving sympathy.'[20] *The Romance of Lust* (1873) is also pretty clued up as to what women want: 'She rapidly came to the ecstatic ending, nearly thrusting my whole face into her vast orbit, and spurting out a very torrent of sperm, all over my face and neck.'[21] And Jack Saul conducts a concerto of orgasms in *Sins of the Cities of the Plain* (1881): 'How

Anonymous Victorian pornographic photograph.

many times I made her spend it would be impossible to say.'[22] As Fern Riddell, one of the leading academics in Victorian sexuality, argues, 'Victorian doctors knew exactly what the female orgasm was; in fact, it's one of the reasons they thought masturbation was a bad idea.'[23]

Not only did Victorian doctors know what an orgasm was, but nineteenth-century medical theories largely taught that orgasms were potentially dangerous and needed to be limited. Masturbation in women was thought to cause hysteria, not cure it. In *The Generative System and Its Functions in Health and Disease* (1883), James George Beaney claimed that a disease 'associated with, and very often closely depending on, female masturbation is hysteria'.[24] Edward John Tilt (1815–1893) wrote that 'habitual masturbation lowers the tone of the whole system, causes an irritable condition of the temper, [and] the milder manifestations of hysteria'.[25] In 1852, Samuel La'mert drew a clear distinction between hysterical paroxysm and masturbation when he wrote 'females devoted to libidinous and solitary pollutions, are more particularly exposed to hysterical paroxysm'.[26] In 1894, Dr A. J. Block of New Orleans in an article entitled 'Sexual Perversion in the Female' referred to female masturbation as a 'moral leprosy'.[27] So dangerous was female masturbation thought to be that it was cited on numerous patient admission forms to Victorian lunatic asylums, and led to quack doctor Isaac Baker Brown routinely carrying out clito-ridectomies.* Now, I ask you, does this sound like a group of people likely to prescribe a session of 'fingerblasting' (2003)?

But it's not all doom and gloom. Although orgasms were not administered by Victorian doctors, they were generally encouraged between

---

* See 'Looking for the Boy in the Boat' for a detailed discussion on Dr Isaac Baker Brown. The 1872 state report to the Governor of California reports that 'masturbation still holds its place at the head of the list of assigned causes' for confinement in an asylum. *Appendix to the Journals of the Senate and Assembly of the Nineteenth Session of the Legislature of the State of California* (Sacramento: T. A. Springer, 1872), p. 211.

husband and wife, and an absence of orgasm when paying the conjugal debt was recognised as a bad thing. An article published by Dr W. Tyler Smith in *The Lancet* in 1842 defined impotence in women as 'failure to produce the sexual orgasm'.[28] One school of medical thought had it that orgasms helped a woman to conceive. For example, in 1872, Dr J. R. Beck argued that an orgasm allowed the cervix to contract and helped the sperm to reach the egg.[29] Others, like Dr John S. Parry, didn't discount the possibility that an orgasm may help things along, but was quite sure that 'an orgasm is not essential to conception'.[30] But whatever the medical profession had to say on the subject of blowing one's lady lumps, Victorian pornography provides substantial evidence that the orgasm was also understood as a very important, and fun, part of sex.

So, what can we salvage from this much-loved and widespread myth? It is true that Victorian doctors were fascinated with the female reproductive system, and, like their medical predecessors, linked madness to the womb. To cure hysteria, in all its weird manifestations, they prescribed all manner of kinky-sounding treatments, including pelvic massage, which is really just fancy fingering. Doctors also had some very strange ideas about orgasm and masturbation damaging health and causing hysteria. There really was such a thing as a 'hysterical paroxysm', which is not an orgasm, but is described as a giggly, farting fit that could last for hours. It's also true that vibrating massagers became popular in the late nineteenth century and were recommended to cure all manner of ills.* But here is the crucial thing: doctors may have been manipulating, sedating, institutionalising and pummelling the pussies of their poor patients – but they were not masturbating them to 'hysterical paroxysm' with steam-powered vibrators to cure them of hysteria. Sorry to be such a buzzkill.

---

* For further reading about the development of the vibrator in the twentieth century, see Hallie Lieberman, *Buzz: A Stimulating History of the Sex Toy* (New York: Pegasus Books, 2017).

On Your Bike

Sex and Cycling

What is the most important invention in the fight for sexual equality? The Pill? The self-cleaning vibrator? Kleenex Mansize? How about the humble bicycle?

Before you panic, this is not a chapter about people having sex with bicycles, although if you are interested in that then both the Erotic Museum in Amsterdam and the Sex Museum in New York have examples of 'dildo bikes'.[1] But there is something quite sexy about bikes. Perhaps it is the saddle rubbing against the genitals, or maybe it is the bent over, arse-up posture that must be assumed to ride one.

Maybe it's just the word 'ride'. But whatever it is, bicycles have long had an air of cheeky 'Carry On' fun about them. Freddie Mercury knew it when he sang about fat-bottomed girls riding their bicycles. Queen even featured just such a fat-bottomed girl riding a bicycle on the picture sleeve of their album *Jazz* (1978).

The role of the bicycle in the sexual emancipation of women is often overlooked, but it allowed

Victorian erotic postcard of a nude woman on a bike.

Victorian erotic postcard showing a nude woman on a bike. How daring.

them a freedom they had never experienced before. And not only the freedom to travel – the bicycle also liberated women's bodies from cumbersome skirts and the tit-crushing corset. The bicycle changed attitudes to health, fitness and exercise and proved women were not desperately delicate little flowers. The popularity of the bicycle forced a medical debate on the stimulating effects of the saddle on the reproductive organs, and the nature of female sexuality.* American suffragette Susan B. Anthony claimed that the bicycle had 'done more to emancipate women than anything else in the world'.[2] For some Victorian moralists, this was all too much, and the bicycle came to be associated with sexual promiscuity, so much so that bicycles feature heavily in nineteenth-century pornographic photographs. Not only because they provide a convenient excuse for bending over, legs akimbo, but because the bicycle signified a sexually liberated woman, who enjoyed pleasure.

The Victorians did not invent the bicycle, but they did refine the design so it could be used without rupturing internal organs and endangering life. One of the earliest designs for a two-wheeled apparatus dates to 1534 and is attributed to Gian Giacomo Caprotti (a pupil of Leonardo da Vinci), but the first usable bicycle was designed by German Baron Karl von Drais in 1817, and was called a 'running machine'. There were no pedals, brakes or suspension, but the device allowed the rider to propel themselves forward in a half run, half cycle motion. Soon, British designer Denis Johnson brought out an

---

* This is a debate that continues to this day. According to research from the University of California, women who regularly cycle enjoy 'better sexual function' than non-cyclists, which directly contradicts previous research that suggested there was a link between cycling and sexual disfunction. (Thomas W. Gaither et al., 'Cycling and Female Sexual and Urinary Function: Results from a Large, Multinational, Cross-Sectional Study', *The Journal of Sexual Medicine*, 15.4 (2018), pp. 510–18 <https://doi.org/10.1016/j.jsxm.2018.02.004>.)

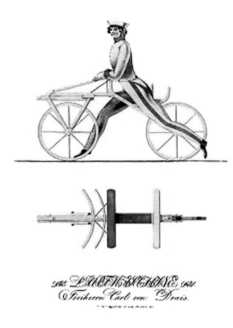

An 1817 illustration of a 'draisine'.

improved, more streamlined version called the 'pedestrian curricle' or the 'velocipede', but it would take another fifty years for the bicycle to become popular.

Four-wheelers, push-bikes, penny-farthings and the 1860 'Boneshaker' were all important points in the evolution of the modern bicycle, but they were dangerous.* They didn't have suspension, brakes or pneumatic tyres, and were notoriously unstable. Falling at speed from the height of a penny-farthing caused horrible injuries and numerous fatalities. The open spokes and precariously placed saddle meant that ladies couldn't ride them in skirts and bustles without their petticoats getting tangled up and their bloomers torn off. As a result, bicycles were associated with thrill-seeking young men who cruised Victorian cobbles on a pimped-up penny-farthing.

---

* For further reading on early bicycles, see Andrew Ritchie, *Early Bicycles and the Quest for Speed* (Jefferson: McFarland & Company, Incorporated Publishers, 2018).

Picture of the Rover Ladies Safety Bicycle, designed by John Kemp Starley, *c.*1889.

Thankfully, the 1880s saw the invention of the 'safety bicycle', which featured steering, brakes, pedals, suspension and, eventually, pneumatic tyres. Finally, the bicycle could be used by anyone. Historians often refer to the 1890s as 'the golden age of the bicycle', and with good reason. The bicycle was suddenly the must-have item, and women started cycling in droves.

As exciting as all this was, the lady cyclist was regarded with suspicion from the get-go. As the bicycle cannot be ridden side-saddle, doctors worried about the potentially stimulating effects all that bouncing about on a saddle would have on a lady's well-being. Men were regarded as robust and physically able to withstand the

LEFT: A Victorian erotic postcard showing a nude woman posing with a penny-farthing.

RIGHT: A Victorian postcard showing 'the new woman' and her sexy bike. Bikes were considered the must-have accessory of the modern woman.

potentially stimulating dangers of the bike, but women were regarded as constitutionally weaker. As the *South Wales Echo* reported in 1897, 'the cycle was invented by the male creature and is still a male creature's vehicle'; women, it reported, 'should beware of the dangers of cycling'.[3]

The dangers of cycling being alluded to were far greater than taking a tumble over the handlebars. Because the saddle rubbed up against the genitals, the dangers a woman faced related to her sexual and reproductive health. One French physician warned that 'the unusual physical exertion, combined with the perilous lack of corsetry, would damage the feminine organs of matrimonial necessity and shake them loose'.[4] Although bicycle anxiety was felt around the world in the 1890s, American and Canadian doctors seemed to be particularly concerned about women cycling and their 'organs of matrimonial necessity', and it's here that the loudest anti-cycling voices were heard.

In 1895, the *St Louis Medical Review* not only stated that cycling was an 'exceedingly ungraceful and unbecoming occupation for young ladies', but it might lead to 'ovarian inflammation, bleeding from the kidney or womb, displacement, and miscarriage'.[5] An article in the *Iowa State Register* warned that cycling 'may suppress or render irregular and fearfully painful the menses, and perhaps sow the seeds for future ill health'.[6] The *Cincinnati Lancet-Clinic* (1895) broadly supported cycling, but had concerns about the saddle acting as a 'frictional agent' and sending a lady into a 'dangerous condition'.[7]

Indeed, it was the 'frictional agent' the saddle provided that concerned most of these medical texts. All the blustering around saddle-induced 'uterine disorders' and 'ovarian inflammation' was little more than a sublimated anxiety that a woman might experience sexual pleasure riding over the cobbles with a wad of leather between her legs. Other doctors were far more direct in voicing their concerns. In 1896, the editor of the Canadian journal the *Dominion Medical Monthly* was widely quoted as saying that 'the consensus of opinion is increasing overwhelmingly day by day that bicycle riding produces in the female a distinct orgasm'.[8] Outraged at the suggestion that Canadian women were putting their bicycles to less than wholesome purposes, a flurry of articles soon followed denouncing the claim, like this one in the *Canadian Medical Practioner* (1896):

> The report that comes to us, indeed, is such that, were it credible, we should be led to despair of the future of the country, for, compared to Canada, or at least to Toronto, Sodom and Gomorrah were as pure as Salvation Army Shelters. It appears that cycling, which, with us is adding so much to the health and beauty and the charm of our women, is in Canada, or at least in Toronto, merely a means of gratifying unholy and bestial desire.

It continues, 'the filthy rubbish to which the *Record* refers is in itself essentially nasty, while the direct charges against the women and girls of Toronto are simply infamous'.[9] It's doubtful that the idea women regularly orgasmed on their bicycles was widely held within the medical community, but the very fact that a public debate was needed to address this is testament to the fact that some people regarded it as a possibility.

The *American Journal of Obstetrics and Diseases of Women and Children* featured an article by Dr Robert Dickinson on 'Bicycling for Women' that addressed the issue of sexual excitement. 'A very grave objection has been made to the use of the bicycle among women, which, if true, would induce us to be exceedingly cautious in ever suggesting this exercise. It has been said to beget or foster the habit of masturbation.' Dickinson continued:

One of the very able women who teach physical culture in New York told a medical friend of mine that a pupil, who claimed a rather varied experience in sexual pleasures, said that she could not ask a more satisfactory development than could be obtained from the saddle of her bicycle. Dr Vance has observed a case of an overwrought, pallid, somewhat emaciated girl of 15, whose saddle was arranged so that the front pommel rode upward at an angle of about 35°, who stooped forward noticeably in riding, and whose actions, during the time when he had good opportunity to observe her, strongly suggested to him the indulgence we are considering.[10]

Thankfully, common sense seems to have prevailed, and although Dickinson knew of some women who arranged their saddles to maintain 'constant friction over the clitoris and labia', he did not believe this was commonplace. He argued that there was only a slight 'danger of the habit being started or fostered' when a woman took up cycling.[11]

Despite several prominent doctors reassuring the public that women were not using bikes to masturbate, the mere suggestion they were was enough for cycling to be condemned by many as indecent.

In 1889, Canada's first woman's page editor, Kit Coleman, wrote:

No girl over 39 should be allowed to wheel. It is immoral. Unfortunately, it is older girls who are ardent wheelers. They love to cavort and careen above the spokes, twirling and twisting in a manner that must remind them of long dead dancing days. They have descended from the shelves in myriads and in a burst of Indian summer are disporting themselves on the highways and byways.[12]

A Victorian postcard of a nude woman celebrating her bike.

In 1896, Charlotte Smith, the president of the American Rescue League, claimed that 'bicycling by young women has helped swell the ranks of reckless girls who finally drift into the standing army of outcast women of the United States more than any other medium'. She went as far as to call the bicycle 'the Devil's advance agent'.[13]

In order to try and maintain modesty, some companies issued 'hygiene saddles' with holes in to try and relieve 'harmful pressure' on a lady's undercarriage. Some bikes came equipped with screens to conceal a lady's ankles. But it wasn't just the indelicate fact that a saddle must be sat upon that was cause for concern.

The bicycle also offered men and women the opportunity for romance and sexual adventure, which no doubt added to their erotic quality. Cycling meant couples could get away from home unchaperoned and easily overcome geographical restrictions to meet up. The freedom the bicycle offered made some suspicious that cycling was being used for 'impure purposes'.[14] Certainly, cycling romances were a hot topic in the late nineteenth century. The English periodical *The Wheelwoman*, for example, reported that fifteen engagements were announced in the days following a cycling club picnic, and declared 'surely no one could possibly desire a better recommendation for cycling than this?'[15]

It is hard to understand how anyone fell in love during a bike ride when doctors started to warn cyclists about a devastating condition called 'bicycle face'. This terrible affliction affected men and women equally, but it was considered particularly upsetting for women. In 1897, Dr A. Shadwell described the symptoms of bicycle face thus: 'set faces, eyes fixed before them, and an expression either anxious, irritable, or at best stony'.[16] In 1897, the editor of *Harper's Magazine* suggested ladies chew gum when riding as 'chewing gum keeps the face mobile and prevents the form of that expression of anxiety that doctors tell us may grow in time to be an essential part of a lady bicyclist's features'.[17]

Thankfully, not all Victorians took this seriously and bicycle face became a long-running joke. Newspapers of the time are full of humorous poems and jokes about bicycle face, such as this one featured in the *Derry Journal* in 1895.

Those women who were prepared to risk bicycle face, damaging their 'matrimonial organs of necessity', cumming on a saddle and being accused of sneaking off for a quick ride, had another 'indecent' obstacle to overcome. It very quickly became apparent that if women wanted to ride a bike, then their dress had to change. The Victorian corset was not compatible with cycling. Victorian corsets restricted women's waists to an 'ideal' circumference of 17–22

THE BICYCLE FACE.

I've a " bicycle face"
Which I wish to replace
　With a face that is not of that kind ;
And if any one can
Provide me a plan
　To exchange, it will quite suit my mind.

I've been reading of late
Some remarks in debate,
　As to whether or not it is true,
That there is such a face.
And I now have a case,
　Which settles the question clear through

There's one eye that's black,
On my cheek is a whack,
　My forehead is scratched like a file ;
While my chin is a fright,
And my lips are a sight,
　Less lovely whenever I smile.

My nose is awry,
Of a tooth I am shy,
　An eyebrow is gone from its place ;
And one of my ears,
I have serious fears,
　Will fall if it hasn't a brace.

There are patches galore,
Till there couldn't be more.
　With plaster and splints and a strap ;
There are black-and-blue spots,
By themselves and in lots,
　Till the face of me looks like a map.

They may stop their debate,
I am ready to state,
　It is true as I find in my case ;
For alack and alas,
When I look in a glass,
　I am sure I've a " bicycle face."

L'ENVOI.

Poem about 'bicycle face', from *Derry Journal*, 23 September 1895.

inches, which precluded anything more strenuous than embroidering doilies and fainting. In an effort to prevent women freeboobing it on their bikes, corset companies tried to sell 'bicycle corsets' that allowed the wearer to 'ride with grace'. They didn't catch on.

As well as ditching the corset, women started to view the miles of skirted crinoline, bustles and petticoats that they donned each day as a pain in the padded arse. In order to cycle safely, some women took to wearing knickerbockers and loose clothing. The knickerbockers

The Perfect Poise
of the woman who wears a Ferris Waist is easily distinguishable. She rides with easy grace because every motion, every muscle is absolutely free. She rides without fatigue because she enjoys perfect respiration.

FERRIS'
Bicycle Corset Waist
is constructed with elastic sides which yield to every motion of the wearer. The hips are short and pliable, the bust is made to give support without restriction. Every woman who rides a wheel or a horse, who plays tennis or golf, should wear a Ferris Waist. They are shown in all their beauty in the Ferris book of Living Models. Sent free.

Ferris' Good Sense Corset Waists are sold by all leading retailers. Do not take substitutes. Ladies', $1.00 to $2.75; Misses', 50c. to $1; Children's, 25c. to 50c. Made only by

THE FERRIS BROS. CO., 341 Broadway, New York.

were deeply shocking to the conservative Victorians as they forced a recognition that women had two legs and that they opened. The image of a woman sitting astride her bicycle, calves on show, her breasts unrestricted by a corset, and a saddle nestled between her legs was an undeniably sexual image. This presented a challenge to women who wanted to cycle comfortably and to avoid accusations of indecency.

In response to this, in 1881 the Rational Dress Society was formed in London, and opposing women's restrictive clothing and cycling was right at the heart of it. Similar groups sprang up all over the world. Rather than viewing cycling outfits as indecent dress, these groups pushed for them to be accepted as 'rational dress'. They emphasised the health and safety aspects of cycle wear, as well as pointing to the immoral and impractical nature of mainstream women's fashions.

The feminist figure of the 'new woman' rose in the late nineteenth century. The new woman was independent, educated and outspoken.

She challenged traditional notions of dress, marriage, gender and equality, and, of course, she rode a bike. The new woman positioned herself against the Victorian 'Angel in the House' version of femininity that was idealised throughout much of the nineteenth century. As a result, the new woman was frequently accused of wanting to be a man, and labelled a 'grown-up tomboy', or an 'adult hoyden'.[18]

Bicycling was held responsible for encouraging all manner of 'masculine' behaviours in women, such as smoking, drinking, swearing and (of course) promiscuity.[19] The new woman also demanded entrance into traditionally male-dominated spaces, such as universities. When Cambridge University proposed granting women full admission to university in 1897, male students protested by dangling an effigy of a woman on a bicycle out of a window in Market Square.

LEFT: 'THE PERFECT POISE of the woman who wears a Ferris Waist is easily distinguishable. She rides with easy grace because every motion, every muscle is absolutely free. She rides without fatigue because she enjoys perfect respiration.'

RIGHT: A 'lady cyclist' is attacked by a mob for wearing socks. From *Illustrated Police News*, 9 October 1897.

'The "New Woman" and Her Bicycle, There Will be Several Varieties of Her', 1895.

At the heart of the hostility towards women cycling was a thinly veiled fear that traditional gender roles were being rejected. As women discarded demure dress, laughed at absurd medical quackery and embraced the independence the bike offered, they cycled out of the domestic and into the public world. As to the fears cycling could led to 'sexual excitement', women were able to disprove this themselves, simply by persisting. The subject of masturbation was shrouded in shame and embarrassment, and was not one your average woman would have voiced their opinion on publicly. But it was the women themselves who provided the evidence that they were not peaking while pedaling. The more women cycled without orgasming, the dafter alarmist doctors looked. It may have been a small victory, but it wrested control of the narrative around female sexuality away from the doctors, and allowed women to challenge it. Of course, there was some

A Victorian lady enjoying her penny-farthing.

BICYCLES FOR WOMEN.

Woman is completing her conquest of the planet. She rows, she smokes, she shoots, she plays billiards, she rides, and now she has lassoed the iron grasshopper that man has hitherto exclusively bestridden, for a manufacturer in St Louis, Missouri, has brought out a bicycle for women. The machine is a safety one, with the connecting bars between the wheels lower than usual, and the contrivance is propelled by pedals attached to the hind wheel, which is directly behind the front one, as in the ordinary bicycle ridden by the male. The manufacturer says he was led to make the invention by the reflection that it was no use of a lady riding a tricycle, the lightest of which weighs 60lb, when she can ride a bicycle that weighs only 35lb, and go a great deal faster with a smaller expenditure of force.

From *Aberdeen Press and Journal*, 14 April 1888.

truth in the panic that cycling encouraged promiscuity, because it did allow men and women far greater freedom to sneak off, meet up and ring each other's bells, but to that I can only say hurrah.

It was the First World War that really forced a change in attitudes towards women's equality (sexual and otherwise), but the lady cyclists had paved the way in the preceding years. They risked ridicule and even violence to do so, but it was clearly worth it. As British writer Louise Jeye wrote in 1895:

> There is a new dawn ... of emancipation, and it is brought
> about by the cycle. Free to wheel, free to spin out in the
> glorious country, unhampered by chaperones ... the young
> girl of today can feel the real independence of herself and,
> while she is building up her better constitution, she is
> developing her better mind.

Boys' Toys

A History of the Sex Doll

Humans are damn clever things, aren't they? I am typing this chapter on a laptop that is streaming a podcast, my smartphone is within reach and it's reasonable to assume that the coffee I am swigging is blessedly free from cholera. If I were writing this a few hundred years ago, it would be an entirely different scene. Not only would I have no computer, coffee or smartphone, but I might well have cholera, and what the hell am I doing thinking with my lady brain anyway? We have advanced enormously, and technology has been at the heart of that all the way along.

Technological advancements do not create new ideas so much as offer new ways to fulfil pretty basic human needs. Take, for example, sex robots. We are finally at a point where we have the technology to create a sex robot. They do not have artificial intelligence just yet, but they do have artificial tits and artificial vulvas. What's more, they can stream your favourite playlist from Spotify out of their orifices while you get down to do the robot-nasty. They aren't cheap though. An average model will set you back about £15,000, and that's without including the cost of all the batteries and wet wipes you'll be getting through.

The prospect of the sex robot has understandably rattled a few cages. An article published in the *British Medical Journal of Sexual and Reproductive Health* in 2018 painted a fairly bleak picture, pointing out that:

> Opponents reject the hypothesis that they reduce sexual
> crimes, and instead raise concerns about the potential

for harm by further promoting the pervasive idea that living women too are sex objects that should be constantly available – 'misogynistic objectification' – and intensifying existing physical and sexual violence against women and children.[1]

In early 2018, two hundred sex workers in Amsterdam protested the opening of more sex doll brothels, understandably pissed off at the threat such self-service poses to their livelihood. Feminist groups have protested against sex robot brothels in Paris, putting pressure on the city council to ban the hire of so-called Xdolls, on the grounds that they objectify and degrade women. And to be sure, the use of sex robots does raise some complex moral issues, but not new ones.

The sex doll is not a new phenomenon. Nor are fears that 'real' women are being replaced, or the concern that something deeply perverse and misogynistic is going on. Of course, dildos are ancient as well. In 2009, researchers in France excavated a 36,000-year-old bison horn penial carving now called 'the Blanchard phallus'.[2] And in 2015, archaeologists found a 28,000-year-old stone phallus in Germany.[3] Generally, archaeologists are reluctant to call these objects 'sex toys' because for all we know they may be Palaeolithic door knockers. But we certainly can't discount the possibility.

Agalmatophilia is a sexual attraction to a statue, doll or mannequin, and examples of this can be found throughout ancient literature. Even in the earliest records of agalmatophilia, we see the anxieties around objectifying and hating women that frame the sex robot debate today. The Roman poet Ovid (43 BC–AD 17), for example, tells the story of a sculptor called Pygmalion who 'loathes women as wantons and vows never to marry'. Instead, Pygmalion devotes all his energy to sculpting the perfect woman from ivory and then falls desperately in love with his creation.

Early twentieth-century image of a man copulating with a model of a woman and models of penises mounted on a board.

His heart desired the body he had formed.

With many a touch he tries it – is it flesh

Or ivory? Not ivory still, he's sure!

Kisses he gives and thinks they are returned;

He speaks to it, caresses it, believes

The firm new flesh beneath his fingers yields...[4]

Pygmalion takes his lady to bed, buys her presents, decorates her with precious jewellery and begs the gods to make her real. Aphrodite eventually takes pity on him and grants his wish.

The statue of 'Aphrodite of Knidos' (or Cnidus) was sculpted by Praxiteles of Athens around the fourth century BC. She is said to be modelled on the courtesan Phryne and is one of the earliest representations of the female body in Greek history. Like the sex robots today, the statue was designed to be the perfect woman. According to Pliny the Elder, 'a certain individual, it is said, became enamoured of this statue, and, concealing himself in the temple during the night, gratified his lustful passion upon it, traces of which are to be seen in a stain left upon the marble'.[5]

The Pygmalion story of trying to create the perfect woman continues to inspire numerous cinematic parallels: *My Fair Lady*, *Pretty Woman*, *The Stepford Wives*, *Mannequin*, *Weird Science*, *Miss Congeniality*, etc. But one of the most important Pygmalion stories is E. T. A. Hoffmann's *Der Sandmann* (1816), where the protagonist Nathaniel falls in love with Olympia, who is a doll-like automaton. Not only is the story one of the first depictions of a humanoid machine (robot), but it also caught the attention of several psychiatrists, most notably Sigmund Freud, who set about trying to understand why dolls are so damn creepy. Freud didn't use the term 'creepy', he said the dolls were 'uncanny', arguing that the 'uncanny' is a 'class of the terrifying which leads back to something long known to us, once very familiar'.[6] Anything

Cnidus Aphrodite. A Roman copy after a Greek original of the fourth century.

that provokes a sense of unease or fear because it distorts something that was once comforting or everyday is uncanny: monstrous mothers, slutty teddy bears, Children of the Corn, etc.

Perhaps it is this sense of uncanny that has provoked a backlash against the sex robots. The grossly exaggerated body of a woman, glassy-eyed and open-mouthed, caught somewhere between being alive and not alive, programmed to gratify the sexual whims of he who wields the remote control is an uncomfortable, nay uncanny, prospect. But things have been 'uncanny' long before anyone thought to hide a USB port in a rubber nipple.

English sexologist Havelock Ellis (1859–1939) also refers to Pygmalionism in volume four of his *Studies in the Psychology of Sex* (1905):

> Pygmalionism, or falling love with statues, is a rare form
> of erotomania founded on the sense of vision and closely
> related to the allurement of beauty. (I here use 'pygmalionism'
> as a general term for the sexual love of statues; it is
> sometimes restricted to cases in which a man requires of a
> prostitute that she shall assume the part of a statue which
> gradually comes to life, and finds sexual gratification in this
> performance alone.)[7]

Pioneering psychiatrist and sexologist Iwan Bloch (1872–1922) also briefly explored sexual attraction to dolls in his work *The Sexual Life of Our Time in its Relations to Modern Civilization* (1905). He argued that the Pygmalion fantasy, or *'Venus statuaria'*, was closely linked to fantasies of necrophilia, and describes a how the 'Pygmalionists' flocked to brothels to masturbate over young women posed as statues, or even just statues of young women.[8] Indeed, in his exposé of Parisian brothels, *Les Maisons De Tolerance* (1892), Louis Fiaux described how one elderly man visited a brothel 'every week to worship, dressed in the costume of Pygmalion' to masturbate over statues of Greek goddesses at a cost of 100 francs.[9]

As well as some gentlemen seeking out some light granite relief, Bloch describes rubber and plastic 'fornicatory dolls' being sold in various catalogues as 'Parisian rubber articles'. Though none survive today, Bloch describes these early sex dolls as being complete with extremely lifelike genitals: 'Even the secretion of Bartholin's glands is imitated, by means of a pneumatic tube filled with oil.'[10] Bloch refers to two 'erotic romances' about rubber dolls to further illustrate how widespread this particular kink was at the turn of the twentieth century: Madame B's *La Femme Endormie* (1899), and René Schwaeblé's *Les Détraquées de Paris* (1904).[11] Both texts fetishise the passive pliability of a doll when compared to the complexity of human women, offering some support for Bloch's theories around necrophilia.

In *La Femme Endormie*, Paul Molaus is a middle-aged man who has sworn off romance, but still wants to have sex with women. Paul reasons that a doll will 'always be compliant and silent, no matter how lewd the act he chose to perform'.[12] The story has a very clever twist as even when Paul gets his doll (named Mea), he cannot control his jealousy and rages at the knowledge that the male creator of Mea was there before him. Paul feels humiliated by his own desire for the doll and angrily abuses her after he has orgasmed.

> 'Slut,' he shouted, 'you didn't want me to spend my time looking at you, studying your postures, feasting upon your various poses, revelling in your cunt, your asshole, your tits, your calves; you didn't want me to cram my cock between your lips, between your breasts; you didn't want me to sprawl over the curves of your buttocks, or rest my head there. Wretched whore, you acted like a bitch, taking advantage of your body,

and you drove me to spear you straight off so as to get rid of me quicker. Here, you harlot, come here. I'm going to whack your bottom to punish you for my stupid behaviour.'[13]

The moral of the story seems to be that Paul's misogyny is not a response to being treated poorly by real women, but is a result of his own sense of inadequacy.

René Schwaeblé's short story 'Homunculus' in *Les Détraquées de Paris* is less sophisticated but also eroticises the lifelessness of the dolls. 'Homunculus' tells the story of Doctor P., who builds artificial women for 'those who do not like women'. The good doctor explains: 'with my dolls there is never any blackmail, or jealousy, argument or illness ... They are always ready, always compliant, no blackmail, no scenes of jealousy, no arguments, no discomfort! They are always ready, always docile.'[14]

Despite sex dolls having a long history, there have been hardly any scientific studies into sex dolls and their owners. A quick keyword search through the leading scientific literature databases for 'sex/love doll' results in only one paper, and that one is about how little scientific research there is on sex dolls.[15] Sex robots have garnered slightly more attention, but it remains a very under-researched subject.[16] Most research on sex dolls and sex robots comes from the humanities, and is concerned with the moral, legal and social implications.[17] There is next to no primary research data with which to try and understand the use of sex dolls.

The early sexologists were convinced having sex with dolls was a type of necrophilia, but the limited research we have suggests otherwise. In her (as yet) unpublished Masters thesis, Sarah Valverde interviewed sixty-one sex-doll users, recruited via various online forums.[18] This piece of research revealed that the majority of doll owners were white, educated, middle-aged males, who did not experience sexual dysfunction with human partners. 'The majority of doll-owners report above average to excellent satisfaction levels for sexual stimulation when using their dolls, which indicates sex doll use is an enjoyable experience.'[19] Obviously, more research is needed, but it seems sex-doll use is not a paraphilia, like necrophilia – it's just a bit of fun.* But, speaking of necrophilia. There have been some unsettling examples of people turning human women into dolls after they had died, which is a whole other level of uncanny.

Martin van Butchell (1735–1814) was an English dentist who decided the best way to mourn his wife's death in 1775 was to embalm her and set up a pay-per-view enterprise. Dr William Hunter and Dr William Cruikshank injected the body with various preservatives and dyes to give colour to her dead cheeks. Her eyes were replaced with glass ones and she was dressed in a very expensive gown. The poor woman was then propped up in the window of Butchell's dental practice to be gawked over by the paying public, where she remained until his second wife objected.[20]

One of the most famous courtesans of the nineteenth century was La Païva (1819–1884). At the height of her powers she held influence over some of the most powerful men in Europe. Her final and richest husband, Count Henckel von Donnersmarck, was so devastated by her death that he had La Païva's body embalmed and kept it in his attic, much to the surprise of his second wife, who had been unaware of her husband's little memento stashed upstairs.[21] All of which makes having sex with a rubber doll look rather tame.

---

* The *Diagnostic and Statistical Manual of Mental Disorders V* diagnosis of paraphilia states that the sufferer must 'feel personal distress about their interest, not merely distress resulting from society's disapproval; or have a sexual desire or behaviour that involves another person's psychological distress, injury, or death, or a desire for sexual behaviours involving unwilling persons or persons unable to give legal consent'. *Diagnostic and Statistical Manual of Mental Disorders*, 5th edn (Washington: American Psychiatric Association, 2013).

About the same time as Freud was thrashing out his essay on uncanny dolls, Austrian artist Oskar Kokoschka (1886–1980) put the theory into practice. When Alma Mahler ended her relationship with Kokoschka, he did what any stable, well-adjusted adult would do, and commissioned doll-maker Hermine Moos to make a life-sized replica of his ex-lover. Kokoschka gave very detailed instructions for Moos to follow.

> Yesterday I sent a life-size drawing of my beloved and I ask
> you to copy this most carefully and to transform it into reality.
> Pay special attention to the dimensions of the head and neck,
> to the ribcage, the rump and the limbs. And take to heart the
> contours of body, e.g., the line of the neck to the back, the curve
> of the belly. Please permit my sense of touch to take pleasure in
> those places where layers of fat or muscle suddenly give way to
> a sinewy covering of skin. For the first layer (inside) please use
> fine, curly horsehair; you must buy an old sofa or something
> similar; have the horsehair disinfected. Then, over that, a layer
> of pouches stuffed with down, cottonwool for the seat and
> breasts. The point of all this for me is an experience which I
> must be able to embrace![22]

Sadly, Kokoschka did not get his Pygmalion ending, as the resulting doll more closely resembled the Gruffalo than it did Alma Mahler. Moos deviated from the instructions and covered the doll's body in fur and feathers. Devastated, Kokoschka took several photographs, immortalised his doll in a painting, and then decapitated her in the garden.

One urban legend you may have heard is that the Nazis manufactured sex dolls to try and staunch the epidemic of syphilis that was decimating their troops, the so-called 'Model Borghild' project. As much fun as this story is, there is very little corroborating evidence to support it. In fact, the only evidence we have for this story is an enthusiastic exposé by a

Oskar Kokoschka's 'Alma Doll', 1919.

journalist calling himself Norbert Lenz.[23] Sadly, none of his claims can be verified and no one has heard anything from Norbert since he posted his extraordinary claims. The Nazi sex doll is a historical hoax. But the Germans did give us one enduring super-sexualised dolly: Barbie.

I know that Barbie isn't a sex doll, per se. But with her enormous boobs, kissy face, tiny waist and feet bent to take a stiletto heel, there can be little doubt that she is a sexual doll. What's more, Barbie is based on a German cartoon character called Bild Lilli, created in the late 1940s by Reinhard Beuthien for the Hamburg-based tabloid *Bild-Zeitung*. If you were feeling euphemistic, you could describe Lilli as a 'good-time girl', but it's pretty clear she is a high-class call girl. Lilli is a woman on the make and determined to use her considerable charms to relieve rich men of their assets. Lilli became so popular that she was immortalised as a saucy, novelty doll. As Barbie historian Robin Gerber wrote,

'Men got Lilli dolls as gag gifts at bachelor parties, put them on their car dashboard, dangled them from the rearview mirror, or gave them to girlfriends as a suggestive keepsake.'[24]

Although marketed to adults, the Lilli dolls were very popular with children as well. When Ruth Handler, a co-founder of the Mattel toy company, was on holiday in Switzerland in 1956, her fifteen-year-old daughter, Barbie, fell in love with the Lilli doll and bought three. Three years later Handler unveiled the Barbie doll at the American International Toy Fair in New York. Since her debut, Barbie has had over 150 careers, but sadly she has never returned to her roots, and 'Sex Work Barbie' has yet to hit the shops.

According to Anthony Ferguson there are three types of contemporary sex doll: vinyl, latex and silicon.[25] Your bog-standard, blow-up vinyl doll, beloved by stag parties around the world, started being mass-produced and advertised in American pornographic magazines in the 1960s.[26] Until 1987, it was illegal to import obscene or indecent items into the UK. But when Conegate Ltd attempted to import blow-up dolls from Germany in 1984, they found themselves caught up in a lengthy legal battle that went all the way to the European Court of Justice. Finally, the Treaty of Rome was evoked, and the British courts had to relent and allow the sex dolls in.

Latex dolls are more expensive than the inflatable vinyl, though arguably not as portable. Latex dolls are more realistic, with glass eyes, wigs, and moulded faces, genitals and extremities. These dolls will set you back a couple of hundred pounds.

The top-of-the-range sex dolls are made from silicon and will set you back anywhere between £5,000 and £20,000, depending on which accessories you opt for. They have flexible joints, very detailed faces, breasts, pubic hair, etc., and detachable genitals to make washing them easier. Many of them are built around a metal skeleton that gives the doll a weight of a 'real woman'.

Simple inflatable vinyl
sex doll, beloved of stag
parties.

Silicon-covered sex robots are currently being manufactured by a range of companies in the US and Japan, including California-based Realbotix, who are leading the race with their Harmony 3.0. Harmony is still in development, but at the time of writing, she can talk, move and answer basic questions. She can't yet respond to touch, but that is the long-term goal of Harmony's creator and Realbotix founder Matt McMullen – that and a self-lubricating vagina.[27]

Sex robots like Harmony have certainly caught the public imagination, and have inspired a host of debate around the ethics, practicalities and feasibility of humans having sex with robots. But these are not new debates. Humans have been having sex with machinery for some time now – the only difference is that vibrators don't ask how your day was, or require their own wardrobe. Sex robots will not replace real people. They are a novelty and no doubt an interesting experience, but sex toys are as old as sex itself, and haven't yet replaced human touch, connection and intimacy. Toys are fun, but they are no substitute for the real deal – for a one thing, no human woman has ever started buffering during a blow-job.

SEX
AND
HYGIENE

Don't Hold
Your Breath
Sex and Smells in the Middle Ages

Although sight is our primary sense, when it comes to sex, it's all about smell. Obviously, looks are important in attracting a mate, but even the hottest of the hot can be undone if they also have ripe BO, bad breath, or cheesy feet. Not being attracted to someone's physical appearance won't make you gag like the sour stink of unwashed genitals. But smelling pleasant goes way beyond improving your chances of getting laid. Our sense of smell motivates human behaviour in truly profound ways. Research has identified a 'behavioural immune system' in humans, meaning we are hardwired to identify and then strongly resist anything that triggers our disgust response. Bad smells trigger an avoidant reaction as a defence mechanism to protect us from health hazards.[1] This may sound obvious, but the behavioural immune system is incredibly powerful and can easily override other instincts, such as sexual attraction or hunger. Research published in *Neuroscience and Behavioural Review* in 2017 revealed that physical disgust, commonly triggered by smell and taste, and moral disgust are inextricably linked in our brains, meaning that if someone smells bad, on one level we are also morally offended by them.[2] So powerful is this response, scientists have actually linked the 2016 election of Donald Trump to our 'body odour disgust sensitivity'. It sounds incredible, but a paper published in the *Royal Society Open Science* journal in 2018 found that right-wing political authoritarians (in this case, Donald

Trump), often promote an avoidance of ethnic and sexual minorities by triggering their audience's primitive disgust reaction. The same primitive reaction to foul odours is triggered by racist rants that present various social groups as a threat to the well-being of others.

> Prejudice can be seen as a social discriminatory behaviour partly motivated by the fact that pathogens represent an invisible threat and individuals with high levels of disgust sensitivity might be more likely to avoid foreign people, and to promote policies that avoid contact with them, because they are perceived as potentially spreading unfamiliar pathogens, or different hygienic or food habits. [3]

When it comes to sexy time, we unconsciously use our sense of smell to assess how healthy our partner is. In 2013, Michael N. Pham theorised humans perform oral sex on each other to secure mating privileges and to try and detect infidelity. He suggested when a man goes down on a woman he is using smell and taste to try and detect foreign sperm.[4] Yum.

In 1989, David Strachan proposed what became known as the 'hygiene hypothesis'.[5] Strachan suggested that in an effort to do away with anything that could trigger our disgust response, we have now killed off bugs we need to develop a resistance to, and collectively weakened our immunity. Strachan's work suggested we need a little muck to be at our best; or as a wise woman once said, if you're not dirty, then you are not here to party. The hygiene hypothesis has been challenged over recent years, but one thing is true: despite Ms Aguilera's protestations, we have never been less dirty, and more aware of cleanliness, hygiene and bacteria than we are today.*

---

* It should be acknowledged that access to clean water, sewage infrastructures and cheap cleaning products is a privilege that people living in urban slums around the world do not enjoy. Inadequate sanitation remains a leading cause of diarrhoeal disease and mortality among children in developing countries,

From face wash for faces to special soaps for your 'special places', almost every part of our bodies has its own specialist cleaning product. Our homes are scrubbed, our clothes are washed, our streets are swept, our air is 'freshened', our odours are eaten, and our food and drink are manufactured within government-specified guidelines. A 2014 UK study conducted by researchers at the universities of Manchester, Edinburgh, Lancaster and Southampton showed that three-quarters of respondents had at least one shower or bath a day.[6] Even if you are reading this sat in the same clothes you've worn for the last two days, with cornflakes in your hair and spaghetti stains on your tits, rest assured: as a society, we have never been so clean.

Which is why if I could transport you back to medieval Europe, the first thing that you would notice would be the smell. The Middle Ages have something of a reputation for being filthy, and this is not without merit. Take almost any fourteenth-century European city at random and you would have to sniff your way through an olfactory assault course of open sewers, mud, animal waste, stagnant water, rotting food, refuse, unwashed bodies and collected filth. In 1332, King Edward III wrote a letter to the mayor of York demanding the city be thoroughly cleaned before he held a parliament meeting there.

> The king, detesting the abominable smell abounding in the said city more than in any other city of the realm from dung and manure and other filth and dirt wherewith the streets and lanes are tilled and obstructed, and wishing to provide for the protection of the health of the inhabitants and of those coming to the present parliament, orders them to cause all the streets and lanes of the city to be cleansed from such filth.[7]

particularly in urban slums. Alison M. Buttenheim, 'The Sanitation Environment in Urban Slums: Implications for Child Health', *Population and Environment*, 30.1-2 (2008), pp. 26–47 <https://doi.org/10.1007/s11111-008-0074-9>.

It is true that the medieval world was far less sanitised than our own, but its people were not unaware of bad smells. Of course, they would have grown accustomed to niffs that would strip the enamel off our teeth, but they feared bad smells. Medieval medicine taught that disease was spread through foul-smelling airs, or 'miasma'. Miasmic theorists were right about the source of bad smells often being a threat to health, but they also believed sweet smells could cure or ward off disease. Comparatively pungent they may have been, but medieval people were just as self-conscious of smelling bad as we are today.*

In his *Canterbury Tales*, written in the fourteenth century, Chaucer gives us visceral portraits of his characters and smell is a key indicator of a pilgrim's moral state. Like many medieval authors, Chaucer links physical ugliness with spiritual ugliness, and he uses foul smells to signify a wrong 'un. The morally bankrupt Summoner's breath smells of onions, garlic and leeks; and Chaucer's cook, a lazy, corrupt thief, is described as a 'stynkyng swyn' whose breath and festering sores are revolting.[8] The hapless fop and forerunner of the metrosexual, Absolon, is heavily perfumed, 'squeamish' about farting, and chews cardamom and liquorice to keep his breath sweet.[9] Absolon souses himself in the medieval equivalent of Lynx Africa because smelling good was a sign of a higher social status. In Malory's *Le Morte d'Arthur* (1485), the poor Sir Gareth is cruelly told to 'stay out of the wind' by the Lady Lynette because he smells of kitchens and 'bawdy clothes'.[10] However, being aware of smelling like the privy on a tuna boat is quite a different thing from being able to do something about it. Bathing requires, at the very least, a river, but, more often than not, it requires bathing facilities and the means to clean yourself and your clothes regularly.

The Romans were famous for bathing. They established lavish bathhouses across the empire, as well as the infrastructure to support

---

* The best book on the history of washing is Katherine Ashenburg, *An Unsanitised History of Washing* (London: Profile, 2009).

Erotic scenes fresco, Memmo di Filippuccio, *c.*1300.

them. Public bathing remained popular across Europe after the collapse of the Roman Empire (*c.* AD 476). But the early Christian Church quickly pulled the plug on the communal soak. As the Christian faith clamped down on sexual freedoms, attitudes to bathing in the buff changed considerably. Not only did public bathing involve nudity, but heat was believed to inflame lustful senses. Theologians like St Jerome (*c.*340–420) had anti-sex agendas that would make the pontiff himself look like a member of Guns N' Roses. Jerome advocated virginity as the supreme moral state, and urged women (in particular) to cultivate 'deliberate squalor' to 'spoil her natural good looks'.[11]

Many monks, hermits and saints saw washing as a sign of vanity and sexual corruption; filth was synonymous with piety and humility. Early Christian militants emphasised spiritual cleanliness over physical cleanliness, even viewing the two as inversely proportional; you could literally stink to high heaven. St Godric (c.1065–1170), for example, walked from England to Jerusalem without ever washing or changing his clothes. Benedictine monks were only permitted to bathe three times a year, at Christmas, Easter and Pentecost. Archbishop of Canterbury, Lanfranc (1005–1089), laid down very precise instructions for monks when bathing. The monks had to gather in the cloister, where a senior monk would guide them one by one to the bathhouse. The monks had to bathe in silence, and on their own. 'When he has sufficiently washed, he shall not stay for pleasure, but shall rise, dress and return to the cloister.'[12] Of course, just because a saintly squad of hardcore soap dodgers shunned the shower, does not mean that every medieval citizen felt the same; but whatever the early medieval washing rota was, by the ninth century, the Roman bath infrastructure had fallen to rack and ruin throughout Christendom.

While the Christians were busy working up a stench that could be weaponised, bathing rituals were widely practised among Jews, Muslims and Buddhists, who believed a holy body was a clean body. Medieval Arab doctors were far more advanced than those in the West and understood the importance of cleanliness and hygiene. The medieval cities of Mecca, Marrakech, Cairo and Istanbul all had their water and bathhouses supplied by well-maintained aqueducts. The *Kitab at-Tasrif* (c.1000) by Al-Zahrawi is a medical encyclopaedia that devotes entire chapters to cosmetics and cleanliness; Al-Zahrawi gives recipes for soap, deodorants, facial creams and hair dyes.[13] In the Muslim world, it was important to smell good and they had the skills to produce perfumes, scented oils and incense. The first recorded perfumer is a woman named Tapputi who lived in Mesopotamia in the second century BC. A cuneiform tablet records that Tapputi made scented oils from flowers, calamus and aromatic spices.[14]

Bathing for ceremonial purposes was widely practised throughout medieval India, especially in sacred rivers that were believed to have

Outer cooling room of a Turkish bathhouse. Wood engraving from *Constantinople and the Scenery of the Seven Churches of Asia Minor*, 1838.

healing powers. Buddhist cleansing rituals soon spread to Tibet, Turkestan, China and Japan. The ancient Chinese text *Liji* (Record of Rites) believed to have been originally composed by Confucius (551–479 BC), contained detailed bathing instructions:

1. A son living with his parents washes his hands and mouth each cockerow.
2. A woman living with her husband's family does likewise.
3. Sons and daughters-in-law attend their parents each morning with hand-washing materials.
4. All children wash hands and mouth at sunup.
5. Household servants do likewise.
6. Children prepare hot water bath for their parents each fifth day, and a hair wash for them every third day.
7. Children heat water to wash their parents' face or feet at any time when they have become dirty.[15]

Yoshitora Utagawa, *Japanese Men and Women Washing in a Traditional Bath House*, 1860.

It was the crusaders who brought the habit of bathing back to medieval Europe. Conversely, for all their 'spiritual purity', the crusaders stank. The medieval Arabian author of *A Thousand and One Nights* was one of many writers appalled at Christian hygiene: 'They never wash, for, at their birth, ugly men in black garments pour water over their heads, and this ablution, accompanied by strange gestures, frees them from the obligation of washing for the rest of their lives.'[16] Happily, the Muslim habit of regular bathing seemed to rub off on the marauding crusaders, and as bathhouses became popular again in medieval Europe once more, bathing became a serious business.

But it wasn't just the habit of social soaking the crusaders brought back from the Holy Lands, they had also learned about the art of perfume. The medieval Europeans had always valued a nice-smelling plant, but oils, soap, colognes and exotic bases for perfume, like civet and musk, were wholly new. Medieval perfumes weren't alcohol-based like modern perfume but were made from oils infused with ingredients such as violet, rose, lavender, rosemary, ambergris, amber or camphor.[17] Rose water, in particular, was the Chanel No. 5 of the Middle Ages. It was regarded as a sacred scent in the Muslim world: it has been argued that mosques were built with rose water mixed into their mortar.[18] In Europe, wealthy hosts would offer guests a bowl of rose water to wash their hands before dinner. Philip the Good, Duke of Burgundy was reported to have owned a statue of a child that peed rose water.[19]

By the thirteenth century there were thirty-two bathhouses in Paris and eighteen in London; even the smaller towns had bathhouses. 'Medicinal' baths were regarded as being very beneficial to health. John Russell's fifteenth-century *Book of Nurture* advises scenting a bath with 'flowers and sweet green herbs', breweswort, chamomile, mallow, fennel and (of course) rose water, to cure all manner of ailments.[20] If you had the money, you could pay for servants to heat water and fill a wooden tub for one, but most people used the public baths.

Historically, wherever you have had public bathing, sex has been working up a lather at the soapy heart of it. This is still the case today, and although all-night saunas can be found in most cities a quick Google of the venue is advised before turning up clutching your soap on a rope. So closely associated are sex and bathing, numerous slang phrases for sex and sex work are derived from bathing: 'lather', as in 'to lather up' was sixteenth-century slang for ejaculation. The word 'bagnio', meaning a brothel, derives from the Latin *balneum*, meaning 'bath'. Likewise, a medieval word for a brothel was a 'stew', which also derives from the bathhouses, where you could literally stew yourself in the hot water and steam. Sex work and saunas were closely associated, and the word 'stew' became synonymous with both.

In the fifteenth century, the city of London officially recognised the Southwark area as a red-light district; it was no coincidence that this was also the area of the city with the highest concentration of bathhouses. One bathhouse in fifteenth-century Avignon was so concerned it might be mistaken for a brothel that they felt it necessary to announce their opening with a clear statement defining themselves as an 'honest' establishment:

> Let everyone of whatever rank be aware that Genin de
> Geline or de Helme, otherwise known as de la Cerveleria,
> has established behind his house at Helme good and honest
> stews for bathing by good and honest women and that these
> are quite separate from the men's bath of de la Cerveleria.[21]

Sebald Benham, *Woman's Bath House*, sixteenth century.

Sanitation was patchy, and Beyoncé's Heat may have been a few centuries off, but the Middle Ages were quite discerning about a sexy smell. In the fourteenth-century *Decameron*, for example, Boccaccio clearly links sex and smell together.

> Without permitting anyone else to lay a hand on him, the lady herself washed Salabaetto all over with soap scented with musk and cloves. She then had herself washed and rubbed down by the slaves. This done, the slaves brought two fine and very white sheets, so scented with roses that they seemed like roses; the slaves wrapped Salabaetto in one and the lady in the other and then carried them both on their shoulders to the bed ... They then took from the basket silver vases of great beauty, some of which were filled with rose water, some with orange water, some with jasmine water, and some with lemon water, which they sprinkled upon them.[22]

The medieval guidebook *Le Ménagier de Paris* (1393) is full of helpful advice on smelling attractive: sage water is recommended, along with 'chamomile, marjoram, or rosemary boiled with orange peel'.[23] William Langham's *Garden of Health* (1579) recommends adding rosemary to a bath: 'Seethe much Rosemary, and bathe therein to make thee lusty, lively, joyfull, likeing and youngly.'[24] *Delights for Ladies* (1609) suggests distilling water with cloves, orris powder, nutmeg and cinnamon. And in a medieval forerunner of the Lynx effect, the civet effect meant musk harvested from the glands of the civet cat became highly desirable, along with castor from the anal glands of a beaver and whale vomit (ambergris), but these were luxury items. If you really want to know the smell of illicit medieval sex, it's lavender.

The word lavender comes from the latin word *lavare*, which means to wash. It has been used for thousands of years for its sweet smell. Unlike the more exotic and expensive perfumes, lavender grows all over Europe and is both cheap and readily available. Lavender was widely used in washing clothes, and washerwomen became known as 'lavenders'; in fact, the word 'launder' derives from lavender. As historian Ruth Mazo Karras identified, one medieval profession that was especially connected to sex work was the washerwoman.[25] Medieval laundresses were very poor, and had a reputation for making ends meet by 'dollymopping' (1859) (subsidising their income with sex work). Chaucer translates Dante's *meretrice* (harlot) as 'lavender' in *The Legend of the Good Woman* (*c*.1380), metaphorically drawing on the double meaning of being at once both dirty and clean.

> Envye (I prey to god yeve hir mischaunce!)
> Is lavender in the grete court I.
> For she ne parteth, neither night ne day.[26]

Walter of Hemingburgh tells a story of King John, who thought he was seducing a married noblewoman, but instead had been sent 'a horrid whore and laundress'.[27] The sixteenth-century poem 'Ship of Fools' includes the following lines:

> Thou shalt be my lavender Laundress
> To wash and keep clean all my gear,
> Our two beds together shall be set
> Without any let.[28]

Given lavender's rather conservative and somewhat old-fashioned reputation today, I take great delight in knowing that elderly women and aromatherapists the world over actually smell like a medieval strumpet.

But the fun was not to last. Public bathhouses went into steep decline across Europe in the sixteenth century. New medical advice suggested bathing weakened the body, and that cleaning the skin left it open to infection. Periodic outbreaks of plague and the arrival of syphilis in the fifteenth century certainly burst the bath bubble. As people became cautious about bathing, washing the body was replaced with washing your shirt instead. Linen, in particular, was thought to draw out and absorb sweat. Therefore, one only needed to swap shirts to be clean. This method of 'bathing' became so popular that French mansions were designed without bathrooms. Bathing would not come back into vogue in Europe until the eighteenth century, with the rise of the spa.

When Monty Python sent up preconceptions about the Middle Ages in *Holy Grail* (1975), the dead collector correctly identifies Arthur as the king, because he is the one who 'hasn't got shit all over him'.[29] In 2004, beloved Python Terry Jones published his *Medieval Lives,* where he set about redeeming the Middle Ages from unjust stigmas such as smelling of shit. Far from living in a ditch, eating twigs and rubbing themselves with sewage, the citizens of the Middle Ages actually smelled quite good; certainly better than the people of the Renaissance, who believed bathing would make them ill. Medieval lovers valued clean bodies, sweet breath, regular scrubbing and an array of perfumes. They also knew the aphrodisiacal qualities of various scents, oils and plants. They enjoyed mixed-sex communal bathing and invested in bathing infrastructure. Sex was very much a part of the culture of communal bathing: at worst it was tolerated, at best it was fully embraced and enjoyed. The medieval period was undeniably grubbier than our own, but they embraced cleanliness as fully as they could, and their harlots smelled of lavender.

Hair Today, Gone Tomorrow

A History of Pubic Hair

O ne of the best and scariest things about Twitter is the instant feedback. I have posted all kinds of historical titbits, which have led to some fairly heated debates in the Twittersphere. But no subject causes the reaction that pubic hair does. Whenever I post an image of a woman with a full 'bush' (1600), inevitably an argument ensues. Interestingly, for as long as I have been tweeting them, no one has ever commented on the state of a gentleman's manscape, but a woman's knicker 'whiskers' (1942) will upset someone every time. A criticism that comes up and again and again is cleanliness. Somehow, a full 'thatch' (1833) has become associated with being dirty and unhygienic.

Twitter users' reactions to a nineteenth-century photograph of a woman with pubic hair.

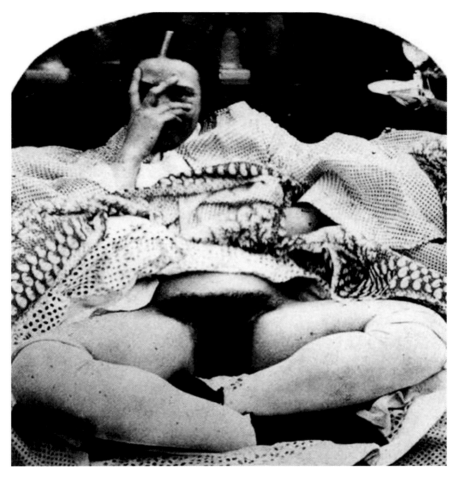

A Victorian lady, resplendent in fuzz.

Let's be clear about one thing: this chapter is not pushing you to cultivate a full bush, nor am I going to recommend fashioning yourself after an eel and marinating in a bathtub of Veet. Whatever the hell you want to do to your own body hair is entirely your choice: wax the lot off and decorate your bald pubis with macaroni pasta and sparkles, or weave dreadlocks and have them hanging down your leg. It's your hair and I fully support whatever you want to do with it. But this is what I do want you to think about: when did our own body hair become alien to us? How have we arrived at the conclusion that pubic hair is 'disgusting' or 'gross'? Because this is always the cause of the arguments: someone recoils in horror at the sight of a woman with pubic hair you could wipe your feet on, and voices this online. Having a 'type' is one thing, but this voicing usually goes well beyond expressing a personal preference, and marches straight into outright revulsion at the prospect of a lady 'garden' (1966) gone to seed.

When did this happen? When did our body hair, hair we have all got, hair that is supposed to be there, start to elicit the same levels of disgust as a matted hairball bunging up the plughole? It gets even stranger when you consider that a mere two foot north of the offending 'silent beard' (1702) is another crop of hair that we collectively devote billions of pounds every year to styling. A cursory glance at any hairstyle magazine reveals adjectives such as 'glamorous', 'sultry', 'flowing' and 'luxurious' being used to describe a mop that tops and tails another barnet capable of making adults wince. Again, I am not trying to convince you to allow your 'pubes' (1721) to go feral, but I do want to pause and ask why are we so anti-fuzz? Because that's where we currently are: our own bodies revolt us, and we shame people for having hair that we have too.

So where did all this start?

Many have pinned our plucking obsession on the *Sex and the City* phenomenon, and there may indeed be some truth to this, but removing body hair goes back much further than Carrie Bradshaw discussing Brazilians over cocktails with the girls. The earliest solid evidence we have of hair removal comes from ancient Egypt and Mesopotamia. I say solid, because it has been speculated that prehistoric man would have managed his beard and hair – but without unearthing a neolithic Gillette Mach Three we are unlikely to be able to confirm this.

The removal of pubic hair is an ancient Islamic tradition and is done for hygiene, as well as religious reasons. Although the Quran doesn't mention body hair, Abu Hurayra (AD 603–681), a companion of Muhammad, once said 'five things are fitra: circumcision, shaving pubic hair with a razor, trimming the moustache, paring one's nails and plucking the hair from one's armpits'.[1] The Niğde Archaeological Museum in Turkey and the Museum of Anatolian Civilisations in Ankara both hold examples of obsidian razors dating to 6500 BC, which are the oldest known examples of hair removal in the world.[2] Removing pubic hair is still a widely observed practice in Islam today.

According to the *Encyclopaedia of Hair*, copper razors dating back to 3000 BC were found among ruins in Egypt and Mesopotamia; tweezers and pumice stones have been found in Egyptian tombs.[3] This was done for aesthetic but also for religious reasons: Ancient Egyptian priests shaved or depilated all over daily, so as to present a 'pure' body before the gods.

Evidence of pubic hair removal becomes less patchy (if you'll excuse the pun) in Ancient Greece and Rome. The Greek playwright Aristophanes (446–386 BC) wrote: if women 'pluck and trim [their] doorways like good spiders; the flies come strolling in'.[4] The very wealthy Romans could even employ a 'picatrix', a young female slave whose job was to style her mistress's pubic hair.[5] But we also have evidence that not everyone in the Ancient World favoured the shaven haven. Written on the walls of the Roman city of Pompeii are the immortal lines: 'A hairy cunt is fucked much better than one which is smooth; it holds in the steam and wants cock.'[6] What this charming sentiment shouted from AD 79 tells us, is that beneath the toga some women were smooth and some were hairy, and some were steaming (apparently).

Of course, the Greeks and Romans were public bathers, so pubic hairstyling was of some consequence, but the coiffured cunt seems to have fallen out of favour in the Middle Ages. The supreme beauty for the medieval women (in Europe, at least) was pale, smooth, slightly plump, with a high forehead and a shiny face; nowhere are a lady's 'tail feathers' (1890) mentioned.[7] But, frustratingly, references to removing hair to achieve this ideal are very rare in medieval texts. A notable exception is Trotula de Ruggiero's eleventh-century treatise *De Ornatu Mulierum* (About Women's Cosmetics), which includes this entry: 'In order permanently to remove hair. Take ants' eggs, red orpiment, and gum of ivy, mix with vinegar, and rub the areas.'[8] As concepts of sexual sin changed, attitudes to pubic preening also changed, and hair removal came to be considered vain, and therefore sinful. In the medieval *Confessionale*, clergymen are encouraged to ask those who came to confession: 'If she has plucked hair from her neck, or brows or beard for lasciviousness or to please men … This is a mortal sin unless she does so to remedy severe disfigurement or so as not to be looked down on by her husband.'[9]

One of the most famous references to pubic hair in medieval literature comes from Chaucer's 'The Miller's Tale' (1400). A love-struck but simpering parish clerk, Absolon, is in love with the miller's young wife, Alison (but she is having it away with her lodger, Nicolas). Absolon sings outside her window late at night and begs for a kiss. Intensely frustrated with his wooing, Alison sticks her 'naked ers' (arse) out the window, where, in the darkness, Absolon kisses 'her hole', believing it to be her mouth; he then jumps back, having 'felte a thyng al rough and long'. Disgusted, Absolon then begins to shout that 'womman hath no berd' (beard), and Alison and Nicolas fall about laughing 'A berd! A berd!' For Alison's Brazilian blowout to be described as 'rough and long', like a 'beard', suggests this sex kitten does not favour the razor.[10]

By the sixteenth century, texts that combined medical treatments with beauty treatments became increasingly popular. A 1532 beauty manual gives this recipe for a homemade depilatory cream: 'Boil together a solution of one pint of arsenic and eighth of a pint of quicklime. Go to a baths or a hot room and smear medicine over the area to be depilated. When the skin feels hot, wash quickly with hot water so the flesh doesn't come off.'[11] There is no detail on this concoction being used on the pubic area, but we all hope it was not. Francisco Delicado's *La Lozana Andaluza* (1528) is about a Roman sex worker, Lozana. She talks about whores 'who pluck their eyebrows and others who shave their private parts'. She also recounts how she accidentally 'burned off all the hair from the private parts of a lady from Bologna' and healed it by salving it with butter.[12] While some women were obviously willing to souse their 'trouser sprouts' (2000) in acid, pubic hair was seen by many Europeans as the must-have sexual accessory. Slang terms for pubic hair from the Renaissance are overwhelmingly positive and include 'feathers', 'fleece', 'flush', 'moss', 'plush', 'plume' and the 'admired abode'.

Shakespeare makes a number of bawdy pubic hair double entendres in his work, suggesting 'muff' (1655) was de rigueur. In his *Venus and Adonis*, Shakespeare writes about 'Sweet bottom-grass' that lies between 'Round rising hillocks';[13] in *Much Ado About Nothing*, Cupid is wryly referred to as a 'good Hare finder',[14] and many have argued that the 'black wires' that grow upon the speaker's mistress in 'Sonnet 130' is a reference to pubic hair.[15] But more than just being the norm, an abundance of pubic hair was a sign of health, youth and sexual vitality. The hero of Richard Head's *The English Rogue* (1665) complains that an elderly woman he sleeps with had no pubic hair: 'I apprehended my danger the greater because I found no rushes growing there, which is an observation of the people; judging the bog passable which hath such things growing there on.'[16] The Renaissance Brit, in particular, favoured a Hairy Potter. Spenser, in *Strange and True Conference* (1660), wonders at 'the Spanish mode of shaving off all the wenches' hairs off their commodities'.[17] And the Earl of Rochester declared, 'My prick no more to bald cunt shall resort.'[18]

Thomas Rowlandson,
*The Hairy Prospect or
the Devil in a Fright*, 1800.

THE HAIRY PROSPECT or THE DEVIL IN A FRIGHT.

Once on a time the Sire of evil
In plainer English call'd the devil
Some new experiment to try
At Chloe cast a roguish eye
But she who all his arts defied
Pull'd it and shew'd her sexes pride
A thing all shagg'd about with hair
So much it made old Satan stare
Who frighten'd at the grim display
Takes to his heels and runs away

One reason for removing hair was pubic lice, which could only be got rid of by shaving, but an even more unpleasant reason for malting muffs was syphilis. Syphilis was first recorded in Naples in 1495, and one of the many unpleasant symptoms of secondary-stage syphilis is hair loss (head hair, eyebrows and pubic hair). Even though this is a rare symptom, the treatment for syphilis was mercury, which most certainly does cause hair loss. As a result, patchy pubes came to be regarded as a sign of disease. Whereas we may view a snatch patch as 'disgusting', your Elizabethan lover would have viewed a 'bald eagle' (1987) in very much the same way. In Thomas Middleton's *Trick to Catch the Old One* (1605), a character called Audrey is attacked as an 'unfeathered, cremitoried quean, you cullisance of scabiosity'.[19] In *Westminster Whore* (1610), one 'lascivious bitch' is cursed to have 'a cunt without hair and ten thousand poxes'.[20] And in *Night Searches* (1640), Mill describes whores who are 'out of date, some tattered; some want a fleece, some a nose'.[21] One 'Loose Song' from 1650 tells of a man who refuses to have sex with a pubeless woman as 'her stuff rustles like buff leather jerkin'.[22]

If a lady had got to the point that a comb-over was no longer disguising her tufty 'tuppence' (1987), she could always go for a pubic wig (merkin). *The Oxford Companion to the Body* points to 1450 as the year 'malkin' – from which the name for a pubic hair wig derives – first appeared.[23] Rochester complains the 'Merkins rub off and spoil the sport'.[24] Mentions of the merkin appears in numerous slang dictionaries from 1600s until the nineteenth century. The merkin is also mentioned in Alexander Smith's *A Complete History of the Lives and Robberies of the Most Notorious Highwaymen* (1714) in a bizarre story of a highwayman selling a cardinal a harlot's merkin and telling him it's St Peter's beard: 'This put a strange Whim in his Head; which was to get the hairy circle of [a] prostitute's Merkin … this he dry'd well, and comb'd out, and then return'd to the Cardinal, telling him he had brought St Peter's Beard.'[25]

Though some ladies may have been wigging it, throughout the eighteenth century bush was most certainly meant to be lush. Despite the introduction of Jean-Jacques Perret's safety razor in 1770, pubic hair was still associated with rude health. *Harris's List of Covent Garden Ladies* 1757–95, an almanac of sex workers available in London, is extremely positive about 'the mossy grot'. Miss Devenport is described as being well thatched, 'though not yet *bushy*, might truly be stiled *Black Heath*'; Miss Betsy has 'ebony tendrils that play in wanton ringlets round the grot', and Madam D—sl—z's 'lower tendrils, which sport on her alabaster mount of Venus, are formed to give delight'.[26] Cleland's heroine, Fanny Hill (1749), describes the 'mossy mounts' of

Two girls and a muff, nineteenth century.

her 'soft laboratory of love', and 'the curling hair that overspread'.[27] Fanny also admires her lover Phoebe, who 'played and strove to twine in the young tendrils of that moss, which nature has contrived at once for use and ornament'.[28]

Victorian erotica is also full of praise for the 'happy trail' (2003), in some cases describing a 'tuzy-muzy' (1672) that, frankly, could scour a greasy pot clean. In *Romance of Lust* (1875), the hero Charlie Roberts describes many furry lovers and finds body hair a turn-on.

> Her position brought out all the beauties of the vast wide-
> spread mass of black curly hair that thickly covered all the
> lower part of her magnificent quim, ran down each thigh,
> up between her buttocks, and opening out on her back,
> had two bunches just below the two beautiful dimples
> that were so charmingly developed below her waist. There
> was as much hair there as most women have on their
> mons Veneris. Her whole body had fine straight silky hair
> on it, very thick on the shoulders, arms and legs, with a
> beautiful creamy skin showing below. She was the hairiest
> woman I ever saw, which, doubtless, arose from or was
> the cause of her extraordinary lustful and luxurious
> temperament. The sight I was indulging in brought out
> my pego in full bloom; as we both rose she saw it sticking
> out under my shirt.[29]

Francisco Goya's *The Nude Maja* (1797) is considered to be the first European painting to show a female subject's pubic hair, but women continued to be depicted with featureless genitals in high art throughout the nineteenth century.

Indeed, it has been suggested that one of the reasons the famous art critic John Ruskin was unable to consummate his marriage to Euphemia

Francisco Goya's *The Nude Maja*, 1797, is considered to be one of the first depictions of pubic hair in Western art.

Gray was because he was horrified to find that, unlike works of art, women have pubic hair. Their marriage was never consummated and was eventually annulled, and the only clue we have as to why is in a letter written by Euphemia in 1848.

> Finally, this last year he told me his true reason (and this
> to me is as villainous as all the rest), that he had imagined
> women were quite different to what he saw I was, and that
> the reason he did not make me his Wife is that he was
> disgusted with my person the first evening.[30]

Despite Ruskin's anxieties, some Victorian women did practise hair removal, as shown on the next two pages; we can even see some of the first 'landing strips' (2014).

The absence of the merkin suggests that a mowed lawn was coming back into fashion once more, or at least it was no longer regarded as a symptom of disease. It seems likely that the retreat of pubic hair in the Western world is linked to the emergence of photography and pornography. It is certainly linked to being 'seen'. Roman and Greek

An anonymous Victorian lady showing that porn can be fun, as well as providing some evidence of pubic hair removal in the nineteenth century.

An anonymous Victorian lady shows off her shaven haven while enjoying the daily news.

women plucked their pudendum because nudity was commonplace, but as bodies were covered up and were called 'sinful', there were far fewer pussies on parade. With the advent of photography and film, genitals were once again seen. Of course, you can look at your own unmentionables, maybe even your friends', but there's nothing quite like looking at a sexualised image of a stranger to have you doubting your own sexual appeal. Fashion has certainly played its part: the removal of underarm hair is directly linked to the new fashion for sleeveless dresses in the 1920s, and a cunning advertising campaign that told women they smelled bad. Leg shaving increased as skirt length decreased, and as underwear shrank to something you could floss with (hello G-string), pubic hair disappeared too.

I've heard many times that the heyday of the bush was the 1960s and 1970s, which simply isn't true. But it was at this time that porn started to become mainstream. It was not that the 'rug' (1939) was back in fashion — it had never been out of fashion — it's simply that we saw more of it. And, of course, the women were splendidly bewhiskered; no one had told them not to be. Pubic hair appeared for the first time in *Penthouse* in 1970. In 1974, *Hustler* published the first 'pink shots' of labial flesh, but hair was still very much on the menu. By the mid-seventies *Playboy*'s circulation surpassed 7 million. That pussy pelt has gone AWOL in recent years is often linked directly to pornography becoming mainstream, but perhaps we should cast our nets a little wider than that. Yes, porn is far more accessible, but we are living in an image-saturated society that constantly reinforces what is 'normal'. But it is not just porn that cue-balls its women: toys, fashion magazines, newspapers, film, television, advertising, music videos, etc., will not show you a single trouser tendril (unless it's in an arty, subversive manner). It's like looking for a pube in a haystack. The reason people react so strongly to women with pubic hair is that they are not used to seeing it; it's not their normal. The less we see it, the 'weirder' it looks when we do.

One of the slightly more disturbing associations with pubic hair removal is hygiene. I hear that all the time; it's just 'cleaner'. Research carried out by University of California found that more than half of 3,000 women surveyed who groomed their pubic hair did so for

Ashes depilatory cream advert that ran in *Harper's Bazaar*, 1922. This advert taps into two major insecurities – avoiding embarrassment and looking attractive.

hygiene reasons, despite evidence that shaving pubic hair can make the vagina more vulnerable to irritation and infection.[31] So, I'll say this only once: if the hair on your head doesn't make your scalp stink, pubic hair will not make your vulva 'dirty'.

In recent years, there have been rumblings that the bush is on its way back. In 2014, American Apparel displayed mannequins with merkins in their New York flagship store. In 2016, society bible *Tatler* announced the 'bush is back'. Caitlin Moran has declared that all women should have a 'big, hairy muff'. Gwyneth Paltrow revealed that she 'works a seventies vibe'. I suspect that as more and more celebrities 'normalise' the mighty muff, it will become acceptable once more. Pubic hair is frequently placed on the frontline of feminism; growing a new band member for ZZ Top in your pants is often seen as a fuzzy fuck you to a patriarchy that leaves you literally tearing your hair out. However, more broadly I hope this chapter has shown that fretting about the quality and quantity of your 'sporran' (1890) has a long, tangled history, and so too do the many painful and dangerous methods of hair removal that we've invented. But for most of our collective history, pubic hair was not only normal, but regarded as sexy, healthy and luscious. So whatever you want to do to yours, I promise, it's all been done before.

Filthy Fannies

A History of Douching

Have you ever wondered why the vulva has specialised cleaning products when the penis can happily make do with a flannel? Your 'pipkin' (1654) is entirely self-cleaning and does not require you to go at it with a scrubbing brush and a bottle of 'Twinkle-Twat' to be happy and healthy. Trust me, it knows what it's doing. But clearly, we do not trust 'Mrs Laycock' (1756) to keep a clean shop. The human body has numerous crevices that can get a bit whiffy from time to time, but this is rarely anything that regular bathing can't keep at bay. While everyone is on the sniff for any kind of body odour, smells coming from 'south of the border' (1945) seem to hold a particular terror for those in possession of a vulva. We would much rather it smelled like an alpine forest than like a healthy human 'madge' (1785).

Anyone who grows up with a vulva soon learns it is a dirty place. No one ever sits us down at school and tells us this, but it's a message that comes through loud and clear when we first trudge through the lexical fields of meat, seafood and general putrescence that characterises vulva slang. When we realise tampons and sanitary pads are sold as 'feminine hygiene products', we learn that periods are unhygienic. We overhear fish jokes, stinky finger jibes and watch people wince at the word 'period' and start to panic about our own bodies. Vaginal deodorants, magazine articles that recommend eating pineapple to 'taste better', and panty pads that will help you 'stay fresh' all tacitly reinforce the message that the 'bearded oyster' (1916) is some kind of a swamp that requires careful maintenance. Little wonder that the 'vaginal odour' business is booming and is projected to expand by 5 per cent every year from 2018 to 2022.[1] But the fear of smelling bad has consequences far more serious than the occasional purchase of specialised lady wipes. Research carried out by Jo's Cervical Cancer Trust in 2018 surveyed over 2,000 women and found that 38 per cent of their respondents didn't attend their smear test because they had 'concerns over smelling "normally"'.[2] The shame around not having a vulva that smells like a bag of bon-bons is now so great that people are putting their lives at risk.

It's a shame we have been so desperate to make pussy smell like potpourri, because all the research shows that the natural smell of your 'flue' (1620) is actually pretty important. Research published back in the 1970s found that on average a vulva contains 21,000 'odoriferous effluents'. The research concluded that 'the olfactory signature of an individual is complex, highly individual and composed of many "mini odours"'.[3] In other words, every vulva has its own signature scent that is completely unique to its owner. Other studies carried out on primates, rats and hamsters found that the odour in vaginal secretions causes a spike in testosterone in a nearby male, which plays a significant role in sexual arousal.[4] Human vulvas produce and secrete a mixture of five fatty acids called 'copulins' – not to be confused with the northern chain of bakeries, Cooplands – which also smell pretty good. Copulin research is still quite new, but studies have already shown that men exposed to copulins experienced an increase in testosterone and after a whiff will rate themselves as more sexually attractive than men in the placebo group. What's more, men exposed to copulins will rate women's faces as being more attractive than men not exposed to copulins do.[5] Why on earth would anyone want to wash this mind-melding superpower away? But sadly, water-boarding one's 'whim-wham' (1602) in order to eliminate anything close to a smell has a very long history indeed.

A mid-fifteenth-century miniature showing a clyster (enema) in a pear-shaped anal douche.

Vaginal deodorants, soaps and wipes are quite late arrivals at the paranoid pussy party. The oldest method of swabbing the decks is douching. A douche is a device that squirts water into the vaginal cavity – or the anal cavity, if you prefer. At its most basic, a shower-head can be used as a douche, but more elaborate contraptions that come equipped with baking soda or alum to add to the water are readily available online. Despite evidence proving that vaginal douching is linked to ovarian and cervical cancer, pelvic inflammatory disease, ectopic pregnancy, bacterial vaginosis, infertility and thrush, as many as one in five women are regularly douching their vaginas for 'hygiene' reasons.[6]

Although douching can be traced back to the Ancient World, it really came into its own in the nineteenth century, when doctors sanctioned it as a reliable method of birth control.*

The douche was the first form of birth control widely advocated

---

* Physicians such as Soranus (*c.* AD 98–138) and Oribasius (*c.* AD 320–400) recommend rinsing the vagina after sex as a form of contraception. Robert Jütte, *Contraception: A History* (Cambridge: Polity, 2008).

by physicians and embraced by women from all races and socioeconomic backgrounds, but this wasn't just about preventing pregnancy. Douching has always been caught up in paranoid narratives about the dirty 'daisy' (1834).

In 1832, Charles Knowlton, a physician from New England, published a medical treatise advocating an antiseptic douche after sex as being 'conducive to cleanliness' and preventing pregnancy.[7] This must have come as welcome news as Victorian doctors were already hell-bent on scrubbing out 'cunny court' (1604) for reasons of hygiene. In 1829, an article in *The Lancet* suggested women wash out their vaginas 'six or eight times in the course of the day' by syringing in tepid water to keep everything in tip-top condition.[8] This kind of advice persisted throughout the nineteenth century. In 1880, for example, Dr Wing announced that 'a woman should have a clean vagina as well as clean face and hands' and recommended regular 'vaginal injections' of hot water and carbolic acid.[9] In 1889, the Massachusetts Medical Society recommended douching women in labour so 'that the woman may start with a clean vagina, not solely for the benefit of the woman but also for the benefit of the child'.[10] And in 1895, *The International Encyclopaedia of Surgery* recommended a vaginal 'injection, night and morning, of one gallon of hot water (110° F), followed by two quarts of a solution of bichloride of Mercury' to treat venereal disease.[11]

The Victorians took their douches very seriously, and in 1843 Parisian doctor Maurice Eguisier (1813–1851) unveiled the Irrigateur Eguisier, a pressure-controlled cylindrical pump and hose made from metal and porcelain. The Irrigateur Eguisier was produced in a variety of sizes and designs. Many were beautifully painted with delicate scenes of flora and fauna, which must have been something of a comfort as you squirted cold water and carbolic acid up your chuff.

In 1866, the Obstetric Society of London held an exhibition of historical gynaecological instruments. The event was hugely successful,

Douches such as this one, although unreliable, were one of the most common methods of contraception in this era. The cylindrical metal supply vessel has a pump mechanism which controls the passage of rinsing fluid to the hose, 1912.

and the Obstetric Society published a catalogue describing all the instruments that had been on show, as well as the most up-to-date instruments used in obstetrics at the time – including douches.[12] Viewing the other contraptions on offer, one can see why Maurice Eguisier's lightweight and portable Irrigateur Eguisier proved to be so popular. One of the most cumbersome douches in the catalogue was designed by John Wiess and looks like a table, holding a large rubber balloon of water. The user would sit down on the balloon, forcing the water into the attached pipe and hose. J. Lazarewitch from Russia, meanwhile, had designed a clunky cylindrical metal douche, which had a sieve at the bottom to prevent anything undesirable entering the vagina (beyond an enormous Russian douche shaped like a fire hydrant, that is).[13]

Douching with water is damaging enough, but in order to prevent pregnancy, doctors started adding all manner of chemicals to douche water in order to kill off the sperm. Charles Knowlton, for example, recommended douching with 'a solution of sulphate of zinc, of alum, pearl-ash, or any salt that acts chemically on the semen'.[14] In 1898, the *Monthly Retrospect of Medicine & Pharmacy* lists the following 'fluids to be used for vaginal douching' to prevent conception: alum, acetate of lead, chloride, boracic acid, carbolic acid, iodine, mercury, zinc and Lysol disinfectant.[15]

Lysol brand disinfectant was introduced in 1889 to control a severe cholera epidemic in Germany.[16] But its antiseptic qualities were soon put to other uses, and by the 1920s Lysol was being aggressively marketed as a vaginal douching agent. Birth control was a highly controversial issue in the 1920s and certainly not something to be openly advertised. By focusing on the issue of 'feminine hygiene' within marriage in their advertising campaign, Lysol could raise the subject of sex and intimacy without ever having to use the word 'sex'. Soon, a product that was used to scrub out bins, drains and toilets was being used to clean vulvas as well. One advert featured in *Ladies' Home Journal* in November 1920 recommended using Lysol to sanitise 'toilets, closets, cuspidors, garbage cans, and places where flies gather', and goes on to point out that 'women find Lysol Disinfectant also invaluable for personal hygiene'. The suggestion that a cleaning product used to clear blocked drains was needed to douche out the 'nether eye' (1902) can have left the public in no doubt: vulvas stink.

Lysol douche adverts are not shy in informing women that vulvas stink, and usually feature a young wife whose husband is on the verge of walking out because she has neglected her 'personal feminine hygiene'. A distraught and humiliated woman is shown left alone and tearful because her husband couldn't stand the smell of her 'old lady' (1885). Homes lie in ruins, children are left fatherless and the poor woman will now die alone, and all because she failed to disinfect her

Still
"the girl he married"

WHEN they were first married, five years ago, they liked to dance together, go motoring together, play golf together. They still like to do those things together today. She is still the girl he married.

During the years following her marriage, she has protected her zest for living, her health and youthfulness, and "stayed young with him" by the *correct* practice of feminine hygiene.

But feminine hygiene, wrongly practiced, does more harm than good. Using the wrong disinfectant may lead to very serious consequences.

Realizing this, the makers of "Lysol" Disinfectant have prepared a booklet called "The Scientific Side of Health and Youth." It gives the facts about this vital subject. Send the coupon now. The booklet will reach you in a plain envelope. It is free.

In the meantime, take no needless, dangerous chances. Buy a bottle of "Lysol" Disinfectant at your druggist's today. Complete, explicit directions come with every bottle.

Made by Lysol, Incorporated, a division of Lehn & Fink Products Company. Sole distributors, Lehn & Fink, Inc., Bloomfield, N.J. In Canada, Lysol (Canada) Limited. Distributed by Lehn & Fink (Canada) Limited.

LEHN & FINK, Inc., *Sole Distributors,* Bloomfield, N.J.
Department 149
Please send me, free, your booklet,
"The Scientific Side of Health and Youth."

Name .... City ....
Street .... State ....

© Lehn & Fink, Inc., 1932

A Lysol douche advert. 'Still "the girl he married"', thanks to scouring her genitals with floor cleaner.

'grumble' (1938). It's an unbelievably cruel campaign.*

Because Lysol could not advertise itself openly as a form of contraception, they had to subtly hint at its spermicidal properties. Many of the adverts mention how effective Lysol is at destroying 'organic matter', which is a coded reference to sperm.

Not only is douching with toilet disinfectant not a reliable method of contraception, but it is also extremely dangerous. In the first half of the twentieth century, drinking Lysol was a common method of suicide and newspapers are crammed full of such tragic cases. Despite repeated

---

* It's worth pointing out here that the company behind the early twentieth-century Lysol douching campaign was Lehn and Fink. Today, Lysol is owned by Reckitt Benckiser who had nothing to do with the original campaign, and whose customer service team are just lovely to random women who email them out of the blue to ask about putting Lysol in their 'fanny' (1834). For the record, although the Lysol product from ninety years ago is not the Lysol product people see on shelves today, they did ask that I make sure everyone reading this book fully understood that 'today's Lysol product should only be used as per label instruction. Any other form of use or exposure is to be avoided.'

claims that Lysol was gentle and would not damage delicate tissue, by 1911 doctors had recorded 193 women who had been poisoned with Lysol douches, and five deaths from 'uterine irrigation'.[17] Despite never admitting liability, Lysol changed their formula in 1952 to be a quarter as toxic as before.

Eventually, contraceptive douching was replaced by the Pill and latex condoms (things that actually work). But this just meant that marketers redoubled their efforts to convince women they smelled bad and only their product could cure this.

Whole-page adverts pushing flavoured douches were common in the 1970s. In 1971, *Essence Magazine* ran an article called 'Beauty Wonders: No Smell So Sweet', which asked women if 'you're getting more attention in a crowd than usual, or if your ole' man turns off the instant you come near, then it's about time to check out why. Could be, your hygiene-thing isn't as up-tight as it should be ... and that's inexcusable, my dears.'[18] The article then recommends all manner of wipes, soaps and deodorants to make sure women could walk down the street without people passing out in their wake. The blunt and

Had she only known the truth ... *earlier*

—*about feminine hygiene*

WHAT regrets, what suffering, might be escaped were women to make *use* of their information concerning this intimate matter of feminine hygiene! And yet, how difficult it *does* seem to get at the truth!

So far as *advice* is concerned, the young woman of today receives plenty of it. This is a frank age. But, unfortunately, wrong advice is just as common as it was in the days of our grandmothers—and just as much to be feared.

*Women can banish their fears
—through Zonite*

"What antiseptic to use?" That is the big problem. For how much suffering has come about because women do not understand the terrible risks attending the use of deadly poisons such as bichloride of mercury and the compounds of carbolic acid.

Physicians know the truth. That is why their recommendation of *Zonite* has real significance. An antiseptic that kills germs yet is absolutely non-poisonous. An antiseptic which cannot irritate sensitive membranes nor cause areas of scar-tissue. An antiseptic actually *far more powerful* than any dilution of carbolic acid that can be allowed on the body. Such are the properties of Zonite.

You will want this booklet

Send for free feminine hygiene booklet. Frank, authentic, really helpful. Zonite Products Corporation, 250 Park Ave., New York, N. Y.

Use Zonite Ointment for burns, abrasions, sunburn or chapped skin. Also as a powerful deodorant in banishing stout form. Large tubes, 30c.

ZONITE PRODUCTS CORPORATION
250 Park Avenue, New York, N. Y.
Please send me free copy of the Zonite booklet or booklets checked below:
☐ The Newer Knowledge of Feminine Hygiene
☐ Use of Antiseptics in the Home
(Please print name)   41-C

Name...
Address..
City...
(In Canada 165 Dufferin St., Toronto)

A 1928 advertisement for Zonite douche liquid in *McCall's Magazine* shows a grumpy woman who regrets not disinfecting her vulva sooner.

FEMININE HYGIENE
YOUR **SUMMER** PROBLEM OF
CLEANLINESS AND DAINTINESS

Don't let doubts haunt
you this vacation! Get
Boro-Pheno-Forms, just
like thousands of women
who KNOW this secret
of poise and charm!
These convenient suppositories are ready-to-
use, EACH COMPLETE in itself; dainty,
soothing, deodorizing, medicated. Ask any
druggist for fact-and-picture booklet or write
DR. PIERRE CHEMICAL CO., Dept. H-26
2020 Montrose Ave., Chicago 18, Ill.
"Ask Any Druggist Anywhere"

BORO DR. PIERRE'S **FORM**
PHENO

1950 advert for 'Dr Pierre's Boro-Pheno-Form Feminine Hygiene Suppositories'.

offensive nature of vintage adverts may shock you, but the vaginal deodorant business continues to boom today. The marketing may have softened its approach since warning young women their husbands will leave them if they haven't scoured themselves raw and installed an air freshener, but these products still make their money by convincing customers their vulvas require a specialist cleaning kit, that it needs extra cleaning that only they can provide – and that stinks.

A word that crops up again and again in vintage douche adverts is 'dainty'. Women must douche to maintain their 'dainty feminine allure', to 'stay dainty', and 'safeguard your daintiness'. The idea that one must remove all vaginal odour in order to be 'feminine' and 'dainty' is telling. There is nothing sexy about dainty. Vulvas aren't dainty. They can eat a penis and push out a baby. They are bloody, sweaty, sticky, hairy, seats of awesome pleasure, and their natural odour is immediately linked to sex. I suspect this is what we have been trying to wash away. A 'dainty' woman is not a sexual woman. Her pussy won't smell of sex, it will smell of furniture polish, or a fondant fancy. The desperation to have germ-free, smell-free genitals stems from a fear of being sexual or being thought of as sexual. A vulva does not need drain cleaner to be healthy. Nor does it require being water-cannoned before it is safe for you to leave the house. Make peace with your smells, they know what they're doing.*

---

* Really do get to know your smells, because a sudden change in smell can indicate a vaginal infection such as bacterial vaginosis. This does not require douching, but it might require an appointment with your GP.

SEX
AND
REPRODUCTION

French Letters, English Raincoats and Mrs Phillips's Wares

A History of the Condom

Despite condoms providing the most effective protection against both pregnancy and STIs, they do come in for a ribbing. Even in countries where they are freely available, many people regard them as a necessary evil, and some don't use them at all. In 2017, a YouGov survey of 2,007 sixteen- to twenty-four-year-olds in the UK found that almost half (47 per cent) of sexually active young people reported having sex with a new partner for the first time and not using a condom. And one in ten sexually active eighteen- to twenty-five-year-olds reported they had never used a condom.[1] In 2017, there were 7,137 cases of syphilis reported in England, a 20 per cent increase from 2016, and a shocking 148 per cent increase from 2008. Gonorrhoea is also on the increase in the UK, with 44,676 diagnoses reported in 2017, a 22 per cent increase from 2016.[2]

I get it. Condoms can be fiddly, they can dull sensation, and they can make the penis look like a clingfilmed bratwurst. But surely a dose of the clap or an unexpected pregnancy are even worse than any of these, so why are some people still so reluctant to wrap it up? I suspect one of the reasons is that antibiotics and antiviral drugs have thankfully provided us with something of a safety net. Of course, if left untreated gonorrhoea and chlamydia can cause infertility, herpes is not curable and HIV remains life-changing (though not necessarily life-threatening with the right medication). I don't mean to minimise the damage of STIs, but I do want to point out that if caught early, the majority of infections require nothing more than a course of antibiotics and a few awkward phone calls with previous partners. This is a luxury our ancestors never had.

But this might not be the case for much longer. So-called 'super gonorrhoea', a multi-drug-resistant strain of the disease, is on the rise, and incidents of antibiotic resistance in both chlamydia and syphilis have been reported.[3] If alternative treatments aren't found, we could find ourselves back in a pre-antibiotic world of STIs, and that's not a pretty place.

For as long as people have been having sex, there have been methods of preventing pregnancy and disease by covering the penis during intercourse. Evidence of such practice is found throughout the Ancient World.* For example, the legend of King Minos of Crete, told by Antoninus Liberalis sometime around the second century AD, tells how his queen, Pasiphae, could not conceive because the king's semen was riddled with scorpions and serpents. King Minos was advised to have intercourse with another woman, but to place a goat's bladder inside her vulva to catch his poisoned seed. Once the king had got it out of his system (so to speak), he was free to make love to his wife and produce a clutch of healthy, scorpion-free babies.[4] Technically, this is a reference to what we might today call a female condom, rather than

---

* A cave in France known as the *Grotte des Combarrelles* has paintings on the wall dating to 11000 BC that some archaeologists have claimed depict condom use, though this is very much open to interpretation. Louis Capitan and Henri Breuil, 'Figures Préhistoriques De La Grotte Des Combarelles (Dordogne)', *Comptes-Rendus Des Séances De l'Année – Académie Des Inscriptions Et Belles-Lettres*, 46.1 (1902), pp. 51–6 <https://doi.org/10.3406/crai.1902.17072>.

a male condom, but it does demonstrate a knowledge of using animal membrane sheaths to prevent exchange of sexual fluids.

Linen sheaths about the length of a finger, with strings to fix them in place, were discovered in the tomb of the boy Pharaoh Tutankhamun who ruled Egypt from c.1332 to 1323 BC.[5] Today these sheaths are exhibited in the Egyptian Museum in Cairo as 'condoms', which would make them the earliest known example of condoms in the world.[6] However, it is by no means certain that these items were condoms, and they may have been some kind of ritual dress instead. Nor is there any other corroborating evidence of condom use in Ancient Egypt, though there is plenty of evidence to suggest birth control was practised. The *Kahun Medical Papyrus* (c.1825 BC), for example, doesn't mention condoms but does recommend a contraceptive pessary made from crocodile dung and honey, which would be inserted into the vulva before sex.[7] Interestingly, this concoction might actually have worked as a spermicide due to the high acidic levels, but please don't try this at home.

The earliest firm evidence we have of venereal protection that resembles a condom is found in the work of Italian physician Gabriele Falloppio (1523–1562). Falloppio was one of many physicians desperately trying to fight the advance of syphilis across Europe in the sixteenth century.[*] Falloppio understood that the 'French Disease', as he called it, was sexually transmitted and he devised a fabric sheath that fitted around the glans of the penis to prevent transmission. Falloppio's

---

[*] The origins of syphilis are intensely disputed by historians, who argue about whether or not syphilis was first picked up in the Americas by Columbus's fleet in 1493, or if it has been around much longer than that. It has been suggested that in the fifteenth century, syphilis mutated into the highly destructive infection that ravaged the world. Fernando Lucas de Melo and others, 'Syphilis at the Crossroad of Phylogenetics and Paleopathology', *Plos Neglected Tropical Diseases*, 4.1 (2010), e575 <https://doi.org/10.1371/journal.pntd.0000575>.

sheath was to be soaked in a mixture of wine, mercury, ashes, salt and wood shavings. Crucially, Falloppio instructed this wrap be applied after sex; he does not suggest attempting to keep this in place during sex. The theory was that his wrap would cleanse the penis of infection. Falloppio boldly claimed he had instructed over a thousand soldiers in how to use his condom and none of them contracted syphilis.[8] As Falloppio's wrap was designed to be used after sex, it was certainly useless, but it is one of the earliest known accounts of wrapping the penis to prevent infection.

Other sixteenth-century 'treatments' for syphilis included steaming and fumigation, guaiacum wood (ground up and drunk, or rubbed

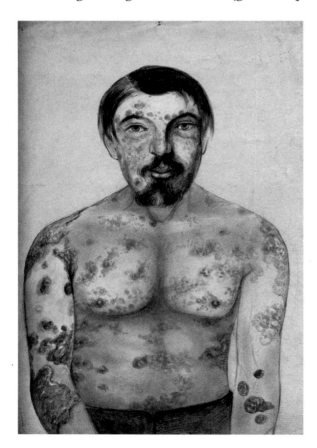

A watercolour of a man suffering from psoriasis and possibly syphilis, by C. D'Alton, 1866. Lettering on back of print states: 'History of primaries [primary syphilis] rather obscure; eruption on arms and shoulders simple psoriasis – the face and chest decidedly copper coloured and syphilitic.'

into the skin), and, of course, mercury – ingested, injected or applied directly to the sores. Mercury had been used to treat skin lesions since Guy de Chauliac advocated its use to cure scabies in 1363.[9] It may have been effective in burning away syphilitic lesions, but it is also highly toxic, causing all manner of neurological problems, as well as swollen gums, rotting teeth and hair loss.

Why would anyone be willing to suffer such hideous treatment? Because the disease itself was even worse. Italian surgeon Giovanni da Vigo (1450–1525) described the progression of syphilis in his 1514 work, *De Morbo Gallicus*.

> The contagion which gives rise to it comes particularly from coitus: that is, sexual commerce of a healthy man with a sick woman or to the contrary ... The first symptoms of this malady appear almost invariably upon the genital organs, that is, upon the penis or the vulva. They consist of small ulcerated pimples of a colour especially brownish and livid, sometimes black, sometimes slightly pale. These pimples are circumscribed by a ridge of callous like hardness ... Then there appear a series of new ulcerations on the genitalia ... Then the skin becomes covered with scabby pimples or with elevated papules resembling warts ... A month and a half, about, after the appearance of the first symptoms, the patients are afflicted with pains sufficiently to draw from them cries of anguish ... Still very much later (a year or even longer after the above complication) there appear certain tumours of scirrhus hardness, which provoke terrible suffering.[10]

In its later stages, syphilis attacks the brain, the soft tissues of the face and causes lesions to form on the bones. It is a truly horrific disease and one that was rightly feared. Useless as they were, when

This condom dates to around 1900, and is made of animal gut membrane, known as caecal.

considering the alternative one can see the appeal of Falloppio's condoms.

Soon, sheaths made of animal guts that were to be worn during coitus replaced Falloppio's linen precautions.* These early condoms were usually made from sheep guts, though sheaths made from fish bladders were also used. The gut would be cut to size and dried out, and required soaking in milk or water to rehydrate it. They were then fastened on the penis with a ribbon or string, and then washed out after use and reused – several times.

The treatment process of turning sheep intestine into a condom is described in Robley Dunglison's *New Dictionary of Medical Science and Literature* (1833).

> The caecum of a sheep, soaked for some hours in water,
> turned inside out, macerated again in weak alkaline lye,
> changed every twelve hours, scraped carefully to abstract
> the mucous membrane, leaving the peritoneal and muscular
> coats exposed to the vapour of burning brimstone, and
> afterwards washed with soap and water. It is then blown
> up, dried, cut to the length of seven or eight inches, and
> bordered at the open end with a riband. It is drawn over

---

* During an excavation at Dudley Castle in the 1980s, a privy was discovered that had been buried during the demolition of the castle's defences in 1647. Contained within were the remains of ten animal gut condoms – the earliest physical evidence of such condoms in Europe. Fahd Khan and others, 'The Story of the Condom', *Indian Journal of Urology*, 29.1 (2013), p. 12 <https://doi.org/10.4103/0970-1591.109976>.

the penis prior to coition, to prevent venereal infection and pregnancy.[11]

It would have been condoms such as these that our favourite libertine John Wilmot, the Earl of Rochester wrote about in a celebratory pamphlet titled *A Panegyric upon Cundum* (1667). Being a thoroughly debauched scoundrel, Rochester was thrilled at the prospect of being able to have sex with as many 'creature[s] obscene' as he could handle without risking either the 'tormenting sores' or 'the big belly and the squalling brat'.

Happy the Man, who in his pocket keeps,
Whether with Green or Scarlet Ribband bound,
A well made CUNDUM – He, nor dreads the ills
Of *Shankers* or *Cordee*, or *Buboes* Dire![12]

Rochester could have certainly used a 'well-made cundum', as he died in 1680, riddled with syphilis and covered in lesions and sores, aged just thirty-three.

The Scottish biographer James Boswell (1740–1795) also placed his faith in the sheep-gut condom to protect him from venereal disease during his considerable sexual exploits. Boswell refers to condoms in his diary as 'machines', 'sheaths' or his 'armour'.*

17 May 1763
I picked up a fresh, agreeable young girl called Alice Gibbs. We went down a lane to a snug place, and I took out my

---

* It's often said it was named after a 'Dr Condom' or 'Colonel Condom', but there is no evidence of that at all. *Oxford English Dictionary*, Oed.com, 2018 <http://www.oed.com/view/Entry/38587?redirectedFrom=condom#eid> [Accessed 15 August 2018].

armour, but she begged that I might not put it on, as the sport was much pleasanter without it, and as she was quite safe. I was so rash as to trust her, and had a very agreeable congress.[13]

One of the many drawbacks about the sheep-gut condom was that it dried out between uses and needed to be soaked to make it malleable enough to fit over the penis. In one diary entry dated 4 June 1763, Boswell describes frantically dipping it in the canal before he could have sex with a 'low Brimstone' he picked up in the park. Despite the setback, Boswell maintained that he had 'performed most manfully'.[14] Manful he may have been, but lucky he was not. Despite his armour, Boswell contacted gonorrhoea at least nineteen times.[15] In his diary, he referred to the repeated infection as 'Signor Gonorrhea'.[16] Despite their popularity, these early condoms may actually have helped to spread venereal disease as their users believed themselves to be safe and didn't take any further precautions.

Condoms were big business in the eighteenth century, as both a contraceptive and a prophylactic. If you needed condoms in eighteenth-century London, you would most likely go to the Green Canister on Half Moon Street and ask either Mrs Phillips or her successor, Mrs Perkins, for one of their 'fine machines'.[17]

The British exported their condoms around the world, and although the Brits referred to them as 'French letters', elsewhere they were known as 'English raincoats'.[18] The great lover Casanova (1725–1798)

A notice for Mary Perkins's London condom shop. Francis Grose, *Guide to Health, Beauty, Riches, and Honour*, 1785.

NUMBER XVI.

MARY PERKINS, fucceffor to Mrs. Philips, at the Green Canifter in Half-moon-ftreet, oppofite the New Exchange in the Strand, London, makes and fells all forts of fine machines, otherwife called C———MS.
Dulcis odor lucri ex re quâlibet.
De quel coté le gain vient.
L'odeur en eft toujours bonne.
Alfo perfumes, wafh-balls, foaps, waters, powders, oils, effences, fnuffs, pomatums, cold cream, lip-falves, fealing-wax.—N. B. Ladies' black fticking-plaifter.

calls condoms *'redingote anglaise'* ('English riding coat') or *'vêtement anglais qui met l'âme en repos'* ('English clothing that brings peace to the soul').[19] Although Casanova disliked using condoms, he understood their value and refused to use 'articles' of inferior quality: 'I did not accept the one she offered as I thought it looked of a common make.'[20] Sadly, this did not prevent him from contracting gonorrhoea four times, cancroids five times, as well as syphilis and herpes.[21]

Richard Carlile (1790–1843), an early activist for universal suffrage, wrote about common methods of contraception in *Every Woman's Book; or, What is Love?* (1826). Carlile describes how many women insert 'into her vagina a piece of sponge as large as can be pleasantly introduced, having previously attached a bobbin or bit of narrow riband to withdraw it, it will, in most cases, be found a preventative to conception...' He also gives a detailed account of condom use:

> To wear the skin, or what, in France, is called the baudruche,
> in England, commonly, the glove. These are sold in London
> at brothels, by waiters at taverns, and by some women and
> girls in the neighbourhood of places of public resort, such as
> Westminster Hall, etc.[22]

Animal-gut condoms were expensive, awkward to use and didn't really work, so when Charles Goodyear (1800–1860) invented vulcanised rubber in 1839 it revolutionised the condom industry, and the first rubber condoms were produced in 1855. These condoms were designed to be reused and had to be made to measure, but they did protect against pregnancy and STIs – as well as against sensation of any kind.

In America, distribution of condoms was severely hampered by the enactment of the Comstock Laws of 1873. The act prohibited 'any drug or medicine or any article whatever for the prevention of conception' being sent through the post. In 1876, the Comstock Act was amended to read:

Every obscene, lewd, or lascivious book, pamphlet, picture,
paper, writing, print or other publication of an indecent
character, and every article or thing designed or intended for the
prevention of conception or procuring of abortion, and every
article or thing intended or adapted for any indecent or immoral
use, and every written or printed card, circular, book, pamphlet,
advertisement, or notice of any kind giving information, directly
or indirectly, where, or how, or of whom, or by what means,
any of the hereinbefore mentioned matters, articles, or things
may be obtained or made, and every letter upon the envelope
of which, or postal card upon which, indecent, lewd, obscene,
or lascivious delineations, epithets, terms, or language may
be written or printed, are hereby declared to be non-mailable
matter, and shall not be conveyed in the mails, nor delivered
from any post-office, nor by any letter-carrier.[23]

The act was named for its most prominent proponent, Anthony
Comstock (1844–1915), a deeply Christian man who had been shocked
by the prevalence of the sex trade and contraceptives in New York. The
Comstock Act did not stop people having sex, but it made having safe
sex much more difficult. But America was not the only country that
placed a ban on condoms. In Ireland, the 1889 Indecent Advertisements
Act forbade advertising condoms, and remained in place until 1980,
and Belgium banned the advertising of all contraceptives until 1973.[24]
Boots, the UK's largest pharmacist, banned the selling of condoms
in 1920 to prevent their staff experiencing any 'awkwardness'. This
policy was not reversed until 1960.[25]

Latex condoms were invented in the 1920s. These condoms were
mass-produced and affordable, and mercifully they were for single use
only. After epidemic levels of STIs among Allied troops in the First
World War, latex condoms were standard issue for all recruits in the

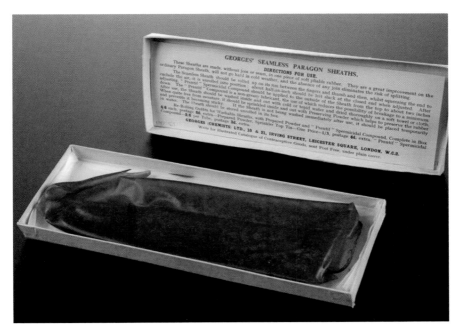

'Paragon' reusable rubber condom, London, England, 1948–50. These condoms were designed to be washed out and reused.

Second World War. The American military also began an aggressive 'sexual hygiene' campaign to try and keep their troops STI-free. The introduction of penicillin in the 1940s meant that infections such as syphilis, gonorrhoea and chlamydia could be cured for the first time. However, STI rates remained extremely high during the Second World War, which suggests the troops were not wrapping up as ordered. But the condom and messages around safe sex were starting to become normalised.

With the introduction of the contraceptive pill in 1960 and antibiotics that could cure most STIs, condom use suffered.[26] It was the discovery of AIDS in the 1980s that thrust condoms back into public view. Despite the reluctance of governments to talk about either safe sex or gay sex, the health crisis forced their hand, and condom use was at the heart of every safe-sex campaign, and has remained so to this day.[27]

This poster warned Second World War soldiers that even the perfect girl next door could not be trusted.

Condoms have never been cheaper, more comfortable, less stigmatised or more effective than they are today. If anyone should ever raise an objection about them to you, remind them of James Boswell stalking London with sheep guts tied onto his weeping penis, or condoms made from linen and ribbons, or the original vulcanised (reusable) condoms that were as thick as a welly boot. And if that doesn't do it, remember the truly horrific, disfiguring diseases our ancestors would go to any lengths to avoid (other than not having sex, obviously). Thank your lucky stars and please, as Spike Milligan once said, use a condom on every conceivable occasion.

Bringing down the Flowers

Abortion in Eighteenth-Century Britain

But, th'aged Neurse calling her to her bowre,
had gathered Rew and Savine and the flower
of Camphora, and Calamint, and Dill.

Edmund Spenser, *The Faerie Queene*[1]

William Buchan's *Domestic Medicine* (1769) was a medical block-buster. It sold over 80,000 copies, was translated into several European languages and was republished to receptive audiences well into the nineteenth century. Buchan claimed he wrote the work with an earnest desire to 'assist the well-meant endeavours ... in relieving distress; to eradicate dangerous and hurtful prejudices; to guard the ignorant and credulous against the frauds and impositions of quacks and imposters'.[2] *Domestic Medicine* covers every subject from nosebleeds and ulcers to croup and water in the head. In his chapters on pregnancy, Buchan outlines the causes and dangers of miscarriage, and morally condemns those women who sought to deliberately termi-nate their pregnancy:*

---

* In the eighteenth century 'abortion' was used interchangeably with 'miscarriage' and did not necessarily mean the deliberate termination of a pregnancy.

Every mother who procures an abortion does it at the hazard
of her life; yet there are not a few who run this risk merely to
prevent the trouble of bearing and bringing up children.
It is surely a most unnatural crime, and cannot, even in
the most abandoned, be viewed without horror; but in
the decent matron, it is still more unpardonable. Those
wretches who daily advertise their assistance to women,
in this business, deserve in any opinion, the most severe
of all human punishments.[3]

Abortion was made illegal in Britain in 1803, when the passing of Lord
Ellenborough's Act made abortion after 'the quickening' (first movement
of the foetus) punishable by death or transportation.[4] Abortion before
the quickening was not regarded as a criminal act as most theologians
and physicians agreed this stage was when ensoulment of the child
occurred. Until then, the woman was not regarded as carrying a
child. But abortion post-quickening was regarded as deeply immoral.
Dr John Astruc called the 'miserable women' seeking an abortion an
'utter shame to human nature and religion'. Barrister Martin Madan
called the women who died through botched abortions 'doubly guilty
of suicide and child murder', and a spouse procuring pills to induce
an abortion is cited as suitable grounds for divorce in a number of
eighteenth-century divorce trials.[5]

As the previous chapter has shown, by the eighteenth century,
rudimentary contraceptives were available, ranging from folklore
and quackery to methods that would have offered limited protection.
The withdrawal method is a time-honoured, if completely unreliable,
option. Animal-gut condoms, which were rinsed out and reused, had
been available from the sixteenth century. In his memoirs, Casanova
records using a linen condom and a lemon slice as a cervical cap.[6]
Post-coital vaginal douching has been used as a method to wash away

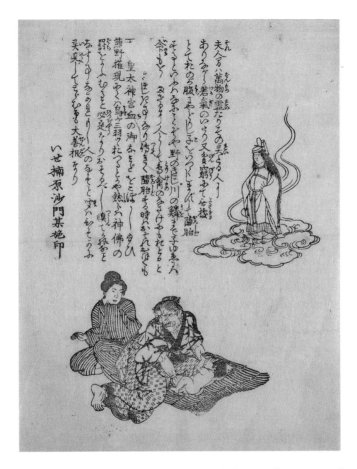

A late nineteenth-century Japanese Ukiyo-e woodblock print showing an admonition against abortion.

semen in the hopes of preventing pregnancy since ancient times.[7] Owing to widespread disease, malnutrition and poor health, fertility rates would have been reduced, but unwanted pregnancies were still widespread. When a girl found herself with a 'bellyful' (1785), pressures of shame, circumstance, poverty and myriad other reasons could lead her to seek a termination.

In eighteenth-century Britain it may not have been illegal, but abortion (post-quickening) was certainly considered a deeply shameful

FRENCH PERIODICAL PILLS.

Warranted to have the desired effect in all cases.

THESE Pills contain a portion of the only article in the whole meteria medica, which can regulate the system and produce the monthly turns of females that can be taken, without hazarding life, and this article is not to be found in any of the pills or nostrums which are pictured forth so largely in the papers of the day. It has frequently occurre that the unhappy patient has by the use of these pills and nostrums given nature such a shock that they have never since enjoyed health, and they never can. It seems that they are got up and advertised merely for the object of making money, regardless of the consequences, and the venders are usually considered beneath responsibility, by all who know them.

The French Periodical Pills are the result of the combined knowledge and experience of some of the oldest and most distinguished physicians of Europe, and have been used by females embracing the gentility and most of the nobility of France, for the last twenty-three years. To eulogize their virtues would not add to their merits. We will only say TRY THEM, and if they do not prove to be what they are here represented to be, your money shall be refunded.

They contain no medicine detrimental to the constitution, but restore all debilitated constitutions to their wonted energy and healthfulness by removing from the system every impurity.

The only precaution necessary to be observed is ladies married should not take them if they have reason to believe they are en ciente, as they are sure to produce a miscarriage, almost without the knowledge of the patient, so gentle yet active are they.

All letters to be directed to DR. L. MONROE, U. S. Agent and Importer. No 58 Union street, Boston.

N. B. The above Pills can only be obtained at 58 Union street, all sold elsewhere in Boston, are counterfeit, and only calculated to deceive.

N. B Full directions accompanying the Pills.

3 w*   d 11

Advertisement by Dr L. Monroe in the *Boston Daily Times* newspaper for 'French periodical pills' for regulation of 'the monthly turns of females' in 1845. Advertisement advises that 'ladies married should not take them if they have reason to believe they are en ciente [sic], as they are sure to produce a miscarriage.'

act, and the practice is shrouded in obscurity. Owing to the paucity of primary evidence, researching the history of abortion is notoriously difficult. Court records tell the stories of the women who died through botched abortions, and those who faced prosecution for attempting to induce one. Physicians and midwives were unwilling to risk their own necks by providing readers with instructions on how to perform an abortion, or what herbs and tonics should be taken to induce one. Rather, euphemistic language is employed in such texts to allude to a plant's abortive properties.

A text may list plants that will induce miscarriage, embedding them within the warning 'not to be taken by pregnant women', just as 'legal highs' advertised themselves as 'research chemicals' and 'not for human consumption' to get around the law. Advertisements for 'women's monthly pills' and 'cures' for 'menstrual blockage' can be read as coded contraceptives and abortifacients. In *English Sexualities* (1990), Tim Hitchcock argued that:

> Throughout the early-modern period recipes for medicines to 'bring down the flowers', or to regulate menstruation, were a common component of any herbal or recipe book, and could certainly be obtained from the local apothecary.[8]

Women seeking to 'bring down the flowers' (1598) would naturally progress from the least to the most dangerous methods of abortion. Certain known herbs were ingested, the most commonly known being savin, pennyroyal, rue and ergot. Savin, a species of juniper used to flavour gin ('mother's ruin'), is referenced in numerous court records regarding abortion once the practice was made illegal in 1803. In 1829, for example, Martha Barrett was accused of taking a 'quantity of savin for the purpose of causing abortion'. In 1834, William Childs was charged with illegal abortion, having given Mary Jane Woolf 'a large quantity of a certain drug, called savin ... with intent thereby to cause and procure her miscarriage'. In 1855, William Longman was charged with 'feloniously administering to Elizabeth Eldred Astins, 10 grains of a noxious thing called savin, with intent to procure miscarriage'.[9] The list goes on. Abortifacients such as savin and pennyroyal are indeed toxic

Savin Juniper Botanical Illustration, 1790.

and consumed in a high enough quantity could induce miscarriage – at too high a dose, they could, and did, kill the mother too.

If these methods proved ineffective (as would usually be the case), the mother was left with increasingly desperate and dangerous methods of abortion. Sitting in scalding hot baths, drinking vast quantities of gin, falling down stairs or being forcefully struck in the stomach have all been recorded as efforts to induce an abortion. But if all these failed, surgical intervention could be sought.[10] Accounts of surgical abortion are extraordinarily rare in the eighteenth century. One of the few detailed accounts of eighteenth-century surgical abortion is the record of the trial of Eleanor Beare of Derby in 1732. Eleanor was indicted on three counts: one account of encouraging a man to murder his wife and two counts of 'destroying the foetus in the womb', by 'putting an iron instrument' into the body. One of the women Beare operated on was 'unknown to the jury', and the other is named as Grace Belfort.[11] Grace Belfort worked briefly for Eleanor, during which time she was raped by a visitor to the house. Grace confessed to Eleanor that she feared she was with child and for thirty shillings (paid by the rapist) Eleanor said she could 'clear' her of the child. The account given of what happened next is so rare, it is worth sharing in full.

> Evidence: Some company gave me Cyder and Brandy, my
> Mistress and I were both full of liquor, and when
> the company was gone, we could scarse get
> upstairs, but we did get up; then I laid me on the
> bed, and my mistress brought a kind of instrument,
> I took it to be like an iron skewer, and she put it up
> into my body a great way, and hurt me.
> Court: What followed upon that?
> Evidence: Some blood came from me.
> Court: Did you miscarry after that?

Evidence: The next day ... I had a miscarriage.

Court: What did the prisoner do after this?

Evidence: She told me the job was done.[12]

Eleanor was found guilty and sentenced to three years imprisonment and to stand in the pillory for the next two market days. The mob was so incensed by Eleanor's crimes that she barely escaped being pilloried with her life. Records describe townsfolk hurling eggs, turnips and rocks at her head until she was bleeding heavily and barely conscious. After trying to wriggle free, she was dragged back to the jail, only to repeat the ordeal the following market day.[13]

In 1760, poet Thomas Brown wrote 'Satire Upon a Quack', where he attacks an abortionist who 'murdered' his friend's child. The poem is a bitter and sustained attack upon the 'graveyard pimp' who 'unborn

The *National Police Gazette*'s depiction of Ann Lohman (aka Madame Restell), 'the female abortionist', in 1847.

NATIONAL POLICE GAZETTE.

Vol. 2. No. 27—99 A YEAR.   NEW-YORK, SATURDAY, MARCH 13, 1847.   FOUR CENTS A NUMBER.

THE FEMALE ABORTIONIST.

infants murder'd in the womb'. Brown curses the abortionist to hear 'the screams of infants' and their dying mothers for all eternity, to be the 'jest of midwives' and 'strumpets without noses', and to be stalked by 'the most solemn horrors of the night'.[14] Brown refers to the abortionist's tools throughout the poem. He does not mention an 'iron skewer' but he does allude to 'baleful potions', 'stabbing verse', 'pointed darts' and a 'murdering quill'.[15] Any thin, sharpened tool, even the sharpened point of a quill pen, would serve as a suitable 'instrument' to pierce the cervix and 'bring down the flowers'. This procedure could be self-induced, or well-meaning friends or family members could attempt to penetrate the womb. How many women suffered irreparable damage, mutilation, infection and death as a result of this practice is not known, but many were willing to risk the dangers.

If this method failed, or if the poor girl simply could not afford the abortionist's fee, there were three options left: keep and raise the child, abandon the child, or murder the child and hide the body.

In Francis Grose's *Lexicon Balatronicum: a Dictionary of Buckish Slang, University Wit, and Pickpocket Eloquence* (1785), there is a truly disturbing entry: 'To stifle a squeaker: to murder a bastard, or throw it into the necessary house [privy]'.[16] This phrase also appears over a hundred years earlier in *A New Dictionary of the Terms Ancient and Modern of the Canting Crew* (1698), and in various collections of slang through the nineteenth century. That infanticide had its own slang suggests that the practice was alarmingly common. Christian Russel, of the Parish of St Paul's Covent Garden, was found guilty of murdering her illegitimate child in 1702 by 'throwing the same into a House of Office'. In 1703, Mary Tudor was put on trial for murdering her 'female bastard child, on the 18th of January last, by throwing the same into a House of Office, whereby it was choked and strangled'. In 1708, Ann Gardner was found guilty of murdering her 'female bastard … by throwing of it into a house of office, where 'twas suffocated with Filth'. Anne Wheeler was indicted for suffocating her 'male bastard' by 'suffocating it in a house of easement' in 1711. Elizabeth Arthur 'drowned' her 'male bastard' in a 'house of office' in 1717. Elizabeth Harrard was found guilty of drowning her 'male bastard' in 1739 — she was one of four women to be hanged for murdering their illegitimate children that year.[17] The list goes on and on. In the court records for the Old Bailey alone, between 1700 and 1800, there are no less than 134 trials for infanticide, the overwhelming majority of which are the killings of illegitimate children. We must remember that this is only one court in one area, and these trials are only for those who were caught. The actual figures of illegitimate infanticide will never be known, but most of the women on trial were poor, unwed, unsupported and alone — they were desperate.

A woman who had sex or fell pregnant outside wedlock was said to be 'ruined' or to have 'fallen', both of which convey the consequences of sex before marriage. If she were wealthy enough, a pregnant woman could avoid scandal by hiding away for the duration of her pregnancy and then placing the baby in the care of relatives or someone who had been paid off. But for those who could not afford to pay for a cover-up, the consequences were bleak indeed. The social stigma was so great that an expectant mother could be turned out of her family home, lose her employment, and would be left to fend for herself in a very hostile world. Eighteenth-century bawdy literature, such as *Fanny Hill,* loves to tell the story of a virgin who was 'debauched' and abandoned, who must turn to the sex trade to survive. The sad truth is that once a girl had been 'ruined' and 'fallen' from polite society, there would have been precious few options available to her. Sex workers would have been familiar with methods of contraception and ways to induce abortion, but 'brothel babies' were inevitable. In 1993, a nineteenth-century New York tenement house in the Five Points district was excavated and the skeletons of two full-term infants, most likely twins, were discovered in the lower soil level of the privy. Evidence

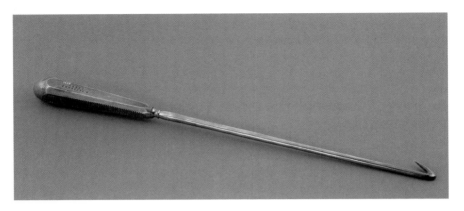

A hooked instrument once used for removing an aborted foetus.

from the time suggested that this particular address, 12 Orange Street, was once a brothel. Although foetal remains have been excavated from privies before, this discovery is significant as it is the only one with strong contextual links to the sex trade.*

In order to escape the noose, the mother's life depended on being able to 'prove' that the child was stillborn. In 1624, parliament passed an act that made it a capital offence for unmarried mothers to conceal the death of an illegitimate child, the presumption being that if the child died, the mother had killed it. In order to prove that the birth was not concealed, the mother had to produce at least one witness statement that the baby was stillborn. The prosecution would also have to prove that the pregnancy and birth had been deliberately concealed. Ann Gardner, mentioned above, was proven to have murdered her baby as she had made no provisions for the baby, and told no one she was pregnant.

---

* In 1973, the remains of a newborn baby were found in an eighteenth-century privy site in Philadelphia. Foetal remains were also found at a site in Minneapolis that used to be a restaurant in 1870. Thomas A. Crist, 'Babies in the Privy: Prostitution, Infanticide, and Abortion in New York City's Five Points District', *Historical Archaeology*, 39.1 (2005), pp. 19–46, p. 19.

The Prisoner could say little in her Defence, it did not appear that she made any Provision for the Birth of the Child, nor was she heard to cry out, or us'd any endeavour to discover it, as the Statute of King James I [the 1624 Act] in such Cases requires. The Fact being clear, upon the whole the Jury found her Guilty of the Indictment.[18]

This was enough to condemn Ann to death; she was executed on 15 January 1708.

The philanthropist Thomas Coram opened the London Foundling Hospital in 1739. His primary aim was to give shelter to the children of the 'unhappy female, who fell victim to the seductions and false promises of the designing man', and had been left to 'irretrievable disgrace'.[19] When it first opened, the hospital expected to receive twenty infants, but was overwhelmed with demand. Eventually, the hospital had to limit admissions to infants under two months, and admittance was done through a ballot system. So that mothers could reclaim their child from the hospital, they were initially encouraged to leave a token with their baby so they could be recognised later. Thousands of ribbons, thimbles, broken coins, lockets, bits of buttons, pieces of paper and shells left with abandoned children are still housed at the Foundling Hospital Museum today. Of the 16,282 babies brought to the hospital between 1741 and 1760, only 152 were reclaimed.[20]

In 1967, when the UK Abortion Act was passed, midwife Jennifer Worth was asked to comment on the morality of abortions. After fourteen years of witnessing the reality of illegal abortion, she replied she 'did not regard it as a moral issue, but as a medical issue. A minority of women will always want an abortion. Therefore, it must be done properly.'[21] Today, most of us would like to think that we are privileged enough to never find ourselves in the situation that women like Ann Gardner found themselves in over three hundred years ago: destitute,

A selection of tokens mothers left with their infants at the London Foundling Hospital. The tokens were to help mothers identify their children if they could come back for them. The thousands still housed at the Foundling Hospital today are testament to the fact that most never came back.

A metal token left with an abandoned infant at the London Foundling Hospital by a mother in the eighteenth century.

ill, alone, stigmatised and pregnant with no maternity rights, medical care, security or means to raise a child. But, the right to safely access abortion is severely under threat. As I write this, the states of Alabama and Georgia are passing two of the most aggressive anti-abortion bills in recent American history. The bills will outlaw abortion after a foetal heartbeat is detected – what was once known as 'the quickening'. And until 2019, Northern Ireland had some of the most restrictive laws around abortion in the world, with women facing long jail sentences if they go through with one. While we have come a long way in terms of social security, medical care and attitudes to sex in general, the debate surrounding abortion is still rooted in religious moralising that seeks to demonise and punish both the women who seek abortions and the doctors who perform them. But as the history of contraceptives shows, abortion will always be sought, risks will always be taken and no amount of criminalisation, not even the death penalty itself, will change that.

Period Drama

A History of Menstruation

*Contact with [menstrual blood] turns new wine sour, crops
touched by it become barren, grafts die, seed in gardens are
dried up, the fruit of trees falls off, the edge of steel and the
gleam of ivory are dulled, hives of bees die, even bronze and
iron are at once seized by rust, and a horrible smell fills the
air; to taste it drives dogs mad and infects their bites with
an incurable poison ... Even that very tiny creature the ant is
said to be sensitive to it and throws away grains of corn that
taste of it and do not touch them again.*

Pliny the Elder[1]

Few bodily functions evoke as strong and universal reaction as
menstruation. Though Pliny ventured his opinion on the apparently apocalyptic properties of menstrual blood almost two thousand
years ago, one merely has to look to the euphemistically titled 'feminine
hygiene products' aisle in modern-day supermarkets to know that,
though we have certainly moved on, as a culture we are still not entirely
comfortable with the subject.

But a coyly worded sign is really the least of it. In 2005, the Nepalese
government criminalised the ancient Hindu tradition of *Chhaupadi*,
which banishes menstruating women from their family home and forces
them to sleep in menstrual huts for the duration of their period.[2] The
practice stems from the belief that menstrual blood and by extension the
menstruating woman is impure; *Chhaupadi* translates to 'untouchable

being'. To prevent others from being polluted, the menstruating woman cannot handle food or freely interact with others. Sadly, the 2005 ruling did not stop the practice. In 2018, following the deaths of several women who froze to death or died of smoke inhalation while trying to keep warm inside the hut, the Nepalese government made the practice of *Chhaupadi* punishable by three months in prison or a fine of 3,000 rupees.[3] The practice of quarantining menstruating women is not unique to Nepal, and although the tradition is disappearing, it has been recorded around the world. In Ethiopia, for example, Jewish women still retire to a hut in the village named *margam gojo*, or 'curse hut', during menstruation.

'Farr's Patent Ladies' Menstrual Receptacle', advertised in *American Druggist*, January 1884.

PLATE 185.—**Páez houses and bridge.** *Top (left):* Family dwelling with menstrual hut at left. San Andrés. *Bottom (right):* *Páez* Indians and house, Calderas, Tierradentro. *Top (right):* Large communal fiesta house, Calderas, Tierradentro. *Bottom (left):* Suspension bridge, Tierradentro. (Courtesy Gregorio Hernández de Alba.)

A 1945 photograph, showing a menstrual hut to the left.

In 1974, the American Anthropological Association researched the menstrual taboos of forty-four societies around the world, and, in descending order, found the most common taboos were as follows:

1. Generalized belief that menstrual fluid is unpleasant, contaminating, or dangerous.
2. Menstruants may not have sexual intercourse.
3. Personal restrictions are imposed upon the menstruants, such as food taboos, restriction of movement, talking, etc.
4. Restrictions are imposed upon contact made by menstruants with men's things, i.e., personal articles, weapons, implements used in agriculture and fishing, craft tools, 'men's crops', and religious emblems and shrines, where men are the guardians.
5. Menstruants may not cook for men.

6. Menstruants are confined to menstrual huts for the duration of their periods.[4]

Historically, menstrual huts were used by the Tohono O'odham (Native American people), the Cheyenne (Native American people), the Ifaluk islanders, the Dahomey in present-day Benin, the Tiv people (West Africa), the Madia Gonds (Chandrapur, India), the Southern Paiute (Native American people), and the Ashanti in West Africa.[5] And Huaulu women in Seram, Indonesia were still being banished to a hut and forbidden from eating certain types of meats until the 1980s.[6]

The 1974 research also explores various origin myths of menstruation within these cultures and found that many of these cultures believed menstruation was caused by the moon, with the exception of the Madia Gond, who believed the vulva once had teeth that were pulled out and menstruation results from a wound that never healed, and the Arunta of Australia, who 'attribute the flow to demons who scratch the walls of vaginas with their fingernails and make them bleed'.[7]

By far the most common belief was that menstrual blood is unpleasant or dangerous, and this was recorded in thirty of the forty-four cultures studied. And although this research is now over forty years old and the menstrual hut is mercifully on the way out, menstruation continues to be viewed as 'unpleasant' by many today. I myself have often found menstruation to be an unpleasant experience. There are those who sail through a 'visit from Auntie Flo' (1954), enduring little more than a twinge in the abdomen. And then there are people like me, who firmly believe their uterus is re-enacting the Battle of the Somme.

For those of you who have never experienced severe PMS, allow me to paint a picture for you. It's fucking ugly. Your body bloats, your tits hurt and you sweat uncontrollably. Your crevices start to feel like a swamp and your head is pounding all the time. You feel like you have a cold – shivering, aching, nauseous – and have the hair-trigger emotions of someone who has not slept for days. But we're not done yet. The intense cramping across your lower abdomen feels like the worst diarrhoea you've ever had – in fact, you'll also get diarrhoea, to help with the crying fits. As your internal organs contract and tear themselves to blooded bits so you can lay an egg, blasts of searing pain rip through you. Sometimes they're so bad, you double over and can't breathe until it's passed, and the dull, constant ache returns. Nothing will satisfy the food monster that has been unleashed in your belly. It's braying for sugar and carbs like a fat yak. Some foods make you feel sick. Some smells turn your stomach and make you retch. You don't know what you want to eat, but you want to eat a lot of it. You bleed so much that all 'intimate feminine hygiene products' fail you – it's like trying to control a lava flow with an oven mitt. You worry people can smell your period. You are terrified to sit on anything or stand up for a week in case you've bled through. And as you're sitting, a crying, sweaty, wobbly, spotty, smelly mess, some bastard asks 'Time of the month, love?' And then you have to eat his head.

It's not much fun, I grant you, but this doesn't explain the out-and-out revulsion even the word PERIOD can elicit from some people. It doesn't justify having to sleep in a shed.

Disgust at menstruation may be a common phenomenon, but it is not a universal one. The Vaishnava Bauls of Bengal believe that menstrual blood is a potent and powerful fluid. A girl's first period is a cause for community celebration and her menstrual blood is mixed with cow's milk, camphor, coconut milk and sugar, and then drunk by family and friends. Tara, a Baul woman interviewed in 2002, recalled the effect drinking her menstrual blood had on those who partook of the ceremony: 'Powers of memory and concentration were enhanced, their skin acquired a brilliant glow, their voices grew melodious, and their entire beings were infused with happiness, serenity, and love.'[8] Perhaps you don't fancy using a tampon as a teabag, but the belief menstrual blood has healing properties is not without historical precedence.

The *Ebers Papyrus* (*c*.1550 BC) includes a number of remedies to stop the breasts from sagging, including one where the menstrual blood of a girl who had just started to menstruate was smeared across the breasts and stomach.[9] Benedictine abbess Hildegard of Bingen (d. 1179) claimed menstrual blood could cure leprosy: 'If a person becomes leprous from lust or intemperance ... He should make a bath ... and mix in menstrual blood, as much as he can get, and get into the bath.'[10] The Jiajing Emperor (1507–1567) was the twelfth emperor of the Chinese Ming dynasty. Every day he would drink a concoction called 'red lead', made from the menstrual blood of virgins that he believed would prolong his life. The girls were aged between eleven and fourteen and were treated so cruelly that in 1542 they attempted to assassinate the emperor. Though he was badly injured, the emperor survived, and his attackers, along with their families, were sentenced to death by slow slicing. The emperor continued to drink red lead for the rest of his life.[11] Twat.

However, most cultures and religions stigmatise menstruation as something impure. Judaism, Christianity, Islam, Hinduism and Buddhism, for example, all place sanctions on menstruating women and view menstrual blood as unclean.[12] Leviticus 20:18 reads: 'if a man has sexual relations with a woman during her monthly period, he has exposed the source of her flow, and she has also uncovered it. Both of them are to be cut off from their people.'[13] The Quran 2:222 says: 'They ask you about menstruation. Say, "It is an impurity, so keep away from women during it and do not approach them until they are cleansed."'[14]

Galen's theory of the four humours – blood, black bile, yellow bile and phlegm – dominated the Western medical understanding of menstruation until the eighteenth century. The Galenic 'plethora theory' taught that menstruation was caused by an excess or 'plethora' of the blood in

LEFT: Female with anatomical view of abdomen, from Jacopo Berengario da Carpi, *Isagoge Breves Prelucide Ac Uberime In Anatomiam Humani Corporis*, 1522.

RIGHT: Woodcut illustration from an edition of 1591 (nineteenth year of the Wanli reign period of the Ming dynasty), showing the acu-moxa locations commonly employed in treating irregular menstruation (yuejing bu tiao).

the body.[15] It logically followed that menstruation was the body's way of redressing such an imbalance, as women were naturally weaker than men and in need of regular bleeding. Galen also taught that menstruation was important to conception and provided nourishment to the foetus.[16]

Early Chinese medicine also viewed menstruation as the result of an imbalance in the body. Blood and yin energy were understood to be the ruling aspects in women and monthly bleeding threatened to cause disharmony. As early as AD 651, doctors like Sun Simiao (孫思邈) linked menstruation with poor physical and psychological health.[17] Therefore, Chinese doctors viewed menstrual health as key to female health overall. In his *Comprehensive Good Formulas for Women* (1237), Chen Ziming (陳自明) wrote, 'when providing medical treatment to women, the first necessity is to regulate the menses, therefore we begin with this'.[18]

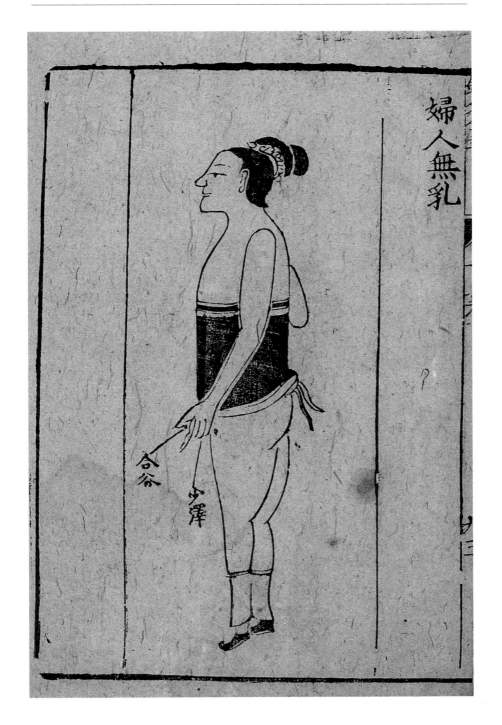

Foundational texts of Indian Ayurvedic medicine such as the *Sushruta Samhita*, composed sometime between 600 BC and the first century AD, taught that menstruation was a form of bodily purification. However, an imbalance of the three dosha energies could lead to 'bad' menstruation that could make women very ill indeed. Such an imbalance could result in blood that smelled 'like a putrid corpse or fetid pus, or which is clotted, or is thin, or emits the smell of urine or fecal matter'.[19] In order to assist the purification, the *Sushruta Samhita* advises that:

> A woman in her menses should lie down on a mattress made of Kusha blades (during the first three days), should take her food from her own blended palms or from earthen saucers, or from trays made of leaves. She should live on a course of Habishya diet and forswear during the time, even the sight of her husband. After this period, on the fourth day she should take a ceremonial ablution, put on a new (untorn) garment and ornaments and then visit her husband after having uttered the words of necessary benediction.[20]

Doctors in the West were still debating whether or not a menstruating woman could pollute food as late as 1878, when the *British Medical Journal* ran a series of letters discussing whether a woman would spoil ham if she touched it while 'the painters were in' (1964).[21] By the nineteenth century, doctors prided themselves on being rational men of science, but their understanding of menstruation was still shaped by narratives of pollution and madness.

Dr William Rowley, professor of medicine at Oxford University and member of the Royal College of Physicians, eagerly wrote of the hysteria that amenorrhea could bring about in women. 'The tongue falters, trembles, and incoherent things are spoken; the voice changes; some roar, scream or shriek immoderately; others sigh deeply, weep or moan

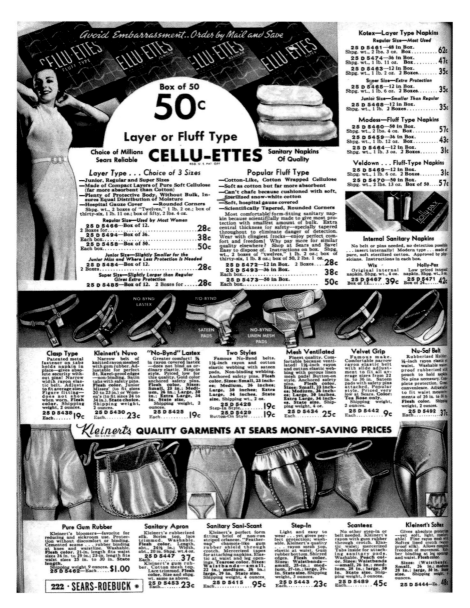

1936 advertisement in the Sears catalogue.

plaintively.'[22] Heavy bleeding was also considered to be dangerous and required purging, opiates and physical restriction. Dr Charles Manfield also believed menstruation and madness were inextricably linked. 'That peculiar states of the uterus have frequently a share in producing madness, appears from the fact that between the years 1784 and 1794 eighty patients were admitted to Bethlem hospital, whose disorders followed shortly after the menstrual state.'[23] In 1848, Dr Althaus agreed

Vaginal examination in vertical position, from J. P. Maygrier, *Nouvelles Démonstrations D'accouchemens: Avec Des Planches En Taille-Douce, Accompagnés D'un Texte Raisonné Propre À En Faciliter L'explication*, 1822.

and wrote that 'hysterical attacks almost always occur after a sudden suppression of the menstrual flow'.[24]

The same arguments, taken to extreme conclusions, served the cause of aggressive anti-feminists such as James McGrigor Allan, who addressed the Anthropological Society of London in 1869 to explain why women should not be granted the vote:

> Although the duration of the menstrual period differs greatly according to race, temperament and health, it will be within the mark to state that women are unwell, from this cause, on the average two days in the month, or say one month in the year. At such times, women are unfit for any great mental or physical labour. They suffer under a languor and depression which disqualify them for thought or action, and render it extremely doubtful how far they can be considered responsible beings whilst this crisis lasts. Much of the inconsequent conduct of women, their petulance, caprice and irritability, may be traced directly to this cause ... In intellectual labour, man has surpassed, does now, and always will surpass woman, for the obvious reason that nature does not periodically interrupt his thought and application.[25]

It was not until the early twentieth century that science began to fully understand menstruation. It is no coincidence that menstrual taboos began to be dispelled as more and more women entered the medical profession. The pioneering work of Dr Mary Putnam Jacobi (whose 1876 essay 'The Question of Rest for Women during Menstruation' won the Boylston Prize at Harvard University), and her intellectual heirs Clelia Duel Mosher and Leta Stetter Hollingworth, finally proved the idea of 'menstrual incapacity' was wrong.[26]

Disposable sanitary towels were available by the late nineteenth century and the first tampons were invented in 1929 by Dr Earle Haas. Until this point, women would use wads of cloth called 'clouts', or simply bleed into their clothes.[27] The practicalities of dealing with a period improved dramatically, but ancient attitudes that viewed menstruation as debilitating and dirty proved stubbornly persistent.

In 1946, Walt Disney released the educational film *The Story of Menstruation*, which was shown to high school students across the United States. The film includes the first documented use of the word 'vagina' on screen and was an attempt to educate young women about their bodies. The narrator, Gloria Blondell, tries to debunk a number of menstrual myths, such as not bathing or exercising while menstruating, and explains the role of neurobiology, hormones and reproductive organs in menstruation. The film also advises young women to 'stop feeling sorry for yourself', to 'keep smiling' and 'keep looking smart'.[28]

Unfortunately, millions of women still suffer with more than cramps each month. 'Period poverty' means that women the world over cannot afford tampons or towels and are still using bundles of cloth. Research has shown that women living in urban slums, refugee camps and rural communities in particular struggle to access basic menstrual sanitary wear.[29] Every month, millions of schoolgirls miss school because of their periods. Ninety-five per cent of schoolgirls in Malawi cannot afford pads or tampons, and report using rags and string to catch the blood. As this often falls out of their underwear, more than half of these girls stayed at home during their period.[30] And research carried out by Plan International UK in 2017 showed that one in ten British fourteen- to twenty-one-year-olds have struggled to afford sanitary products, which has resulted in thousands of girls missing school every month.[31]

Historical narratives around menstruation have rarely been neutral. Menstrual blood has been thought to contain magical and destructive properties; it has been seen as revolting, purifying and sacred.

Menstruation has been linked to madness, irrationality and ill health for thousands of years and in thousands of cultures. While medical texts argued that menstruation weakens the body, references to madness, violence, irrationality and superstitious associations with the moon suggest a power in menstruation. In patriarchal societies, menstruation was evidence that women were not equal to men, that biology had determined a different role

Kotex advert from 1920.

for them. But more than this, it was used to reinforce prejudices that women were not rational creatures and required constant supervision. We may think we have moved past all this now, that we have a purely scientific understanding of menstruation and have done away with such superstitions. But until we can talk about the 'red-headed aunt from Redbank' (1948) openly and without embarrassment or discomfort, we can't claim to be there yet. Period.

SEX
AND
MONEY

The Oldest Profession

Sex Work in the Ancient World

D espite the old adage, sex work is not the world's oldest profession: medicine is. In 1952, anthropologist George Peter Murdock of Yale University published his research on the social customs of hundreds of indigenous people around the world, and while he found no evidence of prostitution, the figure of the medicine man was universal.

> I have personally read accounts of many hundreds of
> primitive societies, and in not a single one of them is genuine
> prostitution reported. Many of them exhibit forms of sex
> behavior that we would regard as exceedingly lax, but such
> laxity does not take the specific form of prostitution except
> in the so-called 'higher' civilizations. The oldest profession is
> actually the one to which you yourselves belong.[1]

Other scholars such as Mary Breckinridge have suggested that midwifery is the oldest profession: 'The midwife's calling is so ancient that the medical and nursing professions, in even their earliest traditions, are parvenus beside it.'[2] Trying to work out what is the 'oldest' profession is actually something of a wild goose chase as professions, and indeed money, are quite recent inventions. *Homo sapiens* has been wandering around the planet for about 200,000 years, and the earliest evidence of coined money dates to 640 BC in Lydia, Asia

Minor. Even systems of bartering goods, rather than money, depend largely on the domestication of cattle and cultivation of crops, and that dates to around 9000 BC.[3] This means that for most of human history, we have done without money. Given that money is arguably the most dominating influence in how we live our lives today, it is sobering to remember that the only value money really has is that which we collectively attach to it. Ultimately, it's pieces of paper and discs of metal which somewhere along the line we have all agreed are special. We managed perfectly well without it until our ancestors thought that those gold rocks were nicer to look at than the other rocks.

Without money and commerce there are no professions. There is no evidence of selling sex among the Maori before Europeans arrived in New Zealand carrying with them syphilis and flags. Victorian explorers were surprised to discover that the Dyak people of Borneo had 'no word to express that vice'.[4] When the Christian missionary Lorrin Andrews translated the Bible into Hawaiian in 1865, he had to invent

Image of a large native missionary family, taken by A. A. Montano for his New Photographic Gallery in Honolulu, c.1878.

new words to teach the islanders about the concepts of sexual shame and infidelity.[5]

There is very little evidence of a sex trade among the Native Americans until the Europeans turned up to 'civilise' everyone. Even then, the only evidence that exists is that the invaders believed all indigenous women were promiscuous.[6] The commodification of sex, and the selling of sexual favours as a profession, is firmly linked to the establishment of money and economic markets. The causal effect of establishing commerce with the selling of sex was seen in a pioneering experiment by economist Keith Chen. In 2006, Chen introduced the use of currency to a group of capuchin monkeys, and taught them to buy grapes, jelly and apples with tokens. The female monkeys began trading sex for tokens almost immediately.[*]

It was Rudyard Kipling who first coined the phrase 'the world's oldest profession' in the short story 'On the City Wall' (1898). The tale opens with the immortal line: 'Lalun is a member of the most ancient profession in the world.'[7] The expression has since fallen into common

---

[*] Keith Chen, Venkat Lakshminarayanan and Laurie R. Santos, 'How Basic are Behavioral Biases? Evidence from Capuchin Monkey Trading Behavior', *Journal of Political Economy*, 114.3 (2006), pp. 517–37 <https://doi.org/10.1086/503550>. Trading sex for gain has also been witnessed in longtailed male macaques. The currency paid by the males was the length of time spent grooming the female before sex, and the price rose and fell with the availability of females. The more females available, the less males paid for sex, and vice versa. Michael D. Gumert, 'Payment for Sex in a Macaque Mating Market', *Animal Behaviour*, 74.6 (2007), pp. 1655–67 <https://doi.org/10.1016/j.anbehav.2007.03.009>. Dr Fiona Hunter, a Cambridge University zoologist, observed that female Adélie penguins on Ross Island in Antarctica traded sex for rocks. Penguins use rocks to build a platform for their nests, which keeps their eggs off the ice. So valuable are the rocks that when the females want to take rocks from male counterparts, they trade sex. The female approaches a male with the rocks she wants and engages him in a mating dance. Once they have had sex, she takes the rocks and returns to her mate, who is none the wiser. 'Pick up a Penguin', *BBC News*, 1998 <http://news.bbc.co.uk/1/hi/world/asia-pacific/60302.stm> [Accessed 17 September 2018].

parlance as a historical truth. But what Kipling wrote after those words perhaps offers more insight into what is, at least, a very ancient profession indeed: 'In the West, people say rude things about Lalun's profession, and write lectures about it, and distribute the lectures to young persons in order that Morality may be preserved.'[8] As Kipling observed, attitudes to selling sex are not fixed but are culturally determined. Researching ancient sexuality is difficult for many reasons, but particularly because historical records are always mediated through the author's world view. What many historical texts understand as prostitution often speaks far more of the author's own cultural prejudices than the practices being described.

For example, when the Spanish conquistadors colonised the Aztecs in 1521, they translated the Aztec Náhuatl word *ahuienime* as 'prostitute' or 'whore'. But this translation was done by Spanish Catholics, and what they saw as 'prostitution' was not what the Aztecs saw at all. The word *ahuienime* is more accurately translated as 'the bringer of joy', and has religious, spiritual connotations. Unable to move beyond their own cultural attitudes, Spanish texts describe the *ahuienimeltin* as whores. As Ulises Chávez Jimenez argued, 'the Spaniards did not understand the role of the *ahuienimeltin* in Aztec religion, where they legitimised cosmic models that allowed a deep communion with the Gods'.[9]

Some of the earliest written evidence of sex work comes from Ancient Mesopotamia. Verses written about the Babylonian goddess Inanna (also known as Ishtar), composed sometime between 2000 and 1000 BC, contain these lines:

> When you stand against the wall your nakedness is sweet,
> When you bend over, your hips are sweet ...
> When I stand against the wall it is one shekel,
> When I bend over, it is one and a half shekels.[10]

Bear in mind it's the goddess Inanna herself who is offering to bend over for one and a half shekels which goes some way to show that the sacred could be sexy as well as funny in the Ancient World.

The Code of Hammurabi, dating to 1754 BC, sets down the Babylonian code of law and covers a number of laws pertaining to the protection of the 'ladies of the town' (1680):

> If a man's wife does not bear him a child but a prostitute [kar.
> kid] from the street does bear him a child, he shall provide
> grain, oil, and clothing rations for the prostitute, and the
> child whom the prostitute bore to him shall be his heir; as
> long as his wife is alive, the prostitute will not reside in the
> house with his first-ranking wife.[11]

Legal protection and state regulation of sex work is found throughout the Ancient World. The *Arthasastra* of Kautilya is an Indian text on politics that was composed sometime between the second century BC and the third century AD. The *Arthasastra* devotes a chapter to discussing the duties of *ganikadhyaksa*, the 'Superintendent of Courtesans', and details rules for women in this profession. Sex work was regulated by the state and sex workers paid taxes each month. As with most professions, sex work was densely layered. For example, a *ganika* was appointed by the state to attend the king and received a salary of 1,000 *panas* every year, whereas *bandhaki* worked in brothels, and *pumscali* worked on the streets. The *Arthasastra* uses the word *rupjiva* to describe a woman selling sex, which translates to 'one who makes a living out of her beauty'.[12]

One of the most contentious areas of study within the history of sex work is the practice of so-called 'Sacred Prostitution' in the Ancient World (also called Temple or Cult Prostitution).[*] It's also an important

---

[*] The historian leading the charge against the existence of sacred sex work is

area of study, as the belief that selling sex was once a sacred exchange directly challenges many of our modern narratives around sexual services. As Mary Beard has argued, the myth of sacred prostitution provides 'a model for alternative humanities paraded by our archives, available for new living, for different lives'.[13] The figure of the 'sacred whore' or 'sexual priestess' is a prominent figure in many spiritualist groups today who use sex as a healing ritual. Sacred prostitution is a notoriously difficult subject to research, let alone verify, and historians continue to debate if the practice existed at all. All that is left to try and decipher is a handful of ancient sources, and we have no way of knowing if they are factual or fictitious.

The ancient Babylonian epic *Gilgamesh* (c.1800 BC) tells the story of a temple 'moll' (1604) called Šamhat who serves Ishtar and tames the wild man Enkidu through her sexual skills.[14] This is one of the earliest written references to sex work ever found, but it does not claim to be anything but a story. The earliest account of sacred sex work in a non-fiction text comes from the Greek historian Herodotus's (c.484–425 BC) account of sixth-century neo-Babylonia:

> The foulest Babylonian custom is that which compels every
> woman of the land to sit in the temple of Aphrodite and have
> intercourse with some stranger at least once in her life. Many
> women who are rich and proud and disdain to mingle with
> the rest, drive to the temple in covered carriages drawn by
> teams, and stand there with a great retinue of attendants. But
> most sit down in the sacred plot of Aphrodite, with crowns
> of cord on their heads; there is a great multitude of women

Stephanie Lynn Budin, in *The Myth of Sacred Prostitution in Antiquity* (New York: Cambridge University Press, 2010). Budin tears into various translations of Herodotus to show that although the sex trade thrived in the Ancient World, it was not considered sacred.

coming and going; passages marked by line run every way through the crowd, by which the men pass and make their choice. Once a woman has taken her place there, she does not go away to her home before some stranger has cast money into her lap, and had intercourse with her outside the temple; but while he casts the money, he must say, 'I invite you in the name of Mylitta'. It does not matter what sum the money is; the woman will never refuse, for that would be a sin, the money being by this act made sacred. So she follows the first man who casts it and rejects no one. After their intercourse, having discharged her sacred duty to the goddess, she goes away to her home; and thereafter there is no bribe however great that will get her. So then the women that are fair and tall are soon free to depart, but the uncomely have long to wait because they cannot fulfil the law; for some of them remain for three years, or four. There is a custom like this in some parts of Cyprus.[15]

Although he writes histories, Herodotus is what might be politely termed an 'unreliable narrator'. He is a historian in much the same way that Disney is a historian. What's more, he is clearly out to smear the reputation of the Babylonians and is projecting his own negative views around sexuality onto them – so, is any of this true? Possibly. There are other accounts of similar customs, but they could just be rehashings of Herodotus. Four hundred years after Herodotus, the historian Strabo (64 BC–AD 21) describes ritual sex practised at Acilisene in Armenia. Here, people honoured the Persian goddess Anaitis by dedicating their daughters to serve her in the temple before they were given in marriage.[16]

In *De Dea Syria,* the Greek writer Lucian of Samosata (AD 125–180) describes a ritual practised in Syria where women would have to have sex with a stranger in a public place as an offering of payment

Edwin Long, *The Babylonian Marriage Market*, 1875.

to the goddess Aphrodite.[17] The Augustan historian Pompeius Trogus wrote: 'There was a custom among Cyprians to send their virgins to the sea-shore before marriage on fixed days, for employment in order to get dowry-money, and to make a first-fruit offering to Aphrodite, a dedication to preserve their virtue in the future.'[18] The Greek lyric poet Pindar (518–438 BC) also writes about sex workers being dedicated to Aphrodite's temple in Corinth after the Olympic games: 'O mistress of Cyprus, here to your grove Xenophon has led the hundred-limbed herd of grazing women.'[19] But because Pindar himself called this work a *skolion* (drinking song), it's unlikely this anecdote is anything more than a good yarn.[20]

There are also several references in the Old Testament to *qadeshes*, a word many have translated to mean male and female temple prostitutes. Kings 23:7 reads 'He also tore down the quarters of the male shrine prostitutes that were in the temple of the Lord, the quarters where women did weaving for Asherah.'[21] But the devil is in the detail, and many historians dispute the translation.

James Tissot, *The Harlot of Jericho and the Two Spies*, 1896.

The most tangible evidence of sacred prostitution is the eight-hundred-year-old Hindu tradition of the devadasi in India. Devadasi means 'female servant of God', and refers to women who are dedicated to the goddess Yellamma. The earliest written records of dancing temple girls called devadasi dates to AD 1230–1240, from the time of Raja Raya III in Maharashtra.[22] A thousand-year-old inscription in Tanjor Temple lists four hundred devadasis in Tanjor, four hundred and fifty in Brahideswara temple and another five hundred in the Sorti Somnath temple.[23] Devadasi looked after the temples, and sang and danced in devotion to the deities. They were also courtesans, supported by wealthy patrons who sought out the devadasi because they were sacred women. They dazzled the courts with their poetry, music and devotion to the goddess. Classical Indian dances such as Bharatnatyam, Odissi and Kathak are all legacies of the devadasi. Sex was a part of their world, but it was incidental: they celebrated art, beauty, love and the divine. When the British colonised India, they brought with them their rigid world view and were unable to see the devadasi as anything but prostitutes. So repulsed were they by

A photograph of two dancing girls, by K. L. Brajbasi & Co., Patna, *c.*1910.

what they saw, the British set about shaming and dismantling the devadasi institution.

In 1892, the Hindu Social Reform Association petitioned the Governor General of India and the Governor of Madras to erase the devadasi: 'There exists in the Indian community a class of women commonly known as nautch-girls. And that these women are invariably prostitutes.'[24] The British missionaries taught India what a 'prostitute' was and why it was so shameful. Support for the devadasi disappeared; they were socially shunned and stigmatised. Cut off from patrons and the temple, they tried to earn money by dancing at private events and selling sexual services. Eventually, the devadasi were outlawed throughout India in 1988. The tradition continues in southern India, but the women are no longer respected. Now they are stigmatised and without protection many abuses occur, but impoverished parents still dedicate young daughters to the service of the goddess.

Selling sex is not the oldest profession in the world, but sex just might be the oldest currency. We've always had sex, always enjoyed sex, and therefore always traded sex. Attitudes to the sex trade are not fixed but are constantly in flux. Sex workers in the Ancient World were often sanctioned by the state, protected by the law, and, if not always respected, then at least accepted as part of day-to-day life. There is also evidence that those who sold sex were once revered as noble and holy. Selling sex is heavily criminalised around the world today and is a far cry from being regarded as socially acceptable, let alone sacred. This change in fortune speaks of dramatic shifts in cultural attitudes towards sex. In cultures where sex was not regarded as inherently sinful, attitudes to sex workers were markedly different from cultures that repressed sexuality. As patriarchal, puritanical attitudes to sex developed in the West, women's sexuality came in for particular censure, and the women selling sex were condemned most of all. Rather than condemning the sex trade wholesale as immoral and dangerous, perhaps we should ask what the world would be like if those selling sex were again respected, instead of marginalised; if they were given rights, instead of rescue. I doubt sex workers will ever again be regarded as priestesses, but at the very least they should be respected as professionals – from one of the oldest professions in the world.

Public Relations

A History of the Tart Card

The sex trade is as old as civilisation itself, and as long as people have bought and sold sexual services, the authorities have been trying to regulate it – usually through criminalisation and punitive measures. Over the centuries, sex workers have been punished with fines, imprisonment, excommunication, exile, mutilation and even the death penalty. Most punishments have involved public humiliation, intended to shame people into better behaviour. For example, 'Cockatrices' (1508) in fourteenth-century Augsburg had their noses cut off if they were found soliciting on holy days.[1] Whereas, in 1713, on the Isle of Man, Kath Kinred, 'a notorious strumpet' who had 'brought forth three illegitimate children', was sentenced to be 'dragged after a boat in the sea at Peele Town ... at the height of market', as an 'example to others'.[2] Despite such punishments, no measure has been successful in abolishing sex work. Criminalisation has only succeeded in forcing the trade underground, and creating dangerous working conditions. The dilemma faced by every 'wagtail' (1553) operating under criminalisation throughout history is how to stay safe and attract clients, but without also attracting the attention of the law. One of the most effective ways to do this is to advertise, and one of the most iconic and recognisable forms of sex-work advertisement is the humble 'tart card' – the brightly coloured calling cards that once covered telephone boxes the length and breadth of Britain.

The 1953 Post Office Act made it illegal to advertise in or 'in any way disfigure' telephone boxes in the UK.[3] When this Act was repealed

London tart cards, c.1995.

in 1984, business-savvy 'flossies' (1900) saw an opportunity to advertise. Although tart cards are still found in the telephone boxes of cities all around the world, they garnered something of a cult following in Britain, and are most immediately associated with London (they are known as 'slag tags' in the North).[4] The 1990s were the heyday of the tart card, and every telephone box from Soho to King's Cross was festooned with a patchwork of porn. The need to keep production costs down in terms of wording and materials, while still standing out, resulted in a truly unique art form.

The early cards were printed on cheap paper and feature simple block designs in black ink against brightly coloured (often neon) backgrounds. Kitsch silhouettes of nude women, stilettos, suspenders or sex toys directly communicate the type of service on offer. Technological advancements influenced the design of the later cards, which feature fancy typesets and glossy photos of erotic fantasy figures puckering up, bending over or staring seductively down the camera. To the disappointment of many clients, these photos were rarely of the providers, who were far too canny to out themselves to the authorities in a phone box.

Tart cards in a British phone box in 2004. It was illegal to advertise there by 2004, but they were still very common.

From the 'strict mistress seeking human toilet', to 'naughty nannies' who will 'rub it better', and 'schoolgirls' seeking some 'hanky spanky', there was something for everyone. Although men were certainly selling sex, most tart cards are from female providers (cis and transgender) advertising to male clients. The cards offered sex workers a basic form of client screening. The only contact information provided was a phone number, which the client would call to discuss what they wanted, as well as arranging a time and a place to meet. The address would only be given out once the provider established that this was someone they wanted to see.

By 2001, tart cards had become such a nuisance in the UK that the Criminal Justice and Police Act made placing them in phone boxes punishable by six months in prison, or a fine of up to £5,000.[5] You can still find the odd card here and there, but as the mobile phone has rendered the phone box redundant, and the internet has created a far safer way for sex workers to advertise to clients, the tart card has had its day.

We might think of advertising as a very modern phenomenon, but sex workers have always understood the value of marketing. The eighteenth-century literary blockbuster *Harris's List* (1757–1795) was an annual almanac of London sex workers, and a masterclass in self-promotion. A forerunner to the modern tart card and TripAdvisor, the list detailed the appearance, skills and prices of up to two hundred

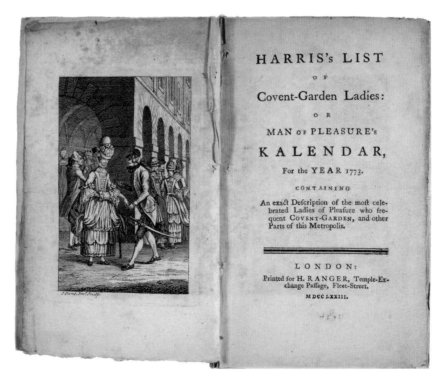

Harris's List of Covent-Garden Ladies: or, Man of pleasure's kalender, 1773.

women selling sex in the capital. The list was a collaboration between Sam Derrick, an Irish Grub Street hack and poet, and a London pimp, Jack Harris. Only nine known volumes of the list survive today (1761, 1764, 1773, 1774, 1779, 1788, 1789, 1790 and 1793), and they are scattered throughout various archives around the world. There have been a handful of reprints, but until 2005, if you wanted to see the list, an appointment at an archive and a pair of white gloves would have been required. It wasn't until historian Hallie Rubenhold undertook the herculean task of researching and editing the list in her publication *The Covent Garden Ladies: Pimp General Jack and the extraordinary story of Harris's List* (2005) that the list was dusted off and shown to the public anew.

As you may well imagine, *Harris's List* was a hugely popular work, functioning as both a practical guide to the sex industry and softcore pornography for those not brave enough to actually arrange a meeting. The list itself straddled the boundaries of fact and fiction, and we will never be able to attest to its accuracy. Was Mrs Howard's 'grove' truly 'ample enough in size to take in any guest?' Did Emma at Mother Grey's really drink whiskey for breakfast and possess a 'magic ring ... as much sought after as the philosopher's stone'? Were Miss Simms's 'low countries' like 'a well-made boot'?[6] We will never know.

Harris's List could make or break the fortune of London's 'horizontal workers' (1870). Like every profession, sex work was (and still is) densely layered, and a favourable review would allow a girl to command more money, richer clients and go up in the world. A bad review, or an accusation of carrying the pox (like Miss Young of Cumberland Court, who is described as spreading 'her contaminated carcass on the town'), would see business dry up quicker than sawdust on sick.[7]

Despite Jack Harris's narrative style of a cheeky scamp about town sampling the delights of the city at random, the selection process was highly competitive, and Harris knew the marketing value of

A Harlot's Progress is a series of six engravings by the English artist William Hogarth. The series shows the story Moll Hackabout, who arrives in London from the country and becomes a sex worker. Although Moll starts her career as a high-flying courtesan, the series ends with her dying in poverty and racked with syphilis. This image shows Moll being lured into the sex trade by the notorious bawd, Mother Needham, 1732.

his list. The memoirs of Fanny Murray, one of the most celebrated eighteenth-century courtesans, provides valuable insight into the processes. Harris described Murray as 'a fine Brown Girl rising nineteen years next Season … Fit for High Keeping with a Jew Merchant'.[8] The favourable review allowed Fanny to command higher prices and court a better class of clientele. But she had to apply to Harris to have her name 'enrolled upon his parchment list'. She then had to be interviewed, submit to a medical examination, agree to give Harris a fifth of the money she earned and sign a contract that stipulated she must forfeit £20 to Harris if she was found to have lied about her health during the examination.[9]

Expensive this may have been, but it could be a worthwhile investment. *Harris's List* helped to launch the careers of several of London's top courtesans, such as Lucy Cooper and Charlotte Hayes. Charlotte Hayes is favourably described in the 1761 edition of *Harris's List*:

> Were we to enter into an exact description of this celebrated
> Thais; that is, were we to describe each limb and feature a
> party, they would not appear so well as taken altogether, in
> which we must acknowledge her very pleasing; and in our
> eye (and sure nobody can better tell what is what) she is as
> desirable as ever.[10]

Charlotte clawed her way up from desperate poverty to become one of the most successful bawds in London, and madam of the King's Place brothel. When she died in 1813, she had amassed a fortune of over £20,000, achieved celebrity status and hobnobbed with royalty – not bad for a girl from the gutter.

Lucy Cooper's life is detailed alongside Charlotte's in *Nocturnal Revels* (1779), and a description of Lucy is also found in the 1761 edition of *Harris's List*.[11] Both women achieved fame and fortune, but Lucy did not have the business acumen Charlotte had and failed to save for the inevitable rainy day. Lucy lived a life of excess and saw her wealthy, elderly protectors die one by one. Finding herself grog-blossomed, partied out and the wrong side of thirty-five, Lucy was unable to replace them. Having set nothing aside from her heyday, she could not meet her debts and soon found herself destitute and in debtor's jail. She died in squalid poverty in 1772, just four years after being immortalised in song as the woman who 'all mankind' wanted to lie with.

Must Lucy Cooper bear the bell
And give herself all the airs?
Must that damnation bitch of hell
Be hough'd by Knights and Squires?
Has she a better cunt than I
Of nut brown hairs more full?
That all mankind with her do lye
Whilst I have scarce a cull?[12]

Just over one hundred years after the last copy of *Harris's List* was published, the city of New Orleans started advertising the services of its sex workers. On 29 January 1897 an ordinance to restrict all 'working girls' (1928) in the city of New Orleans to one area was passed into law. As the ordinance was prepared and sponsored by Alderman Sidney Story the area came to be known as 'Storyville'. It was the first legal red-light district in the history of the United States and operated until 1917, when the USA entered the First World War and the federal government made it illegal to sell sex anywhere within a five-mile radius of any military base.[13] Storyville had its own press, which produced guides to the area, known as the 'Blue Books'; the earliest surviving copies date to 1900. 'Blue' referred to the content rather than the colour of the book. Like *Harris's List*, the 'Blue Books' were widely sold throughout the city. They were available at the railway station, in bars, hotels, and in barber shops. The preface to each edition introduces the reader to the area and explains why the 'Blue Books' are necessary:

Because it is the only district of its kind in the States set aside
for the fast women by law.

Because it puts the stranger on a proper and safe path as
to where he may go and be free from 'Hold-ups,' and other

games usually practised upon the stranger.

It regulates the women so that they may live in one district to themselves instead of being scattered over the city and filling our thoroughfares with street walkers.

It also gives the names of women entertainers employed in the Dance Halls and Cabarets in the District.[14]

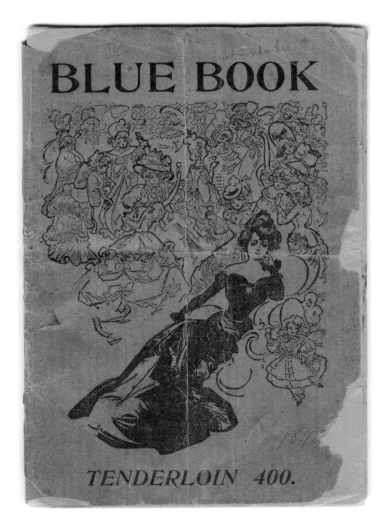

Blue Book, Tenderloin 400, 1901.

The 'Blue Books' contained details of the most prominent working girls, but more commonly advertised the madams at whose establishments they worked, such as Miss Bertha Golden of Iberville Street:

> Bertha has always been a head-liner among those who keep first-class Octoroons. She also has the distinction of being the only classical Singer and Salome dancer in the Southern States. She has had offers after offers to leave her present vocation and take to the stage, but her vast business has kept her among her friends. Any person out for fun among a lot of pretty Octoroon damsels. Here is the place to have it. For ragtime singing and clever dancing, and fun generally, Bertha stands in a class all alone.[15]

'Octoroon' refers to race and means to be one-eighth black. One of the most famous 'Octoroon Parlours' in Storyville was Mahogany Hall, which belonged to Lulu White (c.1868–c.1931). Lulu made an enormous amount of money and was known for wearing ropes of diamonds and rings on every finger. Mahogany Hall housed up to forty 'call girls' (1913), five parlours, and each bedroom had an adjoining bathroom. It boasted mirrored rooms, expensive artwork and plush interiors.[16] E. J. Bellocq (1873–1949) photographed many of the 'wet hens' (1886) of New Orleans and it is believed many of his subjects were shot inside Mahogany Hall.[17]

When Storyville was closed down in 1917 the 'Blue Book' press went with it and the 'totties' (1900) relocated to the French Quarter where they had to work illegally.

About the same time as Bellocq was immortalising the women of Storyville, French photographer Jean Agélou (1878–1921) was making his name with his nude and erotic works. One of Agélou's favourite models was a sex worker known only as Miss Fernande, who became

A woman in striped stockings in New Orleans's Storyville red-light district, 1912.

the world's first pin-up girl. Not much is known about Miss Fernande, not even her full name.[*] In a 1911 edition of the magazine *L'Étude*

---

[*] Some online sources identify Miss Fernande as Fernande Barrey (1893–1960), but there is no evidence to support this beyond a coincidence in age. Christian Bourdon, *Jean Agélou: De L'Académisme À La Photographie De Charme* (Paris: Marval, 2006).

Académique, Agélou featured four pictures of Miss Fernande and gave her age as eighteen, meaning she was born in 1893.[18] We know her name as she would sign her postcards 'Miss Fernande' and provide an address where clients could reach her.[19] Miss Fernande shrewdly marketed herself through her erotic postcards, and came to be known as the first lady of French erotica. Original postcards of Miss Fernande are now highly collectable and change hands for hundreds, if not thousands, of pounds.

Original copies of *Harris's List* and the 'Blue Books' are also now worth enormous amounts of money. The modern tart card has also acquired value as a form of 'accidental' art and there have even been several tart card exhibitions in recent years.[20] Although these are beautiful and fascinating historical artefacts, it is worth remembering the sex workers who relied on them to advertise their services.

Miss Fernande photographed by Jean Agélou, *c*.1910.

Like many industries, sex work has been revolutionised by the internet and the online sector is now the largest of the UK sex industry. But this is no bad thing. 'Beyond the Gaze' was a three-year research project that ran from 2015 to 2018 and looked at the effect of the internet on the UK sex industry. The study found that 89 per cent of UK sex workers felt online platforms had allowed them to work more independently, 85 per cent reported using the internet to screen and monitor their clients, and 78 per cent said that advertising online had improved their quality of life.[21] Sex workers being able to use the internet to advertise has improved safety and working conditions.

The internet has taken most sex work off the street and certainly out of the phone box. It has made sex work safer for those who choose to do it, and largely reduced the need for calling cards. But this is under threat. In 2018, the US Senate passed the Stop Enabling Sex Traffickers Act (SESTA), and the Fight Online Sex Trafficking Act (FOSTA). FOSTA makes posting or hosting online prostitution adverts a federal crime and SESTA makes websites directly responsible for third-party content, the theory being that victims of sexual exploitation can sue websites for any role they played in facilitating their abuse. The result is that multiple internet platforms and website providers have now prohibited sex workers from advertising on them. Without access to online advertising, sex workers are being forced back onto the street and advertising with cheaply produced cards.[22] Sex workers have the right to work safely and to be respected. The tart card, calling card and sex-worker almanacs are relics and must be left in the past. As beautiful as they are, the best place for them is in a museum.

Feasting with the Panthers

A History of Male Sex Work

Writing to his lover Lord Alfred Douglas from a prison cell in 1897, Oscar Wilde reflected on the crimes of 'gross indecency' that had resulted in his serving two years' hard labour at Reading Gaol. Wilde described the young male sex workers he would entertain at dinner as 'the brightest of gilded snakes'. He recalled being intensely aroused by the danger of having sex with these 'delightfully suggestive and stimulating' creatures, and likened his time in their company to 'feasting with the panthers'.[1]

Assumptions around sex work are staggeringly heteronormative: women sell sex, men buy sex, and that's that. Only that's not that. It's not even close. Sex work involves a vast spectrum of gender, sexuality, services, providers and clients. Sex work

Oscar Wilde seen here in a photo with his lover, Lord Alfred Douglas. Wilde lost a defamation lawsuit involving his relationship with Douglas and was imprisoned as a homosexual. He died shortly after his release. Photographed by Gillman & Co. (1882–1910).

is a notoriously difficult subject to research. Criminalisation and stigma means that many sex workers are unwilling to speak to researchers. As a result, gathering reliable data on sex work demographics is tricky and estimates can differ significantly. For example, according to the 2016 Home Office Affairs Committee report on prostitution, about 20 per cent of UK sex workers are male.[2] Yet statistics released by the data collecting website Import.io in 2014 suggested that 42 per cent of all UK sex workers are male.[3] We may never have an exact figure, but one thing we know is true is that there are a lot of fellas on the game and this has been true throughout history.[4]

Although there is considerable evidence of men selling sex to other men, the history of women buying sex from men proves far more elusive and unreliable. The Roman poet Martial, for example, mocks an 'ugly and old woman' who wishes to 'receive services without paying for them'. Elsewhere, he jokes that 'Lesbia swears that she has never been fucked for free. It's true. When she wants to be fucked, she usually pays for it.' But this may be a snide dig at older women, rather than evidence that women paid for sex.

Likewise, many powerful female rulers were smeared as insatiable nymphomaniacs by their enemies, which makes teasing out the facts particularly difficult. For example, Queen Ana Nzinga (1583–1663) of the Ndongo and Matamba Kingdoms in Angola was alleged to have kept a harem of fifty men to pleasure her at will. 'She also maintains fifty to sixty concubines, whom she dresses like women, even though they are young men.'[5] The problem with this account is it was written by Dutch geographer Olfert Dapper, who had never actually visited Africa. Given the arse-kicking Queen Nzinga handed out to the Portuguese, this may be nothing more than slanderous rumour.

One of the few historical accounts of an all-male brothel catering to a female clientele comes from Mary Wilson, a London bawd who owned a string of brothels in the early nineteenth century. In 1824, Mary published *The Voluptarian Cabinet* where she described her creation of an 'Eleusinian Institution'. There, for the right price, a woman could be pleasured by a gentleman of her choosing.

> I have purchased very extensive premises, which are situated between two great thoroughfares and are entered from each by means of shops, devoted entirely to such trades as are exclusively resorted to by ladies ... In these saloons, according to their class, are to be seen the finest men of their species I can procure, occupied in whatever amusements are adapted to their taste, and all kept in a high state of excitement by good living and idleness...[6]

The problem with this account is that it comes to use through the work of sexologist, Iwan Bloch, who wrote about Mary Wilson's brothel in his *A History of English Sexual Morals* (1936). Not that I would want to suggest Bloch is lying, but corroborating evidence of Miss Wilson's premises, and indeed her writing is rather hard to find.

But absence of evidence is not evidence of absence, and women almost certainly will have been paying for sex throughout history. Even today, women buying sex is a taboo and under-researched subject. But this is changing. In 2016, criminologists Dr Natalie Hammond and Dr Sarah Kingston completed one of the first research projects into UK women paying for sex.[7] Dr Kingston recognised her preconceptions were challenged by 'just how similar women's motivations for buying sex are to men's'. Dr Hammond found that women pay for sex for a range of reasons, 'such as wanting to experiment or having a mismatched sex drive with their partner – wanting sex, but not an affair. This parallels what we know about male clients – they come from all walks of life and pay for sex for a range of reasons.'[8]

François Villain, *Ann Zingha, Queen of Matamba*, 1800.

Thankfully, research is now shedding light on the women who pay for sex, but it remains a hidden history.

Same-sex relationships between men were widely accepted throughout the Ancient World, but they were still subject to strict sociosexual 'rules' that dictated what was decent, and what was not. In Greece, for example, an older man (*erastes*) could take a teenage boy (*pais*) for his lover, but he would also become his mentor, and tutor him in the ways of the world. Though today we would recognise this as child sexual abuse and institutionalised paedophilia, the Ancient Greeks not only accepted it, but parents would happily offer up their sons to rich old men in the hope that it would give them a boost up the social ladder. The older man was regarded as the active, more masculine one, and the younger man would be expected to assume the passive role – this extended to the sex itself, where the *pais* would be the one being penetrated (the bottom), and the *erastes* would be doing the penetrating (the top). It was considered quite unseemly for a grown man to be a bottom. Similar pederastic arrangements were regarded as perfectly normal among the Samurai warriors in Japan, where an older warrior (*nenja*) would take an adolescent boy (*chigo*) as his sexual partner in exchange for training him in martial arts and social etiquette.[9]

During his 1895 trial for indecency, Oscar Wilde described his affection for Lord Douglas as 'the love that dare not speak its name'. When pushed by Sir Edward Clarke to explain what he meant by this, Wilde referred to the *erastes/pais* relationships of the Ancient Greeks:

> 'The Love that dare not speak its name' in this century is
> such a great affection of an elder for a younger man as there
> was between David and Jonathan, such as Plato made the
> very basis of his philosophy, and such as you find in the
> sonnets of Michelangelo and Shakespeare ... It is in this
> century misunderstood, so much misunderstood that it may
> be described as the 'Love that dare not speak its name,' and
> on account of it I am placed where I am now. It is beautiful,
> it is fine, it is the noblest form of affection. There is nothing
> unnatural about it. It is intellectual, and it repeatedly exists
> between an elder and a younger man, when the elder man
> has intellect, and the younger man has all the joy, hope and
> glamour of life before him. That it should be so the world
> does not understand. The world mocks at it and sometimes
> puts one in the pillory for it.[10]

All very noble this may have been, but for a man to simply sell sex, rather than exchanging sex for being mentored, did carry a certain

Greek ceramic dating to 480 BC, showing an *erastes* (lover) and his *eromenos* (beloved) kissing.

amount of shame. For example, Greek men who sold sex were forbidden from entering temples, public speaking or taking part in official proceedings. In 346 BC, the Athenian politician Aeschines prosecuted fellow stateman Timarchus for addressing the assembly when he sold sex in his youth: 'The man who has sold the right to his own body would be ready to sell the state as well.'[11] Similar laws existed outside Athens too. In the city of Beroia, modern-day Veria, an inscription from the second century BC bans 'slaves, drunks, madmen, and those who have prostituted themselves (*hetaireukôtes*)' from entering the gymnasium.[12]

However, such shame was not universal. The Ancient Hindu sex manual, the *Kama Sutra*, describes how male sex workers, 'imitating women's dress', give good head to their male clients, with no hint of shame. 'When it is in precisely this state, driven halfway inside the mouth through the force of passion, he mercilessly presses down, and presses down again, and lets it go. This is called sucking the mango.'[13]

Attitudes to sucking the mango were not quite as permissive throughout medieval Christian Europe, but we know a lot of sucking went on. On the evening of 11 December 1394, John Rykener was arrested for selling sex to Yorkshire man John Britby in Cheapside, London. Rykener's questioning and testimony before the mayor's court are recorded in lurid detail in the London Plea and Memoranda Rolls. What makes this case so important is that Rykener then confessed to dressing as a woman and using the name Eleanor to sell sex to Britby, as well as to friars and members of the clergy. Rykener also admitted dressing as a man to seduce laywomen and nuns.

> John Rykener further confessed that on Friday before the
> feast of St Michael [he] came to Burford in Oxfordshire and
> there dwelt with a certain John Clerk at the Swan in the
> capacity of tapster for the next six weeks, during which time
> two Franciscans, one named Brother Michael and the other
> Brother John, who gave [him] a gold ring, and one Carmelite
> friar and six foreign men committed the above-said vice
> with him ... Rykener further confessed that [he] went to
> Beaconsfield and there, as a man, had sex with a certain
> Joan, daughter of John Matthew, and also there two foreign
> Franciscans had sex with him as a woman. John Rykener also
> confessed that after [his] last return to London a certain Sir
> John, once chaplain at the Church of St Margaret Pattens, and
> two other chaplains committed with him the aforementioned

vice in the lanes behind St Katherine's Church by the Tower of London. Rykener further said that he often had sex as a man with many nuns and also had sex as a man with many women both married and otherwise, how many [he] did not know. Rykener further confessed that many priests had committed that vice with him as with a woman, how many [he] did not know, and said that [he] accommodated priests more readily than other people because they wished to give [him] more than others.[14]

On first reading, this document appears to be a rare account of a transgender woman in the Middle Ages. So, why then have I included it in a chapter on men in sex work? Because the document is likely to be a satirical jibe at the Church, rather than a genuine case. When this document first came to light, historians were understandably excited at what this could tell us about sex and gender in the fourteenth century. It wasn't until Jeremy Goldberg did a bit of digging that questions had to be asked about the reliability of the source. Not only are the charges, verdict and punishment missing, but cases of fornication, buggery (anal sex), etc., were not heard before the mayoral courts. Furthermore, the names John Rykener and John Britby appear elsewhere. A John Britby was a vicar in a Yorkshire parish and a John Rykener escaped the Bishop of London's prison in 1399.[15] Which makes it likely that the Church is the target of the satire. It has even been suggested that 'Rykener' is an allusion to 'Richard', King Richard II, meaning the document is mocking the king as whoring himself to the Church for money.[16]

A hoax it may be, but it still gives valuable insight into medieval male sex work. Clearly, it was widely known that men sell sex, and we can see the levels of stigma and shame attached to it. Whereas in the Ancient World, same-sex relationships were not only accepted and actively encouraged, in medieval Britain, they were subject to ridicule and scorn.

In *Anarchia Anglicana* (1649), Clement Walker refers to 'new-erected sodoms and spintries at the Mulberry Garden at S. James's'.[17] A 'spintry' is a Latin word for a male brothel, and the one at Mulberry Garden once stood where Buckingham Palace does today. We don't know the names of the people who worked there, but they all took a terrible risk to do so. The Buggery Act of 1533 had been passed to punish 'the detestable and abominable Vice of Buggery committed with Mankind or Beast'. Those convicted of buggery faced the death penalty. It wasn't until the Offences Against the Person Act of 1861 that buggery stopped being a capital offence in England and Wales. Lord Walter Hungerford had the dubious honour of being the first man convicted and executed for the crime of buggery under the Act on 28 July 1540. The last two men executed for sodomy in Britain were James Pratt, aged thirty-two, and John Smith, aged thirty-four, who were hanged together at Newgate Prison on Saturday 28 November 1835.

In 1710, John Dunton published 'The He-Strumpets: A Satyr on the Sodomite-Club' where he claims that the 'he-whores' (1638) have taken 'all the Trade' away from the 'cracks' (women):

> He-Whore! The Word's a Paradox;
> But there's a Club hard by the Stocks,
> Where Men give unto Men the Pox.[18]

Any self-respecting 'he-whore' in eighteenth-century London would solicit for customers at one of the city's 'molly houses'. A molly house was not strictly a brothel, but rather a public house, such as a tavern, a coffee shop or an alehouse, where gay men could meet up. In 1709, journalist Ned Ward published an exposé of the goings-on at the capital's 'molly-houses' (1726):

There are a particular Gang of Sodomitical Wretches, in
this Town, who call themselves the Mollies, and are so far
degenerated from all masculine Deportment, or manly
Exercises, that they rather fancy themselves Women, imitating
all the little Vanities that Custom has reconcil'd to the Female
Sex, affecting to Speak, Walk, Tattle, Cursy [i.e. curtsey], Cry,
Scold, and to mimick all Manner of Effeminacy, that ever
has fallen within their several Observations; not omitting
the Indecencies of Lewd Women, that they may tempt one
another by such immodest Freedoms to commit those odious
Bestialities, that ought for ever to be without a Name.[19]

One of the most notorious molly houses belonged to 'Mother' Margaret
Clap, who also provided beds for her clients. In 1726, Mother Clap's establishment was raided, and forty men in various states of undress were
hauled off in the middle of the night to Newgate Prison. Although most
were released owing to lack of evidence, the resulting trial later that year
saw three men executed, and two put in the pillory. Mother Clap herself
was sentenced to be pilloried and did not survive the experience.[20]

The case largely depended on the testimony of two sex workers turned
informants. Thirty-year-old Thomas Newton and eighteen-year-old
Edward Courtney had been caught selling sex in London's molly
houses, and to save their own skins both agreed to testify at the trials
following the raid on Mother Clap's molly house. At the trial of George
Kedger, Edward Courtney testified that Kedger had paid to bugger
him at Thomas Orme's molly house. Kedger denied this and claimed he
had 'advised him to leave off that wicked Course of Life; but he said,
he wanted Money, and Money he would have, by hook or by crook;
and, if I would not help him to some, he would swear my Life away'.[21]
Courtney very nearly did 'swear his life away' as Kedger was found
guilty and sentenced to death, though he was later reprieved. Newton

Anonymous same-sex Victorian lovers enjoy a spot of cross-dressing and mutual masturbation.

testified that he regularly sold sex in the molly houses, and had been sodomised by forty-three-year-old William Griffin, forty-three-year-old Gabriel Lawrence and thirty-two-year-old Thomas Wright. All three men were sentenced to death and hanged at Tyburn.

While the threat of capital punishment was not enough to deter the he-strumpets, it was enough to force the trade underground. Subsequently, the names of historical hustlers are primarily left to us in court records as men stood before a judge, shamed, scared and denying everything. But one male sex worker who shocked Britain precisely because he refused to be shamed and proudly called himself 'a professional Mary-Ann' was Jack Saul (1857–1904).

Born John Saul in a Dublin tenement slum, Jack first turns up in the court records of 1878, charged with stealing from Dr John Joseph Cranny, who had employed him as a domestic servant.[22] In 1879 he moved to London to make his fortune as a sex worker. Two years later, Jack put his name to the erotic memoirs, *The Sins of the Cities of the Plain or Recollections of a Mary-Ann, With Short Essays on Sodomy and Tribadism* (1881). How much of this book is fact and how much is fiction is unknown, but it is a deliciously lurid account of Jack turning tricks in Victorian London.

> I wanted to see him spend, so removing my lips, I pointed
> that splendid tool outwards over the hearthrug and frigged
> him quickly. Almost in a moment it came; first a single thick
> clot was ejected, like a stone from a volcano, then quite a
> jet of sperm went almost a yard high, and right into the fire,
> where it fizzled on the red-hot coals.[23]

In 1889, Saul was caught up in what became known as the 'Cleveland Street Scandal', when Postal Constable Luke Hanks found eighteen shillings in the pockets of a fifteen-year-old telegram boy in his employ.

'The West End Scandals, some Further Sketches', *Illustrated Police News*,
4 December 1889.

This was almost twice the boy's weekly salary and Hanks demanded
to know where it had come from. Under questioning, the boy, Charles
Swinscow, confessed that he and many of the other telegram boys had
been being paid to have sex with wealthy men at a gay brothel, owned
by a Charles Hammond, at 19 Cleveland Street in Fitzrovia. The police
put Cleveland Street under surveillance, but by the time they finally
raided the property Hammond had fled to France following a tip-off. The
scandal really got going when the names of those men visiting the house
became public. Lord Arthur Somerset and Henry James Fitzroy the Earl
of Euston were both accused, and rumours abounded that Prince Albert
Victor, the eldest son of the Prince of Wales, was also a regular patron.
Lord Arthur escaped to the continent and Prince Albert laid low in India
until the heat was off, but the Earl of Euston sued journalist Ernest Parke
for criminal libel after he was named in the press.

In court, Henry James Fitzroy claimed he had visited 19 Cleveland
Street to see a '*tableau plastique*' (nude women), and once he realised
what was really going on there he left. Jack Saul was called to testify
that he had regularly had sex with Fitzroy at Cleveland Street. What
was particularly shocking to the British press was not only how open
Saul was about earning his livelihood as a 'sodomite', but that he
actually enjoyed it.[24] Up to this point, the press had described the boys

An anonymous Victorian couple provide ample evidence that there really is nothing new under the sun.

at Cleveland Street as innocents, preyed upon by corrupt men, but Saul described how much he enjoyed 'champagne and drinks' and his 'very comfortable' lodgings.[25] So outspoken was Saul that the presiding judge reprimanded him a number of times. Unable to accept that anyone would be happy as a 'professional sodomite', the press viciously attacked Saul as an 'unquestionably filthy, loathsome, detestable beast'.[26] The judge instructed the jurors to disregard Saul's testimony, calling it 'as foul a perjury as a man could commit'.[27] Ernest Parke was found guilty of libel, and sentenced to one year's hard labour.

Despite Saul's confession the Attorney General declined to prosecute him for indecency. The reason is unknown, but it's been suggested it was to protect Saul's wealthy clients. After the trial, Saul returned to Dublin and domestic service, where he worked as a butler. In 1904, he died of tuberculosis aged forty-six and was buried in an unmarked grave.

All throughout recorded history men have been selling sex, whether as part of a sugar-baby relationship, or as straightforward transactional exchange for cash. Whether it was 'the love that dare not speak its name' or the livelihood of the 'professional sodomite', male sex work has always been with us. Attitudes towards sex work and gay sex have varied from culture to culture, but stigma has consistently dogged both. Even today, when sex work is discussed in the media, the male sex worker is almost always excluded. The narrative of the sexually exploited 'prostituted woman' dominates the rhetoric of those who would abolish sex work. No space is given to discussing the men who sell sex and the women who buy it. Why? Because as Jack Saul discovered in 1889, the abolitionists and those who wish to 'rescue' sex workers will disregard that which challenges the narrative of the abused victim. Stigma and the threat of the law have kept male sex workers in the shadows for thousands of years, but they deserve far better than this. All sex workers do.

Conclusion

So here we are, at the end of our journey together. This is the point where we both roll over, light a cigarette and ask, 'so how was it for you?' I do hope you have enjoyed reading this book. Although, like a well-posed Tinder profile picture, I fear the title may have promised more than could be delivered. This could never have been a comprehensive history of sex. I'm not sure that such a thing could ever be produced, because there is not one history of sex – there are legion.

The history of sex is a notoriously difficult subject to research. Police and court records, medical texts and pornography are generally the 'go to' resources of the sex historian, but these sources always load the dice. What is almost totally absent is the unbiased testimony of everyday folk to tell us how they felt about and experienced sex. Take, for example, the history of sex work. It is quite easy to find sources that will tell us what doctors, moralisers and the media have thought of the sex trade, but trying to find the voices of sex workers themselves is almost impossible. They are always just out of reach, filtered through the pens of men who had their own agenda, sensationalised to titillate, or heavily dictated by circumstance.

For example, when Isabel Barker stood trial on 24 May 1683 for keeping a brothel in Morc-Lane, London, the court records show that she swore blind she 'used honest industry for her living' – despite several women testifying that they had caught their husbands sneaking out of her house late at night.[1] Isabel was eventually found not guilty after managing to find a number of people to provide her with a good character witness. But, given that the penalty for running a brothel in seventeenth-century London was a hefty fine, imprisonment and some time in the pillory, we can perhaps understand why Isabel might not have been completely honest in her claims that she knew absolutely nothing about 'licentious people' or 'carnal wickedness'. Such records tell us a great deal about the law and the sex trade, but what they can't reveal is who Isabel really was, or how she truly felt about her accusation, beyond the fact that she denied it. Nor can it tell us anything about the men and 'lewd women' who were caught by irate wives in Isabel's boarding house, what their background was, or how they felt about Isabel and indeed the law. The lived experiences of everyday people remain frustratingly just out of sight. Like trying to peer through a dirty window, we can glimpse shape, colour and movement within, but we can never quite see the whole picture clearly.

While unbiased individual testimony may be rare, what we do have in abundance is evidence of the structures that frame people's experience of sex. Throughout this book I have traced the various threads of religion, the media, law, politics and economy in an attempt to reveal some of the rich tapestry of human sexuality. But I'll finish by asking what kind of picture we are currently weaving for future historians to unpick.

Current attitudes to sexuality around the globe vary dramatically. Countries such as Saudi Arabia, Pakistan and Somalia have all outlawed adultery. Common punishments include fines, imprisonment, flogging and even the death penalty. Being gay is still illegal in seventy countries, and punishable by death in Mauritania, Sudan, Northern Nigeria and Southern Somalia. Although Western attitudes can be comparatively progressive, they are by no means uniform. For every sex positive, polyamorous, pansexual there is a monogamous heterosexual who believes homosexuality is wrong. For every unrepentant nymphomaniac, there is an asexual wondering what the hell all the fuss is about. And for every placard-touting 'me too' feminist, there is a confused and indignant Hooray Henry who can't understand why he isn't allowed to slap female interns on the ass any more. As anyone who has ever spent more than two minutes on social media can tell you, modern debates around sexuality and gender can be fierce, and often toxic.

But at least people are talking and can talk about their sexuality with a freedom we've never had before. Of course, there is still a long way to go before, as a culture, we are comfortable with sex, but we have never been more inclusive, permissive and tolerant than we are right now. I say that in the full knowledge that this is a privilege that many around the world do not have, but the simple fact that many of us are free to talk about and express our sexuality is remarkable. We have never been more willing to talk, listen and respect one another's viewpoints and experiences. And although there is still considerable prejudice, stigma and sexual ignorance around the world, voices are being heard and ground is being gained.

Perhaps what our own time will be remembered for is our scrutiny of sexual consent. Debates around sexual consent are nothing new – almost every culture in history outlawed sexual violence and understood rape as morally wrong. But what constituted rape varied considerably from culture to culture. In Ancient Rome, for example, rape was illegal, but only if the victim was a freeborn Roman citizen. Slaves weren't recognised as citizens, so as far as the Romans were concerned, it was impossible to rape a slave because they did not have the right to say no.[2]

Likewise, the Anglo-Saxons outlawed rape, but viewed the seriousness of the crime as dependent on the victim's status, rather than the attacker's actions. Some of the earliest extant Anglo-Saxon laws covering the punishment for rape are those of King Æthelberht of Kent (AD 560–616). Æthelberht's laws cover abduction, adultery and assault, but also sexual assault, specifically the sexual assault of freeborn, virgin women. The law reads: 'If anyone carries off a virgin by force, [he has to pay] to the owner 50 shillings, and afterwards buy from the owner his consent [to the marriage]'.[3] To the Anglo-Saxon mind, this all made perfect financial sense. A woman's virginity was highly prized on the marriage market, and the loss of virginity effectively lowered her stock. If a woman could no longer marry, her family (owner) would have to continue to keep her, hence the compensation paid. That the victim is forced to marry her rapist is barbaric, but again, made financial sense to the Anglo-Saxons, who viewed rape as criminal damage; if you break it, you buy it. As far as the Anglo-Saxons were concerned, the injury inflicted was not bodily or emotional, it was financial.

The Victorians also intensely debated sexual consent and fretted over what was assault and what was simply 'banter'. One case that forced a national debate around the difference between 'top bants' and assault occurred on 26 December 1837, in the Artichoke public house in the London district of Holborn when Caroline Newton bit the left nostril off one Thomas Saviland, who had tried to kiss her without asking first. According to various reports she then either 'absolutely swallowed the flesh', or 'was seen to spit it out of her mouth upon the ground'.[4] After spending several weeks recovering, Thomas pressed charges for assault.

But what made this case so famous was not the assault itself, but the court chairman's (Sargent Adams) ruling of it. Having reviewed all the evidence, Adams told Thomas Saviland that although he was truly sorry for the loss of his nose, 'if he would play with cats, he will get scratched'. Adams then told the jury, 'Gentlemen, my opinion is, if a man attempts to kiss a woman against her will, she has a perfect right to bite his nose off, if she has a fancy for doing so.'[5] This ruling was widely reported in the press as 'The Law of Kissing' and set a legal precedent for assault in the nineteenth century.

Oh, fie upon you, Sergeant Jack,
    To go to tell the jury,
That ev'ry man his nose should lack
    Who tries to kiss a fury.

We know that woman-kind may *claw*,
    If due restraint man throws off ;
But never dreamt that it was "law"
    That she might " bite his nose off. "

By the queer mark across your *own*
    We *see* it has been mended,
And *hear* 'twas bitten to the bone
    By prudery offended.

You fished for maids, and *got a bite* ;
    And since they treated *you* so,
You seem to think 'tis only right
    That they should *always* do so.

Your politics are bad enough,
    And so is your theology ;
But all condemn, as wretched stuff,
    Your doctrine of nosology.— *Chronicle.*

'The Law of Kissing', from
The Pilot, 1 May 1837.

The 'law of kissing' ruling genuinely unsettled nineteenth-century Britain, and the idea that a woman had a 'right' to bite off an attacker's nose was criticised and ridiculed in equal measure. Mocking poems were published, like the one in *The Pilot*.

Clearly, the threat of punishment for kissing a woman led to some anxiety amongst the menfolk about what was acceptable behaviour between the sexes. In 1901, Kristoffer Nyrop published *The Kiss and Its History*, in which he not only tries to trace the history of the kiss, but also its legal status. Nyrop cites the 1837 case and uses it to illustrate the great difficulty men have in fully understanding when they should not kiss women and why: 'it is a matter of general knowledge that a woman's "No" is not always to be taken seriously. The refusal may, you know, be merely feigned.' He continues to warn his male readers that if they 'take the girl's feigned "No" seriously, she will only laugh at him afterwards – such is woman's nature'.[6]

What makes our own time and culture historically unique is our understanding that no really does mean no, and that everyone has the right to say no, at any point, under any circumstances, and that must be respected. It's important to acknowledge here that sexual assault remains a major issue today, and there are still far too many people who haven't got the message about ongoing sexual consent. This can't be emphasised strongly enough. But when we look back, we can see just how far we've come.

We are slowly moving towards a place where we understand that there are no mitigating circumstances when it comes to consent. It does not matter what a victim is wearing, drinking, or who else they have had sex with. It doesn't matter if the attacker is a good swimmer, a Supreme Court judge or the president of the United States. It doesn't matter if the attacker thought it was all jolly japes and 'banter' – assault is assault.

We are not there yet. We still live in a world where a victim's underwear can be submitted as evidence of consent in a rape trial, as happened in Ireland in 2018. A twenty-seven-year-old man was acquitted of raping a seventeen-year-old girl in Cork after his lawyer told the jury, 'You have to look at the way she was dressed. She was wearing a thong with a lace front.'[7] This kind of victim blaming, shaming and proclaiming of sexual entitlement can be seen all throughout history, but what happened next is new. The case caused global outrage. Hundreds marched in Cork, Dublin, Limerick and Belfast to protest against the ruling and the absurd idea that underwear can give consent. The hashtag #ThisIsNotConsent trended on social media as women across the world posted pictures of their underwear.[8] Irish MP Ruth Coppinger held up a lace thong in the Dáil (Irish parliament) shortly after the ruling and said 'it might seem embarrassing to show a pair of thongs here … how do you think a rape victim or a woman feels at the incongruous setting of her underwear being shown in a court?' She also told supporters that compulsory training on consent should be introduced for judges and jurors.[9] While misogynistic court rulings and weary narratives around consent and clothing are not new, they are now being challenged and called out on a global scale.

So, we must keep talking about sex. We must keep educating children about sex, and not just about what happens when a sperm gets its hands on an egg. We must talk about consent, pleasure, masturbation, pornography, love, relationships and our own bodies. Because the only way we will dispel shame is to drag sex out in the open and have a good long look at it. History has shown us how damaging shaming sexual practices, in all their myriad forms, can be. Let's learn the lesson.

Notes

INTRODUCTION

1   Philip Kaufman, *Quills* (Fox Searchlight, 2000).
2   Anil Aggrawal, *Forensic and Medico-legal Aspects of Sexual Crimes and Unusual Sexual Practices* (Boca Raton: CRC Press, 2008), p. 369.
3   Gerald S. Martin, *Gabriel Garcia Márquez: A Life* (London: Bloomsbury, 2009), p. 205.
4   2018 Review, '2018 Year in Review – Pornhub Insights', *Pornhub*, 2018 <https://www.pornhub.com/insights/2017-year-in-review> [Accessed 29 September 2018].
5   Jonas Roelens, 'Visible Women: Female Sodomy in the Late Medieval and Early Modern Southern Netherlands (1400–1550)', *BMGN – Low Countries Historical Review*, 130.3 (2015), 3 <https://doi.org/10.18352/bmgn-lchr.10101>.
6   Ibid.
7   William Acton, *The Functions and Disorders of the Reproductive Organs in Childhood, Youth, Adult Age, and Advanced Life* (London: John Churchill, 1857), p. 101.
8   James Douglas, 'A Book That Must be Suppressed' in *Palatable Poison: Critical Perspectives on* The Well of Loneliness, ed. by Laura L. Doan and Jay Prosser (New York: Columbia University Press, 2002), pp. 10–11.

'TIS PITY SHE'S A WHORE

1   Daniel Chandler, *Semiotics: The Basics*, 2nd edn (London: Routledge, 2007), p. 25.
2   Georg Büchner, 'Danton's Death', in *Danton's Death; Leonce and Lena; Woyzeck*, trans. and ed. by Victor Price (Oxford: Oxford University Press, 2008), p. 65.
3   'Bernie Sanders Quickly Condemns Rally Speaker Who Called Hillary Clinton a "Corporate Democratic Whore"', *RealClearPolitics*, 2016 <https://www.realclearpolitics.com/video/2016/04/14/speaker_at_sanders_rally_calls_hillary_clinton_a_corporate_democratic_whore.html> [Accessed 9 August 2018].
4   'Oxford English Dictionary', *Oed.Com*, 2018 <http://www.oed.com/view/Entry/228780?rskey=PMdb56&result=1#eid> [Accessed 9 August 2018].

5   Thomas De Chobham and F. Broomfield, *Thomae De Chobham Summa Confessorum* (Louvain: Nauwelaerts, 1968), pp. 346–7.

6   John Webster, *The White Devil*, in John Webster, *Three Plays,* ed. by David Charles Gunby (London: Penguin Books, 1995), pp. 84–5.

7   Rachael Jayne Thomas, '"With Intent to Injure and Diffame": Sexual Slander, Gender and the Church Courts of London and York, 1680–1700' (unpublished MA, University of York, 2015), pp. 134–5.

8   'Anne Knutsford c. Anne Blagge' (Chester, 1664), Cheshire Record Office, EDC5 1.

9   Quoted in Bernard Capp, *When Gossips Meet: Women, Family, and Neighbourhood in Early Modern England (Oxford Studies in Social History)* (Oxford: Oxford University Press, 2003), p. 193.

10 'Susan Town c. Jane Adams' (London, 1695), London Metropolitan Archives, DL/C/244.

11 'Cause Papers' (York, 1699), Borthwick Institute for Archives, University of York, C.P.H.4562., p. 3.

12 'Elizabeth Young c. Robert Heyward' (Chester, 1664), Cheshire Record Office, CRO EDC5 1663/64.

13 'Peter Leigh c. William Halliwell' (Chester, 1663), Cheshire Record Office, CRO EDC5 1663/63.

14 'Judith Glendering c. Thomas Ellerton' (London, 1685), London Metropolitan Archives, DL/C/241.

15 'Cicely Pedley c. Benedict and Elizabeth Brooks' (Chester, 1652), Cheshire Record Office, PRO Ches. 29/442.

16 Dinah Winch, 'Sexual Slander and its Social Context in England c.1660–1700, with Special Reference to Cheshire and Sussex' (unpublished PhD thesis, The Queen's College, Oxford University, 1999), p. 52.

17 'Martha Winnell c. Abraham Beaver' (York, 1685), Borthwick Institute for Archives, University of York, C.P.H.3641.

18 'Thomas Richardson c. Elizabeth Aborne' (London, 1690), London Metropolitan Archives, DL/C/243.

19 Thomas, 'With Intent to Injure and Diffame', p. 142.

20 'Thomas Hewetson c. Thomas Daniel' (London, 1699), London Metropolitan Archives, C.P.H.4534.

21 William Selwyn, *An Abridgment of the Law of Nisi Prius* (London: Clarke, 1817), p. 1004.

22 'The word "whore" occurs in a total of 163 trials at the Old Bailey up to 1800: From the first occurrence in 1679 through 1739, 66 trials (just over 40 per cent); from 1730 through 1769, 61 (just over 37 per cent); from 1770 through 1799, 36 (22 per cent)'. ('History of the Term "Prostitute"', *Essays by Rictor Norton*, 2018 <http://rictornorton.co.uk/though15.htm> [Accessed 10 August 2018].)

'A NASTY NAME FOR A NASTY THING'

1   Walter Kirn, 'The Forbidden Word', *GQ*, 4 May 2005, p. 136.

2   Christina Caldwell, 'The C-Word: How One Four-Letter Word Holds So Much Power', *College Times*, 15 March 2011.

3   Pete Silverton, *Filthy English* (London: Portobello Books, 2009), p. 52; Matthew Hunt, 'Cunt', *Matthewhunt.Com*, 2017 <http://www.matthewhunt.com/cunt/> [Accessed 03 September 2018].

4   Mark Daniel, *See You Next Tuesday* (London: Timewell, 2008), Kindle edition, location 135.

5   Melissa Mohr, *Holy Sh*T: A Brief History of Swearing* (Oxford: Oxford University Press, 2013), p. 20.

6   Silverton, *Filthy English*, p. 52.

7   Quoted in Mohr, *Holy Sh*T*, p. 149.

8   Ibid.

9   Lanfranco and John Hall, *Most Excellent and Learned Worke of Chirurgerie, Called Chirurgia Parua Lanfranci*, 1st edn (London: Marshe, 1565).

10 'Cunt', *Oed.com*, 2018 http://www.oed.com/view/Entry/45874?redirectedFrom=cunt#eid> [Accessed 7 September 2018].

11 'OE and ME Cunte in Place-Names', *Keith Briggs*, 2017 <http://keithbriggs.info/documents/cunte_04.pdf> [Accessed 5 April 2017].

12 'Oxford English Dictionary', *Oed.Com*, 2018.

13 Russell Ash, *Busty, Slag and Nob End* (London: Headline, 2009), Kindle edition, location 665.

14 'Oxford English Dictionary', *Oed.Com*, 2018.

15 Liz Herbert McAvoy and Diane Watt, *The History of British Women's Writing, 700–1500* (Basingstoke: Palgrave Macmillan, 2011), p. 68.

16 Geoffrey Chaucer, *The Canterbury Tales*, ed. Jill Mann (London: Penguin Books, 2005), p. 226.

17 Chaucer, *The Canterbury Tales*, p. 120.

18 John Florio and Hermann W. Haller, *A Worlde of Wordes* (Toronto: University of Toronto Press, 2013), p. 504.

19 Andrew Marvell, 'To His Coy Mistress', *Poetry Foundation*, 2018 <https://www.poetryfoundation.org/poems/44688/to-his-coy-mistress> [Accessed 7 September 2018].

20 William Shakespeare, *Hamlet*, *Shakespeare.Mit.Edu*, 2018 <http://shakespeare.mit.edu/hamlet/full.html> [Accessed 7 September 2018].

21 William Shakespeare, *Twelfth Night*, *Shakespeare.Mit.Edu*, 2018 <http://shakespeare.mit.edu/twelfth_night/full.html> [Accessed 7 September 2018].

22 Thomas Bowdler, *The Family Shakespeare* (London: Hatchard, 1807).

23 Reprinted in Ian Frederick Moulton, *Before Pornography: Erotic Writing in Early Modern England* (Oxford: Oxford University Press, 2004), p. 127.

24 John Whiteford Mackenzie, *Philotus, A Comedy, Reprinted from the Edition of Robert Charteris* (Edinburgh: Ballantyne, 1835), p. 3.

25 Gordon Williams, *A Dictionary of Sexual Language and Imagery in Shakespearean and Stuart Literature*, vol. 1 (London: The Athlone Press, 1994), p. 350.

26 Geoffrey R. Stone, 'Origins of Obscenity', *New York University Review of Law*, 31 (2007), 711–31, p. 718.

27 James Thomas Law, *The Ecclesiastical Statutes at Large, Extracted from the Great Body of the Statute Law, and Arranged Under Separate Heads*, vol. 4 (London: William Benning and Co., 1857), p. 273.

28 *The History of the C-Word* (BBC3: BBC, 2007).

29 Geoffrey Hughes, *Swearing: A Social History of Foul Language, Oaths and Profanity in English* (London: Penguin, 1998), p. 140.

30 John Wilmot, Earl of Rochester, *The Works of John Wilmot Earl of Rochester*, ed. by Harold Love (Oxford: Oxford University Press, 1999), p. 269.

31 Ibid., p. 79.

32 Ibid., p. 78.

33 Samuel Pepys and Robert Latham, *The Diary of Samuel Pepys*, vol. 4 (Berkeley: HarperCollins, 2000), p. 209; E. J. Burford, *Bawdy Verse: A Pleasant Collection* (Harmondsworth: Penguin, 1982), p. 170.

34 Francis Grose, *A Classical Dictionary of the Vulgar Tongue*, 3rd edn (London: Hooper & Co., 1796), p. 81.

35 Hallie Rubenhold, *Harris's List of Covent Garden Ladies* (London: Doubleday, 2012), p. 11.

36 Marquis de Sade, *Marquis de Sade Collection*, ed. by Anna Ruggieri, Kindle edition, location 8323.

37 Anonymous, *The Pearl* (London, Privately printed, 1879).

38 'Oxford English Dictionary', *Oed.Com*, 2018 <http://www.oed.com/view/Entry/45874?redirectedFrom=cunt#eid> [Accessed 7 September 2018]; see also Mark E. Neely, *The Abraham Lincoln Encyclopedia* (New York: McGraw-Hill, 1982), p. 154.

39 Gerald Gould, 'New Novels', *Observer*, 28 February 1932, p. 6.

40 D. H. Lawrence, *Lady Chatterley's Lover*, ed. by David Ellis (Ware: Wordsworth, 2007), p. 156.

41 James Joyce, *Ulysses* (Ware: Wordsworth, 2010), p. 54.

42 Allen Ginsberg, 'Howl', *Poetry Foundation*, 2018 <https://www.poetryfoundation.org/poems/49303/howl> [Accessed 7 September 2018].

43 Mike Nichols, *Carnal Knowledge* (Los Angeles: AVCO Embassy Pictures, 1971).

44 William Friedkin, *The Exorcist: Extended Director's Cut* (Warner Brothers, 2010).

45 'Oxford English Dictionary', *Oed.Com*, 2018 <http://www.oed.com/view/Entry/45874?redirectedFrom=cunt#eid> [Accessed 7 September 2018].

46 'Ofcom Explores Latest Attitudes to Offensive Language', *Ofcom*, 2016 <https://www.ofcom.org.uk/about-ofcom/latest/media/media-releases/2016/attitudes-to-offensive-language> [Accessed 7 September 2018].

47 Eve Ensler, Jacqueline Woodson and Monique Wilson, *The Vagina Monologues* (London: Virago, 2001), pp. 100–10.

LOOKING FOR THE BOY IN THE BOAT

1 Viz, *Roger's Profanisaurus* (London: John Brown, 1998), pp. 7, 10, 17, 30, 81.

2 Graham Dury and others, *Hail Sweary* (London: Dennis Publishing, 2013), pp. 19, 40, 127.

3 H. C. T. Hamilton, *The Geography of Strabo* (London: Bell and Sons, 1903), 17.2.5.

4 Galen and Margaret Tallmadge May, *Galen on the Usefulness of the Parts of the Body* (New York: Classics of Medicine Library, 1996). Other medical writers from the Ancient World to discuss the anatomy of the 'nymph' were Caelius Aurelianus, Albucasis and Avicenna.

5 Soranus and Owsei Temkin, *Soranus' Gynecology* (Baltimore: Johns Hopkins Univ. Press, 1994), p. 16.

6 Soranos d'Éphèse, *Sorani Gynaeciorum Libri IV. De Signis Fracturarum. De Fasciis. Vita Hippocratis Secundum Soranum*, ed. by Ioannes Ilberg (Lipsiae: Teubneri, 1927). (4.9), p. 370.

7 Cited in Mary Knight, 'Curing Cut or Ritual Mutilation? Some Remarks on the Practice of Female and Male Circumcision in Graeco-Roman Egypt', *Isis*, 92.2 (2001), pp. 327–8.

8 John G. Younger, *Sex in the Ancient World from A to Z* (London: Routledge, 2005), p. 36.

9 Aristophanes and Alan Herbert Sommerstein, *Knights* (Warminster: Aris & Phillips, 1990), pp. 1284–5.

10 Cicero and D. R. Shackleton Bailey, *Epistulae ad Familiares* (Cambridge: Cambridge University Press, 1977), p. 9.

11 Cited in Jacqueline Fabre-Serris and Alison Keith, *Women and War in Antiquity* (Baltimore: Johns Hopkins University Press, 2015), p. 264; Melissa Mohr, *Holy Sh*T: A Brief History of Swearing* (Corby: Oxford Academic Publishing Ltd, 2013), p. 26.

12 Martial, *Epigrams*, trans. by Gideon Nisbet (Oxford: Oxford University Press, 2015), 1.90., p. 27.

13 Mohr, *Holy Sh*T*, p. 28.

14 Samuel Arbesman, *The Half Life of Facts – Why Everything We Know Has An Expiration Date* (London: Penguin, 2004).

15 Geoffrey Chaucer, V. A. Kolve and Glending Olson, *The Canterbury Tales* (New York, N.Y.: Norton & Company, 2005), lines 430–35.

16 M. S. Spink and L. G. Lewis, *Albucasis on Surgery and Instruments. A Definitive Edition of the Arabic Text with English Translation and Commentary* (Berkeley: University of California Press, 1976), p. 456.

17 Avicenna, *Liber Canonis* (Hildesheim: Georg Olms Verlagsbuchhandlung, 1964), p. 377.

18 Danielle Jacquart and Claude Thomasset, *Sexuality and Medicine in the Middle Ages* (Cambridge: Polity, 1988).

19 See Karma Lochrie, *Heterosyncrasies: Female Sexuality When Normal Wasn't* (Minneapolis: University of Minnesota Press, 2005).

20 Thomas Wright and Richard Paul Wülker, *Anglo-Saxon and Old English Vocabularies* (London: Trubner & Co., 1883), p. 549.

21 Ibid. Also see Mohr, *Holy Sh*T*, p. 98.

22 Gabriele Falloppio, *Observationes Anatomicae* (Modena: STEM Mucchi, 1964), p. 193.

23 Realdo Colombo, *De re Anatomica*, trans. by Nicolae Beuilacquae (Venice: Bruxelles, 1969), Book XI, pp. 242–3, Book XV, pp. 262–9.

24 Falloppio, *Observationes Anatomicae*, p. 193.

25 Colombo, *De re Anatomica*, pp. 242–3.

26 Vincent Di Marino and Hubert Lepidi, *Anatomic Study of the Clitoris and the Bulbo-Clitoral Organ* (Cham: Springer International Publishing, 2014), p. 8.

27 Thomas Bartholin and Michael Lyser, *The Anatomical History of Thomas Bartholinus* (London: Printed by Francis Leach for Octavian Pulleyn, 1653), p. 77. For further discussion on lesbianism and large clitorises in the early modern period, see Valerie Traub, *The Renaissance of Lesbianism in Early Modern England* (Cambridge: Cambridge University Press, 2002).

28 Nicolas Venette, *Conjugal Love; Or, The Pleasures of the Marriage Bed*, 20th edn (London, 1750), p. 71.

29 Charles Slackville, 'A Faithful Catalogue of Our Most Eminent Ninnies', in *Poems on Affairs of State: Augustan Satirical Verse, 1660–1714* (New Haven: Yale University Press, 1963), iv, p. 195.

30 Jane Sharp, *The Midwives Book, Or, The Whole Art of Midwifry Discovered*, ed. by Elaine Hobby (Oxford: Oxford University Press, 1999), p. 39.

31 Ibid., p. 40.

32 Ibid., pp. 41–42.

33 See, for example, Rosemary Guiley, *The Encyclopaedia of Witches and Witchcraft* (New York: Facts on File, 1989); Lana Thompson, *The Wandering Womb* (Amherst, N.Y.: Prometheus Books, 1999); Jelto Drenth, *The Origin of the World* (London: Reaktion, 2008).

34   King James I, *Daemonologie in Forme of a Dialogie* (Robert Walde-graue, 1597), p. 70.

35   Diane Purkiss, *The Witch in History* (Hoboken: Routledge, 2012), p. 135.

36   Anon, *The Wonderful Discoverie of the Witchcrafts of Magaret and Phillip Flower, Daughters of Joan Flower Neere Beur Castle: Executed at Lincolne, March II. 1618* (London, 1619), pp. 22–4.

37   H. F., *A True and Exact Relation of the Several Informations, Examinations, and Confessions of the Late Witches, Arraigned and Executed in the County of Essex* (London, 1664), p. 24.

38   Matthew Hale, *A Tryal of Witches at Bury St Edmunds*, 1664, p. 16.

39   Nicolas Chorier, *A Dialogue between a Married Lady and a Maid* (London, 1740), p. 13.

40   de Sade, *The Marquis de Sade: The Complete Justine, Philosophy in the Bedroom, and Other Writings* (New York: Grove Press, 1990), p. 205.

41   *A New Description of Merryland* (London: E Curll, 1741), p. 15.

42   M. D. T. de Bienville and Edward Wilmot, *Nymphomania, Or, A Dissertation Concerning the Furor Uterinus* (London: J. Bew, 1775), p. 36.

43   Alexandre Parent Du Châtelet, *On Prostitution in The City of Paris* (London: T. Burgess, 1837), p. 108.

44   Ibid., p. 109.

45   Robley Dunglison, *Medical Lexicon: A Dictionary of Medical Science* (Philadelphia: Blanchard & Lea, 1854), p. 214.

46   'Masturbation in the Female', *American Homeopathic Journal of Gynaecology and Obstetrics*, 1.I (1885), pp. 338–340; p. 340.

47   Isaac Baker Brown, *On the Curability of Certain Forms of Insanity, Epilepsy, Catalepsy, and Hysteria in Females* (Robert Hardwicke: London, 1866), p. 84.

48   Ibid., p. 17.

49   'Obstetrical Society's Charges and Mr Baker Brown's Replies', *The Lancet*, 1.92 (1867), pp. 427–41; p. 434.

50   Sigmund Freud, *The Question of Lay Analysis* (New York: Norton, 1989), p. 38.

51   Sigmund Freud, *Three Essays on the Theory of Sexuality* (Mansfield: Martino Publishing, 2011), p. 87.

52   A.E. Narjani, 'Considerations Sur Les Causes Anatomiques De La Frigidite Chez La Femme', *Bruxelles Medical*, 27.4 (1924), 768–78.

53   Eduard Hitschmann and Edmund Bergler, *Frigidity in Women: Its Characteristics and Treatment* (Washington: Nervous and Mental Disease, 1936), p. 20.

54   William S. Kroger, 'Psychosomatic Aspects of Frigidity', *Journal of The American Medical Association*, 143.6 (1950), 526–32, p. 526.

55   Alfred C. Kinsey, Individual Variation Lecture, lecture 8, spring 1940 (28 February, 1940), Alfred C. Kinsey Collection.

56   'Clitoral Hood: Size, Appearance, Effect on Orgasm, Reduction, and More', *Healthline*, 2018 <https://www.healthline.com/health/womens-health/clitoral-hood> [Accessed 24 September 2018].

57   Donna Mazloomdoost and Rachel N. Pauls, 'A Comprehensive Review of the Clitoris and Its Role in Female Sexual Function', *Sexual Medicine Reviews*, 3.4 (2015), pp. 245–63.

58   Pierre Foldes and Odile Buisson, 'The Clitoral Complex: A Dynamic Sonographic Study', *Journal of Sexual Medicine*, 2009, 1223–31.

59   Odile Buisson and others, 'Coitus as Revealed by Ultrasound in One Volunteer Couple', *The Journal of Sexual Medicine*, 7.8 (2010), 2750–4.

60   'Female Genital Mutilation', *World Health Organization*, 2018 <http://www.who.int/news-room/fact-sheets/detail/female-genital-mutilation> [Accessed 17 June 2018].

COLONISING THE CUNT

1   Sir Mix-a-Lot, 'Baby Got Back' (Def American, 1992).

2   Darlene Abreu-Ferreira, *Women, Crime, And Forgiveness in Early Modern Portugal* (Florence: Taylor and Francis, 2016).

3   William Smith, *A New Voyage to Guinea*, 2nd edn (London: John Nourse, 1745), p. 221.

4   *Reports of the Lords of the Committee of Council Appointed for the Consideration of all Matters Relating to Trade and Foreign Plantations* (London, 1789), p. 119.

5   Clifton C. Crais and Pamela Scully, *Sara Baartman and the Hottentot Venus* (Princeton: Princeton University Press).

6   François Le Vaillant, *New Travels into the Interior Parts of Africa, by the Way of the Cape of Good Hope* (London: G. G. and J. Robinson, 1796), p. 351.

7   John Barrow, *Travels into the Interior of Southern Africa* (London: T. Cadell and W. Davies, 1801), p. 281.

8   *The Times*, 'The Hottentot Venus', 1810, p. 3.

9   'Baartman, Sara [Performing Name the Hottentot Venus] (1777X88–1815/16), Celebrity and Subject of Scientific Speculation | Oxford Dictionary Of National Biography', *Oxforddnb.com*, 2018 <http://www.oxforddnb.com/view/10.1093/ref:odnb/9780198614128.001.0001/odnb-9780198614128-e-73573;jsessionid=1ABB9A1E6F71D8D1704734C50D86E17D> [Accessed 7 August 2018].

10   *Bell's Weekly Messenger*, 'The Hottentot Venus', 1810, p. 7.

11   Georges Cuvier, 'Extrait D'Observations Faites Sur Le Cadavre D'Une Femme Connue À Paris Et À Londres Sous Le Nom De Vénus Hottentotte',

in *Mémoires Du Musée Nationale D'Histoire Naturelle*, 1817, pp. 259–74.

12   Adrien Charpy, 'Des Organes Genitaux Externes Chez Les Prostituées', *Annales De Dermatologie*, 3 (1870), pp. 271–79.

13   Cesare Lombroso and Gugliemo Ferrero, *La Donna Delinquente* (Turin: Roux, 1893), pp. 38, 361–2.

14   William Lee Howard, 'The Negro as a Distinct Ethnic Factor in Civilization', *Medicine*, 60 (1904), pp. 423–26.

'AS EASILY MADE AS A PUDDING'

1   Rose McKeon Olson and Claudia García-Moreno, 'Virginity Testing: A Systematic Review', *Reproductive Health*, 14.1 (2017) <https://doi.org/10.1186/s12978-017-0319-0>.

2   World Health Organization, 'Interagency Statement Calls For The Elimination Of "Virginity-Testing"', *World Health Organization*, 2018 <https://www.who.int/reproductivehealth/publications/eliminating-virginity-testing-interagency-statement/en/> [Accessed 21 May 2019]

3   'FGM National Clinical Group – Historical & Cultural', *Fgmnationalgroup.org*, 2018 <http://www.fgmnationalgroup.org/historical_and_cultural.htm> [Accessed 11 September 2018].

4   'Female Genital Mutilation', *World Health Organization*, 2017 <http://www.who.int/mediacentre/factsheets/fs241/en/> [Accessed 10 August 2017].

5   'Virginity Testing "Sacred" But Not a Science', *Africa Check*, 2017 <https://africacheck.org/reports/virginity-testing-sacred-but-not-a-science/> [Accessed 21 August 2017].

6   Lucy Pasha-Robinson, 'Doctors Are Being Ordered to Perform "Virginity Tests" on Underage Girls in Russia', *The Independent*, 2018 <https://www.independent.co.uk/news/world/europe/russia-doctors-virginity-tests-russian-investigative-committee-underage-girls-a7783811.html> [Accessed 11 September 2018].

7   Kathleen Coyne Kelly, *Performing Virginity and Testing Chastity in the Middle Ages* (New York: Routledge, 2000).

8   Soranus and Owsei Temkin, *Soranus' Gynecology* (Baltimore: Johns Hopkins University Press, 1994).

9   Danielle Jacquart and Claude Thomasset, *Sexuality and Medicine in the Middle Ages* (Cambridge, UK: Polity Press, 1988), p. 44.

10   'Lacuscurtius Valerius Maximus – Liber VIII', *Penelope.Uchicago.Edu*, 2018 <http://penelope.uchicago.edu/Thayer/L/Roman/Texts/Valerius_Maximus/8*.html> [Accessed 11 September 2018].

11   Aelian, *On the Characteristics of Animals* (Cambridge: Harvard University Press, 1959), p. 358; Michael Rosenberg, *Signs of Virginity: Testing Virgins and Making Men in Late Antiquity* (Oxford: Oxford University Press, 2018), p. 26.

12   Albertus and Helen Rodnite Lemay, *Women's Secrets: A Translation of Pseudo-Albertus Magnus' De Secretis Mulierum with Commentaries* (Albany: University of New York Press, 1992), p. 128.

13   Rosenberg, *Signs of Virginity*, p. 24.

14   Kelly, *Performing Virginity and Testing Chastity in the Middle Ages*, pp. 28–31.

15   Navas, *Book of Women* (Hoboken: Taylor and Francis, 2014), p. 142.

16   Albertus, *Women's Secrets*, p. 128.

17   'Bloody Sheets: An Age-Old Tradition Still Held in Georgia's Regions', *Georgia Today*, 2017 <http://georgiatoday.ge/news/2879/Bloody-Sheets%3A-An-Age-old-Tradition-Still-Held-in-Georgia%E2%80%99s-Regions> [Accessed 20 August 2017].

18   Henry Ansgar Kelly and Alan M Dershowitz, *The Matrimonial Trials of Henry VIII* (London: Wipf and Stock, 2004), pp. 233–4.

19   *The Trotula*, trans. by Monica Helen Green (Philadelphia: University of Pennsylvania Press, 2002), pp. 103–4.

20   Navas, *Book of Women*, pp. 142–4.

21   Nicolas Venette, *The Mysteries of Conjugal Love Reveal'd*, 3rd edn (London, 1712), p. 78.

22   Francis Grose, *A Classical Dictionary of the Vulgar Tongue*, 3rd edn (London: Hooper & Co.,1796), p. 183.

23   *Nocturnal Revels: Or, the History of King's Place* (London: M. Goadby, 1779), p. 164.

24   John Cleland, *Fanny Hill, or, Memoirs of a Woman of Pleasure* (London: LBA, 2007), Kindle edition, p. 146.

25   Tassie Gwilliam, 'Female Fraud: Counterfeit Maidenheads in the Eighteenth Century', *Journal of the History of Sexuality*, 6 (1996), pp. 518–48.

26   'On the Signs of Defloration in Young Females', *London Medical Gazette: or, Journal of Practical Medicine*, 48 (1831), 304–6.

27   Edward B. Foote, *Medical Common Sense* (New York: printed by the author, 1867), p. 173.

28   Rose McKeon Olson and Claudia García-Moreno, 'Virginity Testing: A Systematic Review', *Reproductive Health*, 14.1 (2017) <https://doi.org/10.1186/s12978-017-0319-0>.

29   Independent Forensic Expert Group, 'Statement on Virginity Testing', *Journal of Forensic and Legal Medicine*, 33 (2015), pp. 121–24 <https://doi.org/10.1016/j.jflm.2015.02.012>.

30   Olson and García-Moreno, 'Virginity Testing: A Systematic Review', *Reproductive Health*, p. 14.

SPILLING THE BEANS

1   Elisabeth A. Lloyd, *The Case of the Female Orgasm: Bias in the Science of Evolution* (Cambridge, MA: Harvard University Press, 2005), p. 44.

2   Anne A. Lawrence, 'Sexuality Before and After Male-to-Female Sex Reassignment Surgery', *Archives of Sexual Behaviour*, 34.2 (2005), 147–66 <https://doi.org/10.1007/s10508-005-1793-y>; Imbimbo, C., et al., 'Intersex and Gender Identity Disorders: A report from a single institute's 14-Year experience in treatment of male-to-female Transsexuals', *The Journal of Sexual Medicine*, 6.10 (2009), pp. 2736–45. doi: 10.1111/j.1743-6109.2009.01379.x; Jochen Hess et al., 'Satisfaction With Male-to-Female Gender Reassignment Surgery', *Deutsches Aerzteblatt Online*, 111.47 (2014) <https://doi.org/10.3238/arztebl.2014.0795>.

3   Lisa D. Wade, Emily C. Kremer and Jessica Brown, 'The Incidental Orgasm: The Presence of Clitoral Knowledge and the Absence of Orgasm for Women', *Women & Health*, 42.1 (2005), 117–38 <https://doi.org/10.1300/j013v42n01_07>.

4   John G. Avildsen, *Rocky* (Chartoff-Winkler Productions, 1976).

5   'The Myths of Sex Before Sport', *BBC News*, 2004 <http://news.bbc.co.uk/1/hi/magazine/3555734.stm> [Accessed 27 August 2018].

6   Dr Brooke Magnanti, 'Boxer Carl Froch Has Been Abstaining from Sex – But Is It Ever Worth It?', *Daily Telegraph*, 2014 <https://www.telegraph.co.uk/women/sex/10864506/Sex-ban-Carl-Froch-has-been-abstaining-from-sex-but-is-it-really-good-for-you.html> [Accessed 27 August 2018].

7   N. Maffulli, et al., 'Sexual Activity before Sports Competition: A Systematic Review', *Frontiers in Physiology*, 2016;7:246. doi:10.3389/fphys.2016.00246.

8   Alexandra Sifferlin, 'Can Sex Really Dampen Athletic Performance?', *Time*, 2014 <http://time.com/2911744/can-sex-re/> [Accessed 27 August 2018].

9   'The Classic of Su Nu', in Douglas Wile, *Art of the Bedchamber: the Chinese Sexual Yoga Classics* (Albany: University of New York Press, 1992), p. 93.

10   'Does Frequent Ejaculation Help Ward Off Prostate Cancer?', 2009 <http://www.harvardprostateknowledge.org/does-frequent-ejaculation-help-ward-off-prostate-cancer> [Accessed 13 February 2017]; Jennifer R. Rider and others, 'Ejaculation Frequency and Risk of Prostate Cancer: Updated Results with an Additional Decade of Follow-Up', *European Urology*, 70.6 (2016), 974–82 <https://doi.org/10.1016/j.eururo.2016.03.027>.

11   G. G. Giles and others, 'Sexual Factors and Prostate Cancer', *BJU International*, 92.3 (2003), 211–16 <https://doi.org/10.1046/j.1464-410x.2003.04319.x>.

12   John G. Younger, *Sex in the Ancient World from A To Z* (London: Routledge, 2005), p. 2.

13 Albert the Great, 'Questions on Animals', quoted in *Sexuality and Medicine in the Middle Ages*, trans. by M. Adamson (Oxford: Oxford University Press, 1998), pp. 55–6.

14 Gerald of Wales, *The Jewel of the Church: A Translation of the Gemma Ecclesiastica*, trans. by J.J. Hagen (Leiden: Brill, 1979), p. 109.

15 'Summa Theologica Index', *Sacred-Texts.Com*, 2018 <http://www.sacred-texts.com/chr/aquinas/summa/index.htm> [Accessed 15 September 2018].

16 P. G. Maxwell-Stuart, *The Malleus Maleficarum* (Manchester: Manchester University Press, 2007), Kindle edition, location 1507.

17 Ibid., location 1474.

18 Ibid., location 1524.

19 William Masters and Virginia Johnson, *Human Sexual Response* (London: Churchill, 1966), pp. 7–8.

20 K. R. Turley and D. L. Rowland, 'Evolving ideas about the male refractory period', *BJU International*, 112 (2013), 442–52.

21 S. A. D. Tissot, *Onanism; Or, A Treatise upon the Disorders Produced by Masturbation; Or, The Dangerous Effects Of Secret and Excessive Venery ... Translated from the Last Paris Edition, By A. Hume. The Fifth Edition, Corrected*, 5th edn (London: Richardson, 1781), p. 11.

22 Léopold Deslandes, *A Treatise on the Diseases Produced by Onanism, Masturbation, Self-Pollution, and Other Excesses*, 2nd edn (Boston: Otis, Broader and Company, 1839), p. 3.

23 J. H. Kellogg, *Plain Facts for Old and Young* (Burlington: Segner, 1887), p. 294.

24 Ibid., p. 295.

25 Ibid., p. 296.

26 Robert Baden-Powell, *Boy Scouts of America*, 1st edn (New York: Page and Company, 1911), p. 345.

27 Albert Moll, *Sexual Life of the Child (Classic Reprint)* (London: Forgotten Books, 2015), p. 56.

28 Wilhelm Reich, *The Bioelectrical Investigation of Sexuality and Anxiety* (New York: Farrar, Straus and Giroux, 1982), p. 9; Alfred C. Kinsey, Wardell B. Pomeroy and Clyde E. Martin, *Sexual Behavior in the Human Male* (Philadelphia: W. B. Saunders, 1948).

29 William H. Masters and Virginia E. Johnson, *Human Sexual Response* (London: Churchill, 1966), pp. 3–9.

30 Semir Zeki and Andreas Bartels, 'The Neural Correlates of Maternal and Romantic Love', *Neuroimage*, 21.3 (2004), 1155–66 <https://doi.org/10.1016/j.neuroimage.2003.11.003>.

31 B. Whipple, 'Functional Magnetic Resonance Imaging (FMRI) During Orgasm in Women', *Sexologies*, 17 (2008), S45 https://doi.org/10.1016/

s1158-1360(08)72639-2; Ruth G. Kurtz, 'Hippocampal and Cortical Activity During Sexual Behavior in the Female Rat', *Journal of Comparative and Physiological Psychology*, 89.2 (1975), 158–69 https://doi.org/10.1037/h0076650; Mary S. Erskine, Joseph G. Oberlander and Jasmine J. Yang, 'Expression of FOS, EGR-1, and ARC in the Amygdala and Hippocampus of Female Rats During Formation of the Intromission Mnemonic of Pseudopregnancy', *Developmental Neurobiology*, 67.7 (2007), 895–908 <https://doi.org/10.1002/dneu.20376>.

32   James G. Pfaus and others, 'The Role of Orgasm in the Development and Shaping of Partner Preferences', *Socioaffective Neuroscience & Psychology*, 6.1 (2016), 31815 <https://doi.org/10.3402/snp.v6.31815>.

33   Stuart Brody and Rui Miguel Costa, 'Satisfaction (Sexual, Life, Relationship, and Mental Health) is Associated Directly with Penile-Vaginal Intercourse, but Inversely with Other Sexual Behavior Frequencies', *The Journal of Sexual Medicine*, 6.7 (2009), 1947–54 <https://doi.org/10.1111/j.1743-6109.2009.01303.x>.

34   Beverly Whipple and Carol Rinkleib Ellison, *Women's Sexualities: Generations of Women Share Intimate Sexual Secrets of Sexual Self-Acceptance* (Oakland, CA: New Harbinger Publications, US, 2000).

35   Randolph W. Evans and R. Couch, 'Orgasm and Migraine', *Headache: The Journal of Head and Face Pain*, 41.5 (2001), 512–14 <https://doi.org/10.1046/j.1526-4610.2001.01091.x>.

36   Quentin Crisp, *The Naked Civil Servant* (London: Flamingo, 1996) p. 14.

GLAND LARCENY

1   Glenn Matfin, 'The Rejuvenation of Testosterone: Philosopher's Stone or Brown-Séquard Elixir?', *Therapeutic Advances in Endocrinology and Metabolism*, 1.4 (2010), 151–54 <https://doi.org/10.1177/2042018810385052>.

2   Charles Éduoard Brown-Séquard, *The Elixir of Life: Dr. Brown-Séquard's Own Account of His Famous Alleged Remedy for Debility and Old Age,* ed. by Newell Dunbar (Boston: J.G. Cupples, 1889), pp. 21–6.

3   Ibid., p. 23.

4   Ibid., p. 25.

5   Charles Éduoard Brown-Séquard, 'Note on the Effects Produced on Man by Subcutaneous Injections of a Liquid Obtained from the Testicles of Animals', *The Lancet*, 134.3438 (1889), pp. 105–7 <https://doi.org/10.1016/s0140-6736(00)64118-1>.

6   Le Petit Parisien, 'Jouvence', 8 October 1919. See also Catherine Remy, '"Men Seeking Monkey-Glands": The Controversial Xenotransplantations

of Doctor Voronoff, 1910–30', *French History*, 28.2 (2014), pp. 226–40 <https://doi.org/10.1093/fh/cru042>.

7   John B. Nanninga, *The Gland Illusion: Early Attempts at Rejuvenation Through Male Hormone Therapy* (London: McFarland, 2017), Kindle edition, location 1125.

8   Serge Voronoff, *Quarante-Trois Greffes Du Singe À L'homme* (Paris: G. Doin, 1924), p. 90.

9   *Aberdeen Press and Journal*, 'Monkey Gland Patient Dead', 1923, p. 7.

10   Serge Voronoff, *Rejuvenation by Grafting* (London: G. Allen & Unwin Ltd, 1925), pp. 118–119.

11   Ibid., pp. 68–127.

12   Nanninga, *The Gland Illusion*, location 1232.

13   *The Times*, 'Dr Voronoff's Operations: A Meeting of Protest', 8 June 1928.

14   Nanninga, *The Gland Illusion*, location 1638.

15   R. Alton Lee, *The Bizarre Careers of John R. Brinkley* (Lexington: The University Press of Kentucky, 2015), p. 219.

16   Quoted in Pope Brock, *Charlatan: America's Most Dangerous Huckster, the Man Who Pursued Him, and the Age of Flimflam* (New York: Crown Publishers, 2008), p. 264.

17   George Bernard Shaw, 'Letter to the Editor', in *The Saturday Review of Literature*, 1928, p. 1043.

18   David Hamilton, *The Monkey Gland Affair* (London: Chatto & Windus, 1986), p. 91.

19   Eugen Steinach and Josef Löbel, *Sex and Life: Forty Years of Biological and Medical Experiments* (New York: Viking, 1940), p. 176.

20   E. Steinach, 'Biological Methods Against the Process of Old Age', *Medical Journal and Record*, 25 (1927), p. 79.

21   'Current Comment, "Glandular Therapy"', *Journal of the American Medical Association*, 83 (1924), p. 1004.

22   Sharon Romm, *The Unwelcome Intruder: Freud's Struggle with Cancer* (New York, NY, USA: Praeger, 1983), pp. 17–23.

23   Quoted in Nanninga, *The Gland Illusion*, location 1549.

24   S. Lock, '"O That I Were Young Again": Yeats and the Steinach Operatio', *BMJ*, 287.6409 (1983), pp. 1964–68 <https://doi.org/10.1136/bmj.287.6409.1964>.

25   *Portsmouth Evening News*, 'Gland Rejuvenation', 22 April 1939, p. 8.

26   *Nottingham Evening Post*, 'Seven Methods Explained', 15 July 1924, p. 1.

27   *Dundee Evening Telegraph*, 'Youth Glands Stolen', 16 October 1922, p. 7.

28   Ibid.

TOUGH LOVE

1 John Tozzi and Jared Hopkins, 'The Little Blue Pill: an Oral History of Viagra', *Bloomberg*, 2018 <https://www.bloomberg.com/news/features/2017-12-11/the-little-blue-pill-an-oral-history-of-viagra> [Accessed 25 August 2018].

2 Dawn Connelly, 'Three Decades of Viagra', *The Pharmaceutical Journal*, 2017 <https://doi.org/10.1211/pj.2017.20202847>.

3 'Cover Page', *Time*, 1998.

4 Stanley E. Althof and others, 'Self-Esteem, Confidence, and Relationships in Men Treated with Sildenafil Citrate for Erectile Dysfunction', *Journal of General Internal Medicine*, 21.10 (2006), 1069–74 <https://doi.org/10.1111/j.1525-1497.2006.00554.x>.

5 Stephanie B. Hoffman, 'Behind Closed Doors: Impotence Trials and the Trans-Historical Right to Martial Policy', *Boston University Law Review*, 89 (2009), 1725–52, p. 1732.

6 Rider, *Magic and Impotence in the Middle Ages*, p. 61.

7 Jacqueline Murray, 'On the Origins and Role of "Wise Women" in Causes for Annulment on the Grounds of Male Impotence', *Journal of Medieval History*, 16.3 (1990), pp. 235–49, p. 243. <https://doi.org/10.1016/0304-4181(90)90004-k>.

8 Quoted in Frederik Pedersen, *Marriage Disputes in Medieval England* (London: Hambledon, 2000), p. 117.

9 Frederick Pederson, 'Motives for Murder: The Role of Sir Ralph Paynel in the Murder of William Cantilupe', in *Continuity, Change and Pragmatism in the Law: Essays in Honour of Professor Angelo Forte* (Aberdeen: Aberdeen University Press, 2016), pp. 69–95, p. 83.

10 Quoted in Henrietta Leyser, *Medieval Women: Social History of Women in England 450–1500* (London: Phoenix Press, 1995), p. 116.

11 Quoted in Rider, *Magic and Impotence in the Middle Ages*, p. 44.

12 P. G. Maxwell-Stuart, *The Malleus Maleficarum* (Manchester: Manchester University Press, 2007), Kindle edition, locations 2844–45.

13 Ibid., locations 2897–99.

14 Ibid., locations 2931–3.

15 Hincmar of Rheims, *De Divortio Lotharii Regis Et Theutbergae Regina*, ed. by Letha Böhringer (Hanover: MGH, 1992), p. 217.

16 Hincmar of Rheims, *De Nuptiis Stephani Et Filiae Regimundi Comiti* (Berlin: MGH, 1939), p. 105.

17 See Rider, *Magic and Impotence in the Middle Ages*, pp. 72–4.

18 Hoffman, 'Behind Closed Doors', p. 1727.

STAFF OF LIFE

1 See Johann F. Kinzl and others, 'Partnership, Sexuality, and Sexual Disorders in Morbidly Obese Women: Consequences of Weight Loss After Gastric Banding', *Obesity Surgery*, 11.4 (2001), 455–8 https:// doi.org/10.1381/096089201321209323; Sarah R. Holzer and others, 'Mediational Significance of PTSD in the Relationship of Sexual Trauma and Eating Disorders', *Child Abuse & Neglect*, 32.5 (2008), 561–6 <https:// doi.org/10.1016/j.chiabu.2007.07.011>.

2 'Proverbs 9:17 Commentaries: "Stolen Water Is Sweet; And Bread Eaten In Secret Is Pleasant."', *Biblehub.Com*, 2018 <https://biblehub.com/ commentaries/proverbs/9-17.htm> [Accessed 18 August 2018].

3 Judith Harris, *Pompeii Awakened: A Story Of Rediscovery* (London: Tauris, 2007), p. 121.

4 'Exeter Book Riddles', *Anglo-Saxon Narrative Poetry Project*, 2018 <https:// anglosaxonpoetry.camden.rutgers.edu/exeter-book-riddles/> [Accessed 18 August 2018].

5 Martial, 'Epigrams. Book 14'. *Tertullian.Org*, 2018 <http://www.tertullian. org/fathers/martial_epigrams_book14.htm> [Accessed 18 August 2018].

6 Athenaeus, *The Deipnosophists*, vol. VI, trans. by Charles Burton Gulick (London: Heinemann, 1927), p. 493.

7 Jacques-Antoine Dulaure, *Histoire Abrégée De Différens Cultes*, 2nd edn (Paris, 1825), p. 285.

8 Richard Payne Knight and Thomas Wright, *A Discourse on the Worship of Priapus, and its Connection with the Mystic* (London: Spilbury, 1865), p. 158.

9 Quoted in John Raymond Shinners, *Medieval Popular Religion, 1000–1500: A Reader* (Toronto: UTP, 2009), pp. 451–53.

10 Ibid., p. 455.

11 Ibid., pp. 451–53.

12 Geoffrey Chaucer, 'The General Prologue', in *The Canterbury Tales*, ed. by Jill Mann (London: Penguin Books, 2005), p. 26.

13 Madeleine Pelner Cosman and Linda Gale Jones, *Handbook to Life in the Medieval World,* vol. 3 (New York: Facts on File, 2008), p. 134.

14 Ibid. Theodore of Canterbury (AD 602–690) had a slightly different take on this in his penitential and warned of women baking their husband's semen into his bread to increase his libido. Jacqueline Murray, *Love, Marriage, and Family in the Middle Ages: A Reader* (Toronto: University of Toronto Press, 2001), p. 46.

15 George Peele, *The Old Wives' Tale*, ed. by Patricia Binnie (Manchester: Manchester University Press, 1980), p. 75.

16 Richard Brome, *A Jovial Crew*, ed. by Tiffany Stern (London: Bloomsbury, 2014), pp. 122–33, 30–1.

17 John Aubrey, *Remaines of Gentilisme and Judaisme* (London: Folklore Society, 1881), pp. 43–44.

18 Natasha Hinde, 'Blogger Bakes Sourdough Using Yeast from Vagina, Internet Explodes', *Huffpost UK*, 2018 <https://www.huffingtonpost.co.uk/2015/11/24/woman-makes-sourdough-using-yeast-from-vagina_n_8636372.html> [Accessed 19 August 2018].

THE FOOD OF LOVE

1 'Science Proves Oysters and Mussels are the Food of Love', *The Scotsman*, 2018 <https://www.scotsman.com/future-scotland/tech/science-proves-oysters-and-mussels-are-the-food-of-love-1-740457> [Accessed 20 August 2018].

2 Antimo D'Aniello and others, 'Occurrence and Neuroendocrine Role of d-Aspartic Acid And n-Methyl-D-Aspartic Acid Inciona Intestinalis', *FEBS Letters*, 552.2–3 (2003), 193–8 <https://doi.org/10.1016/s0014-5793(03)00921-9>.

3 Raul A. Mirza and others, 'Do Marine Mollusks Possess Aphrodisiacal Properties?', paper presented at the Chemical Society National Conference in San Diego, March 13–17, 2005.

4 Adam Lusher, 'Raw Oysters Really Are Aphrodisiacs Say Scientists (And Now Is the Time to Eat Them)', *Daily Telegraph*, 2018 <http://www.telegraph.co.uk/news/uknews/4195596/Raw-oysters-really-are-aphrodisiacs-say-scientists-and-now-is-the-time-to-eat-them.html> [Accessed 19 August 2018].

5 C. D. Hunt and others, 'Effects of Dietary Zinc Depletion on Seminal Volume and Zinc Loss, Serum Testosterone Concentrations, and Sperm Morphology in Young Men', *The American Journal of Clinical Nutrition*, 56.1 (1992), 148–57 https://doi.org/10.1093/ajcn/56.1.148; Radhika Purushottam Kothari, 'Zinc Levels in Seminal Fluid in Infertile Males and Its Relation with Serum Free Testosterone', *Journal of Clinical and Diagnostic Research*, 10 (2016), CC05-8 https://doi.org/10.7860/jcdr/2016/14393.7723.

6 Robert C. Walter and others, 'Early Human Occupation of the Red Sea Coast of Eritrea During the Last Interglacial', *Nature*, 405.6782 (2000), 65–9 <https://doi.org/10.1038/35011048>.

7 Hesiod, *Theogony*, ed. by M. L. West (Oxford: Oxford University Press, 2008), p. 9.

8 Vātsyāyana, *Kamasutra*, ed. and trans. by Wendy Doniger and Sudhir Kakar (Oxford: Oxford University Press, 2009), p. 165.

9 Nicolas Culpeper, *The Complete Herbal* (London: CreateSpace, 2018), p. 324.

10 *Historia Augusta* (Boston: Loeb Classical Library, 1921), p. 483.

11   Pliny the Elder, 'Pliny the Elder, Natural History | Loeb Classical
      Library', *Loeb Classical Library*, 2018 <https://www.loebclassics.
      com/view/pliny_elder-natural_history/1938/pb_LCL418.503.
      xml?readMode=recto> [Accessed 19 August 2018].

12   Alain Chartier, *Delectable Demaundes, and Pleasaunt Questions, with their
      Seuerall Aunswers, in Matters of Loue, Naturall Causes, with Morall and
      Politique Deuises. Newely Translated out of Frenche into Englishe, this
      Present Yere of our Lorde God. 1566* (London: John Cawood, 1566), p. 4.

13   Felix Platter, *Platerus Golden Practice of Physick* (London: Peter Cole,
      1664), p. 170; Humphrey Mill, *A Night's Search, Discovering the Nature and
      Condition of Nightwalkers and their Associates* (London, 1646), p. 113.

14   John Marston, *The Scourge of Villanie*, Vol. 2 (London, 1598), p. 107.

15   Thomas Killigrew, *The Parson's Wedding* (London: Henry Herringman,
      1641), p. 78.

16   John Wilmot Rochester, 'A Dream', in *the Poetical Works of the Earls
      of Rochester, Roscomon and Dorset; The Dukes of Devonshire,
      Buckinghamshire, &C. with Memoirs of their Lives in Two Volumes.
      Adorn'd with a New Set of Cuts* (London: Goodourl, 1735), p. 71.

17   Printed in Drew Smith, *Oyster: A Gastronomic History (with Recipes)* (New
      York: Abrams, 2015), Kindle edition, location 866.

18   Henry Randall Waite, *Carmina Collegensia: a Complete Collection of the
      Songs of the American Colleges, with Selections from the Student Songs of the
      English and German Universities* (Boston: Ditson, 1876), p. 73.

19   *Apollo's Medley* (Doncaster, 1790), p. 78.

20   John Whitaker, *Molly Malone* (London: Phipps, 1805), p. 1.

21   Charles Lever, *Charles O'Malley, The Irish Dragoon* (Leipzig: Tauchnitz,
      1848), p. 108.

22   Giacomo Casanova, *The Complete Memoirs of Jacques Casanova de Seingalt*,
      trans. by Arthur Machen (SMK Book, 2014), Kindle edition, location 17545.

23   Ibid., location 61336.

24   Charles Dickens, *The Pickwick Papers* (London: Createspace, 2017), p. 238.

25   Jonathan Swift, *A Complete Collection of Genteel and Ingenious
      Conversation* (London: Printed for B. Motte, and C. Bathurst, at the Middle
      Temple-Gate in Fleet-Street, 1738), p. 120.

26   Trebor Healey, *A Horse Named Sorrow* (Madison, WI: Terrace Books, 2012),
      p. 40.

TURNING DOWN THE HEAT

1   Javed Ali, Shahid H. Ansari and Sabna Kotta, 'Exploring Scientifically
      Proven Herbal Aphrodisiacs', *Pharmacognosy Reviews*, 7.1 (2013), p. 1
      <https://doi.org/10.4103/0973-7847.112832>.

2   Paola Sandroni, 'Aphrodisiacs Past and Present: a Historical
     Review', *Clinical Autonomic Research*, 11.5 (2001), 303–7 <https://doi.
     org/10.1007/bf02332975>.

3   J. Shah, 'Erectile Dysfunction Through the Ages', *BJU International*, 90.4
     (2002), 433–41, p. 433 <https://doi.org/10.1046/j.1464-410x.2002.02911.x>.

4   Plato, *The Republic of Plato*, trans. by John Llewelyn Davies and David
     James Vaughan (Cambridge: Macmillan, 1852), p. 4.

5   Sharman Apt Russell, *Hunger: An Unnatural History* (New York: Basic
     Books, 2008).

6   R. A. Talib et al., 'The Effect of Fasting on Erectile Function and Sexual
     Desire on Men in the Month of Ramadan', *Urology Journal*, 12.2 (2015),
     2099–102.

7   Henry Newell Guernsey, *The Application of the Principles and Practice of
     Homoeopathy to Obstetrics*, 2nd edition (London: Turner, 1878), p. 459.

8   Tierney A. Lorenz and Cindy M. Meston, 'Acute Exercise Improves Physical
     Sexual Arousal in Women Taking Antidepressants', *Annals of Behavioral
     Medicine*, 43.3 (2012), 352–61 <https://doi.org/10.1007/s12160-011-9338-1>.

9   Aristotle, ed. by Jonathan Barnes, *Complete Works of Aristotle, Volume
     2* (Princeton: Princeton University Press, 2014), p. 1352.

10   Pliny the Elder, *Delphi Complete Works of Pliny the Elder*, trans. by John
     Bostock (Hastings: Delphi Classics, 2015), Kindle edition, location 38731.

11   Alexander Morison, *The Physiognomy of Mental Diseases* (London:
     Longman, 1843), page numbers unavailable.

12   Athenaeus, *Delphi Complete Works of Athenaeus*, trans. by C. D. Yonge
     (Hastings: Delphi Classics, 2017), Kindle edition, location 2327.

13   François Rabelais, *Gargantua And Pantagruel* (New York: AMS Press, 1967),
     p. 162.

14   John Davenport and John Camden Hotten, *Aphrodisiacs and Anti-
     Aphrodisiacs* (London: Privately printed, 1869), p. 133.

15   Agnieszka Raubo, 'The Concept of Temperament and the Theory of
     Humours in the Renaissance', *Ruch Literacki*, 57.4 (2016), 408–25 <https://
     doi.org/10.1515/ruch-2017-0071>.

16   Ibid.

17   *The Women's Petition Against Coffee Representing to Publick Consideration
     the Grand Inconveniencies Accruing to their Sex from the Excessive Use of
     that Drying, Enfeebling Liquor* (London, 1674), p. 4.

18   Ibid., p. 2.

19   Ibid., p. 3.

20   Nicholas Culpeper, *A Physicall Directory; or, A Translation of The London
     Dispensatory Made by the Colledge of Physicians in London* (London: Peter
     Cole, 1649), p. 6.

21 Robert Burton, *The Anatomy of Melancholy* (Oxford: John Lichfield and James Short, for Henry Cripps, 1624), pp. 630–31.

22 Davenport and Hotten, *Aphrodisiacs and Anti-Aphrodisiacs*, p. 133.

23 Michael Ryan, *Prostitution in London, with a Comparative View of that of Paris and New York* (London: H. Bailliere, 1839), p. 385.

24 Ibid.

25 Grailey Hewitt, *The Diagnosis, Pathology and Treatment of Diseases of Women* (Philadelphia: Lindsay and Blackiston, 1868), p. 403.

26 John Harvey Kellogg, *Plain Facts for Old and Young: Embracing the Natural History and Hygiene of Organic Life* (Burlington: Segner, 1887), pp. 302–3.

27 Sylvester Graham, *A Lecture to Young Men on Chastity, Intended Also for the Serious Consideration of Parents and Guardians* (Boston: Cornhill, 1838), p. 47.

28 Brian C. Wilson, *Dr John Harvey Kellogg and the Religion of Biologic Living* (Indianapolis: Indiana University Press, 2014).

29 Thomas Douglas and others, 'Coercion, Incarceration, and Chemical Castration: an Argument from Autonomy', *Journal of Bioethical Inquiry*, 10.3 (2013), pp. 393–405 <https://doi.org/10.1007/s11673-013-9465-4>.

30 Jean-Jacques Rousseau, *Confessions of Jean-Jacques Rousseau* (London: Penguin, 1953), p. 303.

31 Davenport and Hotten, *Aphrodisiacs and Anti-aphrodisiacs*, p. 131.

BUZZKILL

1 Helen King, 'Galen and the Widow: Towards a History of Therapeutic Masturbation in Ancient Gynaecology', *Journal on Gender Studies in Antiquity*, 2011, 205–35; Hallie Lieberman and Eric Schatzberg, *Journalof positivesexuality.org*, 2018 <http://journalofpositivesexuality.org/wp-content/uploads/2018/08/Failure-of-Academic-Quality-Control-Technology-of-Orgasm-Lieberman-Schatzberg.pdf> [Accessed 23 September 2018].

2 Rachel Maines, 'The Study that Set the World Abuzz – Video', *Big Think*, 2017 <http://bigthink.com/videos/the-study-that-set-the-world-abuzz> [Accessed 12 March 2017].

3 Cesare Lombroso and others, *La Donna Delinquente, La Prostituta E La Donna Normale*, 1st edn (Milano: Et.al, 2009).

4 Joseph Mortimer Granville, *Nerve-Vibration and Excitation as Agents in the Treatment of Functional Disorder and Organic Disease*, 1st edn (J. & A. Churchill: London, 1883), p. 57.

5 *The Pearl:Victorian Erotica* (2017), Kindle edition, locations 6118–19.

6 Ibid., location 11360.

7 Samuel Ward and others, 'Reports on the Progress of Medicine', *New York Medical Journal*, 23 (1876), 207–10, p. 209.

8   Robert Ziegenspeck, *Massage Treatment (Thure Brandt) in Diseases of Women: For Practitioners* (Chicago: Westerschulte, 1898), p. 26.

9   Ibid., pp. 30–32.

10   Ibid., p. 47.

11   Ibid.

12   Rachel P. Maines, *The Technology of Orgasm* (Baltimore: Johns Hopkins University Press, 2001), p. 3.

13   William John Anderson, *Hysterical and Nervous Affections of Women. Read Before the Harveian Society*, 1st edn (London: Churchill, 1864), p. 26.

14   Andrew Whyte Barclay, *A Manual of Medical Diagnosis: Being an Analysis of the Signs and Symptoms* (Philadelphia: Blanchard, 1864), p. 138.

15   John Henry Walsh, *A Manual of Domestic Medicine and Surgery: Revised Edition* (London, Frederick Warne, 1878), p. 150.

16   William Potts Dewees, *A Treatise on the Diseases of Females* (Philadelphia: Lea and Blanchard, 1843), p. 470.

17   Walsh, *A Manual of Domestic Medicine and Surgery*, p. 150.

18   George B. Wood, *A Treatise on the Practice of Medicine*, 1st edn (Philadelphia: Lippincott, Grambo, 1852), p. 581; W. W. Bliss, *Woman, and Her Thirty Years' Pilgrimage* (Boston: B. B. Russell, 1870), p. 98.

19   'Aretaeus, De Causis Et Signis Acutorum Morborum (Lib. 1), Book II., Chapter XI. On Hysterical Suffocation', *Perseus.Tufts.Edu*, 2018 <http://www.perseus.tufts.edu/hopper/text?doc=Perseus%3Atext-t%3A1999.01.0254%3Atext%3DSA%3Abook%3D2%3Achapter%3D11> [Accessed 22 July 2018].

20   'Sub-Umbra or Sport Among the She-Noodles', in *The Wordsworth Book of Classic Erotica* (Ware: Wordsworth Editions, 2007), p. 1091.

21   'The Romance of Lust', in *The Wordsworth Book of Classic Erotica* (Ware: Wordsworth Editions, 2007), p. 163.

22   Jack Saul, *The Sins of the Cities of the Plain, Or the Recollections of a Mary Ann* (London: Privately printed, 1881), p. 132.

23   Fern Riddell, 'No, No, No! Victorians Didn't Invent the Vibrator', *Guardian*, 2017 <https://www.theguardian.com/commentisfree/2014/nov/10/victorians-invent-vibrator-orgasms-women-doctors-fantasy> [Accessed 12 March 2017].

24   James George Beaney, *The Generative System and its Functions in Health and Disease* (Melbourne: F. F. Bailliere, 1872), p. 359.

25   Edward John Tilt, *A Handbook of Uterine Therapeutics and of Diseases of Women* (London: J. & A. Churchill, 1878), p. 119.

26   Samuel La'mert, *Self-Preservation: A Medical Treatise on the Secret Infirmities and Disorders of the Generative Organs* (London; 1852), pp. 105–6.

27 A. J. Block, 'Sexual Perversion in the Female', *New Orleans Medical Surgery Journal*, 22 (1894), pp. 1–7.

28 W. Tyler Smith, 'Principles and Practices of Obstetricy', *The Lancet*, 2 (1847), 669–71, p. 669.

29 John S. Parry, *Extra-Uterine Pregnancy; its Causes, Species, Pathological Anatomy, Clinical History, Diagnosis, Prognosis and Treatment* (Philadelphia: Henry Lea, 1876), p. 45.

30 Ibid.

ON YOUR BIKE

1   Jaime Rojo and Steven Harrington, '"F**K Art" Opens Wide at Museum of Sex (NSFW)', *Huffpost*, 2018 <https://www.huffingtonpost.com/jaime-rojo-steven-harrington/new-opening-at-museum-of-sex_b_1261589.html> [Accessed 11 August 2018].

2   Quoted in Julie Wosk, *Women and the Machine* (Baltimore: Johns Hopkins University Press, 2003), p. 114.

3   *South Wales Daily News*, 'A Cure for Bicycle Face', 1897, p. 3.

4   Quoted in Katherine Murtha, 'Cycling in the 1890s: An Orgasmic Experience?', *Cahiers De La Femme*, 21.3 (2002), pp. 119–21, p. 120.

5   *St Louis Medical Review*, 32 (1895), p. 209.

6   *Iowa State Register*, 'Taking Chances', 1895.

7   *The Cincinnati Lancet-Clinic*, 74 (1895), p. 674.

8   'Female Cyclists', *The Dominion Medical Monthly*, 7.3 (1896), 235–7.

9   'Immorality in Canada', *The Canadian Practioner* 21, (1896), 848–9.

10 Robert Dickinson, 'Bicycling for Women', *The American Journal of Obstetrics and Diseases of Women and Children*, 31 (1895), 24–35, p. 33.

11 Ibid.

12 Quoted in Ted Ferguson, *Kit Coleman: Queen of Hearts* (Markham: PaperJacks, 1979), p. 92.

13 Sue Macy and Meredith Orlow, *Wheels of Change* (Washington: National Geographic, 2012), p. 18.

14 *New Zealand Wheelman*, 18 August 1897, p. 7.

15 *New Zealand Graphic and Ladies' Journal*, 17 September, 1898, p. 372.

16 Arthur Shadwell, 'The Hidden Dangers of Cycling', *The National Review*, 1897, p. 796.

17 Quoted in *South Wales Daily News*, 'Remedy for Bicycle Face', 1897, p. 3.

18 Clare Simpson, 'A Social History of Women and Cycling in Late-Nineteenth Century New Zealand' (unpublished PhD thesis, Lincoln University, 1998), p. 137.

19 *New Zealand Wheelman*, 30 April 1898, p. 9.

BOYS' TOYS

1   Chantal Cox-George and Susan Bewley, 'I, Sex Robot: The Health Implications of the Sex Robot Industry', *BMJ Sexual & Reproductive Health*, 44, 2018, 161–4. https://doi.org/10.1136/bmjsrh-2017-200012.

2   S. J. De Laet, *History of Humanity* (London: Routledge, 1994), p. 234.

3   Jonathan Amos, 'Ancient Phallus Unearthed in Cave', *BBC News*, 2005 <http://news.bbc.co.uk/1/hi/sci/tech/4713323.stm> [Accessed 24 June 2018].

4   Ovid, trans. by A. D. Melville and E. J. Kenney, *Metamorphoses* (New York: Oxford University Press, 2008), p. 233.

5   'Pliny the Elder, The Natural History, Book XXXVI. The Natural History Of Stones', *Perseus.Tufts.Edu*, 2018 <http://www.perseus.tufts.edu/hopper/text?doc=Perseus:abo:phi,0978,001:36:4> [Accessed 24 June 2018].

6   Sigmund Freud, 'The Uncanny', in *The Standard Edition of the Complete Psychological Works of Sigmund Freud*, ed. by James Strachey (London: Vintage, 2001), p. 220.

7   Havelock Ellis, *Studies in the Psychology of Sex* (Honolulu: University Press of the Pacific, 2001), p. 188.

8   Iwan Bloch, *The Sexual Life of Our Time in Its Relations to Modern Civilization*, trans. by M. Eden Paul (London: Rebman, 1908), p. 648.

9   Louis Fiaux, *Les Maisons De Tolerance* (Paris: G. Carré, 1892), p. 176.

10 Bloch, *The Sexual Life of Our Time*, pp. 648–9.

11 Ibid.

12 Madame B, *La Femme Endormie* (Melbourne, 1899), pp. 11–12.

13 Ibid.

14 René Schwaeblé, 'Homunculus', *Les détraquées de Paris* (Paris: Daragon libraire-éditeur, 1910), pp. 247–53.

15 N. Döring and S. Pöschl, 'Sex Toys, Sex Dolls, Sex Robots: Our Under-Researched Bed-Fellows', *Sexologies*, 27, (2018), 133–8 <https://doi.org/10.1016/j.sexol.2018.05.009>.

16 See Kate Devlin, *Turned On: Science, Sex and Robots* (London: Bloomsbury, 2018).

17 Vic Grout, 'Robot Sex: Ethics And Morality', *Lovotics*, 03.01 (2015) <https://doi.org/10.4172/2090-9888.1000e104>; Cox-George and Bewley, 'I, Sex Robot: The Health Implications of the Sex Robot Industry', *BMJ Sexual & Reproductive Health*, (2018), 44, 161–4 bmjsrh-2017-200012 <https://doi.org/10.1136/bmjsrh-2017-200012>.; Veronica Cassidy, 'For the Love of Doll(s): A Patriarchal Nightmare of Cyborg Couplings', *ESC: English Studies In Canada*, 42.1-2 (2016), pp. 203–215 <https://doi.org/10.1353/esc.2016.0001>.

18 Sarah Valverde, 'The Modern Sex Doll-Owner: A Descriptive Analysis' (unpublished Masters thesis, California State Polytechnic University, 2012).

19   Ibid., p. 34.

20   Lucy Orne Bowditch and Charles Pickering Bowditch, *The Lives and Portraits of Curious and Odd Characters* (Worcester: Thomas Drew, 1853), pp. 11–17.

21   Janine Alexandre-Debray, *La Païva, 1819–1884* (Paris: Perrin, 1986); Melissa Hope Ditmore, *Encyclopaedia of Prostitution and Sex Work* Vol I (Westport, CT: Greenwood Press, 2006), p. 244.

22   Quoted in Derek Sayer, *Prague, Capital of the Twentieth Century – A Surrealist History* (Princeton: Princeton University, 2013), p. 227.

23   Norbert Lenz, Borghild.de <http://www.borghild.de/indexe.htm> [Accessed 13 July 2018].

24   Robin Gerber, *Barbie and Ruth: The Story of the World's Most Famous Doll and the Woman Who Made Her* (New York: Harper, 2010).

25   Anthony Ferguson, *The Sex Doll* (Jefferson, N.C.: McFarland & Co., 2010), p. 31.

26   Ibid., p. 30.

27   Christopher Trout, 'There's a New Sex Robot in Town: Say Hello To Solana', *Engadget*, 2018 <https://www.engadget.com/2018/01/10/there-s-a-new-sex-robot-in-town-say-hello-to-solana/> [Accessed 18 July 2018].

DON'T HOLD YOUR BREATH

1   Megan Oaten, Richard J. Stevenson and Trevor I. Case, 'Disgust as a Disease-Avoidance Mechanism', *Psychological Bulletin*, 135.2 (2009), 303–21 <https://doi.org/10.1037/a0014823>.

2   Carmelo M. Vicario and others, 'Core, Social and Moral Disgust are Bounded: A Review on Behavioural and Neural Bases of Repugnance in Clinical Disorders', *Neuroscience & Biobehavioral Reviews*, 80 (2017), 185–200 <https://doi.org/10.1016/j.neubiorev.2017.05.008>.

3   Marco Tullio Liuzza and others, 'Body Odour Disgust Sensitivity Predicts Authoritarian Attitudes', *Royal Society Open Science*, 5.2 (2018), 171091 <https://doi.org/10.1098/rsos.171091>.

4   Michael N. Pham et al., 'Is Cunnilingus-Assisted Orgasm A Male Sperm-Retention Strategy?', *Evolutionary Psychology*, 11.2 (2013), 147470491301100 <https://doi.org/10.1177/147470491301100210>.

5   D. P. Strachan, 'Hay Fever, Hygiene, and Household Size', *BMJ*, 299.6710 (1989), 1259–60 <https://doi.org/10.1136/bmj.299.6710.1259>.

6   Alison Leigh Browne et al., 'Patterns of Practice: A Reflection on the Development of Quantitative/Mixed Methodologies Capturing Everyday Life Related to Water Consumption in the UK', *International Journal of Social Research Methodology*, 17.1 (2013), pp. 27–43 <https://doi.org/10.108 0/13645579.2014.854012>.

7   *Calendar of Close Rolls preserved in the Public Record Office: Edward III*,
      vol. 2 (London: HMSO, 1898), p. 610.

8   Geoffrey Chaucer and Jill Mann, *The Canterbury Tales* (London: Penguin
      Books, 2005), pp. 821, 17.

9   Ibid., p. 123.

10   Sir Thomas Malory, *Le Morte D 'Arthur*, ed. by Helen Cooper (Oxford:
      Oxford University Press, 2008), p. 129.

11   St Jerome, *The Sacred Writings of Saint Jerome* (London: Jazzybee Verlag,
      2018), Kindle edition, location 7151.

12   C. H. Lawrence, *Medieval Monasticism: Forms of Religious Life in Western
      Europe in the Middle Ages* (London: Routledge, 1984), p. 108.

13   Abū al-Qāsim Khalaf ibn ʿAbbās al-Zahrāwī, *Albucasis on Surgery and
      Instruments* (Berkeley: University of California Press, 1973).

14   Martin Levey, *Early Arabic Pharmacology* (Leiden: E.J. Brill, 1973), p. 9.

15   Edward H. Schafer, 'The Development of Bathing Customs in Ancient
      and Medieval China and the History of the Floriate Clear Palace', *Journal
      of The American Oriental Society*, 76.2 (1956), 57–82, 57. <https://doi.
      org/10.2307/595074>.

16   J. C. Mardrus and E. P. Mathers, *The Book of the Thousand and One
      Nights* (Hoboken: Taylor and Francis, 2013), p. 42.

17   Jonathan Reinarz, *Past Scents: Historical Perspectives on Smell* (Chicago:
      University of Illinois Press, 2014), p. 64.

18   Mandy Aftel, *Essence and Alchemy* (New York: North Point Press, 2001), p. 190.

19   Jacquelyn Hodson, 'The Smell of the Middle Ages', *Trivium
      Publishing LLC*, 2018 <http://www.triviumpublishing.com/articles/
      smellofthemiddleages.html> [Accessed 9 September 2017].

20   John Russell, Wynkyn de Worde and Frederick James Furnivall, *The Boke
      of Nurture* (Bungay: Printed for the Honourable R. Curzon by J. Childs,
      1867), p. 68.

21   Quoted in James A. Brundage, *Law, Sex, and Christian Society in Medieval
      Europe* (Chicago: University of Chicago Press, 2009), p. 527.

22   Giovanni Boccaccio, Guido Waldman and Jonathan Usher, *The
      Decameron* (Oxford: Oxford University Press, 2008), p. 543.

23   Tania Bayard, *A Medieval Home Companion* (New York: Harper, 1992), p. 130.

24   William Langham, *The Garden of Health* (London: Christopher Barker,
      1579), p. 147.

25   Ruth Mazo Karras, *Common Women: Prostitution and Sexuality in Medieval
      England* (New York: Oxford University Press, 1998), pp. 54–5.

26   Geoffrey Chaucer, 'The Legend of Good Women', in *The Complete Works
      of Geoffrey Chaucer*, ed. by Walter William Skeat (London: Cosimo Classics,
      2013), p. 91.

27 Quoted in Karras, *Common Women*, p. 54.

28 Ibid.

29 Terry Gilliam, *Monty Python and the Holy Grail* (EMI, 1975).

HAIR TODAY, GONE TOMORROW

1   Bukhārī, Muḥammad ibn Ismā'īl, and Muhammad Muhsin Khan, *Ṣaḥīḥ Al-Bukhārī* (Riyadh-Saudi Arabia: Darussalam, 1997), 7.777.

2   Didem Muallaaziz and Eyüp Yayci, 'Pubic Hair Removal Practices in Muslim Women', *Basic and Clinical Sciences*, 3 (2014), pp. 39–44, p. 39.

3   Victoria Sherrow, *Encyclopaedia of Hair* (Westport: Greenwood Press, 2006), pp. 111–5.

4   'Aristophanes, Lysistrata, Line 130', *Perseus.Tufts.Edu*, 2018 <http://www.perseus.tufts.edu/hopper/text?doc=Perseus%3Atext%3A1999.01.0242%3Acard%3D130> [Accessed 8 August 2018].

5   John G. Younger, *Sex in the Ancient World from A to Z* (London: Routledge, 2005), p. 75.

6   Kristina Milnor, *Graffiti and the Literary Landscape in Roman Pompeii* (Oxford: Oxford University Press, 2014), p. 179.

7   Kim M. Phillips, *Medieval Maidens: Young Women and Gender in England, c.1270–c.1540* (Manchester: Manchester University Press, 2003), p. 45.

8   Monica Helen Green, *The Trotula* (Philadelphia: University of Pennsylvania Press, 2001), p. 175.

9   This quotation is found in an illuminated manuscript, and attributed to the fourteenth-century Dominican Friar, John of Freiberg. P. J. P. Goldberg, *Women in Medieval English Society* (Gloucestershire: Sutton, 1997), p. 90.

10 Geoffrey Chaucer, *The Canterbury Tales* ed. by Jill Mann (London: Penguin Books, 2005), p. 137, lines 3722–49.

11 *Recettario Novo Probatissimo a Molte Infirmita, E Etiandio Di Molte Gentilezze Utile A Chi Le Vora Provare* (Venice, 1532).

12 Francisco Delicado and Bruno M. Damiani, *Portrait of Lozana* (Potomac: Scripta Humanistica, 1987), p. 72.

13 William Shakespeare, *Venus And Adonis, Shakespeare.Mit.Edu*, 2018 <http://shakespeare.mit.edu/Poetry/VenusAndAdonis.html> [Accessed 8 August 2018].

14 William Shakespeare, *Much Ado About Nothing, Shakespeare.Mit.Edu*, 2018 <http://shakespeare.mit.edu/much_ado/full.html> [Accessed 8 August 2018].

15 William Shakespeare, 'Sonnet 130: My Mistress' Eyes Are Nothing Like the Sun', *Shakespeare-Online.Com*, 2018 <http://www.shakespeare-online.com/sonnets/130.html> [Accessed 8 August 2018].

16   Richard Head, *The Rogue Discovered, Or A Congratulatory Verse upon a Book Newly Published (A Piece Much Desired, and Long Expected) Called the English Rogue, A Witty Extravagant* (London: Francis Kirkman, 1665), p. 67.

17   Megg Spenser, *A Strange and True Conference Between Two Bawds, Damarose Page and Priss Fotheringham, during their Imprisonment in Newgate* (London, 1660), p. 7.

18   John Wilmot, 'The Farce of Sodom', in *Book of Sodom*, ed. by Paul Hallam (London: Routledge, 1995), p. 230.

19   Thomas Middleton, 'A Trick to Catch the Old One', in *Thomas Middleton: The Collected Works*, ed. by Gary Taylor and John Lavagnino (Oxford: Oxford University Press, 2010), p. 407.

20   Quoted in James T. Henke, *Gutter Life and Language in the Early 'Street' Literature of England* (West Cornwall: Locust Hill Press, 1988), p. 77.

21   Humphrey Mill, *A Night's Search, Discovering the Nature and Condition of Night-Walkers with their Associates* (London: H. Shepard and W. Ley, 1640), p. 249.

22   Gordon Williams, *A Dictionary of Sexual Language and Imagery in Shakespearean and Stuart Literature: A–F* (London: Athlone Press, 1994), p. 877.

23   'Pubic Wigs', *Oxford Reference*, 2018 <http://www.oxfordreference.com/view/10.1093/acref/9780198524038.001.0001/acref-9780198524038-e-783> [Accessed 8 August 2018].

24   John Wilmot, 'The Farce of Sodom', p. 230.

25   Alexander Smith and Arthur Lawrence Hayward, *A Complete History of the Lives and Robberies of the Most Notorious Highwaymen, Footpads, Shoplifts & Cheats of Both Sexes* (London: Routledge, 2002), p. 217.

26   *Harris's List of Covent Garden Ladies or Man of Pleasure's Kalendar for the Year, 1788* (London: H. Ranger, 1788), pp. 39, 79, 130.

27   John Cleland, *Fanny Hill: Memoirs of a Woman of Pleasure* (London: LBA, 2007), Kindle edition, p. 125.

28   Ibid., p. 11.

29   'Full Text Of "The Romance of Lust a Classic Victorian Erotic Novel"', *Archive. Org*, 2017 <https://archive.org/stream/theromanceoflust30254gut/30254-8. txt> [Accessed 12 March 2017].

30   John Ruskin and others, *The Story of John Ruskin, Effie Gray and John Everett Millais Told for the First Time in their Unpublished Letters* (London: Murray, 1948), p. 220.

31   Tami S. Rowen and others, 'Pubic Hair Grooming Prevalence and Motivation Among Women in the United States', *JAMA Dermatology*, 152.10 (2016), 1106 <https://doi.org/10.1001/jamadermatol.2016.2154>.

FILTHY FANNIES

1   Technavio Research, *Global Vaginal Odor Control Product Market 2018–2022* (London: Regional Business News, 2018).

2   Jo's Cervical Cancer Trust, 'Body Shame Responsible for Young Women not Attending Smear Tests', *Jo's Cervical Cancer Trust*, 2018 <https://www.jostrust.org.uk/node/1073042> [Accessed 17 February 2019].

3   Louis Keith and others, 'The Odors of the Human Vagina', *Archiv Für Gynäkologie*, 220.1 (1975), pp. 1–10 <https://doi.org/10.1007/bf00673143>.

4   E. B. Keverne and R. P. Michael, 'Sex-Attractant Properties of Ether Extracts of Vaginal Secretions from Rhesus Monkeys', *Journal Of Endocrinology*, 51.2 (1971), pp. 313–22 <https://doi.org/10.1677/joe.0.0510313>; Foteos Macrides, Patricia A. Johnson and Stephen P. Schneider, 'Responses of the Male Golden Hamster to Vaginal Secretion and Dimethyl Disulfide: Attraction Versus Sexual Behavior', *Behavioral Biology*, 20.3 (1977), 377–86 <https://doi.org/10.1016/s0091-6773(77)90931-2>; Ana Lilia Cerda-Molina et al., 'Endocrine Changes in Male Stumptailed Macaques (Macaca Arctoides) As a Response to Odor Stimulation with Vaginal Secretions', *Hormones And Behavior*, 49.1 (2006), 81–7 <https://doi.org/10.1016/j.yhbeh.2005.04.014>.

5   Megan N. Williams and Amy Jacobson, 'Effect of Copulins on Rating of Female Attractiveness, Mate-Guarding, and Self-Perceived Sexual Desirability', *Evolutionary Psychology*, 14.2 (2016), 147470491664332 <https://doi.org/10.1177/1474704916643328>.

6   Didem Sunay, Erdal Kaya and Yusuf Ergun, 'Vaginal Douching Behavior of Women and Relationship Among Vaginal Douching and Vaginal Discharge and Demographic Factors', *Journal of Turkish Society of Obstetric and Gynecology*, 8.4 (2011), 264–71 https://doi.org/10.5505/tjod.2011.57805; 'Douching', *Womenshealth.Gov*, 2018 <https://www.womenshealth.gov/a-z-topics/douching> [Accessed 10 September 2018].

7   Charles Knowlton, *Fruits of Philosophy: A Treatise on the Population Question* (San Francisco: Readers Library, 1891), p. 74.

8   Dr Blundell, 'Incapability of Retaining the Urine', *The Lancet*, 1 (1829), 673–7.

9   Clifton E. Wing, 'The Proper Use of the Hot Vaginal Douche', *The Boston Medical and Surgical Journal*, 102 (1880), 583–4.

10   'Reports of Societies', *The Boston Medical and Surgical Journal*, 14 (1889), 443–5, 444.

11   John Ashurst, *The International Encyclopedia of Surgery: A Systematic Treatise on the Theory and Practice of Surgery* (W. Wood, 1895), p. 1002.

12   *Catalogue and Report of Obstetrical and other Instruments* (London: Obstetric Society of London, 1867).

13 James V. Ricci, *The Development of Gynaecological Surgery and Instruments* (Philadelphia: Blakiston, 1949), p. 526.

14 Knowlton, *Fruits of Philosophy*, p. 74.

15 'Vaginal Douching', *Monthly Retrospect of Medicine & Pharmacy*, 4 (1898), p. 555.

16 'Over a Century of Healthing', *Lysol.Com*, 2018 <http://www.lysol.com/about-us/our-history/> [Accessed 11 September 2018].

17 Andrea Tone, *Devices and Desire: A History of Contraceptives in America* (New York: Hill and Wang), pp. 151–83.

18 'Beauty Wonders: No Smell So Sweet', *Essence*, September 1971, p. 20.

FRENCH LETTERS, ENGLISH RAINCOATS AND MRS PHILLIPS'S WARES

1   'Campaign To Protect Young People From STIs by Using Condoms', gov.uk, 2018 <https://www.gov.uk/government/news/campaign-to-protect-young-people-from-stis-by-using-condoms> [Accessed 14 August 2018].

2   'New Data Reveals 420,000 Cases of STIs Diagnosed In 2017', gov.uk, 2018 <https://www.gov.uk/government/news/new-data-reveals-420000-cases-of-stis-diagnosed-in-2017> [Accessed 14 August 2018].

3   Nicola Low and others, 'Molecular Diagnostics for Gonorrhoea: Implications for Antimicrobial Resistance and the Threat of Untreatable Gonorrhoea', *Plos Medicine*, 11.2 (2014), e1001598 https://doi.org/10.1371/journal.pmed.1001598; Kelsi M. Sandoz and Daniel D. Rockey, 'Antibiotic Resistance in Chlamydiae', *Future Microbiology*, 5.9 (2010), 1427–42 <https://doi.org/10.2217/fmb.10.96>.

4   Jean-Jacques Amy and Michel Thiery, 'The Condom: A Turbulent History', *The European Journal of Contraception & Reproductive Health Care*, 20.5 (2015), 387–402 <https://doi.org/10.3109/13625187.2015.1050716>.

5   Michael Leidig, 'Condom from Cromwell's Time Goes on Display in Austria', *BMJ*, 333.7557 (2006), 10.3 <https://doi.org/10.1136/bmj.333.7557.10-b>.

6   Lesley Smith, 'The History of Contraception', in *Contraception: A Casebook from Menarche to Menopause* (Cambridge: Cambridge University Press, 2013), p. 18.

7   Lesley Smith, 'The Kahun Gynaecological Papyrus: Ancient Egyptian Medicine', *Journal of Family Planning and Reproductive Health Care*, 37.1 (2011), 54–5 <https://doi.org/10.1136/jfprhc.2010.0019>.

8   Gabriele Falloppi, *De Morbo Gallico* (Padua, 1563), chapter 89.

9   Guy de Chauliac, *La Grande Chirurgie* (Paris: F. Alcan, 1890).

10 Quoted in Ralph Hermon Major, *Classic Descriptions of Disease*, 3rd edn (Springfield: Charles C. Thomas, 1978), p. 26.

11   Robley Dunglison, *A New Dictionary of Medical Science and Literature* (Boston: C. Bowen, 1833), p. 223.

12   John Wilmot and others, 'A Panegyric Upon Cundum', in *The Works of The Earls of Rochester, Roscomon and Dorset, the Dukes of Devonshire, Buckingham and Co.* (London, 1667), p. 208.

13   James Boswell, *Boswell's London Journal, 1762–1763*, ed. by Frederick Albert Pottle (New Haven: Yale University Press, 2004), p. 262.

14   Boswell, *Boswell's London Journal, 1762–1763*, p. 272.

15   Daniel Turner, *Syphillis. A Practical Dissertation on the Venereal Disease* (London: J. Walthoe, R. Wilkin, J. and J. Bonwicke, and T. Ward, 1727), p. 74; M. Tampa and others, 'Brief History of Syphilis', *Journal of Medicine and Life*, 7.1 (2014), 4–10.

16   Boswell, *Boswell's London Journal, 1762–1763*, p. 155.

17   Francis Grose, *Guide to Health, Beauty, Riches, and Honour* (London: S. Hooper, 1785), p. 13.

18   Robert Jütte, *Contraception* (Cambridge: Polity, 2008), p. 104.

19   Casanova, Giacomo, *The Complete Memoirs of Jacques Casanova de Seingalt*, trans. by Arthur Machen (SMK Books, 2014), Kindle edition, location 33819.

20   Ibid.

21   M. Tampa and others, 'Brief History of Syphilis'

22   Richard Carlile, 'Every Woman's Book Or What Is Love?', in *What Is Love?: Richard Carlile's Philosophy of Sex*, ed. by M. L. Bush (London: Verso, 1998).

23   Quoted in Andrea Tone, *Controlling Reproduction: An American History* (Wilmington: SR Books, 1997), p. 141.

24   Amy and Thiery, 'The Condom: A Turbulent History', pp. 397–8.

25   Aine Collier, *The Humble Little Condom* (Amherst: Prometheus Books, 2007), p. 209.

26   A. Salem, 'A Condom Sense Approach to AIDS Prevention: A Historical Perspective', *South Dakota Journal of Medicine*, 45.10 (1992), pp. 294–6, p. 294.

27   Samuel Hallsor Booth, 'A Comparison of the Early Responses to AIDS in the UK and the US', *Res Medica*, 24.1 (2017), pp. 57–64 <https://doi.org/10.2218/resmedica.v24i1.1558>.

BRINGING DOWN THE FLOWERS

1   Edmund Spenser, *The Faerie Queene*, 2.3.49.5–7

2   William Buchan, *Domestic Medicine: Or, a Treatise on the Prevention and Cure of Diseases by Regimen and Simple Remedies* (London: Balfour, Auld and Smellie, 1769), p. 3.

3   Ibid., p. 531.

4 William Cobbett, *The Parliamentary History of England, 1801–1803* (London: 1806), p. 36. The 'quickening' referred to the first movements of the foetus in the womb. Typically, a woman starts to feel movement around 18–20 weeks. Levene, Malcolm et al., *Essentials of Neonatal Medicine* (London: Blackwell, 2000), p. 8.

5 John Astruc, *A treatise on all the Diseases Incident to Women* (London: Cooper, 1743), p. 363; Martin Madan, *Thelyphthora; or, A treatise on female ruin* (London, 1785), p. 285; A. Civillian, *Trials for Adultery; or, the History of Divorces, III vols,* (London: Blandon, 1779).

6 Casanova, *The Memoirs of Jacques Casanova de Seingalt*, Kindle Edition, location 33688.

7 Karen Harris, *The Medieval Vagina: A Historical and Hysterical Look At All Things Vaginal During the Middle Ages* (London: Snark, 2014).

8 L. Stone, *The Family, Sex and Marriage in England 1500–1800* (London: Penguin, 1990), pp. 266–7.

9 Old Bailey Proceedings Online, central criminal court (2003), <https://www.oldbaileyonline.org/browse.jsp?id=t18290409-83&div=t18290409-83&terms=Savin#highlight> [accessed 30 August 2016].

10 John M. Riddle, *Eve's Herbs: A History of Contraception and Abortion in the West* (Cambridge, MA: Harvard University Press, 1999).

11 'The Tryal of Eleanore Beare of Derby', *Gentleman's Magazine*, 1732, pp. 933–4.

12 Anon, 'The Tryal of Eleanor Beare of Derby, on Tuesday 15 August, 1732', *The Gentleman's Magazine, or, Monthly Intelligencer*, 2. XXIV (1732), pp. 931–3.

13 Ibid.

14 Thomas Brown, 'A Satire Upon a Quack', in *Works Serious and Comical in Prose and Verse* (London 1760), pp. 62–5.

15 Ibid.

16 Francis Grose, *Lexicon Balatronicum: A Dictionary of Buckish Slang, University Wit, and Pickpocket Eloquence* (London: S. Hooper, 1785), p. 204.

17 Old Bailey Proceedings Online, central criminal court (2003), <https://www.oldbaileyonline.org/browse.jsp?id=t18290409-83&div=t18290409-83&terms=Savin#highlight> [accessed 30 August 2016].

18 Old Bailey Proceedings Online, Ann Gardner, 15 January 1708 (t17080115-1).

19 Dan Cruickshank, *The Secret History of Georgian London: How the Wages of Sin Shaped the Capital* (London: Windmill Books, 2010), p. 249.

20 Foundling Museum, <http://foundlingmuseum.org.uk/about/the-museum/> [accessed 2 September 2016].

21 Jennifer Worth, 'A deadly trade', *Guardian*, 6 January 2005.

PERIOD DRAMA

1   Pliny, *Natural History*, trans. H. Rackham (Cambridge: Harvard University Press, 1961), book 7, p. 549.

2   Kate Hodal, 'Nepal's Bleeding Shame: Menstruating Women Banished to Cattle Sheds', *Guardian*, 2018 <https://www.theguardian.com/global-development/2016/apr/01/nepal-bleeding-shame-menstruating-women-banished-cattle-sheds> [Accessed 13 September 2018].

3   Verity Bowman, 'Woman in Nepal Dies After Being Exiled to Outdoor Hut During Her Period', *Guardian*, 2018 <https://www.theguardian.com/global-development/2018/jan/12/woman-nepal-dies-exiled-outdoor-hut-period-menstruation> [Accessed 13 September 2018].

4   Rita E. Montgomery, 'A Cross-Cultural Study of Menstruation, Menstrual Taboos, and Related Social Variables', *Ethos*, 2.2 (1974), 137–70, p. 152 <https://doi.org/10.1525/eth.1974.2.2.02a00030>.

5   Ibid.

6   Janet Hoskins, 'The Menstrual Hut and the Witch's Lair in Two Eastern Indonesian Societies', *Ethnology*, 41.4 (2002), p. 317 <https://doi.org/10.2307/4153011>.

7   Montgomery, 'A Cross-Cultural Study of Menstruation', p. 143.

8   Kristin Hanssen, 'Ingesting Menstrual Blood: Notions of Health and Bodily Fluids in Bengal', *Ethnology*, 41.4 (2002), 365–79, p. 369 <https://doi.org/10.2307/4153014>.

9   J. F. Nunn, *Ancient Egyptian Medicine* (Norman: University of Oklahoma Press, 2002), p. 197.

10 Hildegard of Bingen, *Hildegard Von Bingen's Physica: The Complete English Translation of Her Classic Work on Health and Healing*, ed. by Priscilla Throop (Rochester: Healing Arts Press, 1998), p. 61.

11 Lily Xiao Hong Lee and Sue Wiles, *Biographical Dictionary of Chinese Women, Volume II: Tang Through Ming 618–44* (London: Routledge, 2014), pp. 59–60.

12 Aru Bhartiya, 'Menstruation, Religion and Society', *International Journal of Social Science and Humanity*, 2013, 523–7 <https://doi.org/10.7763/ijssh.2013.v3.296>.

13 'Bible Gateway Passage: Leviticus 20:18 – New International Version', *Bible Gateway*, 2018 <https://www.biblegateway.com/passage/?search=Leviticus+20%3A18&version=NIV> [Accessed 14 September 2018].

14 'Surah Al-Baqarah [2:222–232]', *Surah Al-Baqarah [2:222–232]*, 2018 <https://quran.com/2/222-232> [Accessed 14 September 2018].

15 Joan Cadden, *Meanings of Sex Difference in the Middle Ages: Medicine, Science and Culture* (Cambridge: University Press, 1993), pp. 21–6; Nancy

Tuana, 'The Weaker Seed: The Sexist Bias of Reproduction Theory', in *Feminism and Science*, ed. by Nancy Tuana (Bloomingdale: Indiana University Press, 1989), pp. 147–71.

16 Galen, 'Ancient Medicine/Medicina Antiqua: Galen: Commentary On: Hippocrates: On The Nature Of Man: De Natura Hominis', *Ucl.Ac.Uk*, 2018 <https://www.ucl.ac.uk/~ucgajpd/medicina%20antiqua/Medant/ GNatHom1.htm> [Accessed 14 September 2018].

17 Simiao Sun and Sabine Wilms, *Bèi Jí Qiān Jīn Yào Fāng* (Portland: The Chinese Medicine Database, 2008).

18 Yi-Li Wu, 'The Menstruating Womb: A Cross-Cultural Analysis of Body and Gender in H. Chun's Precious Mirror of Eastern Medicine (1613)', *Asian Medicine*, 11.1–2 (2016), 21–60 <https://doi. org/10.1163/15734218-12341377>.

19 Kaviraj Kunjalal Bhishagratna, *An English Translation of the Sushruta Samhita Based on Original Sanskrit Text* (Calcutta, 1911), p. 123.

20 Ibid. p. 127.

21 'Letters, Notes, and Answers to Correspondents', *British Medical Journal*, 1 (1878), p. 325.

22 William Rowley, *A Treatise on Female Nervous Diseases, Madness, Suicide, &c.* (London: T. Hookham, 1798), p. 54.

23 Charles Manfield Clarke, *Observations on the Diseases of Females which are Attended by Discharges* (Philadelphia: H. C. Carey, 1824), p. 25.

24 Julius Althanus, *On Epilepsy, Hysteria and Ataxy: Three Lectures* (London: Churchill & Sons, 1866), p. 48.

25 J. McGrigor Allan, 'On the Real Differences in the Minds of Men and Women', *The Anthropological Review* 7 (1869), pp. 196–219.

26 See Carla Bittel, *Mary Putnam Jacobi and the Politics of Medicine in Nineteenth-Century America* (Chapel Hill: University of North Carolina, 2009).

27 Lara Freidenfelds, *The Modern Period: Menstruation in Twentieth-Century America* (Baltimore: Johns Hopkins University Press, 2009).

28 *The Story of Menstruation* (Hollywood: Disney, 1946).

29 Crystal VanLeeuwen and Belen Torondel, 'Improving Menstrual Hygiene Management in Emergency Contexts: Literature Review of Current Perspectives', *International Journal Of Women's Health*, 10 (2018), pp. 169–86 <https://doi.org/10.2147/ijwh.s135587>.

30 'School Menstrual Hygiene Management In Malawi', *Assets.Publishing. Service.Gov.Uk*, 2018 <https://assets.publishing.service.gov.uk/ media/57a08aa8e5274a27b20006d7/MenstrualHygieneManagement_ Malawi.pdf> [Accessed 15 September 2018].

31   '1 In 10 Girls Have Been Unable to Afford Sanitary Wear', *Plan International UK*, 2018 <https://plan-uk.org/media-centre/1-in-10-girls-have-been-unable-to-afford-sanitary-wear-survey-finds> [Accessed 15 September 2018]; 'ALWAYS Donates Feminine Hygiene Products to Help UK Girls Stay in School. #Endperiodpoverty', *Always.Co.Uk*, 2018 <https://www.always.co.uk/en-gb/about-us/endperiodpoverty> [Accessed 15 September 2018].

THE OLDEST PROFESSION

1   George P. Murdock, 'Anthropology and its Contribution to Public Health', *American Journal of Public Health and the Nations Health*, 42.1 (1952), 7–11 <https://doi.org/10.2105/ajph.42.1.7>.

2   Mary Breckinridge, 'The Nurse-Midwife – A Pioneer', *American Journal of Public Health*, 17.11 (1927), 1147–51, p. 1147 <https://doi.org/10.2105/ajph.17.11.1147>.

3   Glyn Davies, *A History of Money* (Cardiff: University of Wales Press, 2002); Graeme Barker, *The Agricultural Revolution in Prehistory* (Oxford: Oxford University Press, 2009).

4   William W. Sanger, *The History of Prostitution* (New York: Harper & Brothers, 1858), p. 414.

5   Sally Engle Merry, *Colonizing Hawaii: The Cultural Power of Law* (Princeton: Princeton University Press, 2000), p. 249.

6   Gordon Morris Bakken and Brenda Farrington, *Encyclopedia of Women in the American West* (Thousand Oaks, CA: Sage, 2003), p. 236.

7   Rudyard Kipling, 'On the City Wall', in *Soldiers Three, and Other Stories* (London: Routledge, 1914), p. 137.

8   Ibid.

9   Ulises Chávez Jimenez, 'How Much for Your Love: Prostitution Among the Aztecs', *Academia.Edu*, 2004 <http://www.academia.edu/2631485/How_much_for_your_love_prostitution_among_the_Aztecs> [Accessed 7 August 2018].

10   Irving L. Finkel and Markham Judah Geller, *Sumerian Gods and their Representations* (Groningen: STYX Publications, 1997), p. 65.

11   Martha T. Roth, 'Marriage, Divorce and the Prostitute in Ancient Mesopotamia', in Christopher A. Faraone and Laura McClure, *Prostitutes and Courtesans in the Ancient World* (Madison: University of Wisconsin Press, 2006), Kindle edition, location 427.

12   Patrick Olivelle, *King, Governance, and Law in Ancient India* (Oxford: Oxford University Press, 2012), pp. 158–60.

13   Mary Beard and John Henderson, 'With This Body I Thee Worship: Sacred Prostitution in Antiquity', *Gender and History*, 9.3 (1997), 480–503, p. 486.

14 Andrew R. George, *The Epic of Gilgamesh* (London: Penguin, 2003), pp. 6–8.

15 Herodotus, *Delphi Complete Works of Herodotus*, trans. by A. D. Godley (Hastings: Delphi Classics, 2013), Kindle edition, location 1718.

16 Strabo of Amaseia, *Delphi Complete Works of Strabo*, trans. by H. C. Hamilton (Hastings: Delphi Classics, 2016), Kindle edition, location 20295.

17 Lucian, *The Syrian Goddess: Being a Translation of Lucian's De Dea Syria, with a Life of Lucian* (London: Dodo, 2010), pp. 40–2.

18 Pompeius Trogus, 'Justin, Epitome of Pompeius Trogus (1886) pp. 90–171 Books 11–20', *Tertullian.Org*, 2018 <http://www.tertullian.org/fathers/justinus_04_books11to20.htm> [Accessed 18 September 2018].

19 Leslie Kurke, 'Pindar and the Prostitutes, or Reading Ancient "Pornography"', *Arion*, 4, 1996, p. 52.

20 Stephanie Budin, 'Sacred Prostitution in the First Person', in Christopher A. Faraone and Laura McClure, *Prostitutes and Courtesans In the Ancient World* (Madison: University of Wisconsin Press, 2006), Kindle edition, location 1166.

21 'Bible Gateway Passage: 2 Kings 23:7 – New International Version', *Bible Gateway*, 2018 <https://www.biblegateway.com/passage/?search=2+Kings+23%3A7&version=NIV> [Accessed 19 September 2018].

22 E. B. Aryendra Sharma and E. V. Vira Raghavacharya, 'Gems from Sanskrit Literature. (Sūktimālā)', *Journal of the American Oriental Society*, 81.4 (1961), 461 <https://doi.org/10.2307/595726>.

23 Samantha Chattora, 'The Devadasi System – Genesis & Growth', *Iml.Jou. Ufl.Edu*, 2002 <http://iml.jou.ufl.edu/projects/Spring02/Chattaraj/genesis.html> [Accessed 7 August 2018].

24 K. Jamanadas, *Devadasis* (Delhi: Kalpaz Publications, 2007), p. 300.

PUBLIC RELATIONS

1 Irina Metzler, *A Social History of Disability in the Middle Ages* (Hoboken: Taylor and Francis, 2013), p. 23.

2 John Keble, *The Life of the Right Reverend Father in God, Thomas Wilson* (Oxford: J. H. Parker, 1863), p. 296.

3 'Post Office Act 1953', *Legislation.Gov.Uk*, 2018 <http://www.legislation.gov.uk/ukpga/Eliz2/1-2/36/crossheading/general-offences/enacted> [Accessed 22 September 2018].

4 Caroline Archer, *Tart Cards* (New York: Mark Batty, 2003).

5 'Criminal Justice and Police Act 2001', *Legislation.Gov.Uk*, 2018 <http://www.legislation.gov.uk/ukpga/2001/16/contents> [Accessed 22 September 2018].

6   Jack Harris, *Harris's List of Covent Garden Ladies or Man of Pleasure's Kalendar for the Year, 1788* (London: Ranger, 1788), pp. 72, 112, 36.

7   Hallie Rubenhold, *Harris's List of Covent Garden Ladies* (London: Doubleday, 2005), p. 144.

8   Hallie Rubenhold, *The Covent Garden Ladies: Pimp General Jack and the Extraordinary Story of Harris's List* (London: History Press, 2006), p. 71.

9   Ibid.

10   Ibid., p. 216.

11   *Nocturnal Revels: or, The History of King's Place and Other Modern Nunneries* (London: M. Goadby, 1779).

12   *The Gentleman's Bottle Companion*, 1st edn (Edinburgh: Harris, 1979), p. 55.

13   Pamela D. Arceneaux, 'Guidebooks to Sin: The Blue Books of Storyville, New Orleans', *Louisiana History: The Journal of the Louisiana Historical Association*, 28.4 (2018), 397–405, p. 397.

14   Ibid., p. 401.

15   Ibid., p. 403.

16   Al Rose, *Storyville, New Orleans* (Tuscaloosa: University of Alabama Press, 1979), p. 206.

17   E. J. Bellocq et al., *E. J. Bellocq: Storyville Portraits, Photographs from the New Orleans Red-Light District* (New York: Museum of Modern Art, 1970), p. 14.

18   *L'étude Académique*, 1 February, 1911.

19   See Ferruccio Farina, *Die Verbotene Venus: Erotische Postkarten 1895–1925* (Stuttgart: Deutscher Bücherbund, 1989).

20   'Tart Cards Exhibition' at Birmingham Institute of Art & Design, 2014, and Plymouth College of Art, 2012.

21   Teela Sanders and others, *Beyond the Gaze: Summary Briefing on Internet Sex Work*, 2018 <https://www.beyond-the-gaze.com/wp-content/uploads/2018/01/BtGbriefingsummaryoverview.pdf> [Accessed 22 September 2018].

22   '"This Bill Is Killing Us": 9 Sex Workers on Their Lives in the Wake of FOSTA', *Huffpost*, 2018 <https://www.huffingtonpost.com/entry/sex-workers-sesta-fosta_us_5ad0d7d0e4b0edca2cb964d9> [Accessed 22 September 2018].

FEASTING WITH THE PANTHERS

1   *The Letters of Oscar Wilde*, ed. by Rupert Hart-Davies (New York: Harcourt, Brace, and World, 1968), p. 492.

2   'The Home Affairs Committee: Prostitution', *Publications.Parliament. Uk*, 2016 <https://publications.parliament.uk/pa/cm201617/cmselect/cmhaff/26/26.pdf> [Accessed 23 September 2018].

3   'How Much Does Prostitution Contribute to the UK Economy?', *Import. Io*, 2014 <https://www.import.io/post/how-much-does-prostitution-contribute-to-the-uk-economy/> [Accessed 23 September 2018].

4   Mack Friedman, 'Male Sex Work from Ancient Times to the Near Present', in Victor Minichiello, John Scott and Victor Scott, *Male Sex Work and Society* (Golden: Columbia University Press, 2014), pp. 2–34.

5   Quoted in Rudi C. Bleys, *The Geography of Perversion: Male-to-Male Sexual Behaviour Outside the West and the Ethnographic Imagination* (London: Cassell, 1996), p. 33.

6   Iwan Bloch, *A History of English Sexual Morals*, trans. by William H. Forstern (London: Francis Aldor, 1936), p. 135.

7   Sarah Kingston and Natalie Hammond, *Women Who Buy Sexual Services In The UK*, 2016 <http://eprints.lancs.ac.uk/130705/2/WWBS_End_Report_final_.pdf> [Accessed 12 February 2019].

8   Kate Lister, 'Women Do Pay for Sex, and This Is Why', *i News*, 2018 <https://inews.co.uk/inews-lifestyle/women/the-women-who-pay-for-sex/> [Accessed 25 September 2018].

9   Gary P. Leupp, *Male Colors: The Construction of Homosexuality in Tokugawa Japan* (Berkeley: University of California Press, 1995), p. 26.

10   Moisés Kaufman, *Gross Indecency: The Three Trials of Oscar Wilde* (New York: Dramatists Play Service, 1999), p. 70.

11   'Aeschines, Against Timarchus, Section 29', *Perseus.Tufts.Edu*, 2018 <http://www.perseus.tufts.edu/hopper/text?doc=Perseus%3Atext%3A1999.01.0002%3Aspeech%3D1%3Asection%3D29> [Accessed 23 September 2018].

12   John G. Younger, *Sex in the Ancient World from A to Z* (London: Routledge, 2005), Kindle edition, location 4155.

13   Vātsyāyana, *Kamasutra*, ed. and trans. by Wendy Doniger and Sudhir Kakar (Oxford: Oxford University Press, 2009), pp. 65–67.

14   Ibid.

15   Jeremy Goldberg, 'John Rykener, Richard II And The Governance Of London', *Leeds Studies In English*, 45 2014, pp. 49–70.

16   Ibid.

17   Clement Walker, *Relations and Observations Historical and Politick upon the Parliament Begun Anno Dom. 1640* (London: 1648), p. 221.

18   John Dunton, 'The He-Strumpets. A Satyr on the Sodomite-Club', in *Athenianism*, 2 vols. London, 1710, Vol. 2, pp. 93–9.

19   Ned Ward, 'Of the Mollies Club', in *Edward Ward's Satyrical Reflections on Clubs*, Vol. V. (London: J. Phillips, 1710).

20 Rictor Norton, 'Mother Clap's Molly House', *The Gay Subculture in Georgian England*, 5 February 2005 <http://rictornorton.co.uk/eighteen/mother. htm> [Accessed 20 September 2018].

21 Rictor Norton, 'The Trial of George Kedger, 1726', *Homosexuality in Eighteenth-Century England: A Sourcebook*, 1 December 1999 <http:// rictornorton.co.uk/eighteen/1726kedg.htm> [Accessed 24 September 2018].

22 Glenn Chandler, *The Sins of Jack Saul*, 2nd edn (Claygate: Grosvenor House, 2016), p. 7.

23 Jack Saul, *The Sins of the Cities of the Plain or Recollections of a Mary-Ann, with Short Essays on Sodomy and Tribadism* (London: Privately printed, 1881), pp. 15–16.

24 Colin Simpson, *The Cleveland Street Affair* (Boston: Little, Brown and Company, 1976), p. 81.

25 Ibid.

26 'The West End Scandal', *Reynolds's Newspaper*, 12 January 1890.

27 'Central Criminal Court', *The Standard*, 17 January 1890.

CONCLUSION

1 *Old Bailey Proceedings Online* (www.oldbaileyonline.org, version 8.0, 01 December 2018), May 1683, trial of Isabel Barker (t16830524-7).

2 Nghiem L. Nguyen, 'Roman Rape: An Overview of Roman Rape Laws from the Republican Period to Justinian's Reign', *Michigan Journal of Gender And Law*, 13.1 (2006), pp. 75–112.

3 Dorothy Whitelock, ed., *English Historical Documents* (London: Eyre & Spottiswoode, 1955), p. 359.

4 *The Morning Chronicle*, 'Police Intelligence', 20 February 1847, p. 4; *Nottingham Review and General Advertiser for the Midland Counties*, 'Judicial Procedures', 5 May 1837, p. 4.

5 *Bury and Norwich Post*, 'Miscellaneous', 3 May 1837, p. 1.

6 Kristoffer Nyro, *The Kiss and Its History* (London: Sands & Co, 1901), pp. 67–8.

7 'Outcry over Teen's Underwear in Rape Trial', *BBC News*, 2018 <https:// www.bbc.co.uk/news/world-europe-46207304> [Accessed 7 December 2018].

8 Siobhan Norton, '"This Is Not Consent": How a Thong Prompted Protests Across Ireland over the Handling of Rape Trials', *Inews.Co.Uk*, 2018 <https://inews.co.uk/news/long-reads/this-is-not-consent-thong-rape-case-ireland-protests/> [Accessed 7 December 2018].

9 Ibid.

Bibliography

Books

Abbott, Elizabeth, *A History of Celibacy* (New York: Scribner, 2000).

Abreu-Ferreira, Darlene, *Women, Crime, and Forgiveness in Early Modern Portugal* (Florence: Taylor and Francis, 2016).

Abū al-Qāsim Khalaf ibn ʿAbbās al-Zahrāwī, *Albucasis on Surgery and Instruments* (Berkeley: University of California Press, 1973).

Acton, William, *The Functions and Disorders of the Reproductive Organs in Childhood, Youth, Adult Age, and Advanced Life* (London: John Churchill, 1857).

Aelian, *On Animals,* trans. by A. F. Scholfield, (Cambridge: Harvard University Press, 1959).

Aftel, Mandy, *Essence and Alchemy* (New York: North Point Press, 2001).

Aggrawal, Anil, *Forensic and Medico-Legal Aspects of Sexual Crimes and Unusual Sexual Practices* (Boca Raton: CRC Press, 2008).

Alberti, Fay Bound, *This Mortal Coil: The Human Body in History and Culture* (Oxford: University Press, 2016).

Albertus, and Helen Rodnite Lemay, *Women's Secrets: A Translation of Pseudo-Albertus Magnus' De Secretis Mulierum with Commentaries* (Albany: University of New York Press, 1992).

Alexandre-Debray, Janine, *La Païva, 1819–1884* (Paris: Perrin, 1986).

Allan, Keith, and Kate Burridge, *Forbidden Words: Taboo and the Censoring of Language* (Cambridge: Cambridge University Press, 2009).

Alloula, Malek, *The Colonial Harem*, translated by Myrna Godzich and Wlad Godzich (Minneapolis: University of Minnesota Press, 1986).

Anderson, William John, *Hysterical and Nervous Affections of Women. Read before the Harveian Society* (Sherriff & Downing: Sydney, 1864).

Anonymous, *Proverbs of Hendyng* (Cambridge: Chadwyck-Healey, 1992).

Anonymous, *A New Description Of Merryland* (London: E Curll, 1741).

Anonymous, 'Sweet Molly Malone', in *Apollo's Medley* (Doncaster, 1790), p. 78.

Anonymous, *The Sins of the Cities of the Plain* (London: Privately printed, 1881).

Anonymous, *The Romance of Lust, or Early Experiences* (London: William Lazenby, 1873).

Appendix to the Journals of the Senate and Assembly of the Nineteenth Session of the Legislature of the State of California (Sacramento: T. A. Springer, 1872).

Arbesman, Samuel, *Half Life of Facts: Why everything we know has an Expiration Date* (London: Penguin, 2004).

Archer, Caroline, *Tart Cards: London's Illicit Advertising Art* (New York: Mark Batty, 2003).

Aretaeus, *The Extant Works Of Aretaeus, The Cappadocian*, 1st edn, trans. by Francis Adams (London: The Sydenham Society, 1856).

Aretino, Pietro, *The Ragionamenti, Or Dialogues of the Divine Pietro Aretino*, 1st edn, trans. by Alcide Bonneau (Paris: Éd. Allia, 1892).

Aristophanes, trans. by David Barrett and Alan H. Sommerstein, *The Knights, Peace, Wealth, The Birds, The Assemblywomen* (London: Penguin Books, 1990).

Aristotle, *Complete Works of Aristotle, Volume 2*, ed. by Jonathan Barnes (Princeton: Princeton University Press, 2014).

Aristotle, and John Gillies, *Aristotle's Ethics and Politics: Politics* (United States: Palala Press, 2016).

Ash, Russell, *Busty, Slag & Nob End* (London: Headline, 2009).

—, *Potty, Fartwell & Knob: Extraordinary but True Names of British People* (London: Headline, 2007).

Ashenburg, Katherine, *An Unsanitised History of Washing* (London: Profile, 2009).

Ashurst, John, *The International Encyclopedia of Surgery: A Systematic Treatise on the Theory and Practice of Surgery* (New York: W. Wood, 1895).

Athenaeus, *The Deipnosophists* (London: Heinemann, 1927).

Athenaeus, *Delphi Complete Works of Athenaeus*, trans. by C. D. Yonge (Hastings: Delphi Classics, 2017). Kindle edition.

Aubrey, John, *Remaines of Gentilisme and Judaisme* (London: Folklore Society, 1881).

Avicenne, *Liber Canonis* (Hildesheim: Georg Olms Verlagsbuchhandlung, 1964).

B, Madame, *La Femme Endormie* (Melbourne, 1899).

Baden-Powell, Robert, *Boy Scouts of America*, 1st edn (New York: Page and Company, 1911).

Bakken, Gordon Morris, and Brenda Farrington, *Encyclopedia of Women in the American West* (Thousand Oaks: Sage, 2003).

Barker, Graeme, *The Agricultural Revolution in Prehistory* (Oxford: Oxford University Press, 2009).

Barrow, John, *Travels into the Interior of Southern Africa* (London: T. Cadell and W. Davies, 1801).

Bartholin, Thomas, and Michael Lyser, *The Anatomical History of Thomas Bartholinus* (London: Francis Leach, 1653).

Bayard, Tania, *A Medieval Home Companion* (New York: Harper, 1992).

Beaney, James George, *The Generative System and Its Functions in Health and Disease*, 1st edn (Melbourne: F. F. Bailliere, 1872).

Beasley, Henry, *The Book of Prescriptions*, 9th edn (London: Churchill, 1907).

Bedford, Gunning S., *Clinical Lectures on the Diseases of Women and Children*, 1st edn (New York: William Wood, 1855).

Benson, Catherine, and Roger Matthews, *The National Vice Squad Survey* (Enfield: Middlesex University, 1995).

Betham, Matilda, 'Arthur and Albina', in *Poems* (London: Hatchard, 1808), pp. 3–13.

Bhishagratna, Kaviraj Kunjalal, *An English Translation of the Sushruta Samhita Based on Original Sanskrit Text* (Calcutta, 1911).

Bienville, D. T. de, and Edward Wilmot, *Nymphomania, Or, A Dissertation Concerning the Furor Uterinus* (London: J. Bewer, 1775).

Blank, Hanne, *Virgin: The Untouched History* (London: Bloomsbury, 2007).

Bliss, W. W., *Woman, and Her Thirty Years' Pilgrimage* (Boston: B.B. Russell, 1870).

Bloch, Iwan, *The Sexual Life of our Time in its Relations to Modern Civilization*, trans. by M. Eden Paul (London: Rebman, 1908).

—, *Anthropological Studies on the Strange Sexual Practices of All Races and All Ages*, 1st edn (Honolulu: University Press of the Pacific, 2001).

Board of Trade, *Reports of the Lords of the Committee of Council Appointed For the Consideration of All Matters Relating To Trade and Foreign Plantations* (London, 1789).

Boccaccio, Giovanni, *The Decameron*, ed. by Guido Waldman and Jonathan Usher (Oxford: Oxford University Press, 2008).

Boswell, James, *Boswell's London Journal, 1762–1763*, ed. by Frederick Albert Pottle (New Haven: Yale University Press, 2004).

Bourguignon D'Anville, Hubert François, and John Cleland, *Memoirs of a Woman of Pleasure: From the Original Corrected Edition, with a Set of Elegant Engravings [Ascribed to Gravelot]. [By John Cleland.]* (London, 1766).

Bowditch, Lucy Orne, and Charles Pickering Bowditch, *The Lives and Portraits of Curious and Odd Characters* (Worcester: Thomas Drew, 1853).

Brock, Pope, *Charlatan: America's Most Dangerous Huckster, the Man Who Pursued Him, and the Age of Flimflam* (New York: Crown Publishers, 2008).

Brome, Richard, *A Jovial Crew*, ed. by Tiffany Stern (London: Bloomsbury, 2014).

Brown, Isaac Baker, *On the Curability of Certain Forms of Insanity, Epilepsy, Catalepsy, and Hysteria in Females* (Robert Hardwicke: London, 1866).

Brundage, James A., and Vern L. Bullough, *Handbook of Medieval Sexuality* (New York: Garland Publishing, 2000).

Brundage, James A., *Law, Sex, and Christian Society in Medieval Europe* (Chicago: University of Chicago Press, 2009).

Buchan, William, *Domestic Medicine: Or, a Treatise on the Prevention and Cure of Diseases by Regimen and Simple Remedies* (London: Balfour, Auld and Smellie, 1769).

Büchner, Georg, *Danton's Death, Leonce and Lena, Woyzeck*, trans. and ed. by Victor Price (Oxford: Oxford University Press, 2008).

Budin, Stephanie Lynn, *The Myth of Sacred Prostitution in Antiquity* (New York: Cambridge University Press, 2010).

Bukhārī, Muḥammad ibn Ismāʿīl, and Muhammad Muhsin Khan, *Ṣaḥīḥ Al-Bukhārī* (Riyadh, Saudi Arabia: Darussalam, 1997).

Burford, E. J., *Bawdy Verse*, 1st edn (Harmondsworth: Penguin Books, 1982).

Burge, Amy, '"I Will Cut Myself and Smear Blood on the Sheet": Testing Virginity in Medieval and Modern Orientalist Romance', in *Virgin Envy: The Cultural Insignificance of the Hymen* (London: Zed, 2016).

Burrows, Daron, *The Stereotype of the Priest in the Old French Fabliaux: Anti-clerical Satire and Lay Identity* (Oxford: Peter Lang Publishing, 2005).

Burton, Robert, *The Anatomy of Melancholy: What it is. With all The Kindes, Causes, Symptomes, Prognosticks, and Seuerall Cures of it. In Three Maine Partitions, with their Seuerall Sections, Members and Subsections. Philosophically, Medicinally, Historically Opened and Cut up*, 5th edn (Oxford: Henry Cripps, 1634).

Burton, Sir Richard, Leonard C. Smithers, *Priapeia: Sportive Epigrams on Priapus* (London: TGS Publishing, 2010).

Caballero-Navas, Carmen, *The Book of Women's Love and Jewish Medieval Medical Literature on Women* (London: Routledge, 2004).

Campbell, R. Joe, *A Morphological Dictionary of Classical Nahuatl* (Madison: Hispanic Seminary of Medieval Studies, 1985).

Capp, Bernard, *When Gossips Meet: Women, Family, and Neighborhood in Early Modern England* (Oxford: Oxford University Press, 2003).

Carlile, Richard, 'Every Woman's Book Or What Is Love?', in *What Is Love?: Richard Carlile's Philosophy of Sex* (London: Verso, 1998).

Casanova, Giacomo, *The Complete Memoirs of Jacques Casanova De Seingalt*, trans. by Arthur Machen (SMK Books, 2014).

Catalogue and Report of Obstetrical and Other Instruments (London: Obstetric Society of London, 1867).

Chandler, Daniel, *Semiotics: The Basics*, 2nd edn (London: Routledge, 2007).

Chartier, Alain, *Delectable Demaundes, and Pleasaunt Questions, With Their Seuerall Aunswers, In Matters of Loue, Naturall Causes, with Morall and Politique Deuises. Newely Translated out Of Frenche into Englishe, This Present Yere of our Lorde God. 1566* (London: John Cawood, 1566).

Chaucer, Geoffrey, *The Canterbury Tales*, ed. by Jill Mann (London: Penguin Books, 2005).

Chauliac, Guy de, *La Grande Chirurgie* (Paris: F. Alcan, 1890).

Chorier, Nicolas, *A Dialogue between a Married Lady and a Maid* (London, 1740).

Cicero, trans. and ed. by D. R. Shackleton Bailey, *Epistulae Ad Familiares* (Cambridge: Cambridge University Press, 1977).

Civillian, A, *Trials for Adultery; Or, the History of Divorces* (London: Blandon, 1779).

Cleland, John, *Memoirs of a Woman of Pleasure* (London: G. Fenton, 1749).

Cleland, John, *Fanny Hill: Memoirs of a Woman of Pleasure* (London: LBA, 2007), Kindle edition.

Coleridge, Samuel Taylor, 'To Matilda Betham, from a Stranger', in *The Collected Works of Samuel Taylor Coleridge, Volume 1* (Princeton: Princeton University Press, 2001), pp. 726–8.

Collier, Aine, *The Humble Little Condom: A History* (Amherst: Prometheus Books, 2007).

Colombo, Realdo, Gianluigi Baldo, and Tiziana Brolli, *De Re Anatomica Libri XV* (Paris: Les Belles lettres, 2014).

Copland, James, and Charles A. Lee, *A Dictionary of Practical Medicine*, 1st edn (New York: Harper, 1860).

Crais, Clifton C., and Pamela Scully, *Sara Baartman and the Hottentot Venus* (Princeton: Princeton University Press, 2009).

Cranach, Lucas, and Stephan Füssel, *The Luther Bible of 1534* (Cologne: Taschen, 2016).

Crisp, Quentin, *The Naked Civil Servant* (London: Flamingo, 1996).

Crooke, Helkiah, *Microcosmographia* (London: William Iaggard, 1615).

Cruickshank, Dan, *The Secret History of Georgian London: How the Wages of Sin Shaped the Capital* (London: Windmill Books, 2010).

Culpeper, Nicholas, *A Physicall Directory; Or, a Translation of the London Dispensatory Made By the Colledge of Physicians in London* (London: Peter Cole, 1649).

—, *The Complete Herbal* (London: CreateSpace, 2018)

Cuvier, Georges, 'Extrait D'Observations Faites Sur Le Cadavre D'Une Femme Connue À Paris Et À Londres Sous Le Nom De Vénus Hottentotte', in *Mémoires du Musée Nationale D'Histoire Naturelle*, 1817, pp. 259–74.

Daniel, Mark, *See You Next Tuesday* (London: Timewell, 2008).

Daniel, Samuel, *The Tragedy of Philotas* (Edinburgh: 1603).

Davenport, John, and John Camden Hotten, *Aphrodisiacs and Anti-Aphrodisiacs* (London: Privately printed, 1869).

Davies, Glyn, *A History Of Money* (Cardiff: University of Wales Press, 2002).

De Chobham, Thomas, *Thomae De Chobham Summa Confessorum*, ed. by
F. Broomfield (Louvain: Nauwelaerts, 1968).

De Graaf, Regnier, *Regnier De Graaf on the Human Reproductive Organs*,
trans. by Henry David Jocelyn and Brian Peter Setchell (Oxford: Blackwell
scientific, 1972).

De Laet, S. J., *History of Humanity* (London: Routledge, 1994).

Delicado, Francisco, and Bruno M. Damiani, *Portrait of Lozana* (Potomac: Scripta
Humanistica, 1987).

Deslandes, Léopold, *A Treatise on the Diseases Produced by Onanism, Masturbation, Self-Pollution, and Other Excesses*, 2nd edn (Boston: Otis, Broader and
Company, 1839).

Devlin, Kate, *Turned On: Science, Sex and Robots* (London: Bloomsbury, 2018).

Di Marino, Vincent, and Hubert Lepidi, *Anatomic Study of the Clitoris and the
Bulbo-Clitoral Organ* (Cham: Springer International Publishing, 2014).

Diagnostic and Statistical Manual of Mental Disorders, 5th edn (Washington:
American Psychiatric Association, 2013).

Dickens, Charles, *The Pickwick Papers* (London: Createspace, 2017).

Ditmore, Melissa Hope, *Encyclopedia of Prostitution and Sex Work* (Westport:
Greenwood Press, 2006).

Doan, Laura L., and Jay Prosser, *Palatable Poison: Critical Perspectives on* The
Well of Loneliness (New York: Columbia University Press, 2002).

Drenth, Jelto, *The Origin of the World* (London: Reaktion, 2008).

Dulaure, Jacques-Antoine, *Histoire Abrégée De Différens Cultes*, 2nd edn (Paris,
1825).

Dunbar, Newell, *The Elixir of Life: Dr. Brown-Séguard's own Account of his
Famous Alleged Remedy for Debility and Old Age* (Boston: J.G. Cupples, 1889).

Dunglison, Robley, *A New Dictionary of Medical Science and Literature* (Boston:
C. Bowen, 1833).

—, *Medical Lexicon: A Dictionary of Medical Science* (Philadelphia: Blanchard &
Lea, 1854).

Dury, Graham, Davey Jones, Simon Thorp and Charlie Brooker, *Roger's
Profanisaurus* (London: Dennis Publishing, 2013).

Ellis, Havelock, *Studies in the Psychology of Sex* (Honolulu: University Press of
the Pacific, 2001).

Elyot, Thomas, *The Dictionary of Syr Thomas Eliot Knyght*, 1st edn (London:
1538).

Fabre-Serris, Jacqueline, and Alison Keith, *Women and War in Antiquity*
(Baltimore: Johns Hopkins University Press, 2015).

Falloppio, Gabriele, *De Morbo Gallico* (Padua, 1563).

—, *Observationes Anatomicae* (Modena: Mucchi, 1964).

Faraone, Christopher A., and Laura McClure, *Prostitutes and Courtesans in the Ancient World* (Madison: University of Wisconsin Press, 2006).

Female Genital Mutilation/Cutting: A Global Concern (New York: UNICEF, 2016).

Ferguson, Anthony, *The Sex Doll: A History* (Jefferson: McFarland, 2010).

Ferguson, Ted, *Kit Coleman* (Markham: PaperJacks, 1979).

Fiaux, Louis, *Les Maisons De Tolerance* (Paris: G. Carré, 1892).

Finkel, Irving L., and Markham Judah Geller, *Sumerian Gods and their Representations* (Groningen: STYX Publications, 1997).

Florio, John, Arnold Hatfield, Edward Blount and John Evelyn, *A Worlde Of Wordes, Or, Most Copious, And Exact Dictionarie In Italian And English*, 1st edn (London: Arnold Hatfield, 1598).

Foote, Edward B., *Medical Common Sense* (New York: the author, 1863).

Freidenfelds, Lara, *The Modern Period: Menstruation in Twentieth-Century America* (Baltimore: Johns Hopkins University Press, 2009).

Freud, Sigmund, trans. by James Strachey, *Three Essays on the Theory of Sexuality* (Mansfield: Martino Publishing, 2011).

—, illustrated by Peter Gay, *The Question Of Lay Analysis* (New York: Norton, 1989)

—, trans. by David McLintock, *The Standard Edition of the Complete Psychological Works of Sigmund Freud*, ed. by James Strachey, Anna Freud, Alix Strachey, and Alan Tyson (London: Vintage, 2001).

Freud, Sigmund, trans. by James Strachey, *The Uncanny* (London: Penguin, 2003).

Friedman, and David M. Friedman, *A Mind of its Own: A Cultural History of the Penis* (New York: The Free Press, 2001).

Galen, *Galen on the Usefulness of the Parts of the Body*, ed. by Margaret Tallmadge May (New York: Classics of Medicine Library, 1996).

George, Andrew R., *The Epic Of Gilgamesh* (London: Penguin, 2003).

Gerald of Wales, *The Jewel Of The Church: A Translation Of The Gemma Ecclesiastica* (Leiden: Brill, 1979).

Gerber, Robin, *Barbie and Ruth: The Story of the World's Most Famous Doll and the Woman Who Made Her* (New York: Harper, 2010).

Gernot, Wilhelm, Diana Stein and Jennifer Barnes, *The Hurrians* (Warminster: Aris and Phillips, 1994).

Gersh, Carolyn J., 'Naming the Body: A Translation with Commentary and Interpretive Essays of Three Anatomical Works Attributed to Rufus of Ephesus' (unpublished PhD, University of Michigan, 2012).

Goldberg, P.J.P., *Women In Medieval English Society* (Gloucestershire: Sutton, 1997).

Graham, Sylvester, *A Lecture to Young Men on Chastity, Intended Also for the Serious Consideration of Parents and Guardians* (Boston: Cornhill, 1838).

Granville, Joseph Mortimer, *Nerve-Vibration and Excitation as Agents in the Treatment of Functional Disorder and Organic Disease*, 1st edn (London: Churchill, 1883).

Green, Jonathon, *Green's Dictionary of Slang* (London: Chambers, 2010).

Green, Monica Helen, ed., *The Trotula*, (Philadelphia: University of Pennsylvania Press, 2001).

Grose, Francis, *A Classical Dictionary of the Vulgar Tongue*, 3rd edn (London: Hooper & Co., 1796).

—, *Guide to Health, Beauty, Riches, and Honour* (London: S. Hooper, 1785).

Guernsey, Henry Newell, *The Application of the Principles and Practice of Homoeopathy to Obstetrics*, 2nd edn (London: Turner, 1878).

Guiley, Rosemary, *The Encyclopedia of Witches and Witchcraft* (New York: Facts on File, 1989).

Gurney, Anna, *A Literal Translation of the Saxon Chronicle* (London: Stevenson, 1819).

Gwerful Mechain, *Gwaith Gwerful Mechain Ac Eraill*, 1st edn, trans. by Nerys Ann Howells (Aberystwyth: University Press, 2001).

H. F., *A True and Exact Relation of the Several Informations, Examinations, and Confessions of the Late Witches, Arraigned and Executed in the County Of Essex* (London: Henry Overton, 1645).

Hakim, Catherine, *Erotic Capital: The Power of Attraction in the Boardroom and the Bedroom* (New York: Basic Books, 2011).

Hale, Matthew, *A Tryal of Witches, at the Assizes Held at Bury St. Edmonds for the County of Suffolk, on the Tenth Day of March, 1664: Before Sir Matthew Hale Kt. then Lord Chief Baron of his Majesties Court of Exchequer* (London: William Shrewsbery, 1682).

Hallam, Paul, *Book Of Sodom* (London: Routledge, 1995).

Hamermesh, Daniel S., *Beauty Pays: Why Attractive People are More Successful* (Princeton: Princeton University Press, 2013).

Hamilton, David, *The Monkey Gland Affair* (London: Catto, 1986).

Hamilton, H.C.T., *The Geography of Strabo* (London: Bell and Sons, 1903).

Hannig, Rainer, *Grosses Handwörterbuch Ägyptisch–Deutsch* (Mainz: Philipp von Zabern, 1995).

Harlan, Michael, *Roman Republican Moneyers and their Coins* (London: Seaby, 1995).

Harris, Judith, *Pompeii Awakened: A Story of Rediscovery* (London: Tauris, 2007).

Harris, Karen, *The Medieval Vagina: a Historical and Hysterical Look at all Things Vaginal During the Middle Ages* (London: Snark, 2014).

Harris's List of Covent Garden Ladies or Man of Pleasure's Kalendar for the Year, 1788 (London: H. Ranger, 1788).

Head, Richard, *The Rogue Discovered, Or A Congratulatory Verse Upon A Book Newly Published (A Piece Much Desired, And Long Expected) Called The English Rogue, A Witty Extravagant* (London: Francis Kirkman, 1665).

Healey, Trebor, *A Horse Named Sorrow* (Madison: Terrace Books, 2012).

Heimerl, Christian, and Guilelmus de Saliceto, *The Middle English Version of William of Saliceto's 'Anatomia'* (Heidelberg: Winter, 2008).

Henke, James T., *Gutter Life and Language in the Early "Street" Literature of England* (West Cornwall: Locust Hill Press, 1988).

Henley, Virginia, *A Woman of Passion* (London: Random House, 2009).

Herbert McAvoy, Liz, and Diane Watt, *The History of British Women's Writing, 700–1500* (Basingstoke: Palgrave Macmillan, 2011).

Herodotus, *Delphi Complete Works of Herodotus*, trans. by A. D. Godley (Hastings: Delphi Classics, 2013), Kindle edition.

Hesiod, *Theogony*, ed. by M. L. West (Oxford: Oxford University Press, 2008).

Hewitt, Grailey, *The Diagnosis, Pathology and Treatment of Diseases of Women* (Philadelphia: Lindsay and Blackiston, 1868).

Hildegard of Bingen, *Hildegard Von Bingen's Physica: The Complete English Translation of her Classic Work on Health and Healing*, trans. by Priscilla Throop (Rochester: Healing Arts Press, 1998).

Hincmar of Rheims, *De Divortio Lotharii Regis Et Theutbergae Regina* (Hanover: MGH, 1992).

—, *De Nuptiis Stephani Et Filiae Regimundi Comiti* (Berlin: MGH, 1939).

Historia Augusta (Boston: Loeb Classical Library, 1921).

Hitschmann, Eduard, and Edmund Bergler, *Frigidity in Women: its Characteristics and Treatment* (Washington: Nervous and Mental Disease Publishing Company, 1936).

Hornung, Erik, *Das Buch Der Anbetung des Re im Westen, Sonnenlitanei. Nach Den Versionen Des Neuen Reiches Herausgegeben von Erik Hornung* (Geneva: Université de Genève, 1975).

Hughes, Geoffrey, *Swearing: A Social History of Foul Language, Oaths and Profanity in English* (London: Penguin, 1998).

Jacquart, Danielle, and Claude Thomasset, *Sexuality and Medicine in the Middle Ages* (Princeton: Princeton University Press, 1988).

Jamanadas, K., *Devadasis: Ancient and Modern* (Delhi: Kalpaz Publications, 2007).

—, *Tirupati Balaji was a Buddhist Shrine* (Chandrapur: Sanjivan Publications, 2009).

James VI and I, *Daemonologie, In Forme of a Dialogue, Divided into Three Books: By the High and Mighty Prince, James &C.* (Edinburgh: Robert Walde-graue, 1597).

James, William, *The Story of John Ruskin, Effie Gray and John Everett Millais told for the First Time in their Unpublished Letters*, ed. by William James (London: Murray, 1948).

Jentzer, A., and Maurice Bourcat, *The Physiotherapy in Gynecology and the Mechanical Treatment of Diseases of the Uterus and its Appendages by Thure Brandt* (Leipzig: Barth, 1895).

Jerome, Saint, *The Sacred Writings of Saint Jerome*, trans. by William Henry Fremantle and Philip Schaff (London: Jazzybee, 2018).

Jones, Terry, and Roger Mellie, *The New Roger's Profanisaurus* (London: Boxtree, 2002).

Jönsjö, Jan, *Studies on Middle English Nicknames*, 1st edn (Lund: LiberLäromedel/Gleerup, 1979).

Joyce, James, *Ulysses* (Ware: Wordsworth, 2010).

Jütte, Robert, *Contraception: A History* (Cambridge: Polity, 2008).

Kammerer, C., R. Manneeprassert, and P. Symonds, 'Vulnerability to HIV Infection among Three Hill Tribes in Northern Thailand', in *Culture and Sexual Risk: Anthropological Perspectives on AIDS* (London: Routledge, 1995), pp. 53–79.

Karras, Ruth Mazo, *Common Women: Prostitution and Sexuality in Medieval England* (London: Oxford University Press, 1996).

Keble, John, *The Life of the Right Reverend Father in God, Thomas Wilson* (Oxford: J.H. Parker, 1863).

Kellogg, John Harvey, *Plain Facts for Old and Young: Embracing the Natural History and Hygiene of Organic Life* (Burlington: Segner, 1887).

Kelly, Henry Ansgar, and Alan M. Dershowitz, *The Matrimonial Trials of Henry VIII* (London: Wipf and Stock, 2004).

Kelly, Kathleen Coyne, *Performing Virginity and Testing Chastity in the Middle Ages* (New York: Routledge, 2000).

Killigrew, Thomas, *The Parson's Wedding* (London: Henry Herringman, 1641).

Kinsey, Alfred C., Wardell B. Pomeroy, and Clyde E. Martin, *Sexual Behavior in the Human Male* (Philadelphia: W.B. Saunders, 1948).

Kinsey, Alfred C., *Sexual Behavior in the Human Female* (Philadelphia: Saunders, 1953).

Kipling, Rudyard, *Soldiers Three, and Other Stories* (London: Routledge, 1914).

Knight, Richard Payne, and Thomas Wright, *A Discourse on the Worship of Priapus, and its Connection with the Mystic* (London: Spilbury, 1865).

—, *Sexual Symbolism: A History of Phallic Worship* (New York: Julian Press, 1957).

Knowlton, Charles, *Fruits of Philosophy: A Treatise on the Population Question* (San Francisco: Readers Library, 1891).

Krafft-Ebing, R. von, *Psychopathia Sexualis*, trans. by Victor Robinson (New York: Pioneer Publications, 1939).

Kramer, Heinrich and Jakob Sprenger, *Malleus Maleficarum*, trans. by P. G. Maxwell-Stuart (Manchester: Manchester University Press, 2007).

La'mert, Samuel, *Self-Preservation: A Medical Treatise on the Secret Infirmities and Disorders of the Generative Organs*, 1st edn (London: James Gilbert, 1852).

Lanfranco, and John Hall, *Most Excellent and Learned Woorke of Chirurgerie, Called Chirurgia Parua Lanfranci* (London: Thomas Marshe, 1565).

Langham, William, *The Garden of Health* (London: Christopher Barker, 1579).

Law, James Thomas, *The Ecclesiastical Statutes at Large, Extracted from the Great Body of the Statute Law, and Arranged Under Separate Heads* (London: William Benning and Co., 1857).

Lawrence, C. H., *Medieval Monasticism: Forms of Religious Life in Western Europe in the Middle Ages* (London: Routledge, 1984).

Lawrence, D. H., *Lady Chatterley's Lover*, ed. by David Ellis (Ware: Wordsworth, 2007).

Le Vaillant, François, *New Travels into the Interior Parts of Africa, By the Way of the Cape of Good Hope* (London: G.G. and J. Robinson, 1796).

Lee, Lily Xiao Hong, and Sue Wiles, *Biographical Dictionary of Chinese Women, Volume II: Tang through Ming 618–44* (London: Routledge, 2014).

Lee, R. Alton, *The Bizarre Careers of John R. Brinkley* (Lexington: University Press of Kentucky, 2015).

Lemay, Helen Rodnite, *Women's Secrets: A Translation of Pseudo-Albertus Magnus's* De Secretis Mulierum *with Commentaries* (New York: Suny Press, 1992).

Lever, Charles, *Charles O'Malley, the Irish Dragoon* (Leipzig: Tauchnitz, 1848).

Levey, Martin, *Early Arabic Pharmacology* (Leiden: E.J. Brill, 1973).

Leyser, Henrietta, *Medieval Women: Social History of Women in England 450–1500* (London: Phoenix Press, 1995).

Lieberman, Hallie, *Buzz: A Stimulating History of the Sex Toy* (New York: Pegasus Books, 2017).

Lloyd, Elisabeth A., *The Case of the Female Orgasm: Bias in the Science of Evolution* (Cambridge: Harvard University Press, 2005).

Lochrie, Karma, *Heterosyncrasies: Female Sexuality when Normal Wasn't* (Minneapolis: University of Minnesota Press, 2005).

Logan, William, *An Exposure, from Personal Observations, of Female Prostitution in London, Leeds, and Rochdale, and Especially in the City of Glasgow* (Glasgow: Gallie, 1843).

Lombroso, Cesare, and Gugliemo Ferrero, *La Donna Delinquente* (Turin: Roux, 1893).

López Austin, Alfredo, *Cuerpo Humano E Ideologia* (Mexico City: National Autonomous University of Mexico, 1984).

Lucas, E.V., *Works Of Charles and Mary Lamb* (London: Methuen and Co., 1904).

Lucian, *The Syrian Goddess: Being a Translation of Lucian's De Dea Syria, with a Life of Lucian* (London: Dodo, 2010).

Mackenzie, John Whiteford, *Philotus, A Comedy, Reprinted from the Edition of Robert Charteris* (Edinburgh: Ballantyne, 1835).

Macy, Sue, and Meredith Orlow, *Wheels of Change* (Washington: National Geographic, 2012).

Maines, Rachel P., *The Technology of Orgasm* (Baltimore: Johns Hopkins University Press, 2001).

Major, Ralph Hermon, *Classic Descriptions of Disease*, 3rd edn (Springfield: Charles C. Thomas, 1978).

Malory, Sir Thomas, *Le Morte d'Arthur*, ed. by Helen Cooper (Oxford: Oxford University Press, 2008).

Mardrus, J. C., and E. P. Mathers, *The Book of the Thousand and One Nights* (Hoboken: Taylor and Francis, 2013).

Marston, John, *The Scourge Of Villanie* (London, 1598).

Martial, *Epigrams*, ed. by Gideon Nisbet (Oxford: Oxford University Press, 2015).

Martin, Gerald S, *Gabriel Garcia Marquez: A Life* (London: Bloomsbury, 2009).

Marvell, Andrew, 'To his Coy Mistress', in *Miscellaneous Poems* (London: Robert Boulter, 1681), pp. 19–20.

Masters, William H., and Virginia E. Johnson, *Human Sexual Response* (London: Churchill, 1966).

Mathes, Bettina, 'The Significance of the Enlarged Clitoris for Early Modern Anatomy', in *Sensible Flesh: on Touch in Early Modern Culture* (Philadelphia: University Press, 2002), pp. 103–25.

Meeks, Dimitri, *Année Lexicographique* (Paris: Cybèle, 1998).

Merry, Sally Engle, *Colonizing Hawaii: The Cultural Power of Law* (Princeton: Princeton University Press, 2000).

Metzler, Irina, *A Social History of Disability in the Middle Ages* (Hoboken: Taylor and Francis, 2013).

Middleton, Thomas, *Thomas Middleton: The Collected Works*, ed. by Gary Taylor and John Lavagnino (Oxford: Oxford University Press, 2010).

Mill, Humphrey, *A Night's Search, Discovering the Nature and Condition of Night-Walkers with their Associates* (London: H. Shepard and W. Ley, 1640).

Milnor, Kristina, *Graffiti and the Literary Landscape in Roman Pompeii* (Oxford: Oxford University Press, 2014).

Milton, John Laws, *On the Pathology and Treatment of Gonorrhoea and Spermatorrhoea* (New York: Wood, 1887).

Mohr, Melissa, *Holy Sh*T: A Brief History of Swearing* (Oxford: Oxford University Press, 2013).

Moll, Albert, *Sexual Life of the Child* (Classic Reprint) (London: Forgotten Books, 2015).

Morison, Alexander, *The Physiognomy of Mental Diseases* (London: Longman, 1843).

Moulton, Ian Frederick, *Before Pornography: Erotic Writing in Early Modern England* (Oxford: Oxford University Press, 2004).

Morton, Mark, *Lover's Tongue: A Merry Romp through the Language of Love & Sex*, 1st edn (London: Insomniac Press, 2003).

Murray, Jacqueline, *Love, Marriage, and Family in the Middle Ages* (Toronto: University of Toronto Press, 2001).

Nanninga, John B., *The Gland Illusion: Early Attempts at Rejuvenation through Male Hormone Therapy* (London: McFarland, 2017).

Neely, Mark E., *The Abraham Lincoln Encyclopedia* (New York: McGraw-Hill, 1982).

Nocturnal Revels: Or, the History of King's Place (London: M. Goadby, 1779).

Nunn, J. F., *Ancient Egyptian Medicine* (Norman: University of Oklahoma Press, 2002).

Nyro, Kristoffer, *The Kiss and its History* (London: Sands & Co, 1901).

Olivelle, Patrick, *King, Governance, and Law in Ancient India* (Oxford: Oxford University Press, 2012).

Ovid, *Metamorphoses*, ed. by A. D. Melville, and E. J. Kenney (Oxford: Oxford University Press, 2008).

Pancoast, S., *The Ladies' Medical Guide* (Philadelphia: S.I. Bell & Co., 1886).

Parent Du Châtelet, Alexandre, *On Prostitution in the City of Paris. From the French of M. Parent Duchatelet. Second Edition* (London: T. Burgess, 1837).

Parry, John S., *Extra-Uterine Pregnancy; its Causes, Species, Pathological Anatomy, Clinical History, Diagnosis, Prognosis and Treatment* (Philadelphia: Henry Lea, 1876).

Peakman, Julie, Alexander Pettit, and Patrick Spedding, *Whore Biographies, 1700–1825* (London: Pickering & Chatto, 2006).

Peakman, Julie, Mark Golden, Peter Toohey, Ruth Evans, Bette Talvacchia, and Chiara Beccalossi and others, *A Cultural History Of Sexuality* (Oxford: Berg, 2011).

Peakman, Julie, *Mighty Lewd Books: The Development of Pornography in Eighteenth-Century England* (London: Palgrave Macmillan, 2003).

Pedersen, Frederik, *Marriage Disputes in Medieval England* (London: Hambledon, 2000).

—, 'Privates on Parade: Impotence Cases as Evidence for Medieval Gender, in *Law and Private Life in the Middle Ages: Proceedings of the Sixth Carlberg Academy Conference on Medieval Legal History 2009* (Copenhagen: DJØF, 2011), pp. 81–103.

—, 'Motives For Murder: The Role of Sir Ralph Paynel in the Murder of William Cantilupe', in *Continuity, Change and Pragmatism in the Law: Essays in Honour of Professor Angelo Forte* (Aberdeen: Aberdeen University Press, 2016), pp. 69–95.

Peele, George, and Patricia Binnie, *The Old Wives' Tale* (Manchester: Manchester University Press, 1980).

Pelner Cosman, Madeleine, and Linda Gale Jones, *Handbook to Life in the Medieval World, Volumes 1–3* (New York: Facts on File, 2008).

Pepys, *The Diary of Samuel Pepys*, ed. by Samuel, Robert Latham and William Matthews (London: HarperCollins, 2000).

Phillips, Kim M., *Medieval Maidens: Young Women and Gender in England, c.1270–c.1540* (Manchester: Manchester University Press, 2003).

Plato, *The Republic of Plato* (Cambridge: Macmillan, 1852).

Platter, Felix, *Platerus Golden Practice of Physick* (London: Peter Cole, 1664).

Pliny the Elder, *Delphi Complete Works of Pliny the Elder*, trans. by John Bostock (Hastings: Delphi Classics, 2015), Kindle edition.

Potts Dewees, William, *A Treatise on the Diseases of Females* (Philadelphia: Lea and Blanchard, 1843).

Purkiss, Diane, *The Witch in History* (Hoboken: Routledge, 2012).

Rabelais, François, trans. by Thomas Urquhart, Peter Anthony Motteux and Charles Whibley, *Gargantua and Pantagruel* (New York: AMS Press, 1967)

Rawson, Hugh, *A Dictionary Of Invective* (London: Hale, 1991).

Reaney, P. H., *The Origin of English Surnames* (London: Routledge & Kegan Paul, 1984).

Recettario Novo Probatissimo A Molte Infirmita, E Etiandio Di Molte Gentilezze Utile A Chi Le Vora Provare (Venice: Zuan Maria Lirico, 1532).

Rees, Emma L. E., *The Vagina: A Literary and Cultural History* (London: Bloomsbury, 2013).

Reich, Wilhelm, *The Function of the Orgasm: Sex-Economic Problems of Biological Energy*, trans. by Vincent Carfagno (New York: Farrar, Straus and Giroux, 1973).

—, *The Bioelectrical Investigation of Sexuality and Anxiety* (New York: Farrar, Straus and Giroux, 1982).

Reinarz, Jonathan, *Past Scents: Historical Perspectives on Smell* (Chicago: University of Illinois Press, 2014).

Ricci, James V., *The Development of Gynecological Surgery and Instruments* (Philadelphia: Blakiston, 1949).

Riddle, John M., *Eve's Herbs: A History of Contraception and Abortion in the West* (Cambridge: Harvard University Press, 1999).

—, *Contraception and Abortion from the Ancient World to the Renaissance* (New York: ACLS History, 2005).

Rider, Catherine, *Magic and Impotence in the Middle Ages* (Oxford: Oxford University Press, 2008).

Ritchie, Andrew, *Early Bicycles and the Quest For Speed* (Jefferson: McFarland, 2018).

Rochester, John Wilmot, *Sodom*, (Paris: H. Welter, 1904).

—, *The Poetical Works Of The Earls Of Rochester, Roscomon And Dorset ; The Dukes Of Devonshire, Buckinghamshire, &C. With Memoirs of Their Lives. In Two Volumes. Adorn'd with a New Set of Cuts* (London: Goodourl, 1735).

Rodriguez, Sarah B., *Female Circumcision and Clitoridectomy in the United States* (New York: University of Rochester Press, 2014).

Romm, Sharon, *The Unwelcome Intruder: Freud's Struggle With Cancer* (New York: Praeger, 1983).

Rosenberg, Michael, *Signs Of Virginity: Testing Virgins and Making Men in Late Antiquity* (Oxford: Oxford University Press, 2018).

Rousseau, Jean-Jacques, *Confessions of Jean-Jacques Rousseau* (London: Penguin, 1953).

Rubenhold, Hallie, *Harris's List of Covent Garden Ladies* (London: Doubleday, 2012).

—, *The Covent Garden Ladies* (London: History Press, 2006).

Russell, John, Wynkyn de Worde, and Frederick James Furnivall, *The Boke of Nurture* (Bungay: J. Childs, 1867).

Russell, Sharman Apt, *Hunger: an Unnatural History* (New York: Basic Books, 2008).

Ryan, Michael, *Prostitution in London, With a Comparative View of That of Paris and New York* (London: H. Bailliere, 1839).

Sachdew, Rachana, 'Sycorax in Algiers: Cultural Politics and Gynaecology in Early Modern England', in *A Feminist Companion to Shakespeare* (Chichester: John Wiley and Sons, 2016), pp. 226-44.

Sade, *The Complete Marquis De Sade*, trans. by Paul J. Gillette (Los Angeles: Holloway House, 2006).

—, *The Marquis de Sade: The Complete Justine, Philosophy in the Bedroom, and Other Writings*, trans. by Richard Seaver (New York: Grove Press, 1990).

Sanger, William W., *The History of Prostitution* (New York: Harper & Brothers, 1858).

Saul, Jack, *The Sins of the Cities of the Plain, or The Recollections of a Mary Ann* (London: Privately printed, 1881).

Savonarola, Michael, *Practica Maior* (Venice, 1498).

Sayer, Derek, *Prague, Capital of the Twentieth Century: A Surrealist History* (Princeton: Princeton University, 2013).

Selwyn, William, *An Abridgment of the Law of Nisi Prius* (London: Clarke, 1817).

Schwaeblé, René, 'Homunculus', *Les détraquées de Paris* (Paris: Daragon libraire-éditeur, 1910).

Shakespeare, William, Thomas Bowdler, H. M. Bowdler and Richard Cruttwell, *The Family Shakespeare* (London: Hatchard, 1807).

Sharp, Jane, *The Midwives Book* (London: Simon Miller, 1671).

Sherrow, Victoria, *Encyclopedia of Hair* (Westport: Greenwood Press, 2006).

Shinners, John Raymond, *Medieval Popular Religion, 1000–1500* (Toronto: University of Toronto Press, 2009).

Silverton, Pete, *Filthy English: The How, Why, When and What of Everyday Swearing* (London: Portobello Books, 2009).

Simpson, Clare, 'A Social History of Women and Cycling in Late Nineteenth Century New Zealand' (unpublished PhD, Lincoln University, 1998).

Slackville, Charles, 'A Faithful Catalogue of our Most Eminent Ninnies', in *Poems on Affairs of State: Augustan Satirical Verse, 1660–1714* (New Haven: Yale University Press, 1963).

Smith, Alexander, and Arthur Lawrence Hayward, *A Complete History of the Lives and Robberies of the Most Notorious Highwaymen, Footpads, Shoplifts & Cheats of Both Sexes* (London: Routledge, 1926).

Smith, Drew, *Oyster: A Gastronomic History* (New York: Abrams, 2015).

Smith, Lesley, 'The History of Contraception', in *Contraception: A Casebook from Menarche to Menopause* (Cambridge: Cambridge University Press, 2013).

Smith, William, *A New Voyage to Guinea*, 2nd edn (London: John Nourse, 1745).

Soranos d'Éphèse, *Sorani Gynaeciorum Libri IV. De Signis Fracturarum. De Fasciis. Vita Hippocratis Secundum Soranum*, ed. by Ioannes Ilberg (Lipsiae: Teubneri, 1927).

Soranus, and Owsei Temkin, *Soranus' Gynecology* (Baltimore: Johns Hopkins University Press, 1994).

Spenser, Megg, *A Strange and True Conference Between two Bawds, Damarose Page and Priss Fotheringham, During their Imprisonment in Newgate* (London, 1660).

Spink, M. S., and L. G. Lewis, *Albucasis on Surgery and Instruments. A Definitive Edition of the Arabic Text with English Translation and Commentary* (Berkeley: University of California Press, 1976).

Steinach, Eugen, and Josef Löbel, *Sex and Life: Forty Years of Biological and Medical Experiments* (New York: Viking, 1940).

Steintrager, James A., *The Autonomy of Pleasure: Libertines, License, and Sexual Revolution* (New York: University of Columbia, 2015).

Strabo of Amaseia, *Delphi Complete Works of Strabo*, trans. by H. C. Hamilton (Hastings: Delphi Classics, 2016), Kindle edition.

'Sub-Umbra, or Sport Among the She-Noodles', in *The Wordsworth Book of Classic Erotica* (Ware: Wordsworth Editions, 2007).

Sun, Simiao, and Sabine Wilms, *Bèi Jí Qiān Jīn Yào Fāng* (Portland: The Chinese Medicine Database, 2008).

Swift, Jonathan, *A Complete Collection Of Genteel And Ingenious Conversation* (London: B. Motte, 1738).

Sykes, Audrey, *Moon Amsterdam* (Manchester: Moon Travel, 2018).

Tait, Lawson, *Diseases of Women and Abdominal Surgery* (Philadelphia: Lea Brothers, 1889).

Taylor, Gordon Rattray, *Sex in History* (New York: Vanguard Press, 1954).

Technavio Research, *Global Vaginal Odor Control Product Market 2018–2022* (London: Regional Business News, 2018).

The New Art and Mystery of Gossiping: Being a Genuine Account of all The Women's Club's in and About the City and Suburbs of London, with the Manner of their Club Orders (Cirencester: Samuel Rudder, 1770).

The School of Venus, Or the Ladies Delight (London, 1680).

The Women's Petition Against Coffee Representing to Publick Consideration the Grand Inconveniencies Accruing to Their Sex from the Excessive use of that Drying, Enfeebling Liquor (London, 1674).

The Wonderful Discoverie of the Witchcrafts of Magaret and Phillip Flower, Daughters of Joan Flower Neere Beur Castle: Executed at Lincolne, March II. 1618 (London, G. Eld, 1619).

The Wordsworth Book of Classic Erotica (Ware: Wordsworth Editions, 2007).

Thomas, Rachael Jayne, '"With Intent to Injure and Diffame": Sexual Slander, Gender and the Church Courts of London and York, 1680–1700' (unpublished MA, University of York, 2015).

Thompson, Lana, *The Wandering Womb* (Amherst: Prometheus Books, 1999).

Thompson, Roger, *Unfit for Modest Ears: A Study of Pornographic, Obscene, and Bawdy Works Written or Published in England in the Second Half of the Seventeenth Century* (Totowa: Rowman and Littlefield, 1979).

Tilt, Edward John, *A Handbook of Uterine Therapeutics and of Diseases of Women* (London: J. & A. Churchill, 1878).

Tissot, S. A. D, *Onanism; Or, A Treatise Upon the Disorders Produced by Masturbation; Or, the Dangerous Effects of Secret and Excessive Venery,* 5th edn, trans. by A. Hulme (London: Richardson, 1781).

Tone, Andrea, *Controlling Reproduction: An American History* (Wilmington: SR Books, 1997).

Traub, Valerie, *The Renaissance of Lesbianism in Early Modern England* (Cambridge: Cambridge University Press, 2002).

Turner, Daniel, *Syphillis. A Practical Dissertation on the Venereal Disease* (London: J. Walthoe, R. Wilkin, J. and J. Bonwicke, and T. Ward, 1727).

Valerius Maximus, and D. Wardle, *Valerius Maximus: Memorable Deeds and Sayings* (Oxford: Clarendon, 1997).

Valverde, Sarah, 'The Modern Sex Doll-Owner: A Descriptive Analysis', (unpublished MA, California State Polytechnic University, 2012).

Varone, Antonio, *Erotica Pompeiana: Love Inscriptions on the Walls of Pompeii*, trans. by R. Berg (Rome: L'Erma Di Bretschneider, 2002).

Vātsyāyana, Mallanaga, *Kamasutra*, trans. and ed. by Wendy Doniger, and Sudhir Kakar (Oxford: Oxford University Press, 2009).

Venette, Nicolas, *The Mysteries of Conjugal Love Reveal'd*, 3rd edn (London, 1712).

Viz, *Roger's Profanisaurus* (London: John Brown, 1998).

Voronoff, Serge, *Quarante-Trois Greffes Du Singe À L'homme* (Paris: G. Doin, 1924).

—, *Rejuvenation by Grafting* (London: G. Allen & Unwin Ltd, 1925).

Waite, Henry Randall, *Carmina Collegensia: A Complete Collection of the Songs of the American Colleges, with Selections from the Student Songs of the English and German Universities* (Boston: Ditson, 1876).

Wajnryb, Ruth, *Expletive Deleted* (London: Free Press, 2014).

Walker, James H., *Studies in Ancient Egyptian Anatomical Terminology* (Wiltshire: Aris and Phillips, 1997).

Walsh, John Henry, *A Manual of Domestic Medicine and Surgery* (London: Routledge, 1858).

Webster, John, and David Charles Gunby, *Three Plays* (London: Penguin Books, 1995).

Weiss, John, *A Catalogue of Surgical Instruments, Apparatus, Appliances, Etc.* (London: Obstetric Society, 1863).

Whipple, Beverly, and Carol Rinkleib Ellison, *Women's Sexualities: Generations of Women Share Intimate Sexual Secrets of Sexual Self-Acceptance* (Oakland, CA: New Harbinger Publications, 2000).

Whitaker, John, *Molly Malone* (London: Phipps, 1805).

Whitelock, Dorothy, *English Historical Documents* (London: Eyre & Spottiswoode, 1955).

Whyte Barclay, Andrew, *A Manual of Medical Diagnosis: Being an Analysis of the Signs and Symptoms* (Philadelphia: Blanchard, 1864).

Wile, Douglas, *Art of the Bedchamber: The Chinese Sexual Yoga Classics* (Albany: University of New York Press, 1992).

Williams, Gordon, *A Dictionary of Sexual Language and Imagery in Shakespearean and Stuart Literature* (London: Athlone Press, 1994).

Williams, Gordon, *Shakespeare's Sexual Language* (London: Continuum, 2006).

Wilmot, John, 'A Panegyric Upon Cundum', in *The Works of The Earls of Rochester, Roscomon and Dorset, The Dukes of Devonshire, Buckingham and Co.* (London, 1667).

—, *The Complete Poems of John Wilmot*, ed. by David Vieth (Yale: Yale University Press, 2002).

Wilson, Brian C., *Dr. John Harvey Kellogg and the Religion of Biologic Living* (Indianapolis: Indiana University Press, 2014).

Winch, Dinah, 'Sexual Slander and its Social Context in England *c*.1660–1700, with Special Reference to Cheshire and Sussex' (unpublished PhD, The Queen's College, Oxford University, 1999).

Wolf, Naomi, *Vagina: A New Biography* (London: Virago, 2012).

Wood, George B., *A Treatise on the Practice of Medicine* (Philadelphia: Lippincott, Grambo, 1852).

Worde, Wynkyn de, *Ortus Vocabulorum 1500. A Scolar Press Facsimile*, 1st edn (Menston: Scolar Press, 1968).

Wosk, Julie, *Women and the Machine* (Baltimore: Johns Hopkins University Press, 2003).

Wright, Thomas, and Richard Paul Wülker, *Anglo-Saxon and Old English Vocabularies* (London: Trubner & Co., 1883).

Younger, John G, *Sex in the Ancient World from A to Z* (London: Routledge, 2005).

Ziegenspeck, Robert, *Massage Treatment (Thure Brandt) In Diseases of Women: For Practitioners* (Chicago: Westerschulte, 1898).

Online Sources and Texts

'1 In 10 Girls Have Been Unable to Afford Sanitary Wear', *Plan International UK*, 2017 <https://plan-uk.org/media-centre/1-in-10-girls-have-been-unable-to-afford-sanitary-wear-survey-finds> [Accessed 15 September 2018].

'2018 Year in Review – Pornhub Insights', *Pornhub.com*, 2018 <https://www.pornhub.com/insights/2018-year-in-review> [Accessed 29 January 2019].

'ALWAYS Donates Feminine Hygiene Products To Help UK Girls Stay In School. #Endperiodpoverty', *Always.co.uk*, 2018 <https://www.always.co.uk/en-gb/about-us/endperiodpoverty> [Accessed 15 September 2018].

Amos, Jonathan, 'Ancient Phallus Unearthed in Cave', *News.bbc.co.uk*, 2005 <http://news.bbc.co.uk/1/hi/sci/tech/4713323.stm> [Accessed 24 June 2018].

Anonymous, 'The Romance of Lust: a Classic Victorian Erotic Novel', *Archive. org*, 2017 <https://archive.org/stream/theromanceoflust30254gut/30254-8. txt> [Accessed 12 March 2017].

Aquinas, Thomas, 'Summa Theologica', *Sacred-texts.com*, 2018 <http://www. sacred-texts.com/chr/aquinas/summa/index.htm> [Accessed 15 September 2018].

Aretaeus, 'De Causis et Signis Acutorum Morborum (Lib. 1), Book II. Chapter XI. On Hysterical Suffocation', *perseus.tufts.edu*, 2018 <http://www.perseus. tufts.edu/hopper/text?doc=Perseus%3Atext%3A1999.01.0254%3Atext% 3DSA%3Abook%3D2%3Achapter%3D11> [Accessed 22 July 2018].

Aristophanes, 'Lysistrata', *perseus.tufts.edu*, 2018 <http://www.perseus.tufts.edu/hopper/text?doc=Perseus%3Atext%3A1999.01.0242%3Acard%3D130> [Accessed 8 August 2018].

'Baartman, Sara', *Oxford Dictionary of National Biography*, <http://www.oxforddnb.com/view/10.1093/ref:odnb/9780198614128.001.0001/odnb-9780198614128-e-73573;jsessionid=1ABB9A1E6F71D8D1704734C50D86E17D> [Accessed 7 August 2018].

Barford, Vanessa, 'The Prevailing Myth of Sex before Sport', 2004 <http://news.bbc.co.uk/1/hi/magazine/3555734.stm> [Accessed 27 August 2018].

Bowman, Verity, 'Woman in Nepal Dies after being Exiled to Outdoor Hut during her Period', *Guardian*, 2018 <https://www.theguardian.com/global-development/2018/jan/12/woman-nepal-dies-exiled-outdoor-hut-period-menstruation> [Accessed 13 September 2018].

Briggs, Keith, 'OE and ME Cunte in Place-Names', 2012 <http://keithbriggs.info/documents/cunte_04.pdf> [Accessed 5 April 2017].

'Campaign to Protect Young People from STIs by using Condoms', *GOV.UK*, 2017 <https://www.gov.uk/government/news/campaign-to-protect-young-people-from-stis-by-using-condoms> [Accessed 14 August 2018].

Cannon, J.A., 'Gerald of Wales', *Encyclopedia.Com*, 2002 <http://www.encyclopedia.com/people/history/historians-british-biographies/gerald-wales> [Accessed 13 February 2017].

'Charles II, 1662: An Act for Preventing the Frequent Abuses in Printing Seditious Treasonable and Unlicensed Bookes and Pamphlets and for Regulating of Printing and Printing Presses', *British-History.ac.uk*, 2017 <http://www.british-history.ac.uk/statutes-realm/vol5/pp428-435> [Accessed 10 April 2017].

'Charles II: Statutes', *Constitution.org*, 2017 <http://www.constitution.org/sech/sech_114.txt> [Accessed 10 April 2017].

Chattora, Samantha, 'The Devadasi System – Genesis & Growth', *iml.jou.ufledu*, 2002 <http://iml.jou.ufl.edu/projects/Spring02/Chattaraj/genesis.html> [Accessed 7 August 2018].

'Douching', *Womenshealth.gov*, 2018 <https://www.womenshealth.gov/a-z-topics/douching> [Accessed 10 September 2018].

'Female Genital Mutilation', *World Health Organization*, 2018 <http://www.who.int/news-room/fact-sheets/detail/female-genital-mutilation> [Accessed 17 June 2018].

'FGM National Clinical Group – Historical & Cultural', *Fgmnationalgroup.Org*, 2015 <http://www.fgmnationalgroup.org/historical_and_cultural.htm> [Accessed 10 August 2017].

'Foundling Museum', 2016 <http://foundlingmuseum.org.uk/about/the-museum/> [Accessed 2 September 2016].

Galen, 'On Hippocrates: On the Nature of Man Part One', *ucl.ac.uk*, 2018 <https://www.ucl.ac.uk/~ucgajpd/medicina%20antiqua/Medant/ GNatHom1.htm> [Accessed 14 September 2018].

Gambone, Phillip, 'Shanghai's Museum of Sex', 2003 <https://www. thefreelibrary.com/Shanghai's+Museum+of+Sex.+(Essay).-a0100727471> [Accessed 14 February 2017].

Garnick, Marc B., 'Does Frequent Ejaculation help Ward off Prostate Cancer?', 2009 <http://www.harvardprostateknowledge.org/does-frequent-ejaculation- help-ward-off-prostate-cancer> [Accessed 13 February 2017].

Ginsberg, Allen, 'Howl', *Poetry Foundation*, 2018 <https://www. poetryfoundation.org/poems/49303/howl> [Accessed 7 September 2018].

Hains, Tim, 'Bernie Sanders Quickly Condemns Rally Speaker Who Called Hillary Clinton a "Corporate Democratic Whore"', *Realclearpolitics.com*, 2016 <https://www.realclearpolitics.com/video/2016/04/14/speaker_at_sanders_ rally_calls_hillary_clinton_a_corporate_democratic_whore.html> [Accessed 9 August 2018].

Hall, Lesley, 'Victorian Sex Factoids', *lesleyahall.net*, 2017 <http://www. lesleyahall.net/factoids.htm#hysteria> [Accessed 12 March 2017].

Hinde, Natasha, 'Blogger Bakes Sourdough Using Yeast from Vagina, Internet Explodes', *Huffpost UK*, 2015 <https://www.huffingtonpost.co.uk/2015/11/ 24/woman-makes-sourdough-using-yeast-from-vagina_n_8636372.html> [Accessed 19 August 2018].

Hodal, Kate, 'Nepal's Bleeding Shame: Menstruating Women Banished to Cattle Sheds', *Guardian*, 2018 <https://www.theguardian.com/global-development/ 2016/apr/01/nepal-bleeding-shame-menstruating-women-banished-cattle- sheds> [Accessed 13 September 2018].

Hodson, Jacquelyn, 'The Smell of the Middle Ages', *Triviumpublishing.com*, 2002 <http://www.triviumpublishing.com/articles/smellofthemiddleages. html> [Accessed 9 September 2017].

Hostetter, Aaron K., 'Exeter Book Riddles', *Anglosaxonpoetry.camden.rutgers.edu*, 2017 <https://anglosaxonpoetry.camden.rutgers.edu/exeter-book-riddles/> [Accessed 18 August 2018].

'Humours', *Science Museum*, 2019 <http://www.sciencemuseum.org.uk/ broughttolife/techniques/humours> [Accessed 14 February 2017].

Hunt, Matthew, 'Cunt: a Cultural History of the C-Word', *Matthewhunt.com*, 2000 <http://www.matthewhunt.com/cunt/> [Accessed 29 September 2017].

Jimenez, Ulises, 'How Much for your Love: Prostitution among the Aztecs', *academia.edu*, 2004 <http://www.academia.edu/2631485/How_much_for_ your_love_prostitution_among_the_Aztecs> [Accessed 7 August 2018].

Jo's Cervical Cancer Trust, 'Body Shame Responsible for Young Women not Attending Smear Tests', *Jo's Cervical Cancer Trust*, 2018 <https://www.jostrust.org.uk/node/1073042> [Accessed 17 February 2019].

Kale, Sirin, 'Why is Virginity Testing Still a Thing in so Many Parts of the World?', *Grazia*, 2016 <https://graziadaily.co.uk/life/real-life/virginity-testing-around-world/> [Accessed 11 September 2018].

Kelly, Kathleen Coyne, 'How to Cheat on a Virginity Test', *medievalists.net*, 2017 <http://www.medievalists.net/2016/06/how-to-cheat-on-a-virginity-test/> [Accessed 20 August 2017].

'Kings 23:7', *Bible Gateway*, 2018 <https://www.biblegateway.com/passage/?search=2+Kings+23%3A7&version=NIV> [Accessed 19 September 2018].

Kingston, Sarah, and Natalie Hammond, *Women Who Buy Sexual Services in the UK*, 2016 <http://eprints.lancs.ac.uk/130705/2/WWBS_End_Report_final_.pdf> [Accessed 12 February 2019].

'Kinsey Institute Faqs and Statistics', 2017 <https://www.kinseyinstitute.org/research/publications/faq.php> [Accessed 14 February 2017].

Lenz, Norbert, *Borghild.De* <http://www.borghild.de/indexe.htm> [Accessed 13 July 2018].

'Leviticus 20:18', *Bible Gateway*, 2018 <https://www.biblegateway.com/passage/?search=Leviticus+20%3A18&version=NIV> [Accessed 14 September 2018].

Lusher, Adam, 'Raw Oysters really are Aphrodisiacs say Scientists', *Telegraph.co.uk*, 2005 <http://www.telegraph.co.uk/news/uknews/4195596/Raw-oysters-really-are-aphrodisiacs-say-scientists-and-now-is-the-time-to-eat-them.html> [Accessed 19 August 2018].

Magnanti, Brooke, 'Boxer Carl Froch has been Abstaining from Sex – But is it Ever Worth it?', *Telegraph.co.uk*, 2014 <https://www.telegraph.co.uk/women/sex/10864506/Sex-ban-Carl-Froch-has-been-abstaining-from-sex-but-is-it-really-good-for-you.html> [Accessed 27 August 2018].

Maines, Rachel, The Study that Set the World Abuzz', *Big Think*, 2009 <http://bigthink.com/videos/the-study-that-set-the-world-abuzz> [Accessed 12 March 2017].

'Mapping Anti-Gay Laws in Africa', *Amnesty.org.uk*, 2018 <https://www.amnesty.org.uk/lgbti-lgbt-gay-human-rights-law-africa-uganda-kenya-nigeria-cameroon> [Accessed 5 December 2018].

Martial, 'Epigrams. Book 14', *tertullian.org*, 2018 <http://www.tertullian.org/fathers/martial_epigrams_book14.htm> [Accessed 18 August 2018].

Maximus, Valerius, 'Factorum et Dictorum Memorabilium, Liber VIII', *penelope.uchicago.edu*, 2018 <http://penelope.uchicago.edu/Thayer/L/Roman/Texts/Valerius_Maximus/8*.html> [Accessed 11 September 2018].

'Mercurius Fumigosus or the Smoking Nocturnal Archives', *Newspaperarchive. com*, 2017 <https://newspaperarchive.com/uk/middlesex/london/mercurius-fumigosus-or-the-smoking-nocturnall/> [Accessed 9 April 2017].

Mojapelo, Lebohang, 'Virginity Testing "Sacred" but not a Science', *Africa Check*, 2016 <https://africacheck.org/reports/virginity-testing-sacred-but-not-a-science/> [Accessed 21 August 2017].

Movlud, Gunel, 'Bloody Sheets: An Age-Old Tradition Still Held in Georgia's Regions', *Georgia Today on the Web*, 2016 <http://georgiatoday.ge/news/2879/Bloody-Sheets%3A-An-Age-old-Tradition-Still-Held-in-Georgia%E2%80%99s-Regions> [Accessed 20 August 2017].

'New Data Reveals 420,000 Cases of STIs Diagnosed In 2017', *gov.uk*, 2018 <https://www.gov.uk/government/news/new-data-reveals-420000-cases-of-stis-diagnosed-in-2017> [Accessed 14 August 2018].

Norton, Rictor, 'History of the Term "Prostitute"', *Rictornorton.co.uk*, 2006 <http://rictornorton.co.uk/though15.htm> [Accessed 10 August 2018].

Norton, Siobhan, '"This is not Consent": How a Thong Prompted Protests across Ireland over the Handling of Rape Trials', *Inews.co.uk*, 2018 <https://inews.co.uk/news/long-reads/this-is-not-consent-thong-rape-case-ireland-protests/> [Accessed 7 December 2018].

'Ofcom Explores Latest Attitudes to Offensive Language', *Ofcom*, 2016 <https://www.ofcom.org.uk/about-ofcom/latest/media/media-releases/2016/attitudes-to-offensive-language> [Accessed 7 September 2018].

Old Bailey Proceedings, 'Central Criminal Court', 2003 <https://www.oldbaileyonline.org/browse.jsp?id=t18340515-47&div=t18340515-47&terms=savine#highlight> [Accessed 30 August 2016].

Old Bailey Proceedings, 'May 1683, Trial of Isabel Barker', *Oldbaileyonline. org*, 2018 <https://www.oldbaileyonline.org/browse.jsp?id=t16830524-7-off26&div=t16830524-7#highlight> [Accessed 1 December 2018].

'Outcry over Teen's Underwear in Rape Trial', *BBC News*, 2018 <https://www.bbc.co.uk/news/world-europe-46207304> [Accessed 7 December 2018].

'Over a Century of Healing', *Lysol.com*, 2018 <http://www.lysol.com/about-us/our-history/> [Accessed 11 September 2018].

'Oxford English Dictionary', *Oed.com*, 2018 <http://www.oed.com/view/Entry/45874?redirectedFrom=cunt#eid> [Accessed 7 September 2018].

Pasha-Robinson, Lucy, 'Doctors are being Ordered to Perform "Virginity Tests" on Underage Girls in Russia', *The Independent*, 2017 <https://www.independent.co.uk/news/world/europe/russia-doctors-virginity-tests-russian-investigative-committee-underage-girls-a7783811.html> [Accessed 11 September 2018].

'Pick up a Penguin', *News.bbc.co.uk*, 1998 <http://news.bbc.co.uk/1/hi/world/asia-pacific/60302.stm> [Accessed 17 September 2018].

Pillitteri, Sally Piper, 'School Menstrual Hygiene Management in Malawi', *Assets.publishing.service.gov.uk*, 2012 <https://assets.publishing.service.gov.uk/media/57a08aa8e5274a27b20006d7/MenstrualHygieneManagement_Malawi.pdf> [Accessed 15 September 2018].

Pliny the Elder, 'Natural History', *Loeb Classical Library*, 2018 <https://www.loebclassics.com/view/pliny_elder-natural_history/1938/pb_LCL418.503.xml?readMode=recto> [Accessed 19 August 2018].

Pliny the Elder, 'The Natural History, Book XXXVI. The Natural History Of Stones', *perseus.tufts.edu*, 2018 <http://www.perseus.tufts.edu/hopper/text?doc=Perseus:abo:phi,0978,001:36:4> [Accessed 24 June 2018].

'Post Office Act 1953', *Legislation.gov.uk*, 2018 <http://www.legislation.gov.uk/ukpga/Eliz2/1-2/36/crossheading/general-offences/enacted> [Accessed 22 September 2018].

'Proverbs 9:17', *Biblehub.com*, 2018 <https://biblehub.com/commentaries/proverbs/9-17.htm> [Accessed 18 August 2018].

'Pubic Wigs – Oxford Reference', *Oxfordreference.com*, 2018 <http://www.oxfordreference.com/view/10.1093/acref/9780198524038.001.0001/acref-9780198524038-e-783> [Accessed 8 August 2018].

Quran, 'Surah Al-Baqarah 2:222-232', *quran.com*, 2018 <https://quran.com/2/222-232> [Accessed 14 September 2018].

Riddell, Fern, 'No, No, No! Victorians didn't Invent the Vibrator', *Guardian*, 2014 <https://www.theguardian.com/commentisfree/2014/nov/10/victorians-invent-vibrator-orgasms-women-doctors-fantasy> [Accessed 12 March 2017].

Rojo, Jaime, and Steven Harrington, '"F**K Art" Opens Wide at Museum of Sex (NSFW)', *Huffpost*, 2012 <https://www.huffingtonpost.com/jaime-rojo-steven-harrington/new-opening-at-museum-of-sex_b_1261589.html> [Accessed 11 August 2018].

'Science Proves Oysters and Mussels are the Food of Love', *Scotsman.com*, 2005 <https://www.scotsman.com/future-scotland/tech/science-proves-oysters-and-mussels-are-the-food-of-love-1-740457> [Accessed 20 August 2018].

Shakespeare, William, *Hamlet*, *shakespeare.mit.edu*, 2018 <http://shakespeare.mit.edu/hamlet/full.html> [Accessed 7 September 2018].

Shakespeare, William, *Much Ado About Nothing*, *shakespeare.mit.edu*, 2018 <http://shakespeare.mit.edu/much_ado/full.html> [Accessed 8 August 2018].

Shakespeare, William, 'Shakespeare Sonnet 130', *shakespeare-online.com*, 2018 <http://www.shakespeare-online.com/sonnets/130.html> [Accessed 8 August 2018].

Shakespeare, William, *Twelfth Night*, *shakespeare.mit.edu*, 2018 <http://shakespeare.mit.edu/twelfth_night/full.html> [Accessed 7 September 2018].

Shakespeare, William, *Venus and Adonis*, *shakespeare.mit.edu*, 2018 <http://shakespeare.mit.edu/Poetry/VenusAndAdonis.html> [Accessed 8 August 2018].

Siebert, Eve, 'Chaucer's Cunt', *Skeptical Humanities*, 2011 <https://skepticalhumanities.com/2011/01/18/chaucers-cunt/> [Accessed 8 April 2017].

Sifferlin, Alexandra, 'Can Sex Really Dampen Athletic Performance?' *Time*, 2014 <http://time.com/2911744/can-sex-re/> [Accessed 27 August 2018].

Smith, David Livingstone, 'Dehumanization, Genocide, and the Psychology of Indifference', *Psychology Today*, 2011 <https://www.psychologytoday.com/blog/philosophy-dispatches/201112/dehumanization-genocide-and-the-psychology-indifference-0> [Accessed 1 April 2017].

Smith, Lizzie, 'Dehumanising Sex Workers: what's "Prostitute" got to do with it?', *The Conversation*, 2013 <http://theconversation.com/dehumanising-sex-workers-whats-prostitute-got-to-do-with-it-16444> [Accessed 23 June 2017].

Sprenger, James, and Kramer, Heinrich, *The Malleus Maleficarum*, 2002 <http://www.malleusmaleficarum.org/downloads/MalleusAcrobat.pdf> [Accessed 13 February 2017].

'The Medieval Canon Law Virtual Library', *web.colby.edu*, 2018 <http://web.colby.edu/canonlaw/category/canon-law/> [Accessed 26 August 2018].

Tozzi, John, and Jared Hopkins, 'The Little Blue Pill: an Oral History of Viagra', *Bloomberg.com*, 2017 <https://www.bloomberg.com/news/features/2017-12-11/the-little-blue-pill-an-oral-history-of-viagra> [Accessed 25 August 2018].

Trogus, Pompeius, 'Justin, Epitome of Pompeius Trogus', *tertullian.org*, 2018 <http://www.tertullian.org/fathers/justinus_04_books11to20.htm> [Accessed 18 September 2018].

Trout, Christopher, 'There's a New Sex Robot in Town: Say Hello to Solana', *Engadget*, 2018 <https://www.engadget.com/2018/01/10/there-s-a-new-sex-robot-in-town-say-hello-to-solana/> [Accessed 18 July 2018].

Journals

Althof, Stanley E. et al, 'Self-Esteem, Confidence, And Relationships in Men Treated with Sildenafil Citrate for Erectile Dysfunction', *Journal of General Internal Medicine*, 21 (2006), 1069–74 https://doi.org/10.1111/j.1525-1497.2006.00554.x.

Amy, Jean-Jacques, and Michel Thiery, 'The Condom: A Turbulent History', *The European Journal of Contraception & Reproductive Health Care*, 20 (2015), 387–402 https://doi.org/10.3109/13625187.2015.1050716.

Aryendra Sharma, E.B., and E. V. Vira Raghavacharya, 'Gems From Sanskrit Literature. (Sūktimālā)', *Journal of the American Oriental Society*, 81 (1961), 461 (one page) https://doi.org/10.2307/595726.

Beard, Mary, and John Henderson, 'With This Body I Thee Worship: Sacred Prostitution in Antiquity', *Gender and History*, 9 (1997), 480–503.

Beaulieu, Kiara, 'Stephanie Budin, The Myth of Sacred Prostitution in Antiquity', *Past Imperfect*, 15 (2009), 476–84 https://doi.org/10.21971/p79p4h.

Berliner, Brett A., 'Mephistopheles and Monkeys: Rejuvenation, Race, And Sexuality in Popular Culture in Interwar France', *Journal of the History of Sexuality*, 13 (2004), 306–25 https://doi.org/10.1353/sex.2005.0003.

Bhartiya, Aru, 'Menstruation, Religion and Society', *International Journal of Social Science and Humanity*, 2013, 523–7 https://doi.org/10.7763/ijssh.2013.v3.296.

Block, A.J., 'Sexual Perversion in Female', *New Orleans Medical Surgery Journal*, 22 (1894), 1–7.

Blundell, Dr, 'Incapability of Retaining the Urine', *The Lancet*, 1 (1829), 673–7.

Booth, Samuel Hallsor, 'A Comparison of the Early Responses to AIDS in the UK and the US', *Res Medica*, 24 (2017), 57–64 https://doi.org/10.2218/resmedica.v24i1.1558.

Breckinridge, Mary, 'The Nurse-Midwife—a Pioneer', *American Journal of Public Health*, 17 (1927), 1147–51 https://doi.org/10.2105/ajph.17.11.1147.

Brewer, Catherine, 'The Status of the Jews in Roman Legislation: The Reign of Justinian 527–565 CE', *European Judaism*, 38 (2005), 75–112 https://doi.org/10.3167/001430005781203826.

Brody, Stuart, and Rui Miguel Costa, 'Satisfaction (Sexual, Life, Relationship, and Mental Health) is Associated Directly with Penile-Vaginal Intercourse, but Inversely with Other Sexual Behavior Frequencies', *The Journal of Sexual Medicine*, 6 (2009), 1947–54 https://doi.org/10.1111/j.1743-6109.2009.01303.x.

Brody, Stuart, 'Vaginal Orgasm is Associated with Better Psychological Function', *Sexual and Relationship Therapy*, 22 (2007), 173–91 https://doi.org/10.1080/14681990601059669.

Brown-Séquard, Charles Éduoard, 'Note on the Effects Produced on Man by Subcutaneous Injections of a Liquid Obtained from the Testicles of Animals', *The Lancet*, 134 (1889), 105–7 https://doi.org/10.1016/s0140-6736(00)64118-1.

Browne, Alison Leigh, et al., 'Patterns of Practice: A Reflection on the Development of Quantitative/Mixed Methodologies Capturing Everyday Life Related to Water Consumption in the UK', *International Journal of Social Research Methodology*, 17 (2013), 27–43 https://doi.org/10.1080/13645579.2014.854012.

Buisson, Odile, et al., 'Coitus as Revealed by Ultrasound in One Volunteer Couple', *The Journal of Sexual Medicine*, 7 (2010), 2750–4 https://doi.org/10.1111/j.1743-6109.2010.01892.x.

Buttenheim, Alison M., 'The Sanitation Environment in Urban Slums: Implications for Child Health', *Population and Environment*, 30 (2008), 26–47 https://doi.org/10.1007/s11111-008-0074-9.

Capitan, Louis, and Henri Breuil, 'Figures Préhistoriques De La Grotte Des Combarelles (Dordogne)', *Comptes-Rendus Des Séances De L Année: Académie Des Inscriptions Et Belles-Lettres*, 46 (1902), 51–6 https://doi.org/10.3406/crai.1902.17072.

Cassidy, Veronica, 'For the Love of Dolls: A Patriarchal Nightmare of Cyborg Couplings', *ESC: English Studies in Canada*, 42 (2016), 203–15 https://doi.org/10.1353/esc.2016.0001.

Cerda-Molina, et al., 'Endocrine Changes in Male Stumptailed Macaques (Macaca Arctoides) as a Response to Odor Stimulation with Vaginal Secretions', *Hormones And Behavior*, 49 (2006), 81–7 https://doi.org/10.1016/j.yhbeh.2005.04.014.

Charpy, Adrien, 'Des Organes Genitaux Externes Chez Les Prostituees', *Annales Des Dermatologie*, 3 (1870), 271–9.

Chen, M. Keith, Venkat Lakshminarayanan, and Laurie R. Santos, 'How Basic Are Behavioral Biases? Evidence from Capuchin Monkey Trading Behavior', *Journal of Political Economy*, 114 (2006), 517–37 https://doi.org/10.1086/503550.

Cicurel, Inbal, and Rachel Sharaby, 'Women in the Menstruation Huts: Variations in Preserving Purification Customs among Ethiopian Immigrants', *Journal of Feminist Studies in Religion*, 23 (2007), 69–84 https://doi.org/10.2979/fsr.2007.23.2.69.

Conard, Nicholas J., 'A Female Figurine from the Basal Aurignacian of Hohle Fels Cave in Southwestern Germany', *Nature*, 459 (2009), 248–52 https://doi.org/10.1038/nature07995.

Connelly, Dawn, 'Three Decades of Viagra', *The Pharmaceutical Journal*, 2017 https://doi.org/10.1211/pj.2017.20202847.

Cox-George, Chantal, and Susan Bewley, 'I, Sex Robot: The Health Implications of the Sex Robot Industry', *BMJ Sexual & Reproductive Health*, 44 (2018), 161–4. https://doi.org/10.1136/bmjsrh-2017-200012.

'Current Comment, "Glandular Therapy"', *Journal of the American Medical Association*, 83 (1924).

D'Aniello, Antimo, et al., 'Occurrence and Neuroendocrine Role Of d-Aspartic Acid And n-Methyl-D-Aspartic Acid Inciona Intestinalis', *FEBS Letters*, 552 (2003), 193–8 https://doi.org/10.1016/s0014-5793(03)00921-9.

Dickinson, Robert, 'Bicycling For Women', *The American Journal of Obstetrics and Diseases of Women and Children*, 31 (1895), 24–35.

Döring, N., and S. Pöschl, 'Sex Toys, Sex Dolls, Sex Robots: Our Under-Researched Bed-Fellows', *Sexologies*, 27, (2018), 133–8 https://doi.org/10.1016/j.sexol.2018.05.009.

Douglas, Thomas, et al., 'Coercion, Incarceration, and Chemical Castration: an Argument from Autonomy', *Journal of Bioethical Inquiry*, 10 (2013), 393–405 https://doi.org/10.1007/s11673-013-9465-4.

El-Damanhoury, I., 'The Jewish and Christian View on Female Genital Mutilation', *African Journal of Urology*, 19 (2013), 127–9 https://doi.org/10.1016/j.afju.2013.01.004.

Emans, S. J., E. R. Woods, E. N. Allred, and E. Grace, 'Hymenal Findings in Adolescent Women: Impact of Tampon Use and Consensual Sexual Activity', *Journal of Clinical Forensic Medicine*, 2 (1995), 167 https://doi.org/10.1016/1353-1131(95)90087-x.

Erskine, Mary S., Joseph G. Oberlander, and Jasmine J. Yang, 'Expression Of FOS, EGR-1, And ARC in the Amygdala and Hippocampus of Female Rats During Formation of the Intromission Mnemonic of Pseudopregnancy', *Developmental Neurobiology*, 67 (2007), 895–908 https://doi.org/10.1002/dneu.20376.

Evans, Randolph W., and R. Couch, 'Orgasm and Migraine', *Headache: The Journal of Head and Face Pain*, 41 (2001), 512–14 https://doi.org/10.1046/j.1526-4610.2001.01091.x.

Fahs, Breanne, and Elena Frank, 'Notes from the Back Room: Gender, Power, and (In)Visibility in Women's Experiences of Masturbation', *The Journal Of Sex Research*, 51 (2014), 241–52 https://doi.org/10.1080/00224499.2012.745474.

'Female Cyclists', *The Dominion Medical Monthly*, 7 (1896), 235-7.

Foldes, Pierre, and Odile Boussain, 'The Clitoral Complex: A Dynamic Sonographic Study', *Journal Of Sexual Medicine*, 2009, 1223–31.

Francis, A. G. 'On a Romano-British Castration Clamp used in the Rites of Cybele', *Proceedings of the Royal Society of Medicine*, 19, 1926, 95–110.

Frank, Lily, and Sven Nyholm, 'Robot Sex and Consent: Is Consent to Sex Between a Robot and a Human Conceivable, Possible, and Desirable?', *Artificial Intelligence And Law*, 25 (2017), 305–23 https://doi.org/10.1007/s10506-017-9212-y.

Frese, Achim, et al., 'The Impact of Sexual Activity on Idiopathic Headaches: An Observational Study', *Cephalalgia*, 33 (2013), 384–9 https://doi.org/10.1177/0333102413476374.

Frith, John, 'Syphilis: Its Early History and Treatment until Penicillin and the Debate on Its Origins', *Journal of Military and Veterans' Health*, 20 (2012) <https://jmvh.org/article/syphilis-its-early-history-and-treatment-until-penicillin-and-the-debate-on-its-origins/> [Accessed 15 August 2018].

Gaither, Thomas W., et al., 'Cycling and Female Sexual and Urinary Function: Results from a Large, Multinational, Cross-Sectional Study', *The Journal of Sexual Medicine*, 15 (2018), 510–18 https://doi.org/10.1016/j.jsxm.2018.02.004.

Gamson, Joshua, 'Rubber Wars: Struggles Over Condoms in the United States', *Journal of the History of Sexuality*, 1 (1990), 262–82.

Gesselman, Amanda N., Gregory D. Webster, and Justin R. Garcia, 'Has Virginity Lost its Virtue? Relationship Stigma Associated with Being a Sexually Inexperienced Adult', *The Journal of Sex Research*, 54 (2016), 202–13 https://doi.org/10.1080/00224499.2016.1144042.

Giles, G.G., et al., 'Sexual Factors and Prostate Cancer', *BJU International*, 92 (2003), 211–16 https://doi.org/10.1046/j.1464-410x.2003.04319.x.

Gottner-Abendroth, H., 'The Structure of Matriarchal Societies', *Revision*, 21 (1999).

Graham, John R., Campbell R. Harvey, and Manju Puri, 'A Corporate Beauty Contest', *Management Science*, 2016 https://doi.org/10.1287/mnsc.2016.2484.

Grout, Vic, 'Robot Sex: Ethics and Morality', *Lovotics*, 03 (2015) https://doi.org/10.4172/2090-9888.1000e104.

Gwilliam, Tassie, 'Female Fraud: Counterfeit Maidenheads in the Eighteenth Century', *Journal of the History of Sexuality*, 6 (1996), 518–48.

Hanssen, Kristin, 'Ingesting Menstrual Blood: Notions of Health and Bodily Fluids in Bengal', *Ethnology*, 41 (2002), 365 https://doi.org/10.2307/4153014.

Hess, Jochen, Roberto Rossi Neto, Leo Panic, Herbert Rübben, and Wolfgang Senf, 'Satisfaction with Male-To-Female Gender Reassignment Surgery', *Deutsches Aerzteblatt Online*, 111 (2014) https://doi.org/10.3238/arztebl.2014.0795.

Hobday, A.J., L. Haury, and P.K. Dayton, 'Function of the Human Hymen', *Medical Hypotheses*, 49 (1997), 171–3 https://doi.org/10.1016/s0306-9877(97)90223-1.

Hoffman, Stephanie B., 'Behind Closed Doors: Impotence Trials and the Trans-Historical Right to Martial Policy', *Boston University Law Review*, 89 (2009), 1725–52.

Holzer, Sarah R., et al., 'Mediational Significance of PTSD in the Relationship of Sexual Trauma and Eating Disorders', *Child Abuse & Neglect*, 32 (2008), 561–6 https://doi.org/10.1016/j.chiabu.2007.07.011.

Horváth, Aleksandra Djajić, 'Of Female Chastity and Male Arms: The Balkan "Man-Woman" In the Age of the World Picture', *Journal of the History of Sexuality*, 20 (2011), 358–81 https://doi.org/10.1353/sex.2011.0034.

Hoskins, Janet, 'The Menstrual Hut and the Witch's Lair in Two Eastern Indonesian Societies', *Ethnology*, 41 (2002), 317 https://doi.org/10.2307/4153011.

Howard, William Lee, 'The Negro as A Distinct Ethnic Factor in Civilization', *Medicine*, 60 (1904), 423–6.

Hunt, C. D., P. E. Johnson, J. Herbel, and L. K. Mullen, 'Effects of Dietary Zinc Depletion on Seminal Volume and Zinc Loss, Serum Testosterone Concentrations, and Sperm Morphology in Young Men', *The American Journal Of Clinical Nutrition*, 56 (1992), 148–57 https://doi.org/10.1093/ajcn/56.1.148.

Imbimbo, Ciro, et al., 'Intersex and Gender Identity Disorders: A Report from a Single Institute's 14-Year Experience in Treatment of Male-To-Female Transsexuals', *The Journal of Sexual Medicine*, 6 (2009), 2736–45 https://doi.org/10.1111/j.1743-6109.2009.01379.x.

'Immorality in Canada', *The Canadian Practioner*, 21, (1896), 848–9.

Independent Forensic Expert Group, 'Statement on Virginity Testing', *Journal of Forensic and Legal Medicine*, 33 (2015), 121–4 https://doi.org/10.1016/j.jflm.2015.02.012.

Jannini, Emmanuele A., Odile Buisson, and Alberto Rubio-Casillas, 'Beyond the G-Spot: Clitourethrovaginal Complex Anatomy in Female Orgasm', *Nature Reviews Urology*, 11 (2014), 531–8 https://doi.org/10.1038/nrurol.2014.193.

Jones, Kelley A., and Elizabeth Miller, 'Associations between Condom Attitudes, STI Diagnosis and Treatment, Condom use, and Non-Condom Contraceptive Use', *Journal of Pediatric and Adolescent Gynecology*, 29 (2016), 204 https://doi.org/10.1016/j.jpag.2016.01.105.

Keith, Louis, et al., 'The Odors of the Human Vagina', *Archiv Für Gynäkologie*, 220 (1975), 1–10 https://doi.org/10.1007/bf00673143.

Keverne, E. B., and R. P. Michael, 'Sex-Attractant Properties of Ether Extracts of Vaginal Secretions from Rhesus Monkeys', *Journal of Endocrinology*, 51 (1971), 313–22 https://doi.org/10.1677/joe.0.0510313.

Khan, Fahd, Saheel Mukhtar, Seshadri Sriprasad, and Ian K. Dickinson, 'The Story of the Condom', *Indian Journal of Urology*, 29 (2013), 12 https://doi.org/10.4103/0970-1591.109976.

King, Helen, 'Galen and the Widow: Towards A History of Therapeutic Masturbation in Ancient Gynecology', *Journal on Gender Studies In Antiquity*, (2011), 205–35.

Kinzl, Johann F., et al., 'Partnership, Sexuality, and Sexual Disorders in Morbidly Obese Women: Consequences of Weight Loss after Gastric Banding', *Obesity Surgery*, 11 (2001), 455–8 https://doi.org/10.1381/096089201321209323.

Knight, Mary, 'Curing Cut or Ritual Mutilation: Some Remarks on the Practice of Female and Male Circumcision in Graeco-Roman Egypt', *Isis*, 92 (2001), 317–38 https://doi.org/10.1086/385184.

Kothari, Radhika Purushottam, 'Zinc Levels in Seminal Fluid in Infertile Males and Its Relation with Serum Free Testosterone', *Journal of Clinical and Diagnostic Research*, 10 (2016), CC05-8 https://doi.org/10.7860/jcdr/2016/14393.7723.

Kotta, Sabna, et al., 'Exploring Scientifically Proven Herbal Aphrodisiacs', *Pharmacognosy Reviews*, 7 (2013), 1 https://doi.org/10.4103/0973-7847.112832.

Kroger, William S., 'Psychosomatic Aspects of Frigidity', *Journal of the American Medical Association*, 143 (1950), 526–32 https://doi.org/10.1001/jama.1950.02910410012003.

Kurtz, Ruth G., 'Hippocampal and Cortical Activity during Sexual Behavior in the Female Rat', *Journal of Comparative and Physiological Psychology*, 89 (1975), 158–69 https://doi.org/10.1037/h0076650.

Lawrence, Anne A., 'Sexuality before and after Male-To-Female Sex Reassignment Surgery', *Archives of Sexual Behavior*, 34 (2005), 147–66 https://doi.org/10.1007/s10508-005-1793-y.

Leidig, Michael, 'Condom from Cromwell's Time Goes on Display in Austria', *BMJ*, 333 (2006), 10.3 https://doi.org/10.1136/bmj.333.7557.10-b.

Lerner, Gerda, 'The Origin of Prostitution in Ancient Mesopotamia', *Signs: Journal of Women in Culture and Society*, 11 (1986), 236–54 https://doi.org/10.1086/494218.

'Letters, Notes, and Answers to Correspondents', *British Medical Journal*, 1 (1878), 918–20.

Liuzza, Marco Tullio, et al., 'Body Odor Disgust Sensitivity Predicts Authoritarian Attitudes', *Royal Society Open Science*, 5 (2018), 171091 https://doi.org/10.1098/rsos.171091.

Lock, S., '"O That I Were Young Again": Yeats and the Steinach Operation', *BMJ*, 287 (1983), 1964–68 https://doi.org/10.1136/bmj.287.6409.1964.

Lorenz, Tierney A., and Cindy M. Meston, 'Acute Exercise Improves Physical Sexual Arousal in Women Taking Antidepressants', *Annals of Behavioral Medicine*, 43 (2012), 352–61 https://doi.org/10.1007/s12160-011-9338-1.

Lorenzo, Genevieve L., Jeremy C. Biesanz, and Lauren J. Human, 'What is Beautiful is Good and More Accurately Understood', *Psychological Science*, 21 (2010), 1777–82 https://doi.org/10.1177/0956797610388048.

'Louise De Keralio-Robert; The History of Elizabeth Queen of England', *The Monthly Review, or, Literary Journal*, 77 (1787), 561–7.

Low, Nicola, et al., 'Molecular Diagnostics for Gonorrhoea: Implications for Antimicrobial Resistance and the Threat of Untreatable Gonorrhoea', *Plos Medicine*, 11 (2014), e1001598 https://doi.org/10.1371/journal.pmed.1001598.

Maclachlan, Bonnie, 'Sacred Prostitution and Aphrodite', *Studies in Religion/Sciences Religieuses*, 21 (1992), 145–62 https://doi.org/10.1177/000842989202100202.

Macrides, Foteos, Patricia A. Johnson, and Stephen P. Schneider, 'Responses of the Male Golden Hamster to Vaginal Secretion and Dimethyl Disulfide: Attraction Versus Sexual Behavior', *Behavioral Biology*, 20 (1977), 377–86 https://doi.org/10.1016/s0091-6773(77)90931-2.

Maffulli, Nicola, et al., 'Sexual Activity before Sports Competition: A Systematic Review', *Frontiers in Physiology*, 7 (2016) https://doi.org/10.3389/fphys.2016.00246.

'Masturbation in the Female', *American Homeopathic Journal of Gynaecology and Obstetrics*, 1 (1885), 338–40.

Matfin, Glenn, 'The Rejuvenation of Testosterone: Philosopher's Stone or Brown-Séquard Elixir?' *Therapeutic Advances in Endocrinology and Metabolism*, 1 (2010), 151–4 https://doi.org/10.1177/2042018810385052.

Mazloomdoost, Donna, and Rachel N. Pauls, 'A Comprehensive Review of the Clitoris and Its Role in Female Sexual Function', *Sexual Medicine Reviews*, 3 (2015), 245–63 https://doi.org/10.1002/smrj.61.

Melo, Fernando Lucas, et al., 'Syphilis At The Crossroad of Phylogenetics and Paleopathology', Plos Neglected Tropical Diseases, 4 (2010), e575 https://doi.org/10.1371/journal.pntd.0000575.

Michael, Richard P., and E. B. Keverne, 'Primate Sex Pheromones of Vaginal Origin', *Nature*, 225 (1970), 84–5 https://doi.org/10.1038/225084a0.

Mirza, Raul A., et al., 'Do Marine Mollusks Possess Aphrodisiacal Properties?', presented at the Chemical Society National Conference in San Diego, March 13–17, 2005.

Montgomery, Rita E., 'A Cross-Cultural Study of Menstruation, Menstrual Taboos, and Related Social Variables', *Ethos*, 2 (1974), 137–70 https://doi.org/10.1525/eth.1974.2.2.02a00030.

Mostafa, Taymour, Ghada El Khouly, and Ashraf Hassan, 'Pheromones in Sex and Reproduction: Do they have a Role in Humans?', *Journal of Advanced Research*, 3 (2012), 1–9 https://doi.org/10.1016/j.jare.2011.03.003.

Muallaaziz, Didem, and Eyüp Yayci, 'Pubic Hair Removal Practices in Muslim Women', *Basic and Clinical Sciences*, 3 (2014), 39–44.

Murdock, George P., 'Anthropology and Its Contribution to Public Health', *American Journal of Public Health and the Nation's Health*, 42 (1952), 7–11 https://doi.org/10.2105/ajph.42.1.7.

Murray, Jacqueline, 'On the Origins and Role of "Wise Women" in Causes for Annulment on the Grounds of Male Impotence', *Journal of Medieval History*, 16 (1990), 235–49 https://doi.org/10.1016/0304-4181(90)90004-k.

Murtha, Katherine, 'Cycling in the 1890s: An Orgasmic Experience?', *Cahiers De La Femme*, 21 (2002), 119–21.

Mustafa, Asim Zaki, 'Female Circumcision and Infibulation in the Sudan', *BJOG: An International Journal of Obstetrics and Gynaecology*, 73 (1966), 302–6 https://doi.org/10.1111/j.1471-0528.1966.tb05163.x.

Narjani, A. E., 'Considerations Sur Les Causes Anatomiques De La Frigidité Chez La Femme', *Bruxelles Medical*, 27 (1924), 768–78.

Nguyen, Nghiem, 'Roman Rape: An Overview of Roman Rape Laws From the Republican Period to Justinian's Reign', *Michigan Journal of Gender and Law*, 13 (2006), 75–112.

Oaten, Megan, Richard J. Stevenson, and Trevor I. Case, 'Disgust as a Disease-Avoidance Mechanism', *Psychological Bulletin*, 135 (2009), 303–21 https://doi.org/10.1037/a0014823.

'Obstetrical Society's Charges and Mr Baker Brown's Replies', *The Lancet*, 1 (1867), 427–41.

Olson, Rose McKeon, and Claudia García-Moreno, 'Virginity Testing: A Systematic Review', *Reproductive Health*, 14 (2017) https://doi.org/10.1186/s12978-017-0319-0.

'On Prostitution in the City of Paris', *The Lancet*, 28 (1837), 755–60 https://doi.org/10.1016/s0140-6736(02)79496-8.

'On the Signs of Defloration in Young Females', *London Medical Gazette: Or, Journal of Practical Medicine*, 48 (1831), 304–6.

Pan, Shu, et al., 'Clinical Anatomy of the G-Spot', *Clinical Anatomy*, 28 (2015), 363–7 https://doi.org/10.1002/ca.22523.

Pfaus, James G., et al., 'The Whole Versus the Sum of Some of the Parts: Toward Resolving the Apparent Controversy of Clitoral Versus Vaginal Orgasms', *Socioaffective Neuroscience & Psychology*, 6 (2016), 32578 https://doi.org/10.3402/snp.v6.32578.

——, 'The Role of Orgasm in the Development and Shaping of Partner Preferences', *Socioaffective Neuroscience & Psychology*, 6 (2016), 31815 https://doi.org/10.3402/snp.v6.31815.

Pham, Michael N., et al., 'Is Cunnilingus-Assisted Orgasm a Male Sperm-Retention Strategy?', *Evolutionary Psychology*, 11 (2013), 147470491301100 https://doi.org/10.1177/147470491301100210.

Pungent, Pierce, 'Men and Manners', *Fraser's Magazine*, 10 (1834), 161–74.

Puppo, Vincenzo, 'Anatomy of the Clitoris: Revision and Clarifications about the Anatomical Terms for the Clitoris Proposed (Without Scientific Bases) By Helen O'connell, Emmanuele Jannini, And Odile Buisson', *ISRN Obstetrics and Gynecology*, 2011 (2011), 1–5 https://doi.org/10.5402/2011/261464.

Raubo, Agnieszka, 'The Concept of Temperament and the Theory of Humours in the Renaissance', *Ruch Literacki*, 57 (2016), 408–25 https://doi.org/10.1515/ruch-2017-0071.

Remy, Catherine, '"Men Seeking Monkey-Glands": The Controversial Xenotrans-plantations of Doctor Voronoff, 1910–30', *French History*, 28 (2014), 226–40 https://doi.org/10.1093/fh/cru042.

Rengachary, Setti S., Chaim Colen, and Murali Guthikonda, 'Charles-Édouard Brown-Sequard: An Eccentric Genius', *Neurosurgery*, 62 (2008), 954–64 https://doi.org/10.1227/01.neu.0000318182.87664.1f.

'Reports of Societies', *The Boston Medical and Surgical Journal*, 14 (1889), 443–5.

'Review of a Literal Translation of the Saxon Chronicle', *The European Magazine, and London Review*, 78 (1820), 248.

Rider, Jennifer R., et al., 'Ejaculation Frequency and Risk of Prostate Cancer: Updated Results with an Additional Decade of Follow-Up', *European Urology*, 70 (2016), 974–82 https://doi.org/10.1016/j.eururo.2016.03.027.

Roelens, Jonas, 'Visible Women: Female Sodomy in the Late Medieval and Early Modern Southern Netherlands (1400–1550)', *BMGN – Low Countries Historical Review*, 130 (2015), 3 https://doi.org/10.18352/bmgn-lchr.10101.

Rowen, Tami S., et al., 'Pubic Hair Grooming Prevalence and Motivation among Women in the United States', *JAMA Dermatology*, 152 (2016), 1106 https://doi.org/10.1001/jamadermatol.2016.2154.

Rowland, David L., and Kenneth R. Turley, 'Evolving Ideas about the Male Refractory Period', *BJU International*, 112 (2013), 442–52 https://doi.org/10.1111/bju.12011.

Ruuskanen, Deborah, 'There Is No Word for "Adultery" In Hawaiian: The Translation of Non-Existent Concepts', *Afinla Yearbook*, 1993, 235–44.

Salem, A., 'A Condom Sense Approach to AIDS Prevention: A Historical Perspective', *South Dakota Journal of Medicine*, 45 (1992), 294–6.

Sandoz, Kelsi M., and Daniel D. Rockey, 'Antibiotic Resistance in Chlamydia', *Future Microbiology*, 5 (2010), 1427–42 https://doi.org/10.2217/fmb.10.96.

Sandroni, Paola, 'Aphrodisiacs Past and Present: A Historical Review', *Clinical Autonomic Research*, 11 (2001), 303–7 https://doi.org/10.1007/bf02332975.

Schafer, Edward H., 'The Development of Bathing Customs in Ancient and Medieval China and the History of the Floriate Clear Palace', *Journal of the American Oriental Society*, 76 (1956), 57 https://doi.org/10.2307/595074.

Schips, Luigi, et al., 'The Influence of Ejaculation and Abstinence on Urinary Flow Rates', *Neurourology and Urodynamics*, 30 (2011), 1571–5 https://doi.org/10.1002/nau.21157.

Schultheiss, D., J.J. Mattelaer, and F.M. Hodges, 'Preputial Infibulation: From Ancient Medicine to Modern Genital Piercing', *BJU International*, 92 (2003), 758–63 https://doi.org/10.1046/j.1464-410x.2003.04490.x.

Senf, Wolfgang, et al., 'Satisfaction with Male-To-Female Gender Reassignment Surgery', 111 (2014) <https://www.ncbi.nlm.nih.gov/pmc/articles/PMC4261554/> [Accessed 15 February 2017].

Shah, J., 'Erectile Dysfunction through the Ages', *BJU International*, 90 (2002), 433–41 https://doi.org/10.1046/j.1464-410x.2002.02911.x.

Smith, Lesley, 'The Kahun Gynaecological Papyrus: Ancient Egyptian Medicine', *Journal of Family Planning and Reproductive Health Care*, 37 (2011), 54–5 https://doi.org/10.1136/jfprhc.2010.0019.

Smith, W. Tyler, 'Principles and Practices of Obstetricy', *The Lancet*, 2 (1847), 669-671.

Sommer, Marni, et al., 'Pilot Testing and Evaluation of a Toolkit for Menstrual Hygiene Management in Emergencies in Three Refugee Camps in Northwest Tanzania', *Journal of International Humanitarian Action*, 3 (2018) https://doi.org/10.1186/s41018-018-0034-7.

Stanger-Hall, Kathrin F., and David W. Hall, 'Abstinence-Only Education and Teen Pregnancy Rates: Why We Need Comprehensive Sex Education in the US', *Plos ONE*, 6 (2011), e24658 https://doi.org/10.1371/journal.pone.0024658.

Steinach, E., 'Biological Methods against the Process of Old Age', *Medical Journal and Record*, 25 (1927).

Stone, Geoffrey R., 'Origins of Obscenity', *New York University Review of Law*, 31 (2007), 711–31.

Strachan, D. P., 'Hay Fever, Hygiene, and Household Size', *BMJ*, 299 (1989), 1259–60 https://doi.org/10.1136/bmj.299.6710.1259.

Stringer, Mark D., and Ines Becker, 'Colombo and the Clitoris', *European Journal of Obstetrics & Gynecology and Reproductive Biology*, 151 (2010), 130–3 https://doi.org/10.1016/j.ejogrb.2010.04.007.

Sunay, Didem, Erdal Kaya, and Yusuf Ergun, 'Vaginal Douching Behavior of Women and Relationship among Vaginal Douching and Vaginal Discharge and Demographic Factors', *Journal of Turkish Society of Obstetrics and Gynecology*, 8 (2011), 264–71 https://doi.org/10.5505/tjod.2011.57805.

Talib, R. A., et al., 'The Effect of Fasting on Erectile Function and Sexual Desire on Men in the Month of Ramadan', *Urology Journal*, 12 (2015), 2099–102.

Tampa, M., et al., 'Brief History of Syphilis', *Journal of Medicine and Life*, 7 (2014), 4–10.

'The Bicycle: its Judicious and Injudicious Use, *St. Louis Medical Review*, 32 (1895), 208–10.

'The Progress of Romance', *Town and Country Magazine*, 1785, 427–8.

T.M.T. 'Parisian Medical Chit Chat', *The Cincinnati Lancet-Clinic*, 74 (1895), 647–50.

Tolman, Deborah L., 'In a Different Position: Conceptualizing Female Adolescent Sexuality Development within Compulsory Heterosexuality', *New Directions for Child and Adolescent Development*, 2006 (2006), 71–89 https://doi.org/10.1002/cd.163.

Tyson, Diana B., 'Des Grantz Geanz – A New Text Fragment', *Nottingham Medieval Studies*, 50 (2006), 115–28 https://doi.org/10.1484/j.nms.3.395.

'Vaginal Douching', *Monthly Retrospect Of Medicine & Pharmacy*, 4 (1898), 555.

VanLeeuwen, Crystal, and Belen Torondel, 'Improving Menstrual Hygiene Management in Emergency Contexts: Literature Review of Current Perspectives', *International Journal of Women's Health*, Volume 10 (2018), 169–86 https://doi.org/10.2147/ijwh.s135587.

Vicario, Carmelo M., et al., 'Core, Social and Moral Disgust are Bounded: A Review on Behavioral and Neural Bases of Repugnance in Clinical Disorders', *Neuroscience & Biobehavioral Reviews*, 80 (2017), 185–200 https://doi.org/10.1016/j.neubiorev.2017.05.008.

Wade, Lisa D., Emily C. Kremer, and Jessica Brown, 'The Incidental Orgasm: The Presence of Clitoral Knowledge and the Absence of Orgasm for Women', *Women & Health*, 42 (2005), 117–38 https://doi.org/10.1300/j013v42n01_07.

Walter, Robert C., et al., 'Early Human Occupation of the Red Sea Coast of Eritrea During The Last Interglacial', *Nature*, 405 (2000), 65–9 https://doi.org/10.1038/35011048.

Ward, Samuel, George Cutter, Edward Frankel, and W.T. Bull, 'Reports On the Progress of Medicine', *New York Medical Journal*, 23 (1876), 207–10.

Ward, Samuel, 'Reports on the Diseases of Women', *International Record of Medicine and General Practice Clinics*, 23 (2017), 209.

Westenholz, Joan Goodnick, 'Tamar, Qědēšā, Qadištu, and Sacred Prostitution in Mesopotamia', *Harvard Theological Review*, 82 (1989), 245–66 https://doi.org/10.1017/s0017816000016199.

Whipple, B., 'Functional Magnetic Resonance Imaging (FMRI) During Orgasm in Women', *Sexologies*, 17 (2008), S45 https://doi.org/10.1016/s1158-1360(08)72639-2.

Williams, Megan N., and Amy Jacobson, 'Effect of Copulins on Rating of Female Attractiveness, Mate-Guarding, and Self-Perceived Sexual Desirability', *Evolutionary Psychology*, 14 (2016), 147470491664332 https://doi.org/10.1177/1474704916643328.

Wing, Clifton E., 'The Proper Use of the Hot Vaginal Douche', *The Boston Medical and Surgical Journal*, 102 (1880), 583–4.

Wu, Yi-Li, 'The Menstruating Womb: A Cross-Cultural Analysis of Body and Gender in Hŏ Chun's Precious Mirror of Eastern Medicine (1613)', *Asian Medicine*, 11 (2016), 21–60 https://doi.org/10.1163/15734218-12341377.

Zeki, Semir, and Andreas Bartels, 'The Neural Correlates of Maternal and Romantic Love', *Neuroimage*, 21 (2004), 1155–66 https://doi.org/10.1016/j.neuroimage.2003.11.003.

Newspapers and Magazines

Aberdeen Press and Journal, 'Monkey Gland Patient Dead', 6 September 1923, p. 7.

Bell's Weekly Messenger, 'The Hottentot Venus', 2 December 1810, p. 7.

Belfast Commercial Chronicle, 15 January 1816.

Bury and Norwich Post, 'Miscellaneous', 3 May 1837, p. 1.

Chicago Tribune, 'Gland larceny', 15 October 1922.

College Times, Christina Caldwell, 'The C-Word: How One Four-Letter Word Holds So Much Power', 15 March 2011.

Dundee Evening Telegraph, 'Youth Glands Stolen', 16 October 1922, p. 7.

Evening Chronicle, 'Bow Street', 2 February 1837, p. 4.

Gentleman's Magazine, 'The Tryal of Eleanore Beare of Derby', 1732, pp. 933–4.

GQ, Walter Kirn, 'The Forbidden Word', 4 May 2005, p. 136.

Guardian, Jennifer Worth, 'A Deadly Trade', 6 January, 2005 <https://www.theguardian.com/film/2005/jan/06/health.healthandwellbeing> [Accessed 2 September 2016].

Iowa State Register, 'Taking Chances', 28 August 1895.

Le Petit Parisien, 'Jouvence', 8 October 1919, p. 2.

Morning Chronicle, 'Police Intelligence', 20 February 1847, p. 4.

National Review, Arthur Shadwell, 'The Hidden Dangers of Cycling', 1897, pp. 787-96

New Zealand Graphic and Ladies' Journal, 17 September 1898, p. 372.

New Zealand Wheelman, Edna Taylor, 18 August 1897, p. 7.

New Zealand Wheelman, 30 April 1898.

Nottingham Evening Post, 'Seven Methods Explained', 15 July 1924, p. 1.

Nottingham Review and General Advertiser for the Midland Counties, 'Judicial Procedures', 5 May 1837, p. 4.

Observer, Gerald Gould, 'New Novels', 28 February 1932, p. 6.

Pilot, 'Sargent Adams and the Law of Kissing', 1837, p. 3.

Portsmouth Evening News, 'Gland Rejuvenation', 22 April 1939, p. 8.

Saturday Review of Literature, George Bernard Shaw, 'Letter to the Editor', 14 July 1928, p. 1,043.

South Wales Daily News, 'Remedy for Bicycle Face', 4 September 1897, p. 3.

Time Magazine, 'The Potency Pill', 4 May 1998, cover.

The Times, 'The Hottentot Venus', 26 November 1810, p. 3.

Archives

'Anne Knutsford c. Anne Blagge' (Chester, 1664), Cheshire Record Office, EDC5 1.

'Cause Papers' (York, 1699), Borthwick Institute for Archives, University of York, CP.H.4562.

'Cicely Pedley c. Benedict And Elizabeth Brooks' (Chester, 1652), Cheshire Record Office, PRO Ches. 29/442.

'Elizabeth Young c. Robert Heyward' (Chester, 1664), Cheshire Record Office, CRO EDC5 1663/64.

Fane, Francis, 'Iter Occidentale, or the Wonders of Warm Water' (London, 1674), British Library, Harley.

'Judith Glendering c. Thomas Ellerton' (London, 1685), London Metropolitan Archives, DL/C/241.

'Martha Winnell c. Abraham Beaver' (York, 1685), Borthwick Institute for Archives, University of York, C.P.H.3641.

'Peter Leigh c. William Halliwell' (Chester, 1663), Cheshire Record Office, CRO EDC5 1663/63.

'Susan Town c. Jane Adams' (London, 1695), London Metropolitan Archives, DL/C/244.

'Thomas Hewetson c. Thomas Daniel' (London, 1699), London Metropolitan Archives, C.P.H.4534.

'Thomas Richardson c. Elizabeth Aborne' (London, 1690), London Metropolitan Archives, DL/C/243.

Film, Radio and Music

Avildsen, John G., *Rocky* (Chartoff-Winkler Productions, 1976).

Friedkin, William, *The Exorcist: Extended Director's Cut* (Warner Brothers, 2010).

Gilliam, Terry, *Monty Python and the Holy Grail* (EMI, 1975).

Kinney, Jack, *The Story of Menstruation* (Hollywood: Disney, 1946).

Mercury, Freddie, *Bicycle Race* (London: EMI, 1978).

Mix-a-Lot, Sir, *Baby Got Back* (Def American, 1992).

Nichols, Mike, *Carnal Knowledge* (Los Angeles: AVCO Embassy Pictures, 1971).

Smith, Will, *The C Word: How We Came to Swear by it* (BBC, 2007).

Images

All images of Victorian erotica are from the author's own collection, or from the archives of Delta of Venus.

PAGE

8   Cranach, Lucas, and Stephan Füssel, *The Whore of Babylon* from the Luther Bible of 1534 (Cologne: c. Taschen, 2016).

12   *The New Art and Mystery of Gossiping: Being a Genuine Account of All the Women's Clubs In and About the City and Suburbs of London, With the Manner of Their Club Orders* © The British Library Board. All Rights Reserved / Bridgeman Images (Cirencester: Samuel Rudder, 1770).

16   Courbet, Gustave, *L'Origine du Monde* © RMN-Grand Palais (Musée d'Orsay) / Hervé Lewandowski.

21   Speed, John, *Map of Oxfordshire and the University of Oxford* (Huntercombe: Nuffield Place, 1605). Historic Images / Alamy Stock Photo.

22   *Sheela Na Gig*, Kilpeck, Herefordshire: Kilpeck church, twelfth-century (© Nessy-Pic, Wikicommons).

27   *The School of Venus, or The Ladies Delight* (London, 1680).

29   *'Les charmes de Fanny exposés'* (plate VIII) by Édouard-Henri Avril, 1887. First published in an illustrated edition of *Fanny Hill* by John Cleland. Art Collection 4 / Alamy Stock Photo.

31   Tait, Lawson, *Diseases of Women and Abdominal Surgery* (Philadelphia: Lea Brothers, 1889). Gibson1 / Alamy Stock Photo.

32   *Invocation a l'amour*, c.1825 (London: Wellcome Collection, CC BY).

44   D'Alton, Christopher, 'Female Genitalia Showing Severely Diseased Tissue and Hypertrophy of the Clitoris' (London: Wellcome Trust, 1857, CC BY).

45   Roman fresco from the Terme Suburbane in Pompeii (Wikicommons).

47   'A woman caresses another woman who uses a root vegetable as a dildo' Gouache Painting (London: Wellcome Collection, 1900, CC BY).

51   L'opere Chirurgiche, 'Vaginal Speculum' (London: Wellcome Collection, 1678, CC BY).

54   Norris, T., *The History of Witches and Wizards: Giving a True Account of all their Tryals in England, Scotland, Swedeland, France, and New England; with their Confession and Condemnation* (London: Wellcome Collection, 1720, CC BY).

56   Boulton, Richard, *The Witches of Warboyse* (London: Wellcome Collection, 1720, CC BY).

58   Bourguignon D'Anville, and John Cleland, *Memoirs of a Woman of Pleasure: From the Original Corrected Edition, with a Set of Elegant Engravings [Ascribed To Gravelot]*. (London, 1766).

62   Kobelt, Georg Ludwig, 'Dissected Clitoris' in *The Male and Female Organs of Sexual Arousal in Man and Some Other Mammals* (Strasbourg: Berger-Levrault et fils, 1844).

63   'Marie Bonaparte Princess Giorgios of Greece' (the lost gallery, Wikicommons, CC BY 2.0, https://www.flickr.com/photos/59159563@N04/14901259040).

65   Anatomy of the clitoris (Wikicommons).

70   *Sartjee the Hottentot Venus* (London: British Museum, 1810). © The Trustees of the British Museum. All rights reserved.

72   'The Hottentot Venus', *Belfast Commercial Chronicle*, 15 January 1816. Newspaper image © The British Library Board. All rights reserved. With thanks to The British Newspaper Archive (www.britishnewspaperarchive.co.uk).

74 Lombroso, Cesare, 'Cuscinetto Posteriore in Africane', in *La Donna Delinquente La Prostituta e la Donna Normale* (Turin, L. Roux, 1893).

75 Oosterhoff, Inge, 'Greetings from the Colonies: Postcards of a Shameful Past', *Messy Nessy Chic*, 2015 <https://www.messynessychic.com/2015/06/11/greetings-from-the-colonies-postcards-of-a-shameful-past/> [Accessed 12 November 2018].

75 Malek Alloula, *The Colonial Harem*, trans. by Myrna Godzich and Wlad Godzich (Minneapolis: University of Minnesota Press, 1986).

76 du Noüy, Jean Jules Antoine Lecomte, *Rhamsès Dans Son Harem*, in Louis Enault, *Paris-Salon* (Musée d'Orsay). The History Collection / Alamy Stock Photo.

76 Delacroix, Eugène, *Jewish Wedding in Morocco* (Paris: Louvre Museum, 1841). Age footstock / Alamy Stock Photo.

79 O'Neil, Henry, *Jephthah's Daughter Contemplating her Virginity and her Imminent Death, Surrounded by Woeful Attendants with Musical Instruments* (London: Wellcome Collection, 1846, CC BY).

81 1960s advert for Pursette tampons (*Woman's Day*, May 1962).

84 Saja, Pietro, *Vestal Virgin Condemned to Death* (Caserta: Palazzo Reale, 1800). akg-images / MPortfolio / Electa.

86 Dou, Gerrit, *A Physician Examining a Urine Flask* (London: Wellcome Collection, seventeenth century, CC BY).

89 Painting on a cowrie shell, 'A man unlocking a chastity belt of a reclining woman' (London: Wellcome Collection, CC BY).

91 Monk of the Order of St Francis, *Nocturnal Revels: Or, the History of King's-Place, and Other Modern Nunneries* (London: M. Goadby, 1779).

93 Goya, Francisco, *A Young Woman Casting Aside her Virginity to Become a Prostitute* (London: Wellcome Collection, 1798, CC BY).

102 Seminal Emission Moxibustion Point Chart. Caption: Jinggong (Palace of Essence/Semen), C19 Chinese MS moxibustion chart: Seminal emission point by Zhang Youheng (London: Wellcome Collection, CC BY).

103 Chinese woodcut: *Jiang niu zhuo yue* (Dismounting from the ox to catch the moon), Qigong exercise to treat involuntary seminal emission (London: Wellcome Collection, 1513, CC BY).

105 A giant penis copulating with a female devil. Gouache painting. *c.*1900 (London: Wellcome Collection, CC BY).

108 Milton, John Laws, 'Four Pointed Urethral Ring', in *On the Pathology and Treatment of Gonorrhoea and Spermatorrhoea*, originally published in New York: Wood 1887 (London: Wellcome Collection, CC BY).

109 Brodie, R.J., *The Secret Companion: A Medical Work on Onanism or Self-Pollution* (London, 1845).

111 Milton, John Laws, 'Toothed Urethral Ring', in *On the Pathology and Treatment of Gonorrhoea and Spermatorrhoea* originally published in New York: Wood 1887 (London: Wellcome Collection, CC BY).

112 'The Electric Alarum', *On the Pathology and Treatment of Gonorrhoea and Spermatorrhoea* originally published in New York: Wood 1887 (London: Wellcome Collection, CC BY).

115 Portrait of Charles-Édouard Brown-Séquard (Bethesda: National Library of Medicine, Science Source).

116 Portrait of Dr Serge Abrahamovitch Voronoff (Washington: Library of Congress collections).

121 Eugen Steinach. Photograph by J. Scherb after a painting (London: Wellcome Collection, CC BY).

124 Reports of the case of testicular theft, *Dundee Evening Telegraph*, 16 October 1922). Newspaper image © Successor copyright holder unknown. With thanks to The British Newspaper Archive (www.britishnewspaperarchive. co.uk).

126 'Rejuvenating Tablets', *Sporting Times*, 13 February, 1926. Newspaper image © Successor copyright holder unknown. With thanks to The British Newspaper Archive (www.britishnewspaperarchive.co.uk).

126 'Anti-ageing face cream made from glands', *Britannia and Eve*, 1 December 1938. © Illustrated London News/Mary Evans Picture Library.

128 Beuckelaer, Joachim, *Brothel* (Baltimore: Walters Art Museum, 1537).

140 One man makes dough as another stokes the fire for the oven, there is bread on the tables and trays and baskets are piled in stacks. Sixteenth-century coloured etching (London: Wellcome Collection, CC BY).

141 'A baker is loading uncooked dough into an oven, as baked loaves are carried away by a woman', by J. Amman, Der Beck from Jost Amman's Stände und Handwerker, (London: Wellcome Collection, CC BY).

145 'Sixteenth-century woodcarving of two people making bread'. Two people are making bread in a great brick-built oven. Process print (London: Wellcome Collection, CC BY).

149 'Illustrations of six types of shellfish' by Shizhen, Li, in *Compendium of Materia Medica*, Bencao Gangmu – c.16 Chinese materia medica, Shellfish (London: Wellcome Collection, 1596).

150 Botticelli, Sandro, *The Birth of Venus* (Florence: Uffizi Gallery, 1484). The Picture Art Collection / Alamy Stock Photo. By permission of the Ministry for Cultural Assets and Activities.

152 'Oyster' (Tzomqe/imgur.com).

154 'A young girl is selling oysters to a customer in the street', nineteenth-century coloured lithograph, J. Brydone & Sons (London: Wellcome Collection, CC BY).

156 *Molly Milton, the Pretty Oyster Woman* (London: British Museum, 1788). © The Trustees of the British Museum. All rights reserved.

158 *A woman, with light shining on her face from a lamp, standing in front of a barrel of oysters, opening one with a knife.* Wood engraving by H. Linton after H. Morland (London: Wellcome Collection, CC BY).

160 Nakhshabi, Ziya' al-Din, *Lizzat Al-Nisa* (Pleasures of Women) (London: Wellcome Collection, 1824, CC BY).

162 Reynolds, John, et al., *A Discourse upon Prodigious Abstinence* (London: R.W., 1669).

165 Title page for *Women's Petition Against Coffee* (Houghton Library, Harvard University, 1674).

167 Portrait of John Harvey Kellogg (Washington: George Grantham Bain Collection at the Library of Congress).

175 Granville, Joseph Mortimer, 'Granville Hammer', in *Nerve-Vibration and Excitation as Agents in the Treatment of Functional Disorder and Organic Disease* (London: Churchill, 1883).

176 'VeeDee' Mechanical vibrator, London, England, 1900–1915 (London: Science Museum CC BY).

181–3 Pelvic massage illustrations from Dr A. Jentzer, *Die Heilgymnastik in der Gynaekologie: und die mechanische Behandlung von Erkrankungen des Uterus und seiner Adnexe, nach Thure Brandt* (Leipzig: Verlag Von Johann, 1895).

194 Illustration of a 'Draisine' (Wikimedia Commons, 1817).

195 'Rover Ladies Safety Bicycles', designed by John Kemp Starley (Wikimedia Commons, *c*.1889).

203 'Bicycle face', from Derry Journal, 23 September, 1895. Newspaper image © The British Library Board. All rights reserved. With thanks to The British Newspaper Archive

204 Ferris Good Sense Corset Waist advert, 1901.

205 'A "lady cyclist" is attacked by a mob for wearing socks', *Illustrated Police News*, 9 October 1897. Newspaper image © The British Library Board. All rights reserved. With thanks to The British Newspaper Archive (www.britishnewspaperarchive.co.uk).

206 Opper, F., 'The "New Woman" and Her Bicycle, There will be Several Varieties of Her', in *Puck* (New York: Published by Keppler & Schwarzmann, 1895 June 19. Library of Congress Prints and Photographs Division Washington, D.C. 20540).

208 *Aberdeen Press and Journal*, 14 April, 1888. Newspaper image © The British Library Board. All rights reserved. With thanks to The British Newspaper Archive.

211 'Early twentieth-century image of a man copulating with a model of a woman and models of penises mounted on a board' (London: Wellcome Collection, 1900, CC BY).

213 Cnidus Aphrodite, Roman copy of fourth-century Greek original, Ludovisi Collection (National Museum, Palazzo Altemps, Rome).

219 Kokoschka, Oskar, Alma Doll (Private collection, Fine Art Images/Heritage Images/Getty Images, 1919).

221 Inflatable vinyl sex doll (Wikicommons).

229 Filippuccio, Memmo di, Erotic scenes fresco (Musei Civici di San Gimignano, *c.*1300).

231 Prior, T.A. after Thomas Allom, 'Outer cooling room of a Turkish bathhouse', in *Constantinople and the Scenery of the Seven Churches of Asia Minor* originally published by Fisher and Sons, 1838 (London: Wellcome CC BY).

232 *Japanese Men and Women Washing in a Traditional Bath House*, Utagawa, Yoshitora (London: Wellcome Collection, 1860 CC BY).

234 Benham, Sebald, *Fountain* (London: Wellcome Collection, sixteenth century CC BY).

244 Rowlandson, Thomas, *The Hairy Prospect or the Devil in a Fright* (London: British Museum, 1800). © The Trustees of the British Museum. All rights reserved.

248 Goya, Francisco, *The Nude Maja* (Madrid: Prado Museum, 1797).

252 Ashes depilatory cream advert that ran in *Harper's Bazaar*, 1922.

256 Miniature: *Clyster with Pear-Shaped Douche in Use* (London: Wellcome Collection, fifteenth century CC BY).

258 'Vaginal Douche', *Handbook of Obstetric Nursing*, 1902, by Francis W. N. Haultain and James Haig Ferguson (London: Young J Pentland, 1898).

260 'Lysol douche advertisement', in *McCall's Magazine*, July 1928.

261 'Zonite douche liquid advertisement', in *McCall's Magazine*, 1928.

262 'Dr Pierre's Boro-Pheno-Form Feminine Hygiene Suppositories advertisement', 1950. Published in *Secrets* magazine, July 1950, Vol. 28 No. 2.

268 D'Alton, C., 'A watercolour of a man suffering from psoriasis and possibly syphilis' (London: Wellcome Collection, 1866 CC BY).

270 'Re-usable condom in original' (London: Science Museum / Science & Society Picture Library).

272 Grose, Francis, *Guide to Health, Beauty, Riches, and Honour* (London: S. Hooper, 1785).

275 '"Paragon" Re-usable condom in original' (London: Science Museum / Science & Society Picture Library).

276 *She May Look Clean* (Bethesda: National Library of Medicine, 1940).

279 Late Nineteenth-Century Japanese Ukiyo-e Woodblock Print (London: Wellcome Collection CC BY).

280 'French periodical pills', *Boston Daily Times*, 6 January 1845 (Washington: Library of Congress).

281 'Savin Juniper', botanical illustration, W. M. Woodville, Medical Botany, vol. 2 (London: Wellcome Collection CC BY).

283 'Female Abortionist', in *National Police Gazette*, 13 March 1847, p. 1.

286 'Hooked instrument once used for removing an aborted foetus' (London: Wellcome Collection CC BY).

288 'Foundling hospital tokens' © The Foundling Museum (London: Foundling Museum).

289 'This is a token' © The Foundling Museum (London: Foundling Museum).

291 'Farr's Patent Ladies' Menstrual Receptacle', *American Druggist*, January, 1884.

292 *Páez Houses and Bridge*, image showing menstrual hut (Washington: Smithsonian, 1946).

296 Berengario da Carpi, Jacopo, *Isagoge Breves Prelucide Ac Uberime In Anatomiam Humani Corporis. A Communi Medicorum Academia Usitatam* originally published by Benedictus Hector, 1522 (Wellcome Collection CC BY).

297 'Gynaecological acu-moxa locations for treating irregular menstruation' (London: Wellcome Collection, 1591, CC BY).

299 *Sears Catalogue*, 1936 (Harry Finley, Museum of Menstruation).

300 Maygrier, J.P., 'Vaginal examination in vertical position', in *Nouvelles Démonstrations D'accouchemens/Avec Des Planches En Taille-Douce, Accompagnées D'un Texte Raisonné Propre À En Faciliter L'explication* (Paris: Béchet, 1822), plate XXIX. (London: Wellcome Collection CC BY).

303 Kotex advert, 1920 (Wikicommons).

308 Montano, A.A., 'Image of a large native missionary family' (Wikicommons, 1878).

314 Long, Edwin, *The Babylonian Marriage Market* (London: Royal Holloway College, 1875). Chronicle / Alamy Stock Photo.

315 Tissot, James, *The Harlot of Jericho and the Two Spies* (New York: The Jewish Museum, 1896).

316 'Two dancing girls' (photograph by K.L. Brajbasi & Co., Patna, India, 1910).

320 'Tart cards' (London: Wellcome Collection, *c*.1995).

321 'Tart cards in telephone box' (Wikicommons).

322 *Harris's List of Covent-Garden Ladies: or, Man of pleasure's kalendar* (London: British Museum, 1733).

324 Hogarth, William, *A Harlot's Progress,* Norton Simon Art Foundation, 1732 (London: Wellcome Collection CC BY).

327 *Blue Book, Tenderloin 400* (New Orleans: The Historic New Orleans Collection, 1969.19.4).

329 Image by E. J. Bellocq © Lee Friedlander, courtesy Fraenkel Gallery, San Francisco.

330 *Miss Fernande*, Jean Agélou (*c*.1910) (Wikicommons).

332 Gillman & Co., *Oscar Wilde and Lord Alfred Douglas* (photograph, date unknown, 1882–1910, Wikicommons).

335 Villain, François, *Ann Zingha, Queen of Matamba* (New York: New York Public Library, 1800).

337 Greek ceramic (Paris: Louvre Museum, 480 BC).

344 'The West End Scandals, some Further Sketches', *Illustrated Police News*, 4 December 1889. Newspaper image © The British Library Board. All rights reserved. With thanks to The British Newspaper Archive (www.britishnewspaperarchive.co.uk).

351 'Sargent Adams and the Law of Kissing', *The Pilot*, 1837.

Index

A Note on the Author

Dr Kate Lister a university lecturer. She researches the history of sexuality and curates the online research project *Whores of Yore*. Kate is also a columnist for *iNews* and the Wellcome Trust where she writes about the history of sex. Kate won the Sexual Freedom Award for Publicist of the Year, 2017.

Supporters

Unbound is the world's first crowdfunding publisher, established in 2011.

We believe that wonderful things can happen when you clear a path for people who share a passion. That's why we've built a platform that brings together readers and authors to crowdfund books they believe in – and give fresh ideas that don't fit the traditional mould the chance they deserve.

This book is in your hands because readers made it possible. Everyone who pledged their support is listed below. Join them by visiting unbound.com and supporting a book today.

<'((><
A friend
Celia Aaron
Tom Abba
Seye Abimbola
Modesty Ablaze
Edward Aboufadel
Amy Adams
Jad Adams
Zoe Aiano
Colin Aiken
H S Ainsworth
Ken Akehurst
Lani Kai Akers
Jutta Albrecht
Beth Alcock
Ian Alldis
Bob Allen
Louise Allen
Sophie Allen
Dan Allsobrook
Sophie Almond
Joao Amado
Sophie Ambrose

Elaina Amhurst
Kerry Anderson
Tor Andersson
Tamsin Andrews
Mary Andries
Igor Andronov
Gemma Angel
Lucy Angel
Nicole Antoku
C Appleby
Victoria Aragon
Winter Arcane
Kim Archer
Shannon
　Archuleta-
　Burton
Alba Arnau Prado
Angie Arnold
Elisabeth Aroney
Karla Arteaga
Janine Ashbless
Adrian Ashton
Leigh-Anne
　Asperin

Philippe Auclair
Indigo August
Daphne Austin
Helen Avery
Jessica Avery
Janna Avon
Clare Axton
James Aylett
Rachel B
Christopher Baach
Rebecca L.C.
　Bailey
Jodie Baker
Colrain Balch
Marian Baldwin
John Balfe
Eleanor Ball
Deborah J
　Ballantyne
Jason Ballinger
Yuri Banens
Dennis Barassa
Geraldine Barker
Ruby Barker

Peanuts Barkum
Michael Barnes
Gary Barnett
Ann Marie Barrett
Gemma Barrett
George Barrie
Bruce Barrow
Gape Bartfaster
Glenn Basden
Lance Basler
Laura Bassett
Chloe Bates
Jackie Bates
Kirsty Bates
Terry Bates
Susannah Batstone
Kate Baty
Debbie Bauerle
Aurélie Bavaud
Atty Bax
Josh Bazell
A Stephen Beach
Edward Beake
Andrew Beale

K. R. Bear
Michelle Beazley
Cherie Bebe
Thomas Beckett
Shazza Bee
Sophie Bee
Sub Bee
Joshua Beeman
Ruth Behan
Sarah Beharry-
　Goss
Catherine Bell
Lucy Bell
Emily Benita
Mike Bennett
Oliver Bennett
Phil Bennett
Daniel Benoliel
Jamie Bernthal-
　Hooker
Scott Berry
Yan Berthier
Matthew Bess
Joanne Beswick

Dave Betts
David Bibby
David Bickerstaff
Laura Biesiadecki
Bill Biggles
Drew Bigglestone
Anna Bigland
Christian Bikle
Rachel Bilski
Binary Bad
Andrew Binstead
Birdcloud
Dr Lori Beth
   Bisbey
Matthew Bishop
Shayne Bither
Alexandra Black
Clare Black
Miss Black
Black Club Books
Brandi Blackburn
Barbara Blake
Matthew Blake
Mickey Blake
Alexandra Blake-
   Turner
Don Blevins
Amelia Bliss
Naomi Bloomer
   (they/them)
Sarahjane Blum
Leif Bodnarchuk
Arthur Boff
Sylvain Boissel
Annelies Bon
Raymonde Bonin
Christine Boning
Charles Boot
Ruth Boreham
Per Börjeson
Christian
   Borschberg
Jeff Bosko
Hayley Bosworth
Elizabeth
   Bourgault
Aude Boutillon
Raven Bowen
Satin Bowerbird
John Boxall
Julie Bozza
Becca Bradford
Bill Bradford

Jennifer Brady
Shawn Brady
Mark Brandon
Stephen Brann
Lucinda Brant
Charlotte Breeze
Kim Kristin
   Breitmoser
Pieter Breitner
Gillian Brent
Tina Brescanu
Annick
   Breugelmans
Adrian Briggs
Jules Bristow
Debbie Brix
Cameron Brockett
Talia Brodie
Chris Brookmyre
Jess Brooks
Jessica Brooks
Nathaniel
   Broughton
Lilith Brouwers
Antony Brown
Arlene Brown
Chris Brown
Emily Brown
Emma M. Brown
Martin Brown
Sharon Brown
Jeremy Browning
Michelle Brownlee
Grant Brunner
Luis Bruno
Kelli Bryan
A BS
Mel Buckpitt
Zachary Budesa
Emma Bull
Helen Burbage
Jay Burgess
Melvin Burgess
Chris Burlingame
Keiran Burnett
Simon Burney
David Colin Burns
Merri Burns
Nicole Burstein
Joel Bushart
Stephanie Butland
Megan Butler
Jonny Butter

Morven
   Butterworth
Cara Buttitta
Indigo Byrd
Regina Caldart
Tom Calderbank
Dean Calkins
Alex Callaghan
Breanna Calvin
Isobel Cameron
Brian Campbell
Kevin Cannell
Antonio Cantafio
Amandine
   Canville
Pamela Joy
   Capistrano
Rose Caraway
James Carne
Jonathan
   Carpenter
Peggy Carpenter
Rose Carrigan
Victoria Carroll
Benjamin Carruth
Brent Carson
Linda Carson
Alison Carter
Sarah Carter
Stephen Carter
Mark Casarotto
Chloe Cassens
Christopher Cate
Andrew Catlin
Phil Cawley
@cdf_lover
Chelsea Cebara
Elizabeth
   Chadwick
Chloë Chandless
Claire Chapman
Sarah Chappell
KJ Charles
Charlotte's Boss
Paul Charlton
J. D. Chase
Gilbert Chavez
Tanya Cheadle
Sajesh Cherian
Kimberly Cherrix
David Chess
Steve Chevis
David Cheyne

Chianti
Miriam Chin
Johnny Chiodini
chipkali
Alex Chis
Michael Chlopicki
Vera Chok
Juan Christian
Barbara Chubak
Hazel Chudley
Em Clark
Carolyn Clarke
Dr Jan Clarke
Clarissa Clement
Laura Clements
Harriet Clifford-
   Varley
Gemma Clunie
   and Alex Foley
Garrett Coakley
Angela Coburn
Thea Cochrane
Scott Cohan
Sophie Cohen
Vikki Cohen
Robert Cole
Alex Coles
Stevyn Colgan
Adria Colletti
Megan Collier
Samantha Comfort
Kirsty Connell-
   Skinner
Joele Connolly
Lauren Connolly
Eva Conti
Erik Contreraz
Sarah Cook
Natalie Cooke
Susannah Cooke
Tim Cools
Paul Coombes
Philip Coombes
Laura Coombs
Ashlyn Cooper
Erin Cooper
Jeremy D Cooper
Stephen Cooper
Helen Copeman
Allen Copsey
Helen Corday
Mary Cosgrove
Christie Costello

Dan Cozzuol
Stephen Crabtree
Mark Crail
Stephanie
   Cranford
CrankyOtter
@CrankyPants68
Andy Cranston
Victoria L. Craven
Claire Crawford
Timothy Crawford
Jenni Crawley
CRCC
Jess Crees
Scott Creley
Sophie Cremen
Dee Crescitelli
Andrew Cresswell
Matt Cresswell
James Crider
Becky Crofts
Kat Crooks
Stuart Crosse
Kerstin Crosson
Courtney Croteau
Stella Crowhurst
Chris Crowther
Kathrine Cuccuru
Donald Cumming
Ken Cunningham
Mary Curry
Jude Curtin
Angela Curtis
Gabrielle Curtis
Pippa Cuthbert
Jaclyn Cuyno
Richey D
Emma Dalby
   Bowler
Ben Dalton
Claire Daly
Sean Daniels
Jason
   Danischewski
Mick Dann
Willow Darksong
Geoffrey Darnton
Stephanie Davey
fucking
   davidbishop
Beth Davies
Charlotte Davies
Elin Haf Davies

Emma Davies
Rosie Davies
Steph Davies
William "Ewill" Davies
Catherine Davis
Eleanor Davis
Nathalie Davis
Ginny Dawe-Woodings
Norman Day
Emmanuelle de Maupassant
Phoebe de Sade
Casper de Weerd
Jennifer Debley
Giolla Decair
Zoe Dee
Anna Dellavignia
Liz Denholm
Allan Dennis
Paul Dennis
Moira Dennison
Imogen Denny
Paul Dettman
Lauren Devereux
Kate Devlin
Kirsty Devlin
Athens Diamond
Giotis Dimotikalis
Dirty Words
Scout Dixon
Andy Doddington
Sarah Dodge
Dollymopp
Kimberley Domican
Chloe Dominique
Paige Donaghy
Ray Donelly
Christine Donlan
Darla Donna
Helen Donnelly
Michael Donnelly
Lorna Doon
Kelly Doonan
Sarah Dorman
Ben Dornan
Peter Dray
Stefan Drazkowski
S. R. Dreamholde
Paul Dredge
Pieter Driessen

Katy Driver
Simon Druce
Ewan Drysdale
Phebe du Pont
Jolie DuBarry
Holly Duffey
Lisa Duffy
Catherine Duggan
Annie Duncan
Steve & Sue Duncan
Peter Dungey
Matthew Dunleavy
Keith Dunn
April Durall
Miss E.
Abbie Eales
Imogen Ebsworth
Tony Eccles
Roxanne Edgar
Abi Edwards
Eric Edwards
Melody Edwards
Susan Edwards
Gray Egerton
Daimon Eklund
Tom Ellett
Karen Ellis
Richard Ellis
Steve Elrond
John Elsbree
Miramira Endevall
Kirstie English
Liz English
Mike English
Maya Erickson
Eve Eschenbacher
Peter Esmonde
Lisa Etherson
M Etherton
Marina Etienne
Aaron Evans
Jude Evans
Kate Evans
Will Evans
Mistress Evilyne Exposing 40
Dr Simon Exton
Liam Eyers
Kate Eyres
Thomas Fabbri
Karena Fagan

Bill Fairclough
Barbara Fairfax
Alan Fairley
Marcus Didius Falcos
Richard Fall
Mr Fantasy
Elen Farkas
Simon Farnworth
Finbarr Farragher
Hugh Farrell
Dawn Fedorowicz
L Felix
Gillian Fennell
Madeleine Fenner
Douglas Ferguson
Sam Ferguson
Jacqui Fernie
Rob Ferrari
Pierre Fhtagn
Ryan Finger
Alison Finlay
B Finnegan
Gesine Fischer
Paul Fischer
Lunabelle Fish
Samantha Fish
Billie Fisher
C. R. FitzGerald
Colin Fitzpatrick
Emily Flack
Alexander Fleming
Ben Fletcher-Watson
Emma Flint
Stefanie Flood
James Ford
Nat Foreman
Matthew Forrester
Susanne Förster
Cait "mainly coffee" Fortier
Andy Fortytwo
Michele Foulger
Clare Fowler
Hailie Fowler
Alix Fox
D Franklin
Selena Franklin
Naomi Frears
Paul Freelend
Sophie Freiermuth

Eric Frey
Tabetha Frey
Zacharias Fuchs
Thomas Fuglseth
Steve Fuller
Cat Funkhouser
Dr G
Lesley Gabriel
Clarisse Gallaher
Matt Gambrill
Ben Gandee
David Gansen
Alex Gardner
Martina Gärtner
Colin Gavan
Denise Gawron
Danny Gee
Sarah Gee
Lisa Gemino
Fuzzy Gerdes
Eli Gerzon
Lena Ghazarian
Meghan Thérèse Ghent
Olivia Gianelli
GIANT
Jennifer Gibson
Michael Gibson
Dobrochna Giedwidz
Alexandra Gillgrass
Nora Gillooly
Giovanna Gioli
Antonio Giovinazzo
Anne Katrine Gjerløff
Kenneth Gjesdal
Philip Gladstone
Joanna Glascodine
Chris Glinski
Tara Glover
Volker Göbbels
Celine Godeau
Sasha Goeringer
Trisha Goerlitz
Dawn Goldsberry
Brian Gomoll
Alice-Mary-Elizabeth Goodenough

George Goodfellow
Katelyn Goodheart
Anna Goodridge
Christopher Gordon
Helen Gordon
Amy Gore
Amala Goring
Luci Gosling
Emma Gottesman
Imogen Hermes Gowar
Sue Grabber
Lisa Graddage
Alan Graham
Gibson Grand
Caspar Gray
David Green
Megan Green
Rachel Green
William Green
Julie Greig
Alex Grey
Morag Grey
Morgan 'LaRasa' Grey
Leo Griffaton
Kelly Griffin
Sinéad Griffin
Hannah Griffiths
John Grigas
Linda Groth
Victoria Grundle
Caroline Grunwell
Dr Gruss
Janette Gryniewicz
Neil Gulliver
Mirko Gutjahr
Rachel Guyett
Jenni Gwiazdowski
Gwern Gwynfil
Bean Hackett
John Paul Haden
Geoff Haederle
Sunneva Hafsteinsdóttir
Emil Hagstrom
Phil Hague
Per Hagwall
Andy Haigh

Haiku
Mark Hainsworth
Ian Hales
Bessie Hamilton
Steve Hamilton
Tim Hammond
Reinhard Hampel
Lydia Hand
Edward Handley
Ian Hands-
Portman
Nathan
Haneysmith
Maike Hank
Helen Hanna
Dave Hannah
James Hannah
Lindsay Hannah
Hannah
Ewan Hannay
Briony Hannell
Miss Hannelore
Christian
Hannibal
Emma Hansen
Torsten Hansen
Honey Happy-
ComeLucky
Oz Hardwick
Tim & Ros Hardy
Carolyn Harlow
Lisa M. Harney
Becca Harper-Day
Miss Ria
Harpsichord
Amanda
Harrawood
Sam Harris
Sharon Harris
Shelley Harris
Annie Harrison
Christy Harrison
Mark Harrison
Alison Harvey
Michael Hassett
Shelli Haswell
Jessica Hathway
Brenda Hattersley
Michael Hawkes
Sarah Hayden
Ann Marie Hayes
Brigette Hayes
Kari Hayes

Melissa Hayes
Chris Haynes
Kate Haywood
Becky Alice Head
Celeste Headlee
Theresa Healy
Kevin Heaney
Rosie Enorah
Heart
Ellie Heath
Paula Heathwaite
Kimberley
Heitman
Brittany
Hellegaard
Meg Helmes
Alison Henderson
Emilia Henderson
Jude Henderson
Colin Hendrie
Missy Hermes
Olivia Hersant
Siân Hewitt
David Hicks
Michael Hicks
Amy Hill
Mischa Hiller
Jonathan Hixson
Robert Hoare
Emily Hodder
Graham Hodgson
James Edward
Hodkinson
Rosie Hodsdon
Emma Hodson
Kate Hogan
Bethan Holdridge
Anne Holland
Marius Hollenga
Iain Holmes
Rachael Holmes
Tess Holmes
Sophie Hooper
Jonathan Hope
Chloe Hopkins
Max Hopkinson
Bob Horan
Conor Houghton
Rufus Hound
Craig Houston
Carolyn Howitt
Dara Howley
Holly Howren

Heather Huang
Keil Hubert
Edwina Hughes
Glenn Hughes
Marikka Hughes
Susan Hughes
Jim Hughett
Fiona Hulme
Hannah Hulme
Hunter
Gerry Humphreys
Irene Hunter
Kevin Hunter
Mo Hunter
Steve Huntsman
Steve Hutchings
Brendan Hutt
Jörn Huxhorn
Karrie Hyatt
Ian
IanTheCar
Theresa Ikard
Chigbo Ikejiani
Mark Iliff
Robert Ince
Stig Inga
Marjorie Ingall
Carl Inglis
Rick Innis
Alan Ip
Patricia Irvine
Cat Irving
Corey J
Dan Jackson
Emma Jackson
Nicola Jacobson
Mike James
Rebecca James
Marcin Janczyk
Mary Janda
David Janes
Zak Jarvis
Lee Jaschok
Peter Jenkins
Jenny
Jay Jernigan
Jenn Jersey
Noelia Jiménez
Martínez
JK
Catarina João
Rebecca Jobes
Gurney

Manja Johansen
Jasmine Johansson
Marjorie Johns
Sarah Johnson
Al Johnston
Adele Jolliffe
Alan Jones
Alex Jones
Bree Denise Jones
Helen Jones
Jonathan Jones
Margaret Jones
Mary Ann Jones
Peter Jones
Soapy Jones
Sue Jones
Tanya Jones
Zoey Jones
Tom Jordan
Hiren Joshi
Katherine Joyce
Julie Juliff
Ellen K
Olaf K.
Lulu Kadhim
Rebecca Kahn
Monica Kaminski
Marcus Kamps
Stella Kane
Michael Kannisto
Dimitris Kardaras
Kate Karnage
Richa Kaul Padte
Milja Kaunisto
Aaron Kavanagh
Joanne Kearns
Tony Keen
Christopher Keiser
Rae Kelcou
Kim Kelly
Peter Kelly
Nancy Kelso
Ella Kennedy
Niamh Kennedy
Michael Kerekes
Mark Kernes
Alison Kershaw
Hayley Kershaw
Nick Kershaw
Rik Kershaw-
Moore
Amy Kertesz
Glenn Kessler

Jordan Khan
Ellie Kidger
Yvonne Kiely
Dan Kieran
Torsten Kieslich
Peta Kilbane
Nora Kilkelly
Georgina
Killingworth
A Kimbell
Kinkee Panda
Carolyne Kinsman
Amelia Kirby
Pipsa Kirjavainen
Laurence Kirkby
Jason Kitcat
Phoebe Kitcher
Dan Kitson
Christine Klein-
Lebbink
Samira
Kleinschmidt
Rebecka Klette
Rix Kloss
Doreen Knight
Matt Knight
Sarah Knight
Katrina Knizek
John Knowler
Amy Koester
Anja Kominicki
Korhomme
Sara Kory
Diane K. Kovacs
Alex Kowalczyk
Kayleigh
Krackenberger
Mark Kriegsman
Paul Kruczynski
Edwin Kruglov
Michelle Ksher
Andrew Kucy
Robin Kuller
Kurarin
Lauri Kurki
Devon Kurtz
Melissa Kutner
Kym
Pierre L'Allier
Sabrina La Mantia
Samantha La
Rocco
Becki Labine

Elizabeth
Labovitch
Karen Ladomery
Courtney Laine
Mary Laing
Annalise Laird
Teemu Laitinen
Ai Lake
Ray Lakeman
Morgan Lakey
Gill Lambert
Melissa Lambert
Patricia Lambert
Simon Landmine
Anna Lange
Ali Larkin
Mat Larkin
Bjørn Egil Larsen
Megan Larsen
Richard Larsen
Dave Latham
Stacia Laurence
Ben Laurie
Lin Lawhn
Elizabeth
Lawrence
Thomas Lawrence
Drew Lawson
James Lawson
Geof. Lay
Leah Layman-Pleet
Antonios Lazaridis
Jenet Le Lacheur
Jason Le Page
David LeBer
Annelise
Lecavalier
Neil Lee
Ferdy Leemput
L Lelis
Gavin Lenaghan
Alison Lennie
Fiona Lensvelt
Kyle Lerfald
unqualified
lesbian
Sara Levy
Bonnie Lewellyn
Jessica Lewinsky
Nita L. Lewis
Otis Lewis
Lian Li
Liberating Ideas

Alex Liddell
Nicholai Lidow
Laura Light
Steve Lightfoot
Scott Lillehaug
Georgia Lillie
Daniel Lilliehöök
Grace Marie Lily
Maria Lima
Matthew Lister
Sally Lister
Aruhn Littlejohn
littlepurplegoth
LittleSoleil
Emma Litva-Bailey
Chris Llewellyn
Victoria Lloyd-
Hughes
Leanne Lockwood
Jane Loewen
Steve Lomax
Eva London
Darvell Long
Sarah Longfield
Berislav Lopac
Michelle Lopes
Charlie Lord
Lauren Louise
Faith Love
Seani Love
Elizabeth
Lovegrove
Sian Loxston-Beed
Judi Loy
Estelle Lucas
Amanda Luker
R. Lumsden
Jose Miguel
Vicente Luna
Tobias Luther
Dan Lyke
Richard Lyle
Marit Elise
Lyngstad
Heather Lynn
Laurie Lyon
Natasha Lyons
Marit M
LJ MA
Rowan MacBean
David MacCallum
Gillian
MacDonald

Seonaid
Mackenzie
Ellie Mackin
Roberts
Rebecca Maclean
Sarah Maclean
Rebecca
MacMillan
Cait MacPhee
Seamus
MacPherson
Huw Maddock
Juliet Magee
Paul Maginn
Carlo Mainardis
Emma Major
Jonah Malamud
Dave Malcolm
John Mallon
Aaron Malone
Liam Maloney
Tiia Männistö
Dan Marchant
Bex Marshall
Jen Marshall
Keith Marshall
Deborah Martin
Rebecca Martin
Sarah Martindale
Angela Martini
Brian Masselink
Hjalte Måstrup
Poulsen
Mistress Matisse
Adam Maxwell
Eddie May
Tim May
Amanda Maynard
Cheri Mays
Patricia
McCafferty
Lucy McCahon
Hannah McCleary
Peter McCowie
Clair McCowlen
Marylyle McCue
Meghan McCusker
Caroline
McDermott
Polly Fiona
McDonald
Rory Christine
McDonald

Sandra McDonald
Kevin McGee
Ian McGill
Neil McKenna
Megan McKenzie
Jane McLauchlan
Alex McLauchlan
Gray
Francesca
McLaughlan
June Mcloughney
Paddy McMahon
Calvin Mcphaul
Laura McQuaid
Bairbre Meade
Laurie Medeiros
Iain Meek
Freja Meethan
Janet Megoran
Christin Meisel
Stephen Meister
Nicola Melarkey
Alex Melichar
Nick Mellish
Björn Melzer
P A Mercer
Bel Merel
Maria Merian
Marie Merillat
Alex Metcalf
Brent Midyett
Marcin
Miedziejewski
N. Miles
Neil Miles
Daryl Miller
Eilidh Miller
Elaine Miller
Jonathan Miller
Dave Minter
Sean Mintz
Katie Mirobelli
Chris Mitchell
Lesley Mitchell
Sara Mitchell
John Mitchinson
C R Mitton
Katy Moat
Suzette Mocarski
Jaka Mo nik
Lucy Moffatt
Lorraine Moir
James Monaghan

Ken Monaghan
Gardner Monks
Penny Montague
Emily Montaperto
Nicky Montes
Gabriel Montoya
Diego Montoyer
Jim Mooney
Dave Moore
David Moore
Kathryn Moore
Kathy Moore
Peter Moore
Liz Moores
Sarah Moraghan
Pamela Morelos
G Rhydian
Morgan
Kendall Morgan
Lauren Morgan
Helen Morris
Steve Morrison
Camille Morrow
Ruth Morrow
Leela Moses
Karen Motyl
Steven Moye
Helen Moyes
Mulberry
Lauren Mulvihill
Sophie Munday
Kira Mundhenk
Jenni Murphy
Helen Victoria
Murray
Kirsty Murray
Jeff Murri
Jane Myers
Myszka (Mrs Fox)
MzFee
Ann-Kathrin N
Rhel ná DecVandé
Maurice Naftalin
Raymond Nassar
Carlo Navato
Alyssa Neely
Alyssa Neely
Warda Nejjari
Megan Nell
Nell
Benjamin Nelson
Craig Nelson
Naomi Nelson

453

Lux Neon
Lady Ness /
  Nympho-
  maniac Ness
Andrew Neve
Lucy Neville
Alison Newman
Rob Newstead
Eirik Newth
Elissa Nguyen
Connor Nicholaus
Aaron Nicholson
Gary Nicol
Lasse Nielsen
Mary Lynne
  Nielsen
Kira Nilan
Sarah Njeri
Jack Nolder
Emma Norman
Alice Norton
Rictor Norton
Pete Nottage
Now then
Áron Ó Dubháin
Deb O'Brien
Peter O'Brien
Kristin O'Connor
Karl O'Doherty
Ian O'Donnell
Katie O'Donnell
Grace O'Malley
Marie O'Meara
Cáit O'Riordan
Rebecca O'Shea
Karen O'Sullivan
Chauncey O'Dell
Geraldine
  O'Donnell
Nichole O'Duffy
Georgia Odd
Robin Oliver
Orlando Olmo
Amanda Olsson
Joe Ondrechen
Maggie ONeill
Suzan Öngel
Ingrid Oomen
Niki E. Ortega-
  Diaz
Sally Osborn
Are Osen
Alba Ouro

Lynne Owen
Marcella Paez
Jeffrey Paffett
Dex Page
Kate Paice
Kristen Palazzo
Marco Palmieri
Pan Eros
  Foundation
Ana Panigassi
ParallelSecret
Gaylene Parish
Ian Parish
Cait Parker
Steph Parker
Jennifer Parnell
Jan Parsons
William Pate
Anand Patel
Patrick
Patti
Carle Paul
Beth Pavelka
Micah Payeur
Steve Peake
Catherine Pearson
Neil Pearson
Bruce Peirce
Braden Pence
Amanda
  Penlington
Mike Pennell
Sarah Penner
Meli Pennington
Esteban Peralta
  Losilla
Andre Percant
Harry Percival
Lorenzo Perego
Jo Pérez
Naomi Perilli
Ruth Peters
Christophe Pettus
Nish Pfister
Sarah Phelps
Amy Phillips
Bob Phillips
Jennie Phillips
Jim Phynn
Catherine
  Pickersgill
William Pickwell
Ruth Pietroni

Julianne Pigott
Marieke Pingen
Mx Pinky
William Pitchers
Charles Pitter
Marvin Pittman
Mark Plattner
Thomas Pluck
Bob Pockney
Shannon Poe-
  Kennedy
Steve
  Polkinghorne
Justin Pollard
Lucinda Pollard
Ben Ponton
Olivia Pooley
Oliver Poppelwell
Jason Porath
Henriette Pordan
Gina Porreco
Jennifer Porrett
Matthew Porter
Holly Potier
Hannah Powley
Kirsti Pretty
Pierrick Prévert
Beth Price
Rhian Heulwen
  Price
Stuart Pryde
Fiona Purdie
Jesse Purdom
Sean Purdy
Grainne Purkiss
Meghan Purvis
Maureen Putz
brning pyre
Denis Pyshev
Wayne Quigg
Arran Quigley
Dylan Quigley
Suzan Quilliam
Robert Quindazzi
Jordan Quinn
Neil Quinn
Rosemary Quinsey
Hèctor Quinto
Natalie Quist
Anna Radcliffe
Liza Radley
Sean Raffey
Henning Rambow

Keith Ramsey
Andy Randle
Margaret
  Ransdell-Green
Anointinointi
  Rashbrook
Illkae Rayne
Tabitha Rayne
Andrew Rayson
Angela Rayson
Martin Reed
Travis Reese
Heather Reeves
Anne Sigrid
  Refsum
Susanne Reinhardt
James Rhodes
Paul Rhodes
Kathleen
  Richcreek
Jennie Rigg
Charles Riviere
Main Roads
Elaine Roberts
Emily Roberts
Wyn Roberts
Emma Elizabeth
  Robinette
Heather Robinson
Kevin Robinson
Rachael Robinson
Bryan Rodgers
Catherine Rogan
Emily Rogers
Paul Rogers
Cassie Rogerson
Melanie Romine
Claire Ronald
Lucy Ronald
David Ronder
Avi Rope
Charlotte Rose
Hidori Rose
Lanei Rose
Zebra Rose
Craig Ross
Catherine Rossi
Greg Rothwell
Martyn Roussel
Georgie Rowe
Lauren Rowe
Peter Rowe
Lucy Rowett

Angie Rowntree
Simon Rundell
Lukas Rush
Bonnie J. Russell
Jean Russell
Sam Russell
Euphus Ruth
Erik Ruud
Maebh Ryan
Chris Ryder
Mark S
Caroline S.
K Safford
Carla Salczynska
Ray Salim
Mike Salundi
Sammy #42
Amanda Samuels
David Sanderson
Jennifer Sano
Katy Sardeson-Coe
Michelle Sarnelli
Kathryn Saxon
Kimberley Saye
Arthur Schiller
Jennifer Schilling
Lisa Schimmer
Teresa Schinwald
Leslie Schipa
Schizo Something
Jo Schlekewy
Wolfgang
  Schlueter
Cynthia Schmidt
Adam Schmitt
Adam Scholfield
Chad Schrock
Steven P. Schubert
Kevin Schuetz
Adam Schuster
Anne-Marie Scott
Kirstin Scott
Rachel Scoular
Michael Scully
Lynsey Searle
Holly Seddon
Steve Sedor
Anna Segerström
Clive Selwyn
Madeleine Severin
Kiana Shakeraneh
Tom Shakespeare
Laurence Shapiro

Megan Shaw
Jeremy Shaw-
    Munderback
Lisa & Andrew
    Sheader
Mistress Sheba
Eric Sheley
Susannah
    Shepherd
Sara Sheridan
Keith Sherratt
Christiane Shillito
Jo Short
SilverDomUK
Anna Simmons
Bryan Simpson
Jardine Simpson
Scott Simpson
Matt Sinclair
Gill Singh
Ezada Sinn
Lorelei Siren
Shelley Skidmore
Anna Sky
Debbie Slater
Hazel Slavin
Cath Slessor
Veda Sloan
Allegra Sloman
Mr. Smallens
Lindsey Sminks
Clive Smith
Danielle Smith
Fraser Smith
Hannah Smith
Karen Smith
Matthew Smith
Randall Smith
Stephen Roy
    Smith
Tim Smith
Ryan Smith-Burns
Lucy Smyth
Kate Snook
Dan Snow
Robert Sobecke
Lili Soh
Sara Solatycki
Emma Southon
Jane Spencer
Richard Spencer
Rossanne Spencer
Roy Spencer

Patrick Spicer
Ilona Spiro
Eric Sprankle
Erin Spratley
Annie Sprinkle
Marc St-Laurent
Peter St. Marie
David Stahl
Denise Stainer
Ceri Staley
Roland Standaert
Ruth Stanley
David Stapleton
Oleg Starko
Keith Stattenfield
Cathryn Steele
Daniel Steele
Matt Steffler
Alec Steidl
Lindy Stephens
Melissa Stephens
Jessica Stevens
Vicki Stevens
Elizabeth Stewart
James Stewart
Jason Stewart
Ishen Stewart-
    Dowding
Eric Stiff
L Stigter
Matthew Stillman
E.L. Stillwell
Lois Stone
Shawn Stone
Michael R. Storer
Rebecca Storevik
Greg Stovall
David Stow
Lauren Strauss-
    Jones
Charles Strebor
Angelika
    Strohmayer
Kit Stubbs, Ph.D.
Clayton Sue
Emma Sullivan
Jay Sullivan
William Sutton
Robin Swindell
Deborah Swinney
T. Taggart
Titus Tallang
Cecilia Tan

Andrea Tatjana
Vera Tavares
Deb Taylor
Frans Temme
John Templeton
David ten Have
Avy Tennison
Donna Terpack
Adela Terrell
theotherdave
thesecretwriter
Oliver Thiessen
Allan Third
Hannah Thomas
Caroline
    Thompson
Joseh Thompson
Mark M
    Thompson
Ross Thompson
Tory Thompson
Corinne Thomsett
K Thornhill
Robert Tienken
Andrea Ting
Anna-Marie
    Tipping
Staci Tipsword
Becca Tizzard
Giles Todd
Vhairi Tollan
Oda Tolsrød
Gerard Tomczak
Andrew Tomlin
Marsha-Jean Toms
Ruth Tonge
Shelley Tonkin
A Toulmin
TPOK Network
Torsten Tramm
Peter Tranter
David Traynier
David Traynor
Michiel Trimpe
Julia Trocme-
    Latter
Martin Trotter
Mark Trounce
Jonathan Trout
Michael Trubshaw
Anna Tsukroff
Leslie Tuck
Jean Tucker

Jonny Tucker
Rowena Tucker
Charlie Tuff
Margaret Turman
    Kidd
Abby Turner
Andrew Turner
Kevin Turner
Mark Turner
Allan Tyler
Lewis Tyrrell
Jennifer U-B
Haile Unlikely
Finn Upham
Dafne Valdivia
    Yllades
Hester van der
    Vinne
Louis van
    Dompselaar
Ann Van Haney
Derek Vance
Heather
    VanZuÿlen
Claire Vaughan
Carlos Vazquez
Henry Velick
Brigid Venables
Renee Verburg
Betony Vernon
Kate Verone
Evie Veronica
Clare Vickers
Emilie Viel
Cat Vincent
Amanda Vinson
Madam Violet
Marcel Volker
Reid von Borstel
Broadhildt von
    der Busch
Gabriele von
    Tessin
Rebecca Wadeley
Vicky
    Wagenbaugh
M Walk
Allison Walker
Judy Walker
Meghan Walker
Rachel Walker
Mia K Wallace
Chloe Walls

Andrew Walsh
Eleanor Walsh
Kim 'Swan-
    Puncher'
    Walsh
Tady Walsh
Karen Walton
Chee Lup Wan
Katie Ward
Nicki Ward
Ellie Warmington
Elinor Warner
Christopher
    Warren
Stephanie Wasek
Laura Watkins
Bj Watson
Lilly Watson
Emma Watts
Chrystine Weaver
Charlie Webb
Claire Webb
Richard Webb
Andrew Webber
Julie Weber-Roark
Weebum &
    Amplebutt
Mer Weinhold
Arun Welch
Jo Weldon
Alexandra Welsby
Elizabeth Welsh
@welsh_belle
Claire Wenzler
Nicholas
    Wereszczynski
Katie West
Pete West
Nancy Wetmore-
    Mathews
Alexis Wheeler
Hannah Whelan
Ginette White
Graham White
Peter White
Annalise
    Whittaker
David Widdick
Kristoffer
    Wiklund
Peter Wilde
Zoe Wilde
Lady Wildflower

Scarlett Wilkie
Tamara Will
Paul Willett
Annette Williams
Fiona Williams
Jonathan M. L.
  Williams
Kimberly Williams
Nathan Williams
Neil Williams
Zoë-Elise
  Williamson
David Robert
  Willis
Gabby Willis
Julian Willis

Amber Wilson
Daniel Wilson
Derek Wilson
Gavin Wilson
James A Wilson
Jennifer Wilson
Jenny Wilson
Johanna Wilson
Justin Wilson
Laura Wilson
Andrew Wiltshire
Robert
  Winckworth
Winston
Sara Witte
Hannah Witton

Theresa Witziers
Amber Wojcek
Morgan Wolf
Alyx Wolfe
Becki Wolfe
Ting Wong
Simon Woodrup
Julia Woods
Tracy Woods
Myke Woodwell
Denise Woolley
Aaron Wooster
Wendalynn
  Wordsmith
Rachel Wotton
Sabine Wren

George Wright
Robert Wright
Mandy Wultsch
Josef Wyczynski
Elias X
Margaux Andrea
  Yap
Kerryn Yarwood
Cristina
  Yelvington
Elizabeth Yerke-
  Robins
Gareth Young
Katie Young
Martin Young
Peter Young

Wayne Young
YT
Michael Zerbe
Joachim Ziebs
Jean-Pierre
  Zigrand
Zoo Yorker
Hannah Zuercher
Zugzwang
Хаклбери Фина @
  katiestrummer